THE NATURE OF DISASTER IN CHINA

In 1931, China suffered a catastrophic flood that claimed millions of lives. This was neither a natural nor a human-made disaster. Rather, it was created by an interaction between the environment and society. Regular inundation had long been an integral feature of the ecology and culture of the middle Yangzi, yet by the modern era floods had become humanitarian catastrophes. Chris Courtney describes how the ecological and economic effects of the 1931 flood pulse caused widespread famine and epidemics. He takes readers into the inundated streets of Wuhan, describing the terrifying and disorientating sensory environment. He explains why locals believed that an angry Dragon King was causing the flood, and explores how Japanese invasion and war with the Communists inhibited both official relief efforts and refugee coping strategies. This innovative study offers the first in-depth analysis of the 1931 flood, and charts the evolution of one of China's most persistent environmental problems.

Chris Courtney is an environmental and social historian of modern China. He has lived for more than five years in the city of Wuhan, and is passionate about the history and culture of the region. Having completed his PhD at the University of Manchester, he was awarded research fellowships at Gonville and Caius College, University of Cambridge, and at the Asia Research Institute of the National University of Singapore.

D1595608

Studies in Environment and History

Editors

J. R. McNeill, *Georgetown University*
Edmund P. Russell, *University of Kansas*

Editors Emeritus

Alfred W. Crosby, *University of Texas at Austin*
Donald Worster, *University of Kansas*

Other Books in the Series

(*continued after Index*)

THE NATURE OF DISASTER IN CHINA

THE 1931 YANGZI RIVER FLOOD

Chris Courtney
University of Cambridge

CAMBRIDGE
UNIVERSITY PRESS

University Printing House, Cambridge CB2 8BS, United Kingdom

One Liberty Plaza, 20th Floor, New York, NY 10006, USA

477 Williamstown Road, Port Melbourne, VIC 3207, Australia

314-321, 3rd Floor, Plot 3, Splendor Forum, Jasola District Centre, New Delhi - 110025, India

79 Anson Road, #06-04/06, Singapore 079906

Cambridge University Press is part of the University of Cambridge.

It furthers the University's mission by disseminating knowledge in the pursuit of education, learning and research at the highest international levels of excellence.

www.cambridge.org
Information on this title: www.cambridge.org/9781108405799
DOI: 10.1017/9781108278362

First published 2018
First paperback edition 2020

A catalogue record for this publication is available from the British Library

ISBN 978-1-108-41777-8 Hardback
ISBN 978-1-108-40579-9 Paperback

Cambridge University Press has no responsibility for the persistence or accuracy of URLs for external or third-party internet websites referred to in this publication, and does not guarantee that any content on such websites is, or will remain, accurate or appropriate.

For Wei Juan 魏娟 *and Isobel* 魏心悦

CONTENTS

FIGURES

TABLES

ACKNOWLEDGEMENTS

This book began its life as a doctoral thesis written at the University of Manchester. I am indebted to Sharon Macdonald for offering unstinting intellectual support as I underwent the metamorphosis from ethnographer to historian, and for reading my thesis even as the River Ouse advanced ominously towards her garden. Zheng Yang-wen offered valuable insights into Chinese history, as did Aaron A. Moore, Astrid Nordin, Linsay Cunningham, Carl Kilcourse, David Woodbridge, Bart van Malssen, Hou Jiaqi and Ouyang Donghong. Cormac Ó Gráda's research on famine was a great inspiration, so I was extremely grateful that he agreed to examine my thesis, and, together with Pierre Fuller, offered excellent advice on revisions. The British Inter-University China Centre provided full financial support for my postgraduate training; without this organisation my career and those of many of my peers would not have been possible. I would also like to thank my Chinese instructors at the University of Manchester, Wuhan University and Peking University for making lessons so enjoyable. Several Peking University comrades have continued to offer friendship and support during the writing of this book. Special thanks are due to Mark Baker, who offered invaluable advice on several drafts. Thanks also to Gordon Barrett, who accompanied me on numerous trips to archives. In the latter stages of writing this book I received support from the Singapore Ministry of Education grant 'Governing Compound Disasters in Urbanising Asia'. I would like to thank Mike Douglass and Michelle Miller for facilitating this, and for providing a stimulating intellectual environment in which to think about disasters.

My doctoral thesis began to evolve into a book at the University of Cambridge. I am grateful to Hans van de Ven for much sage advice and to colleagues at the Chinese Research Seminar, helmed by Adam Yuet Chau. My research fellowship at Gonville and Caius College proved invaluable, and although there are too many people to thank individually,

I would be remiss not to mention Sujit Sivasundaram, Melissa Calaresu, Peter Mandler, Richard Staley, Katherine McDonald, Rob Priest, Emma Hunter, John Gallagher, Susan Raich, David Motadel, Tom Simpson, Matt Pritchard and Jeremy Prynne. I am grateful to the staff of the Needham Research Institute, and particularly John Moffett, who shared his formidable knowledge of Chinese history and helped to procure some very useful sources.

On a brief trip to Singapore a few years ago a torrential downpour destroyed all my early fieldwork notes. A kind hotel manager bought me a new computer, enabling me to return to Wuhan with an empty hard drive and a newfound interest in flooding. Undaunted, I later returned to the National University of Singapore, where this book was completed. I learned an inestimable amount from the wonderful scholars at the Asia Research Institute, including Prasenjit Duara, Greg Clancey, Ken Dean, Fiona Williamson, Dhiman Das, Michiel Baas, Shekhar Krishnan, Chen Lang, Rongdao Lai, Huang Jianli, Lee Seung-Joon, Creighton Connolly, Desmond Sham, Shuang Wen, Jonathan Rigg, Bob Wasson, Arunima Datta, Rita Padawangi and many more.

Kathryn Edgerton-Tarpley and Greg Bankoff have each, in different ways, inspired my approach to disasters, so it has been a pleasure to hear their thoughts about my own research, and to receive feedback on papers from scholars including Isabella Jackson, Toby Lincoln, Huang Xuelei, Rana Mitter, Henrietta Harrison, Micah Muscolino, Barend ter Haar, Shirley Ye, Joe Lawson, Robert Bickers, James Warren, Qian Jiwei, Tang Yun, Katiana Le Mentec, Zhang Yuan, Rohan D'Souza and Arupjyoti Saikia. I would like to thank Wei Wenxiang and his colleagues at Huazhong Normal University for their insights into the history of Wuhan. I am extremely grateful to Kitty Kavanagh and Elinor Hope-Simpson for sharing memories of their relatives' experiences in China.

I would like to thank the two anonymous reviewers at Cambridge University Press for their invaluable suggestions, Lucy Rhymer for shepherding this book through the editorial process with great patience and enthusiasm, and John McNeill and Edmund Russell for including my work in a series alongside some of my favourite books. Material used in Chapter 3 was published in a different form in *Twentieth Century China* (Vol. 40, no. 2, 2015, pp. 83–104). Missouri History Museum, Trinity College Library, Cambridge University Library and the United Society all kindly allowed me to reproduce their images.

This book would not have been possible without the support of my friends and family. I began to learn about floods over dinner tables in

Wuhan, as I shared lively baijiu-fuelled conversations with my in-laws. I am grateful to all of them for welcoming me with such warmth, particularly Wei Minxiang, Xu Yunhua and the late Wei Chengxiang, a great champion of wetland culture. It has been an honour to make so many good 九头鸟 friends, especially Zhang Libing, who, together with Simon Galloway, accompanied me on many Wuhan misadventures. I owe a tremendous debt to my family in the United Kingdom, for incubating many of the ideas in this book long before I had travelled to China. I am grateful to my sisters, Laura and Ellen, for their company and support, and to my parents Ann and Alan, who have not only provided invaluable advice, but have also each read more about Chinese floods than could reasonably be expected of any human being. This book is dedicated to my daughter Isobel, who has provided me with limitless joy while I researched a tragic topic, and to my wife Wei Juan, without whom it would not have been possible.

NOTE ON LANGUAGE

This book provides Pinyin followed by Simplified Chinese characters for the names of almost all individuals. In the early twentieth century, those who mixed in cosmopolitan circles often adopted Romanised versions of their names that were considered more accessible to non-Chinese speakers. For the sake of consistency, I have rendered all names in Pinyin, yet have provided such variants in the footnotes. For the convenience of non-specialist readers, I have chosen to use the well-known names Sun Yat-sen – instead of Sun Zhongshan 孙中山– and Chiang Kai-shek – instead of Jiang Jieshi 蒋介石. I refer to the Guomindang 国民党 (or Kuomintang) as the Nationalists and the Chinese Communist Party 共产党 as the Communists throughout. I provide the characters for less well-known toponyms. For the sake of accessibility I have chosen to retain a few inaccurate geographical conventions – in Chinese the Yangzi (or Yangtze) actually refers to a short section of the Long River or Changjiang 长江, and Manchuria is referred to as Dongbei 东北, meaning simply the Northeast. The city known today as Wuhan is a conurbation that comprises the three historically independent municipalities of Hankou (or Hankow), Wuchang and Hanyang. In the early 1930s these cities had yet to be fully unified, yet for the sake of convenience I use the anachronistic term Wuhan throughout. Unless otherwise stated, all financial figures are provided in Chinese yuan. Citations of Chinese literature are provided with a short Pinyin title in the notes. Chinese characters and English translations can be found in the bibliography. Unless otherwise stated, all translations are by the author.

INTRODUCTION

There is no point saying that this was a Heaven-sent-disaster, or that it was a caused by humans ... When disasters strike, neither Heaven nor humans are prepared to take the blame.

Guan Xuezhai 管雪斋, 1931[1]

In early January 1932, a journalist took a walk around Sun Yat-sen Park in the north of Wuhan.[2] Originally constructed as a private garden in the dying days of the Qing dynasty, this park had been opened to the public by the new Nationalist government in 1928, and named in honour of the recently deceased father of the nation.[3] Less than four years after this grand opening, Sun Yat-sen Park presented a grim spectacle. The flood of the previous summer had flattened its decorative gates, ornate pagodas and attractive teahouses. Whole avenues of trees had been washed away. Receding water had left the once manicured lawns sodden, and had deposited a thick layer of sediment on the flowerbeds and fountains. At the height of the flood, small boats known as sampans had come to rule the canal-like city streets. Now several of these vessels that had been abandoned by their owners lay strewn across the park, grass growing through their broken hulls. A repugnant odour of faeces emanated from the park swimming pool, which had been used as a makeshift latrine. Confronted with these dismal scenes, our journalist, whose name has been lost to history, wrote of an overwhelming emotional reaction. Rather than compassion for the suffering of their fellow citizens, they were instead filled with a deep sense of hatred. They detested the terrible disaster that had threatened to choke the life out of their city.

---

[1] Guan 'Shuishang san dian zhong', *Yaxi Yabao*, in HSSDX.
[2] The following accounts are based on an article that can be found in *Wuhan Ribao*, 13 January 1932.
[3] Liu, 'Hankou Zhongshan Gongyuan'.

Yet life continued to exist if one knew where to look. The earth that covered the park, which to the human eye looked like dirt, was actually a nutrient-rich alluvium, alive with the potential for new flora and fauna. Indeed, the very ground upon which the journalist walked had been forged by the gradual accretion of similar deposits over the course of millennia. The annual infusion of silt-laden water that had built up the plains had also fostered a complex wetland ecosystem, which thrived because of floods. Humans had depleted the biodiversity of this area by draining the land. In place of a wetland habitat they constructed a bizarre simulation of nature. Delicate flowerbeds and grass lawns usurped a rich assemblage of wild aquatic and riparian plants. Marshes and mudflats gave way to artificial lakes and rockeries. Fish, waterfowl and amphibians were evicted so that they might be replaced by the leopards, monkeys and turkeys that were caged in the park zoo.[4] The flood that struck the park in 1931 had purged these alien species, leaving an expanse of open territory that could by recolonised by local species. This cycle of death and rebirth was not unusual in the wetlands. It was one of the vital processes that had helped to maintain the ecosystem. For nature, a flood was not a disaster. Were the park to be left untouched by human hands, it would have soon become a wetland once again. This was not to be.

The existence of wildlife was of little consequence to our journalist. It was the loss of cultural life that was of primary concern. The irresistible force of water had destroyed a refined municipal space, obliterating a key symbol of order and progress at the centre of a modernising city. If one looked closely, however, human culture had already begun to recolonise the park. A refugee encampment had been constructed on the waterlogged lawns. Young children in tattered clothing emerged from makeshift huts to play on the muddy ground. For the journalist, this settlement was a depressing enclave of poverty and suffering. A collection of squalid hovels occupied the space in which young women had once promenaded in all their finery. Outside observers showed little consideration for the formidable knowledge and skill involved in forging liveable dwellings from flood detritus. Yet this too was a form of culture – one that had evolved in an environment dominated by rivers, lakes, and wetlands, where flooding was a way of life. The rulers of modern Wuhan did not value this wetland culture, and were not prepared to tolerate unsightly huts and other vernacular technologies that had helped ordinary people to survive flooding. Over the next few months the refugees were cleared

---

[4] Lu and Tang, 'Hankou Zhongshan Gongyuan dongwuyuan de pianduan huiyi'.

from the park, their huts demolished so that the municipal government could begin the job of reconstruction. When the renovation was complete, a statue was erected at the centre of an expanded park depicting Chiang Kai-shek riding a horse: the premier of a nation that was struggling to cope with water, atop an animal highly unsuited to the wetland environment.[5]

This book provides the first comprehensive history of the 1931 China floods.[6] It describes what happened when one of the most populous regions on earth found itself under water. The floods inundated approximately 180,000 km² – an area equivalent in size to England and half of Scotland, or the states of New York, New Jersey and Connecticut combined.[7] Although this book focusses primarily on the Yangzi, the disaster was not limited to this river basin. The Chinese term used most frequently to describe this event is the Yangzi-Huai Flood Disaster 江淮水灾 (Jiang-Huai Shuizai). Even this does not capture the true scale of the flood, which affected waterways throughout the country. Eight provinces in central China were severely affected, with the Yellow River and Grand Canal experiencing particularly severe inundations. Beyond these regions there was flooding as far south as Guangdong, as far north as Manchuria, and as far west as Sichuan.[8] This was a national disaster.

An image that recurs in numerous witness accounts is that of a vast ocean swallowing the landscape (see Figure I.1).[9] The flood lake was 900 miles long and at some points stretched to 200 miles in width.[10] This was three times larger than the area inundated by the famous Mississippi floods of 1927, a key reference point for many of those describing the events of 1931.[11] One air passenger remarked that flying over the Yangzi

---

[5] Liu, 'Hankou Zhongshan Gongyuan'. On the struggle of keeping horses in Hubei see Gao, 'The Retreat of The Horses'.

[6] This is the first book-length study of this disaster. There have been several Chinese articles and chapters describing the flood, including Li et al., *Zhongguo jindai shi da zaihuang*; Zhang, 'Lun zhengfu'; Kong, 'Minguo Jiangsu.' English readers can find brief descriptions in Li, *Fighting Famine*. Zanasi, *Saving the Nation*; Borowy, 'Thinking Big'; and Lipkin, *Useless to the State*. The most comprehensive treatment to date is a chapter in Pietz, *Engineering the State*.

[7] RNFRC, p. 7.

[8] These provinces were Anhui, Hubei, Hunan, Jiangsu, Zhejiang, Jiangxi, Henan and Shandong. For a description of the geographic extent of the flood see Li et al., *Zhongguo jindai shi da zaihuang*, p. 203.

[9] See for example 'Wuhan yi cheng canghai', *Guowen Zhoukan*, 8 (1931); F. G. Onley (Letter Extract), 28 August 1931, SOAS Archives 10/7/15; Hu Yu-tsen (Letter Extract), 28 August 1931, SOAS Archives 10/7/15.

[10] RNFRC, p. 3.   [11] Ibid., p. 5.

Figure I.1. An aerial photograph of the flood. (The Charles Lindbergh
Collection. Reproduced courtesy of the Missouri History Museum)

felt more like 'cruising in the China Sea or the Pacific Ocean'.[12] This deluge had horrific humanitarian consequences. At the time observers estimated that as many as 25 million people may have been affected.[13] More
recently, historians have suggested that the figure may have been as
high as 53 million.[14] As much as a tenth of the Chinese population
found themselves living under water. Hundreds of thousands were said
to have drowned as flood waves swept across the landscape. Others were
crushed to death by falling debris or swallowed by disintegrating earthen
homes. Devastating though these initial hazards were, the secondary consequences of inundation proved far more lethal. With the summer harvest gone and no chance of planting a winter crop, an already highly
impoverished society began to starve. Millions of people left their homes
to tramp and float across the inundated landscape, swelling into a vast
population of refugees who scoured the land for food and shelter. Often
excluded or expelled from cities, refugees had little choice but to gather
in overcrowded settlements with little sanitation. The diseases that swept
through the displaced population were the most lethal consequences of

[12] *The Chinese Recorder*, November 1931.
[13] RNFRC, p. 7.   [14] Li et al., *Zhongguo jindai shi da zaihuang*, p. 231.

the flood. In some areas, they accounted for as much as 70 per cent of all fatalities.

While this was certainly one of the deadliest disasters of its kind in history, exactly how many people died remains unknown.[15] Credible estimates have ranged between 400,000 and 4 million. At the time, government relief workers suggested that around 2 million people had been killed. This figure was based on the direct observation of those who possessed the most accurate data at the time, and is, therefore, perhaps the most credible estimate. Yet given the dysfunctional state of the civil registration system at the time, we can never hope to know the true death toll. This book concerns itself neither with quantifying mortality nor with proving the superlative status of the flood. The question of how many died may be one of the most pervasive asked of disasters, yet it is rarely the most interesting. Instead this book asks what caused the disaster, why the humanitarian consequences were so profound, what it was like to live through a catastrophe of this magnitude and how the government and society responded.

The Nature of Disaster

The question of what caused the 1931 disaster is at once extraordinarily simple and yet also fiendishly complicated. At the most basic level, it was a problem of too much rain. The winter of 1930 was particularly cold, causing large deposits of snow to gather in the highlands of western China.[16] These melted in early 1931, engorging the rivers of the middle Yangzi at the very same time that the region was experiencing unusually heavy spring rains. By the early summer the water table was already dangerously high. Then, in July, seven devastating storms swept down the valley in quick succession. As much rain fell in one month as would normally be expected in one and a half years.[17] The middle Yangzi continued to experience heavy precipitation throughout the summer and early autumn, causing a flood that was not only unusually severe but also unusually prolonged. The flood peak – when the river reached its maximum height – travelled relatively slowly downstream, striking Sichuan in early August before flowing through the Three Gorges and swallowing the plains of Hubei and Hunan. It arrived in Wuhan on 19 August, and then continued to Jiangxi, where it engulfed an area 200 miles to the

---

[15] See the Appendix.
[16] Barrett, *Red Lacquered Gate*, p. 265.   [17] Buck, *1931 Flood in China*, p. 8.

south of Poyang Lake 鄱阳湖. It coursed downstream into Anhui and Jiangsu, reaching Nanjing on 16 September, almost a month after it had left Wuhan.[18] It continued to the Yangzi delta, before finally flowing into the ocean. Figure I.2 shows a map of the areas affected by the flood.

Given the primary importance played by the environment, it is understandable that history has tended to remember the flood as a *natural disaster*. Yet the idea that any disaster can be entirely natural is highly problematic, as it fails to recognise the crucial anthropogenic dimensions that convert environmental hazards into humanitarian catastrophes. Despite the repeated protests of historians and social scientists, the notion of the natural disaster maintains a tenacious grip on the popular imagination.[19] It not only dominates media reporting but all too often also creeps into historical narratives. This is more than just a semantic problem. The term natural disaster implies an absence of human influence and culpability. Having assumed that the environment was to blame, scholars often exclude disasters from their analysis. Millions of deaths are left unexplained or expunged entirely from the historical record. Unlike the casualties of war, revolution or terrorist atrocities, those who perish during floods, earthquakes or droughts are seen simply as nature's victims.

Historians who are not content to submit to such environmental determinism have deployed a wide range of tactics designed to emphasise the anthropogenic aspects of disasters. Environmental historians have highlighted the extent to which unsustainable patterns of settlement and resource extraction exacerbate hazards such as floods and droughts.[20] Institutional historians have suggested that disasters can be read as infrastructural failures.[21] Political historians have shown how authoritarian governments exacerbate or even precipitate disasters.[22] Historians of war have highlighted the critical role that conflict plays in inducing disasters, especially famines.[23] Economic historians have revealed that subsistence crises occur when people lose their entitlement to food rather than just

---

[18] RNFRC, p. 3; *The Chinese Recorder*, November 1932; Barrett, *Red Lacquered* Gate, p. 274.

[19] See for example Wisner et al., *At Risk;* Oliver-Smith, 'Anthropological Research'; Bankoff, *Cultures of Disaster;* Pfister, 'Learning from Nature-Induced Disasters'.

[20] See for example Worster, *Dust Bowl;* Morris, *Big Muddy.*

[21] Li, *Fighting Famine.*; Will and Wong, *Nourish the People;* Will, *Bureaucracy and Famine.*

[22] This is a prevalent theme in studies of disasters that occurred under imperialistic or other authoritarian regimes. See for example Davis, *Late Victorian Holocausts;* Hall-Matthews, *Peasants, Famine and the State;* Yang, *Tombstone;* Dikötter, *Mao's Great Famine;* Wheatcroft, 'Towards Explaining Soviet Famine.'

[23] See for example de Waal, *Famine Crimes;* Muscolino, *Ecology of War;* Mukherjee, *Hungry Bengal.*

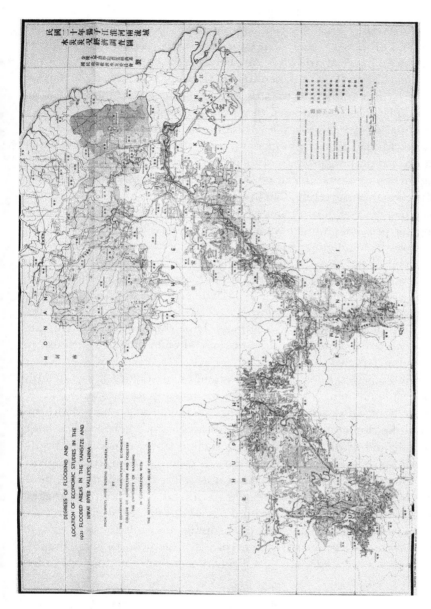

Figure I.2. A map of the 1931 flood. (John Lossing Buck, *The 1931 Flood in China: An Economic Survey* Nanking: University of Nanking, 1932. Reproduced courtesy of the Cambridge University Library)

7

their harvests.[24] Finally, social historians have insisted that we view disasters as processes rather than events, recognising that vulnerability is embedded in social structures long before hazards strike.[25]

Vital though these interventions have been, it is important that we guard against a slow drift towards social determinism. Some of the most influential studies have been those that have argued that the environment played virtually no role in disaster causation.[26] Such analyses are praised for having cut through our intuitive understanding to reveal that nature was nothing more than a passive witness to human folly. Suggesting that all disasters are caused by human action is no less reductive an approach than suggesting that they are entirely natural. This book resists both manoeuvres. It is at pains to demonstrate the critical role of anthropogenic processes, while having no desire to erase the agency of nature. It strives to highlight the environmental dimensions of processes typically considered social – how rivers help to design cities, how snails can generate poverty and how fish behaviour helps humans to survive floods. This should not, however, be taken as a defence of environmental determinism. This book also examines the social dimensions of processes usually considered natural – how farmers shape river valleys, how communities nurture pathogens and how oxen and water buffalo perish due to economic famines.

Although this book pays close attention to nature it is primarily about human beings. As such, it uses the anthropocentric term disaster throughout. Of course, for many species, there was nothing disastrous about the flooding of a floodplain. Ecologists once believed that large climatic and physical disturbances – such as storms, floods and fires – had a destructive effect on ecosystems, preventing them from progressing towards their climax state. Most now reject such equilibrium models, instead recognising that regular disturbances are often an integral component of ecosystems.[27] Within many river basins flood pulses have numerous beneficial effects. They encourage nutrient transfers, expand the territory of wetland species and promote biodiversity. Large inundations certainly kill millions of individual organisms, but they also bring

[24] Sen, *Poverty and Famines*. For a discussion of the entitlements approach see Ó Gráda, *Famine*.
[25] This approach dominates social science literature. See for example Wisner et al., *At Risk*; Oliver-Smith, 'Anthropological Research on Hazards and Disaster'. For a critical appraisal of the discourse of vulnerability see Bankoff, *Cultures of Disaster*.
[26] See Sen, *Poverty and Famines*; Yang, *Tombstone*.
[27] For an overview of these debates see Reice, *Silver Lining*.

new life to ecosystems. This book argues that the human world must be understood within the broader ecology of the flood pulse. Just as the regular inundation of a landscape forged the ecosystem of Hubei, so too it gave shape to the human culture that developed in the region. Just as certain species survived and even thrived during inundations, so too people found ways to exploit the endowments of nature. Unfortunately, humans were not the only species adept at drawing benefits from inundation. The mosquitoes, molluscs and flies that thrived when water rushed into human settlements had a devastating ecological effect on human life.

The Disaster Regime

Historians have been slower than ecologists in recognising the formative role of disasters. They still tend to characterise hazards as unpredictable shocks that disrupt the equilibrium in which humans supposedly live. Yet, as Greg Bankoff has argued, in many part of the world coping with hazards has been a normal part of the human experience.[28] Hostile environments have played an important role in the development of cultural, economic and political institutions. Disasters did not simply interrupt history; they helped to make it. Nowhere was this more the case than in modern China, a society that suffered many of the most lethal disasters in world history. Like much of Asia, China had always been naturally hazard-prone, subject to shocks including floods, droughts, locust attacks and earthquakes. Even in a region long habituated to catastrophes, however, the frequency and magnitude of the disasters that struck China between the mid-nineteenth and mid-twentieth centuries were exceptional. Hundreds of thousands of people perished with grim regularity, and on a number of occasions the death toll reached well into the millions. Long treated simply as a background context against which the grander narratives of history unfolded, scholars are only now beginning to come to terms with the critical role that disasters played in the making of modern China.[29]

---

[28] Bankoff, *Cultures of Disaster.*
[29] See for example Edgerton-Tarpley, *Tears from Iron;* Janku, '"Heaven-Sent Disasters"'; Snyder-Reinke, *Dry Spells*; Fuller, 'North China Famine Revisited'; Muscolino, *Ecology of War*; Li et al., *Zhongguo jindai shi da zaihuang*; Xia, *Minguo shiqi ziran zaihai.* There is also a somewhat distinct literature covering the topic of the famines that occurred in the Maoist state in the late 1950s. See Ens Manning and Wemheuer, *Eating Bitterness*; Thaxton, *Catastrophe and Contention*; Dikötter, *Mao's Great Famine*; Yang, *Tombstone.*

Quite why China became so critically vulnerable to disasters at this stage in its history remains a matter of debate. Pierre-Étienne Will and R. Bin Wong have argued that the capacity of the state declined precipitously from its peak in the eighteenth century, when the Qing state boasted the most sophisticated system of disaster governance in the premodern world.[30] Mike Davis has linked this decline to a broader trend in global history, with South Asia, South America and East Africa all suffering a marked increase in disasters during the late nineteenth century. He attributes these 'late Victorian holocausts' to a deadly combination of climate and politics – extreme El Niño events coincided with a particularly predatory period of European imperialism.[31] While Lillian Li does not ignore the restructuring the global economy, she stresses that domestic factors also contributed to the decline of the Qing, including social unrest, bureaucratic factionalism and environmental degradation. These problems continued into the twentieth century and were exacerbated by internecine warfare.[32]

Most studies that have sought to explain why China descended into this long century of disasters have concerned themselves primarily with the issue of governance. Historians examining flooding have tended to concentrate on two areas of human endeavour – dykes and granaries. They ask first why hydraulic systems failed, and second how well governments fed their subjects. Critically important though both these issues are, there are plenty more questions we can ask about floods. This book develops a more holistic approach, examining how the 1931 flood was embedded within a very particular *disaster regime*.[33] This term is designed to encompass all the basic ingredients – both environmental and anthropogenic – that help to translate natural hazards into humanitarian disasters. The disaster regime concept helps to explain how different strands of causality intertwine on various temporal scales, generating the three major components of catastrophes – hazards, famines and epidemics. Like all regimes – be they political or ecological – disaster regimes change over time. Although every catastrophe is *sui generis*, each is also a product of its era. The same constellation of causes that made

---

[30] Will and Bin Wong, *Nourish the People.*

[31] Davis, *Late Victorian Holocausts.*   [32] Li, *Fighting Famine in North China.*

[33] The use of the term regime is informed by two influences. First, ecologists refer to the profile of physical hazards within an environment as a 'disturbance regime.' See Del Moral and Walker, *Environmental Disasters*, p. 123. Second, historians of urban conflagrations have described how the configuration of material and political relations in cities helps to create 'fire regimes'. See Bankoff et al., *Flammable Cities.*

the 1931 flood so lethal could also be found, in varying forms, during the other catastrophes of early twentieth century China. The disaster regime can be defined, then, as the configuration of human–environmental relations that conditions the humanitarian impact of a hazard in a particular geographic region and time period. One of the central objectives of this book – the spine to which binds it disparate limbs together – is to interrogate the numerous factors that shaped the modern Chinese disaster regime.

Although the 1931 flood was a product of its time, like all disasters it had its own unique features. The most lethal and well-studied catastrophes of the era were the droughts that struck the North China Plain. In examining a devastating flood that struck the middle Yangzi, this book offers an original contribution to the burgeoning historiography of Chinese disasters. Another unusual feature of the flood was the extent to which it affected urban areas. The famines that struck China in the early twentieth century were often seen as the product of a society bound inextricably to the soil. The flood inundated not only the earthen world of rural villagers, but also the modern homes of their urban neighbours. No city was more profoundly affected than Wuhan, the capital of Hubei province and the most technologically advanced city in inland China. Images of starving refugees trudging towards cities during the flood were hardly anything new. Pictures of the wholesale destruction of a modern city were somewhat more novel. The inundated streets of Wuhan recalled iconic images from other modern disasters – the crumbled remains of Tokyo following the 1923 Great Kantō Earthquake, the chic streets of Paris filled with filthy floodwater in 1910 or the charred skeletal remains of San Francisco in the wake of the earthquake and fire of 1906.[34] Modern cities generated their own disaster regimes. The population of Wuhan had to cope not only with a familiar litany of hunger and disease but also with the novel forms of risk that emerged as water subverted the urban landscape. Chemical fires blazed on the surface of the floodwater and collapsing pylons caused electric shocks. These were thoroughly modern ways to die in a disaster.

This book is not just an urban history, as a good deal of the narrative unfolds in the countryside. Yet much of its attention is focussed on Wuhan, a city that has been somewhat neglected by historians of modern China. From the Song poet Lu You 陆游 to the Victorian travel writer Isabella Bird, the most famous accounts we have of this vast conurbation

---

[34] Jackson, *Paris Under* Water; Rozario, *Culture of Calamity*; Clancey, *Earthquake Nation*.

tend to have been written by people on their way somewhere else.[35] Historians have often treated the city in a similarly perfunctory manner. It is impossible to traverse the terrain of modern Chinese history without alighting in Wuhan on several occasions, as the city so often found itself at the heart of national politics. Yet having observed these momentous events, historians are often content to return to more familiar locales, such as Beijing, Nanjing and Shanghai. Those who linger a little longer soon find themselves seduced by a fascinating and rich urban culture.[36] Although this book focuses primarily on the events that unfolded during the flood, it also offers readers the opportunity to dip into the history of this neglected yet fascinating region.

Like much of Republican China, Wuhan was a city riven by deep cultural divides. The collapse of the Qing dynasty and an influx of new foreign ideas inspired intellectuals to challenge many beliefs that their fellow citizens still held sacred. This cultural schism had a profound effect on the way that people understood the environment and disasters. Regardless of their cultural predilections, almost everyone continued to use the term *tianzai* 天灾, which translates literally to mean 'Heaven-sent-disaster'. For many people, this term retained its literal meaning – they believed that they lived beneath judgemental skies, capable of sending floods and droughts as punishments for human immorality.[37] Others subscribed to a more scientific approach, seeing disasters as the product of the inanimate physical processes of climate, hydrology and seismology. They continued to use the term *tianzai*, but only as a colloquial synonym for *ziran zaihai* 自然灾害 – a more literal translation of the English term 'natural disasters'.[38] Yet new meanings could not wash away old concepts. As disparate groups were forced to cohabit a common lexicon, they had to negotiate an ambiguous path between radically differing ideas about

---

35 Watson, *Grand Canal*; Bird, *Yangtze Valley*.

36 William Rowe's classic two-volume history of Hankow remains one of the best resources for scholars of this region, and for urban historians more generally. See Rowe, *Hankow: Commerce and Society* and *Hankow: Conflict and Community*. More recently two books have focussed upon the city: Rahav, *Rise of Political Intellectuals*; MacKinnon, *Wuhan, 1938*. Edward McCord frequently mentions the city in his histories of warlordism. See for example McCord, *Military Force*. There are, of course, numerous Chinese language studies of the city, including, for example, Pi Mingxiu's multivolume urban history and Tian Ziyu's history of the May Fourth movement in the city. See Pi, *Wuhan Tongshi*; Tian, *Wusi Yundong shi*.

37 Elvin, 'Who Was Responsible'; Janku, 'Heaven-Sent Disasters.'

38 As it entered the modern lexicon the term *tianzai* underwent what Lydia Liu has described as a 'relational transformation' – its definition changed while its usage remained consistent. See Liu, *Translingual* Practice, esp. p. 41.

the environment. In the course of examining the 1931 flood, this book offers an insight into a society that was struggling to comprehend the nature of disasters.

Six Histories of the 1931 Flood

This book is divided into six chapters, each of which offers a different historical perspective on the flood. Although individual chapters can be read separately as an exposition of a particular theme and approach, when taken as a whole they offer readers a multidimensional perspective, in which the disaster is viewed at differing temporal and geographic scales and from a range of historiographical approaches. Chapter 1 charts an *environmental history* of flooding in Hubei since the earliest period of human settlement. There is a rich historiography on the theme of water control in this region, which has done much to illuminate how human beings have transformed the environment by building dykes and draining land.[39] This approach is critically important if we are to understand the issue of flooding, yet it has also created something of a hydraulic paradigm. This encourages us to view floods from the perspective of dyke builders, and so to see them primarily as technical failures. This chapter offers a different view, demonstrating how the regular inundation of the landscape was an integral part of the ecology and culture of the region. The vogue for flood suppression, which came to dominate Hubei and much of the world over the last two millennia, was not the historical norm. The local population found numerous ways to coexist with water, developing a sophisticated wetland culture based on accommodating rather than simply suppressing floods. Natural flooding became a physical hazard with the rise of agriculture. Farming not only made rivers more dangerous, but also helped to lay the foundations for the famines and epidemics that would eventually occur in the wake of inundations. The modern disaster regime in Hubei did not simply emanate from nature. It emerged as human communities interacted with river ecosystems over the course of millennia.

In Chapter 2 we narrow the aperture to examine an *ecological history* of a single flood pulse. To understand what happened to humans in 1931 we must examine how water affected the other species that inhabited

---

[39] Liu, 'Dike Construction in Ching-chou'; Will, 'Un cycle hydraulique'; Will, 'State Intervention'; Perdue, *Exhausting the Earth*; Rowe, 'Water Control'; Zhang, *Coping with Calamity*; Gao, 'Retreat of the Horses'.

their ecosystem. Historical studies of flooding tend to concentrate on a single ecological effect – the loss of edible plants. This nutrition-centred approach, which asks us to focus exclusively on agriculture and granaries, distorts our understanding of humanitarian catastrophes. For flood victims rarely succumb to literal starvation, and more often perish because of a synergy of hunger and disease. The mortality crisis in 1931 was no exception. A precipitous decline in available food, amplified by a failure of economic entitlements, resulted in a subsistence crisis that significantly weakened human beings, both individually and collectively. Yet it was the epidemics that swept through the flood zone that proved most lethal. Recognising the formative role that diseases play during disasters does not mean we need to submit to a form of pathogenic determinism, in which humans become nothing more than the hapless victims of bacteria and viruses. Instead it suggests that we must develop an appreciation for the complex interactions among natural, social and microbial ecologies.

Chapter 3 explores the various religious and philosophical responses that emerged in the inundated streets of Wuhan, charting a *cultural history* of the flood. It examines the system of ethnometeorology that the local population employed to explain the weather and mediate with the forces of nature. One of the most potent deities within this system of was the Dragon King, a figure responsible for controlling rainfall and rivers. Shortly before the flood the municipal authorities in Wuhan took the fateful decision to demolish a temple dedicated to this deity. Many locals interpreted the catastrophic flood that followed as spiritual retribution for this act of iconoclasm. The media quickly seized on this religious theory, deriding it as an expression of the ignorant superstition of the common people. What they failed to appreciate was that the processions during the flood were about more than just the Dragon King. Beyond their explicit functions, rituals and processions served as modes of popular protest. Religion played a complicated role in the disaster regime, serving as an idiom through which hazard-stricken communities called their leaders to account.

Chapter 4 brings us closer to the immediate phenomenological experience of the flood by charting a *sensory history* of the disaster in Wuhan. Witnesses frequently referred to the traumatic sight of bodies, the sounds of terror-stricken refugees, the discomforts of living exposed to the elements and the all-pervasive stench of death and faeces. Scholarly accounts often omit such unsavoury details, preferring instead to analyse disasters in terms of dispassionate quantitative data. This chapter rehabilitates the adjectives that have been purged from history. It argues that by examining the sensory and affective dimensions of disaster we can not only appreciate the full range of historical experience, but also gain an insight into how people behave during crises. To understand what people did during the flood we must attempt, as far as possible, to appreciate how they felt. The many sensory traces that have been preserved in the documentary record offer a key insight into refugee behaviour, which is a vitally important component of any disaster regime.

The final two chapters of this book contrast two forms of expertise – the technical expertise of elite relief workers and the vernacular expertise of refugees. Chapter 5 charts an *institutional history* of the flood. It describes how relief organisations were governed by an insular ideology, predicated on shared assumptions about the causes of famine and the nature of poverty. This created a barrier against dissenting voices, and obscured the many practical failings of the relief effort. Though their efforts were later heralded as a triumph of a modern state, in reality relief institutions were plagued by financial and political difficulties. As the Japanese invasion plunged China into even greater economic difficulties, the Nationalist government turned to the United States for wheat loans. Represented as a form benevolent charity, these loans were designed to benefit their creditor, offering the United States government a means to stabilise its own ailing rural economy. This pattern of bilateral disaster aid seemed to anticipate certain features of an international order that would appear in the postcolonial world. Republican China, as a nominally sovereign state, found itself operating in an international system defined by profound asymmetries of wealth and power. As grain rotted in Chinese warehouses, refugees found themselves eating wheat grown on the other side of the world.

Similar asymmetries defined the local experience of the flood in Wuhan, albeit in microcosmic form. Chapter 6 offers a *social history* of the refugee crisis that unfolded in this city. Rather than seeing refugees as a problem in need of expert governance, it focusses on the expertise of refugees themselves, examining how they coped with the disaster and negotiated the difficulties of being governed. Contrary to the received wisdom, many refugees did not want to be institutionalised by the state, preferring to remain autonomous. Unfortunately, the municipal authorities almost invariably interpreted autonomous coping strategies as social problems; water taxis were a public nuisance, begging led to pauperisation, prostitution was immoral and selling children was akin to slavery. Although these social problems caused a degree official paranoia, the local administration remained concerned primarily with the threat of Communism. Fear of political subterfuge led military commanders to initiate a brutal clampdown on the displaced population. Refugees were rehoused hastily at gunpoint in relief camps on the outskirts of Wuhan, where they suffered extremely high death tolls. Like all of those who perished during the flood, those who died in the camps were not simply nature's victims. They were locked into a lethal disaster regime, defined by interactions among hydrology, meteorology, economics, ecology, culture and politics.

1

THE LONG RIVER 长江

Floods would not be a hazard were not man tempted to occupy
the floodplain.

Gilbert White[1]

Cartographers have always struggled to represent rivers. To render
nature legible, they are forced to freeze water in time, turning complex
evolving systems into fixed blue lines, which cut simplistic linear tra-
jectories from origins to destinations. If it were possible to view history
on a time-lapse – condensing millennia to minutes – we would see
rivers writhing across their plains like living entities; expanding and
contracting with the pulse of the seasons, rising and falling with long-
and short-term climatic changes. This chapter reconstructs the history
of one such river – the Yangzi – a watercourse that shaped and was
shaped by the people who made their homes on its plains. We focus, in
particular, on Hubei, a province in the middle reaches of the Yangzi that
is dominated by rivers, lakes and wetlands, and, as a result, is naturally
highly flood-prone. Humans did not always see this as a problem, as
abundant water could be a blessing as well as a curse. It took a particular
mode of human interaction with the environment to transform natural
floods into humanitarian disasters. This chapter describes the history
of this transformation, tracing the long-term evolution of the modern
disaster regime from which the 1931 flood emerged.

The epigraph from the renowned geographer of disasters Gilbert
White encapsulates much of what is argued in this chapter. Flooding, as a human hazard rather than a hydrological process, is never
entirely natural. Disastrous inundations occur when people interact with
water in particular ways. Succinct as it may be, however, White's assessment does not do justice to the complexity of environmental history.

---

[1] White, *Natural Hazards*, p. 3.

For floodplains do not remain static; their contours change continuously under the influence of environmental and anthropogenic processes. Hence, people may settle in a dry area that may become a floodplain over time. Furthermore, living on a floodplain does not necessarily put one at risk of disaster. Inundation becomes truly disastrous only under particular configurations of subsistence and settlement. The population of Hubei constructed a lifestyle that depended on flood-supressing technologies. When these failed, they faced calamitous consequences. The fact that such hydraulic strategies have become ubiquitous in the modern world should not be taken as evidence that they were the historical norm. People can learn to accommodate and even benefit from regular infusions of water, while avoiding larger floods by tactical evacuation or by using technologies to float on water.[2] We might augment White's conclusions, therefore, with the observation that floods would not be hazards if humans could adapt themselves to the environment rather than adapting the environment to themselves.

The story of how floods became disasters in Hubei can be read as part of the broader history of the human transformation of the hydrosphere. Throughout the world people have drained wetlands, channelised rivers, and denuded forested catchments. Much of Hubei was once a vast wetland, which fostered a highly biodiverse ecosystem. As wetland became farmland, the environment was deprived of complex biogeochemical systems. The ecologists William Mitsch and James Gosselink have described wetlands as the 'kidneys of the landscape' – they cleanse water, recharge aquifers and absorb flood pulses.[3] Losing these kidneys is a serious blow, not just to the environment but also to human beings. In detailing the evolution of flooding, this chapter also describes the decline of biodiversity and the loss of the wetland culture practised by a people who found ways to live between water and land. Yet this should not be read solely as a declensionist narrative.[4] Wetland species and wetland culture were never erased entirely. Both survived, albeit in muted forms, offering vital resources for flooded communities. Unfortunately, residents of Hubei

---

[2] Examples of societies that have learned to accommodate and benefit from flooding include certain pre-colonial cultures in the lower Mississippi and the flood recession agriculturalists on the Zambezi in Mozambique. See Morris, *Big Muddy*; Isaacman and Isaacman, *Dams, Displacement*.

[3] Mitsch and Gosselink, *Wetlands*, p. 4.

[4] William Cronon has rightly criticised the tendency for environmental historians to favour tragic narrative arcs, in which humans are pictured inflicting irreparable damage upon nature. See Cronon, 'A Place for Stories'.

had to cope not only with the primary hazard of inundation but also with flood-induced famines and epidemics. By the twentieth century, these secondary risks killed far more people than the physical impact of inundation itself. In detailing the long-term evolution of the modern disaster regime, this chapter provides an environmental history not only of flooding, but also of the hunger and disease that came in the wake of water.

Natural Floods

Forty-five million years ago, the Indian and Eurasian tectonic plates collided, lifting the Himalayas and creating the Tibetan–Qinghai Plateau.[5] As water drained off these new highlands over millions of years, it etched the basins of many of the greatest rivers in Asia.[6] Some flowed south to create the Indus and Brahmaputra, which would shape the lives of millions of South Asians. Some flowed southeast to form the Mekong and Salween, which would nurture the forests and farms of mainland Southeast Asians. Some flowed east, creating two major rivers. The first of these was the Yellow River, an unpredictable watercourse that cut a meandering path through a loess soil landscape. The second would become the greatest river in Asia – and the third longest in the world. Known in the English-speaking world as the Yangzi – a name that locals use to refer to a small eastern stretch of its course – to Chinese people this is the Long River or Changjiang 长江.[7]

The valley carved out by the Yangzi would eventually drain over a million square kilometres.[8] As water cut through the surface of the land it met ancient seams of granite and quartzite, which formed ridges that divided the valley into distinct basins.[9] These basins came to define the three major reaches of the river. The upper Yangzi flows down from Tibet, across Yunnan, and then through the distinctive red sandstone of the Sichuan basin. As it funnels through a mountainous area in western Hubei, it carves the scenic yet treacherous rapids of the Three Gorges. Beyond this point the river is known as the middle Yangzi, a broad watercourse distinct in character from the fast-flowing upper reaches. In its journey across the alluvial and lacustrine plains of Hunan and Hubei, the middle Yangzi drinks up vast quantities of water, increasing in size

---

[5] Flad and Chen, *Ancient Central China*, p. 19.   [6] Hodges, 'Tectonics of the Himalaya'.

[7] Flad and Chen, *Ancient Central China*, p. 19.

[8] Del Moral and Walker, *Environmental Disasters*, p. 116.

[9] Van Slyke, *Yangtze*, pp. 9–10, 30–1.

dramatically before narrowing to cut between the highland ridges that form the border with Jiangxi.[10] Having met Poyang Lake, the river continues to Anhui and Jiangsu, where it becomes the lower Yangzi. It splits into multiple streams, forming a delta, and finally, having travelled 6,380 kilometres, completes its journey by flowing into the East China Sea.

Long before humans set foot in Hubei, the region was already experiencing natural floods. These occurred when the stream flow of rivers exceeded the discharge capacity of their channels.[11] Much of Hubei is located within a geological depression tapering into a mountainous bottleneck in the east. Water accumulates easily yet is slow to discharge.[12] In the east of the province, the Yangzi meets the Han River 汉江, its largest single tributary. The plains formed by these two great watercourses are crisscrossed with smaller rivers and dotted with lakes and marshes. These once formed part of a vast network of wetlands, more extensive than any others found in the temperate world, which stretched continuously along plains of the middle and lower Yangzi.[13] The stream flow of rivers in Hubei varies in accordance with the cycle of seasons. In average years, the basin experiences three surges of high water, in the spring, summer and autumn.[14] The water table is at its lowest in the winter. Relatively little rain falls between October and May, and precipitation in highland catchments gathers as snow. These frozen reservoirs melt in the spring, infusing rivers with large volumes of water at the same time that the region experiences the first of its three annual waves of precipitation.[15] In the summer, cold fronts collide with humid air masses from the subtropics, causing the heaviest rainfall.[16] These summer deluges tend to be the trigger for major flooding.

The middle Yangzi is the intermediary zone between the hammer and anvil of two monsoon systems. The East Asian monsoon determines the

[10] Flad and Chen, *Ancient Central China*, pp. 27–8.
[11] White, 'Human Adjustment to Floods', p. 36. A river or stream has base flow, which is the discharge derived from groundwater excluding runoff from precipitation and snowmelt. It also has a bankfull discharge, which is the level at which a stream may flow without rising above its banks. The average flow of a river will be somewhere between base flow and bankfull discharge. See Reice, *Silver Lining*, p. 108.
[12] Yin et al., 'On the River–Lake Relationship'. See also Rowe, 'Water Control'.
[13] Li, 'Domestication of Plants', p. 40.
[14] Gemmer et al., 'Seasonal Precipitation Changes'; Zhang *Coping With Calamity*, p. 30.
[15] Oxenham, 'On the Inundations of the Yang-tse-Kiang'; Wang et al., 'Terrestrial Contributions', p. 2.
[16] Yu, Zhu and Wang, 'Radiocarbon Constraints'.

level of precipitation in the basin itself. The South Asian monsoon affects rain- and snowfall in the upper Yangzi, thereby helping to determine how much water is discharged downstream.[17] Both monsoon systems are subject to external climatic influences. The sulphur dioxide emitted during volcanic eruptions affects atmospheric temperatures and may have an influence on the stream flow of the Yangzi, though the exact nature of volcanic–monsoon linkages remains unclear.[18] Fluctuating sea surface temperatures in the Pacific Ocean – the infamous El Niño Southern Oscillation (ENSO) – have a more discernible influence. There is some evidence to suggest that large floods, including those of 1954 and 1998, are caused by El Niño and La Niña events. Caution should be exercised before drawing direct causal links, however. Unlike the well-established teleconnection between El Niño and rainfall patterns on the North China Plain, the exact role that ENSO plays in Yangzi flooding remains a matter of debate.[19]

The annual rise and fall of rivers and lakes helped to forge a highly diverse ecosystem in Hubei. As with many river systems, the flood pulse came to play a vital role in the biogeochemical cycle, transferring valuable nutrients between aquatic, terrestrial and wetland areas. Fast flowing water stripped millions of organisms from riverbeds and floodplains, creating empty patches that were colonised by a wide range of biota.[20] Floods also helped to distribute seeds and fruit, increasing the range of local plants, and purged invasive species that may otherwise have become overly dominant. Far from being simply destructive, regular flood pulsing was, as the ecologist Seth Reice has put it, 'an essential recharge mechanism', bringing life to both rivers and

---

[17] Jiang et al., 'Yangtze Floods and Droughts'.

[18] Atwell, 'Volcanism and Short-Term Climatic Change'.

[19] The exact teleconnection between ENSO and Yangzi floods remains an issue of debate. Some have argued that during El Niño years 'the enhanced subtropical high at the western North Pacific strengthens the summer East Asian monsoon, and brings larger amounts of precipitation to the Yangtze River catchment than the normal years.' See Yu et al., 'Analysis of Historical Floods', p. 210. See also Zhang et al., 'Possible influence of ENSO'; Jiang et al., 'Yangtze Floods and Droughts'; Gough et al., 'The Variation of Floods'.

[20] Various ecological models are used to describe the dynamic interaction of rivers and plains during flooding. These include the *river continuum concept, flood pulse concept* and the *river productivity concept*. See Arthington, *Environmental Flows*, esp. pp. 50–2. Recent evidence suggests that the fluvial ecology of the middle Yangzi conforms more closely to the flood pulse concept, as lateral transfers of nutrients are more important than transfers from headwaters stressed in the River Continuum Concept. See Wang et al., 'Terrestrial Contributions'.

floodplains.[21] The biodiversity created by natural flooding would have been extremely attractive to early humans, who could exploit a rich mosaic of aquatic, riparian and terrestrial habitats. From the outset, then, people did not settle Hubei in spite of floods, but because of them.

Settling Floodplains

For much of human history Hubei looked quite different from the way it does today. At the beginning of the Holocene, around 11,500 years ago, the Yangzi was a branched river, flowing in three distinct streams that were prone to shifting course and wandering across the basin. Most of central and eastern Hubei was home to a vast wetland known as the Yunmeng Marsh 云梦泽.[22] Though hard to imagine today, the zoologist Samuel Turvey suggests that the middle Yangzi was then the 'Amazon of the East', home to a vast assemblage of flora and fauna.[23] Rivers and lakes teemed with fish, turtles, alligators, finless porpoises and Yangzi river dolphins. The plains were covered with thick forests of coniferous and deciduous trees, home to pandas, elephants, giant tapirs, gibbons and rhinoceroses. The wetlands supported abundant waterfowl and wading birds, including five species of crane that nested in thick reed beds.[24] This natural abundance was attractive to hunter-gatherers, and later helped to support early experiments in plant and animal domestication.[25]

Early settlers were particularly drawn to a form of semi-aquatic grass known as wild rice. Although there remains some debate about when and where this species was first domesticated, we know that communities in the middle Yangzi region were cultivating it deliberately, rather than simply foraging for it, by at least as early as 7500–6000 BCE.[26] Rice became central to the economy and society of this region not least because it proved to be the perfect biological technology to colonise wetlands. Unlike dry land crops, which require aerated soil, rice can grow under water, thanks to its specialised aerenchyma tissue that diffuses oxygen down its stems to its roots.[27] This water resistance may help to explain

---

[21] Reice, *Silver Lining*, p. 120. See also Middleton, *Flood Pulsing in Wetlands*.

[22] Yin Hongfu et al., 'On the River–Lake Relationship'.   [23] Turvey, *Witness to Extinction.*

[24] Lu, *Transition from Foraging to Farming*, pp. 75–82; Li, 'Domestication of Plants'; Turvey, *Witness to Extinction.*

[25] Christian, *Maps of Time*, p. 238.

[26] Stark, *Archeology of Asia*, pp. 83–4. Theories that suggested a Southeast Asian origin of rice have now been disproven by genetic evidence. See Anderson, *Food and Environment*, p. 39.

[27] Kellman and Tackaberry, *Tropical Environments*, p. 232.

the rapid growth of rice cultivation between 6000 and 3000 BCE, which was a particularly warm and therefore wet climatic epoch.[28] Flood pulses were the lifeblood of rice agriculture, bathing the land in a nutrient-rich cocktail of minerals and water, leaving fertile deposits of nitrogen and phosphorus in their wake.[29] This natural redistribution of biomass meant that rice farmers had to introduce far less fertiliser than those cultivating dry land.[30]

Rice domestication allowed farmers to maximise yields, yet it also created a nutritional system that was dependent on predictable patterns of meteorology. Wild rice (*Oryza rufipogon*) articulates its seeds individually, maximising the chance of sustained reproduction in a wetland environment subject to fluctuating water levels. By encouraging the seeds of domesticated rice (*Oryza sativa*) to ripen synchronously, people could harvest the grain much more easily, yet this process made the plant less flood resistant.[31] Should the rains prove overabundant, farmers would lose a whole generation of crops and a source of nutrition that represented significant inputs of labour and time. In this sense, the subsistence crises that would, in later eras, help to make floods substantially more dangerous, were, as David Christian has argued, 'a paradoxical by-product of the agricultural revolution'.[32] The catastrophic famines of the modern era had deep roots in an ancient interaction between people and plants.

Just as humans changed rice, rice also changed humans. To furnish their chosen plant with a habitat conducive to successful propagation, people transformed their patterns of settlement. In doing so, they fundamentally altered their relationship with rivers. Early rice farmers practised flood-recession agriculture, planting their crops on mud banks after the annual inundation had abated. Over time this minimally invasive form of cultivation was augmented with a form of

---

[28] Yu, Zhu and Wang, 'Radiocarbon Constraints'.

[29] On nutrient flows during flood pulses see Del Moral and Walker, *Environmental Disasters*, pp. 100, 115.

[30] Thorbjarnarson and Wang, *Chinese Alligator*, p. 144. For added fertility farmers would allow fields to remain fallow for a year and then burn off weeds and vegetation, leaving a layer of fertilising ash, and then flooding fields with water. See Lewis, *Early Chinese Empires*, p. 106.

[31] On the difference between wild and domesticated rice see Stark, *Archeology of Asia*, p. 78. Humans change the nature of domesticated grains by choosing to replant particular seeds. For example, people tend to gather and replant more tightly clustered seeds. See Christian, *Maps of Time*, p. 217.

[32] Christian, *Maps of Time*, p. 223.

landscape modification, in which farmers transplanted rice shoots onto bunded terraces known as paddy fields. By 2500 BCE these structures were beginning to spread throughout the Yangzi Valley.[33] Paddy fields were essentially artificial wetlands, allowing farmers to imitate the flood pulse while guaranteeing its regularity. They formed part of a suite of technologies that would eventually spread across a vast rice belt in Asia, which continues to feed much of the population of the world today. By the early modern era, paddy fields were helping colonists to transform wetlands as far afield as the lower Mississippi. Before commercial crops such as tobacco and cotton lured plantation owners to drain the land in this region, the lower Mississippi was known as the China of America.[34]

The rise of sedentary agriculture marked a key conceptual shift in the relationship between humans and water. Hunter-gatherers and flood-recession agriculturalists could evacuate with relative ease when threatened by floods. This is also a strategy favoured by many wetland animals, which retreat from water to shelter in areas known as refugia. Those who had modified the landscape risked losing significant investments of labour and time if they simply abandoned their homes. Being stuck in the path of a flood was one of the many consequences of what David Christian has described as 'the trap of sedentism'.[35] Later, growing populations and changing modes of social organisation made it virtually impossible for people to return to the nomadic solution for flooding. By the modern era, evacuees had become refugees. To ameliorate the trap of sedentism somewhat, communities in Hubei constructed elevated pilings or platforms, which turned into islands when the plains were flooded.[36] These platforms are still in evidence today, and can be identified by the character *tai* 台, a common component in local toponyms.[37] Similar pilings were used historically to avoid floods in regions as diverse as the lower Mississippi and the Gangetic Plain.[38] Unable to retreat to natural highland refugia, people built their own.

Though the environment had already been marked significantly by agriculture by the first century CE, for those from the relatively developed north, the middle Yangzi was still a wild region. The historian Ban

[33] Chang, 'Domestication and Spread'; Marks, *China*, p. 86.
[34] Morris, *Big Muddy*, p. 121.   [35] Christian, *Maps of Time*, p. 235.
[36] Marks, *China*, p. 26.
[37] Gao, 'Transformation of the Water Regime', p. 59. For a nineteenth-century description see Blakiston, *Five Months on the Yang-tsze*, pp. 65–6.
[38] Morris, *Big Muddy*, p. 20; Wisner et al., *At Risk*, p. 136.

Gu 班固 described how those living in the region had a mixed system of subsistence, augmenting cultivated rice with food they had foraged, hunted, and fished from the wild.[39] By this stage human predation had already depleted biodiversity significantly, having pushed appetising and slow-moving species, such as tapirs and wetland deer, to the brink of extinction.[40] Over the next two millennia species loss would increase dramatically, as humans homogenised the ecosystem to furnish their agricultural needs. This was not only ecologically damaging, but also diminished the capacity of humans to survive floods as it deprived them of water-resistant flora and fauna. By replacing wetland species with cultivated grain, humans deprived themselves of vital reservoirs of wild food.[41] Yet these reservoirs were never drained entirely. As we shall see, even in the twentieth century flood-stricken populations often fell back upon the wild wealth of the wetlands.

Agriculture did not erase the natural environment, but rather created agro-ecosystems.[42] Paddy fields were remarkably diverse habitats. Farmers used them to rear a variety of species alongside rice, including cultivated aquatic plants such as lotus and water chestnuts. They also encouraged the growth of ferns that helped improve soil quality.[43] Fish and frogs either were introduced or naturally colonised paddy fields. They not only provided farmers with valuable protein, but also consumed harmful weeds and insects and fertilised crops with their faeces. These species in turn attracted predators, including birds and turtles, which provided a source of nutrition for humans and for larger predators, including wolves and tigers, that left the forests and mountains to hunt on the fringes of the human world.[44] When floods struck, the remnants of the agro-ecosystem offered a valuable source of nutrition to inundated communities. Eventually, salvaging various species of wild and domesticated flora and fauna from inundated farmland was probably more important to human survival than gathering them from wild areas.

As well as hunting, the population of Hubei formed alliances with animals.[45] While domesticated pigs, chickens, and ducks provided useful

---

[39] Quoted in Oxenham, 'History of Han Yang', p. 367; Marks, *China*.
[40] Lu, *Transition from Foraging*; Turvey, *Witness to Extinction*.
[41] Elvin, *Retreat of the Elephants*.   [42] Marks, *China*.
[43] Li, 'Domestication of Plants'; Gorman, *Story of N*, p. 37.
[44] Marks, *China*, pp. 116, 136–7.
[45] On domestication see Christian, *Maps of Time*, pp. 216–17.

protein and manure, ruminant species such as water buffalo, oxen and yellow cows proved the most useful.[46] Far too valuable to eat, these animals were kept primarily for their formidable energy output. Alongside rice, they were a vital biological technology that helped farmers modify the environment. Domestic animals both benefited and suffered from their alliance with humans.[47] Farmers crafted excellent habitats for them, protecting them from competitors, pests and predators. Yet they also placed them in flood-prone areas, constraining them with tethers and fences that inhibited their natural survival behaviours. By the modern era floods were more lethal for domesticated animals than they were for people. As animals drowned, starved or succumbed to epizootics, people lost a vital source of nutrition and energy.

Not all species suffered as humans modified the environment. Pathogens thrived in the agro-ecosystem. Malaria had travelled with early humans into the middle Yangzi. Over time, the plasmodia responsible for the disease became locked into the flood pulse, thriving as mosquito populations swelled during the wet summer months. The draining of wetlands deprived these insects of their natural habitats, yet they found an excellent replacement in paddy fields and irrigation channels.[48] The agro-ecosystem also proved to be an accommodating habitat for freshwater snails, which were the vector of the waterborne disease schistosomiasis, also known as 'snail fever'.[49] The blood fluke that causes this disease has a complicated lifecycle, starting in the intestinal tracts of humans and other mammals, travelling via faeces to freshwater snails and then returning to a mammalian host. Snail fever thrived in areas where humans and cattle spent a long time submerged in water contaminated with faeces. The wetlands and paddy fields of the middle Yangzi offered a perfect habitat. Thus, through fostering the development of an agro-ecosystem, the population of Hubei had laid the foundations of a disaster regime. By encouraging people to settle on floodplains, increasing their reliance on vulnerable plants, and incubating endemic and epidemic diseases, farming helped to make floods much more dangerous.

[46] Smil, *China's Past*, pp. 29–30.   [47] Bankoff, 'Bodies on the Beach'.
[48] Marks, *China*, pp. 116, 130; Webb, *Humanity's Burden*, pp. 42–3.
[49] Schistosoma, or blood flukes, lay eggs in the intestinal tracts of humans and other mammals. These are deposited in faeces, becoming larvae that infect freshwater snails. Mature larvae, which are left behind in snail slime trails, burrow through the skin of mammals and then travel to the intestines to lay their eggs, beginning the lifecycle anew. Gross, *Farewell to the God of Plague*, pp. 3–4; Marks, *China*; Elvin, 'Three Thousand Years'.

Engineering Risks

For the inhabitants of northern China, the south had long been considered a land of swamps, jungles, disease, poisonous plants, dangerous animals and savage people.[50] This did not stop successive waves of northern migrants from flocking to the Yangzi beginning in the fourth century. The traditional story is that these migrants brought with them new ideologies and technologies of river management that helped to transform the hydrography of the middle Yangzi. Recently, Brian Lander has unearthed documents that question this narrative, dating the use of hydraulic technologies in Hubei to centuries earlier. It seems likely that the reason that locals employed these structures rather modestly in comparison to their northern neighbours was not because they were technologically backward, as has often been assumed, but rather because they could feed themselves adequately without modifying their environment.[51] Whatever their true provenance, hydraulic technologies would have a profound impact on the relationship between people and rivers in Hubei.

The artificial topography of dykes and polders prevented water from encroaching upon arable land, thereby precipitating a dramatic increase in agricultural productivity. Yet it also created new risks. Inherent within the structure of hydraulic technology is the possibility of hydraulic failure, which tends to be a much more catastrophic form of flooding than anything that exists in the natural world. Rapid-onset inundations can occur naturally, such as during large storm surges or when natural ice dams collapse. Yet for the most part, the natural rising of rivers and lakes is a far slower process than the bursting of retained water through a broken dyke or dam.[52] Roger del Moral and Lawrence Walker observe that the 'more engineering that is done to control a river's path, the greater are the floods when they burst the barriers – as they always do, eventually.'[53] The catastrophic deluges that poured into communities in 1931 were a product of this form of engineered risk.

Avoiding hydraulic failures is hard work. Dykes require regular maintenance and river channels must be dredged regularly.[54] Communities that neglected these tasks have often found themselves under water.

[50] Lewis, *China between Empires*, p. 13.   [51] Lander, 'State Management'.
[52] An ice dam break happened, for example, on Lake Missouri 12,000 years ago. See Del Moral and Walker, *Environmental Disasters*, p. 24.
[53] Ibid., p. 115.
[54] For a classic discussion of dredging in disaster prevention see Deng. *Zhongguo jiuhuang shi*, pp. 386–8.

Mark Elvin has suggested that in China hydraulic structures created a form of 'technological lock-in' – by building them, communities encumbered future generations with an arduous and expensive task of maintenance, which they had to continue no matter how limited the returns on their investments became over time.[55] Furthermore, by constructing dykes to mitigate natural uncertainties, those living under their protection became vulnerable to human uncertainties. Social phenomena such as financial collapses and armed conflicts often resulted in the neglect of vital hydraulic infrastructure. As people intervened in river flow, floods were no longer determined solely by climate and hydrology but also by economics and politics. Human agency became a key variable in the disaster regime.

Hydraulic agriculture developed incrementally over the course of two millennia. Using techniques first pioneered in the construction of paddy fields, the local population gradually created larger dykes to surround its communities, before beginning to construct larger river defences.[56] By the fourth century the population had begun to construct large dykes in central Hubei along the northern banks of the Yangzi. These would eventually evolve into the Great Jingjiang Dyke 荆江大堤.[57] Dykes were not only a useful agricultural tool, but were sometimes also used as weapons. They allowed defenders to unleash huge quantities of water onto oncoming enemies.[58] The Great Jingjiang Dyke seems to have been constructed at least in part to serve as a rampart against northern invasions.[59] The ancient strategy of 'militarising rivers', as Micah Muscolino has put it, would remain a prominent tactic well into the twentieth century, as modern armies continued to use flooding as a weapon.[60]

River dykes became a vital technology of agricultural colonisation in Hubei, allowing farmers to settle previously inaccessible areas to the north of the Yangzi. At the same time, to the south of the river in Hunan,

---

[55] Elvin, 'Three Thousand Years'; see also Newell and Wasson, 'Social System vs Solar System'.

[56] Lander, 'State Management'.

[57] The Great Jingjiang Dyke is the modern name for a structure that was known throughout much of its history as the Wancheng Dyke 万城提. There are regional differences in the English terms used for hydraulic structures. What British people refer to as dykes Americans call dikes or levees. Here I distinguish polder dykes from river dykes, in keeping with Chinese descriptions, which use the character *di* 堤 in both compound terms. The term *dadi* 大堤 – literally 'great dyke' – which I translate as river dyke, might otherwise be translated as embankment. In this book I use this particular term only to refer to embanked railways, which, confusingly, were sometimes also used as dykes.

[58] Ball, *Water Kingdom*, p. 180.   [59] Will, *State Intervention*, p. 300.

[60] Muscolino, *Ecology of War*.

communities were building dykes between the Yangzi and Dongting Lake 洞庭湖. With dykes on both banks, the Yangzi would eventually become consolidated into a single powerful stream. This process is known as channelisation.[61] It not only changes the flow of rivers but also has profound effects on their ecosystems. Channelisation had been occurring naturally in Hubei for thousands of years, as sedimentation and the inclined uplift of the eastern mountain ranges consolidated the unpredictable branched Yangzi into a more fixed stream. The same processes also caused the major flood basin to shift to the south, draining the Yunmeng Marsh and creating Dongting Lake.[62] From the drained wetlands emerged the Jianghan Plain 江汉平原, a fertile rice basket that became the economic heart of Hubei. Though nominally a plain, this area never quite forgot its marshy origins and remained chronically flood-prone.[63]

Meanwhile in Hunan, nature quickly adapted to the new hydrographic realities. Dongting Lake became a spawning ground for numerous aquatic species, including Yangzi river dolphins and finless porpoises, which swam in large pods throughout the region.[64] Over the next 2,000 years these species would find themselves in direct competition with human beings. Though fisherfolk caught them and starved them of prey, it was farmers who harmed them the most, draining their habitats and dividing their territories with dykes. Today the Yangzi river dolphin is functionally extinct and the finless porpoise is critically endangered.[65] Though pushed over the brink by dams and industrial pollution, it was hydraulic agriculture that initiated the retreat of the cetaceans.

Expanding agriculture built thriving cities. Urbanisation tended to occur at major intersections within the river system where communities could exploit trading opportunities. John McNeill has observed that, prior to the construction of railways, no inland transportation system in the world could rival the Chinese riverine network.[66] Convenience came at a heavy price, as port cities would suffer periodic inundations. Hubei boasted some of the best-located and most flood-prone cities in all of China. The east of the province formed a natural transportation hub,

---

[61] Brookes, *Channelized Rivers*. Channelisation should not be confused with canalisation, a process designed less for flood control and more to turn rivers into navigable waterways, much like artificial canals. Many rivers in Hubei were both channelised and canalised.
[62] Yin et al., 'On the River–Lake Relationship'.   [63] Perdue, *Exhausting the Earth*.
[64] Zhang et al., 'Yangtze River Dolphin'. These creatures once ranged from the Yichang to the Yangzi Delta.
[65] Turvey, *Witness to Extinction*.   [66] McNeill, 'China's Environmental History'.

as it was the point where the Yangzi was at its closest proximity to the Yellow River. Junks and sampans were able to navigate a relatively easy path between two major arterial trade routes by sailing along tributary rivers. Lying between Dongting and Poyang Lakes, eastern Hubei was also an access point for the southern trading networks that drained into these watercourses.[67] By the Song dynasty (960–1279) several urban settlements had developed around the confluence of the Yangzi and Han. These would eventually evolve into the conurbation known today as Wuhan.

When the scholar-official Fan Chengda 范成大 visited the Wuhan area in the twelfth century, he found thriving market cities, home to tens of thousands of households and rows of shops 'as thick as teeth in a comb'. There was, apparently, nothing known in the world that was not sold here.[68] Urban commerce would play an important role in transforming the environment of Hubei. Merchants rarely deforested catchments or reclaimed wetlands with their own hands, but they made great profits by selling timber and rice. Port cities also changed the epidemiological environment. Their dense populations provided sustainable chains of infection for crowd diseases, which were unable to persist in their most virulent forms in smaller human communities.[69] Meanwhile, urban trade networks acted as conduits for rapid dissemination of pathogens across large areas.[70] The diseases incubated by cities would transform the disaster regime, escalating to epidemic proportions in the wake of floods.

Hydraulic agriculture may have begun its inexorable rise, but by the beginning of the second millennium many residents of Hubei still retained elements of an earlier wetland culture. When the scholar-official Lu You visited Hubei in the twelfth century he noticed an obvious divide between those living on higher ground, who farmed millet and buck-wheat, and those living among the marshes and lakes, who hunted, fished and gathered lotus and water chestnuts.[71] Lu painted an idyllic picture of the latter population, describing them as living freely among lakes and marshes. In reality, wetland communities could not escape the stric-tures of state regulation, as the use of wild resources was subject to rigid controls.[72] Over the next few centuries hunting and fishing would be

[67] Worcester, *Junks and Sampans*, pp. 18, 145–58.
[68] Hargett, *Riding the River Home*, p. 147.
[69] Crawford, *Deadly Companions*; Elvin, 'Three Thousand Years'.
[70] Marks, *China*, p. 130.   [71] Watson, *Grand Canal*, pp. 124–35.
[72] Elvin, 'Three Thousand Years', pp. 25–7.

curtailed as wild areas were incorporated into a regime of property and usufructuary rights. Yet the wetland world that Lu described was not a complete fiction. Many people truly did manage to find ways to evade some of the worst consequences of sedentism.

Some did so by living outside the law. Like the dark forests of northern Europe, the wetlands of China had always been imagined as spaces of mystery and crime. Fan Chengda described the trepidation that he and his crew had felt when they sailed through an area to the west of Wuhan known as the Hundred Miles of Wasteland百里荒 (Baili Huang). This was 'all lakes and meres, and stalks and reeds, with no further traces of humans, and where powerful bandits appear and disappear'.[73] Others found legal ways to live in the wetlands. One of the most remarkable adaptations to regular inundation was the use of floating fields, which could be found on rivers and lakes. Lu described seeing large structures formed of knitted aquatic grass covered with earth. They were large enough to support entire communities – complete with chickens and dogs, vegetable allotments, wine shops, and temples.[74] Floating fields represented a radical alternative to hydraulic agriculture – a way of life based on accommodating rather than suppressing water.

Fighting Water for Land

Two interlinked processes defined the history of flooding in Hubei over the course of the second millennium. The first was the repetitive growth and collapse of floodplain agriculture that Pierre-Étienne Will has described as the 'hydraulic cycle'.[75] This began with heavy investment in dykes, which helped to precipitate a period of rapid agricultural expansion and economic growth. When growth exceeded the capacity of hydraulic technology, the region experienced increased flooding and a concomitant economic recession. A period of crisis could be ameliorated only when the state renewed its investment in water control, thereby beginning the hydraulic cycle anew. The hydraulic cycle played out twice over the course of the second millennium, roughly corresponding with the rise and fall of the Ming and Qing dynasties. History may not have repeated itself but it certainly rhymed. These cycles were nested within

[73] Fan quoted in Hargett, *Riding the River Home*, p. 146.
[74] Watson, *Grand Canal*, p. 147.
[75] Will, 'Un cycle hydraulique,' pp. 261–88. Peter Perdue identified a similar pattern in the Dongting Lake area of neighbouring Hunan. See Perdue, *Exhausting the Earth*.

a second, more profound process of environmental change, in which all available land was gradually turned over to agricultural production. Mark Elvin has described this as a trajectory towards the 'maximal arablization' of the environment.[76] To feed an insatiable appetite for land, people trapped rivers in channels, drained wetlands, and denuded forests. Together, these environmental encroachments helped to increase the frequency and intensity of flooding.[77]

Song engineers consolidated the piecemeal river dykes in Hubei into continuous hydraulic systems. They were careful to incorporate outlets and sluice gates that would allow rivers to discharge excess water and silt onto their floodplains.[78] At the same time, local communities began to construct dykes to encircle their communities known as polders or *yuan* 垸.[79] These would become the primary units of cultural and social organisation in Hubei, serving a role similar to that played by villages in other regions.[80] River dykes and polders – together with new technologies such as waterwheels and treadle paddle pumps – allowed farmers to drain wetlands.[81] This process expanded dramatically during the Ming dynasty (1368–1644), due, in part, to a large influx of migrant colonists from downstream Jiangxi.[82] This period of growth corresponded roughly with the onset of a period of global cooling known as the Little Ice Age. As cold periods tend to precipitate a decline in flooding in the middle Yangzi, it is possible that the climate may have made it easier for colonists to drain the wetlands.[83] Soon the Jianghan and Dongting plains became largest rice-exporting area in the empire, exceeding even Jiangnan region in the prosperous eastern provinces. 'If Hubei and Hunan have a good harvest', it was said, 'All-under-Heaven will be fed' 湖广熟, 天下足 (Huguang shu, Tianxia zu).[84] Hydraulic agriculture – an inherently risky business – was now a vital constituent of one of the largest regional economies in the world.

---

[76] Elvin, 'Three Thousand Years'.

[77] On this increase see Yu, Chen and Ren, 'Analysis of Historical Floods'.

[78] Will, 'State Intervention'.

[79] Gao, 'Transformation of the Water Regime'; Perdue, *Exhausting the Earth*; Zhang, 'Environment, Market, and Peasant Choice'.

[80] Gao, 'Transformation of the Water Regime'.

[81] Elvin, *Pattern of the Chinese Past*, pp. 126–7.   [82] Will, 'State Intervention', pp. 307–8.

[83] Ts'ui-jung Liu notes that the period between 1470 and 1520 was particularly cold. Liu, 'A Retrospection of Climate Changes.' Timothy Brook has noted that the broad transformation to the Little Ice Age was punctuated by a succession of nine 'sloughs', during which China experienced bouts of severe weather. Brook, *Troubled Empire*, 6–24.

[84] Di, 'Xin Zhongguo'; Zhang, *Coping with Calamity*, p. 101.

In 1465, Hubei experienced one of its most historically significant floods. The Han River suddenly shifted course, revealing a thin strip of land at the point of its former confluence with the Yangzi. This would eventually become named Hankou 汉口, literally the Mouth of the Han. With an unrivalled position in the riverine network, by the late imperial period this was the greatest inland entrepôt in China, and one of the biggest cities in the world.[85] Like so many other great trading centres – such as Paris, New Orleans, Kolkata and Saint Petersburg – Hankou was a city designed by rivers. Water defined its economic life, forged its urban morphology, influenced its vernacular architecture and saturated its religious life. This intimate relationship with water came at a heavy cost. A city that owed its very existence to the capricious nature of rivers would remain at their mercy throughout its history, as time and again Hankou would find itself under water.

The rapid growth of the agricultural economy eventually proved unsustainable. Excessive wetland reclamation deprived rivers of natural flood reservoirs. As the surface area of marshes and lakes decreased, the wetlands no longer absorbed excess water.[86] Poor hydraulic governance hastened the systemic decline. The outlets that Song engineers had included in river dykes silted up or were deliberately blocked. This allowed agriculturalists to colonise more land but also prevented rivers from discharging excess water and silt.[87] Siltation would eventually elevate the Han and Yangzi above their plains, and lead to disastrous dyke breaches. In the 1560s Hubei was struck by a succession of catastrophic floods.[88] These inundations marked the beginning of a deeper hydraulic crisis. Waterlogging and localised flooding became the norm, and basin wide floods struck Hubei in 1592 1593 and 1600. Although we know that this was an era of intense El Niño activity in areas such as Burma and India, the general pattern of flooding in the sixteenth and seventeenth centuries does not correspond neatly with ENSO activity.[89] The political climate was at least as important, as the collapse of Ming governance prevented effective hydraulic reforms. The most significant factor

---

[85] Rowe, *Hankow: Commerce and Society*; Rowe, *Hankow: Conflict and Community*.

[86] Yin et al., 'On the River–Lake Relationship'; Will, 'Un cycle hydraulique'.

[87] In most cases sluice gates were sealed so that colonists could open new land, yet some were also deliberately sealed for geomantic reasons, as officials wished to prevent the flooding of an imperial tomb. See Will, 'State Intervention', pp. 311–13.

[88] Will, 'Un cycle hydraulique'.

[89] Ricklefs et al., *New History of Southeast Asia*, p. 96. A chronology compiled by Brook cites five El Niño events in the 1560s and three in the 1590s. See Brook, *Nine Sloughs*.

34   *The Long River* 长江

was the unsustainable pattern of river basin settlement. By the time that the Ming dynasty fell, the hydraulic crisis had become so severe that the Jianghan Plain had reverted to being a depopulated wetland once again.[90]

Although hydraulic agriculture had proven vulnerable to climatic and political stress, its economic benefits were hard to resist. Hence, when the Qing dynasty (1644–1912) took over Hubei, its governors began to invest heavily in dyke reconstruction. From the mid-seventeenth century the wetlands and floodplains of Hubei were reoccupied. This time the impetus was provided by internal demographic growth rather than immigration.[91] The population increased dramatically as New World crops such as maize, corn, peanuts and sweet potatoes improved nutrition. These hardy plants allowed agriculturalists to colonise inhospitable highland environments with acidic soils.[92] As agriculture climbed hills the pace of deforestation increased dramatically. Meanwhile merchants continued to strip highland forests and float timber rafts along rivers to urban markets.[93] The denuding of catchments exacerbated the problem of flooding. Removing trees and vegatation caused water to drain off hillsides faster and in much greater volumes. Increased water runoff stripped the topsoil, which was no longer bound by forest root systems, from the land. As soil leached into watercourses the silt-load of rivers increased, meaning that their beds were raised and their discharge channels were blocked.[94]

---

[90] Oxenham, 'On the Inundations', p. 175; Will, 'Un cycle hydraulique'; Perdue, *Exhausting the Earth*.

[91] Zhang, *Coping with Calamity*. The 225 million people who populated the empire in 1750 had risen to 420 million by 1870. See Marks, *China*, p. 170.

[92] Osborne, 'Highlands and Lowlands'. Although the late imperial increase of deforestation, starting in the eighteenth century, was by far the most intense, there had been several major waves of deforestation in Chinese history. The loss of forests first began to have a discernible impact in the first millennium CE, increasing dramatically at the start of the second millennium CE, around the same time that the dyke network in Hubei was evolving. This was a period of relative climatic and economic stability, known as the medieval economic revolution. See Elvin, *Retreat of the Elephants*. China was far from unique in decimating its forest resources in the early modern period. See Richards, *Unending Frontier*.

[93] Worcester, *Junks and Sampans*, p. 420.

[94] There remains some debate among hydrologists regarding the link between deforestation and flooding. For a view in support of the link see Bradshaw et al., 'Global Evidence that Deforestation Amplifies Flood Risk'. For an argument that rejects simple causation see Dijk et al. 'Forest–Flood Relation Still Tenuous'. Qing scholars such as Wei Yuan seem to have believed strongly in the link. See Wei, 'Huguang shuili lun'.

While colonists drained wetlands and denuded forested slopes, administrators failed to address the structural problems in the river dyke system. Rather than opening blocked outlets, Qing engineers consolidated dykes into uninterrupted networks, finally separating rivers from their floodplains entirely.[95] Farmers later exacerbated this process by building polders next to the river dykes.[96] The Yangzi and Han Rivers, which had once wandered across their plains in a continuum of multiple streams, were now effectively channelised. As they were unable to discharge water and silt, alluviation raised their riverbeds.[97] Communities on the plains now lived below the level of rivers, with only dykes to protect their homes and livelihoods. When these dykes failed, as they inevitably did from time to time, the constructed landscape funnelled water down onto these communities. Hydraulic agriculture had helped to create a mutant form of flooding, far more destructive than any natural inundation.

In 1788, the Yangzi burst through the Great Jingjiang Dyke. Water poured onto the Jianghan Plain and turned polders into reservoirs.[98] This was the first in a series of mega-floods that would devastate Hubei over the next two centuries. The ultimate cause of this disaster lay in the human interaction with the environment, but its proximate cause was meteorological. The final two decades of the eighteenth century were a period of extreme weather worldwide, with droughts in Egypt, India and Mexico killing millions. The common link seems to have been a powerful and prolonged El Niño event.[99] This may well have contributed to the flooding of Hubei in 1788.

The climate could not have precipitated such a calamitous inundation, however, were it not for the profound anthropogenic transformation of the environment. Observers at the time were not unaware of this fact. The great nineteenth century polymath Wei Yuan 魏源 wrote an incisive account of how excessive deforestation and polder construction had exacerbated flooding. Inundation is inevitable, he observed, when 'people fight water to derive the benefits of land.'[100] To prevent flooding, Wei

---

[95] Yin et al., 'On the River–Lake Relationship of the Middle Yangtze.' The Great Jingjiang Dyke was further elongated in the Republican period and finally extended to Jianli County in 1954, thereby reaching a total length of 182.35 km. Zhang, 'Water Calamities and Dike Management', p. 70.

[96] Wei, 'Hubei difang yi'; Wei, 'Huguang shuili lun'.

[97] Zhang, *Coping with Calamity*, p. 30.

[98] Will, 'State Intervention', p. 342.

[99] Grove, 'Great El Niño.' See also Grove and Chappell, *El Niño*, p. 17.

[100] '*Ren yu shui zheng di wei li* 人与水争地为利', Wei, 'Hubei difang yi', p. 399.

argued, the people of Hubei would have to allow rivers to reclaim some of their natural floodplains. This sustainable approach to river management had a long pedigree in Chinese environmental thinking. Though water conservancy had long been dominated by a Confucian doctrine of decisive environmental interventionism, there had always been a counterculture of intellectuals who advocated a more Daoist approach, suggesting that rivers be allowed to follow their own courses.[101] In the years since Wei Yuan offered his analysis of flooding, his non-interventionist perspective tended to be marginalised. In China, as elsewhere, modern states have been determined to fight water for land.[102]

It took two decades for Hubei to recover from the 1788 flood. The provincial government eventually funded an extensive rehabilitation of the dyke network, which bought temporary respite but could not arrest the incipient hydraulic crisis.[103] Over the next century the frequency and intensity of flooding would increase dramatically. This was partly a matter of perception. As Eduard Vermeer has observed, when agricultural colonists occupied marginal land in the late Qing, the previously unremarkable ebb and flow of water suddenly came to be recorded in local gazetteers as flooding.[104] This observer bias cannot explain the increase in flooding in established agricultural areas such as the Jianghan Plain, which had long been under official surveillance. In 1831 Hubei experienced one the most devastating inundations of the nineteenth century. One hundred thousand refugees descended upon Hankou, where they were fed for months at rice porridge kitchens. Later, Wuhan itself was flooded to such an extent that large ships could sail through the streets – scenes that would be repeated exactly a century later.[105]

Zhang Jiayan has argued that the hydraulic crisis that Hubei experienced between the mid-nineteenth and mid-twentieth centuries was due largely to poor governance. Administrators embezzled tax revenue, neglected dyke management and used substandard construction materials.[106] These localised failures were part of a broader pattern. Historians today rightly eschew the teleological view of the late Qing, which pictures it as a polity limping meekly to an inevitable demise. Beset by serious domestic and international pressures, governors often responded with flexibility and innovation. Yet the capacity of the state

[101] Pietz, *Yellow River*; Ball, *Water Kingdom.*   [102] McNeill, *Something New*, p. 150.
[103] Will, 'State Intervention', p. 342.   [104] Vermeer, 'Population and Ecology'.
[105] *Wuhan shi zhi: Minzheng zhi*, p. 141.
[106] Zhang, 'Environment, Market, and Peasant Choice', p. 39; Zhang, 'Water Calamities', p. 97.

undoubtedly declined, helping to set the stage not only for the hydraulic crisis in the middle Yangzi but also for the long century of disasters more generally. This ailing state not only failed to maintain its hydraulic infrastructure, but also underfunded its once formidable granary network. This meant that not only were floods more devastating but the famines they caused were also significantly worse. Politics and economics had helped to forge a modern disaster regime, which left people chronically vulnerable to hazards.

Living with Floods

In the 1840s Évariste Huc wrote one of the first European travel accounts of Hubei. Among numerous remarkable sights, he described whole communities living on floating fields. These seem to have changed remarkably little in the seven centuries since Lu You had travelled through the region. Whole villages sat on bamboo rafts covered with soil, floating in a leisurely fashion across lakes and rivers. Huc characterised the existence of those thereon as a life of 'peace and abundance'. These nomads of the wetlands, who cultivated rice and caught fish, had 'constructed themselves a little solitude in the midst of civilisation.'[107] These were not the only people who found ways to accommodate water by floating on its surface. River merchants and fisherfolk often lived their entire lives aboard sampans and junks, which had kitchens and sleeping areas in the aft.[108] This floating population enjoyed a way of life that was radically different from that of the sedentary majority.

Though farmers were far more vulnerable to inundation, they also found ways to live with floods, as the historian Zhang Jiayan has described eloquently. For those at the ecological fringes, living on land prone to inundation, the threat of water formed an imperative far stronger than the market. They eschewed profitable cash crops in favour of water-resistant varieties such as deep-water rice and sorghum.[109] They also continued to practise older forms of wetland culture, supplementing their nutritional intake by foraging and hunting. Habitat loss and human predation had severely depleted biodiversity, but as the accounts of foreign travellers and hunters in the late nineteenth century attest, Hubei

[107] Huc, *Journey Through the Chinese* Empire, pp. 95–7. See also Zhang, *Coping with Calamity*.
[108] Worcester, *Junks and Sampans*, pp. 466–7.
[109] Although a dry land crop, sorghum is relatively water resistant. See Zhang, *Coping with Calamity*, p. 109.

was far from the ecological wasteland that the North China Plain was becoming.[110] Thomas Blakiston, who sailed up the Yangzi in the 1860s, saw a wide variety of flora and fauna, including pods of porpoises 'disporting themselves in the still muddy current' of the Yangzi, which followed him for much of his journey through the region.[111] Great flocks of water birds still gathered in the region to exploit the wide variety of fish species, including bream, carp, catfish and perch, which could be found in great abundance in the many rivers and lakes of the region.[112]

Fish still formed an important part of the diet of the local population. The Japanese diplomat Mizuno Kokichi, who made a detailed study of the markets in Wuhan in the first decade of the twentieth century, remarked on the huge variety available to local consumers.[113] Though many of these fish were raised in ponds, aquaculture still relied heavily on the natural environment, as the spawn of most species was harvested from the wild.[114] Fisherfolk cast lines or dip-nets into rivers and lakes, or caught fish using lime, which deprived their quarries of oxygen.[115] Some people even exploited the fishing expertise of wetland animals. Cormorants and egrets were domesticated and used to catch fish, their throats bound to prevent them from swallowing their catch.[116] In western Hubei people trained otters to flush fish into their nets.[117] As the main fishing season coincided with a slack period in the agricultural year, farmers often took to the water to supplement their diets and incomes.[118] Fish stocks were also sufficient to support a large population of occupational specialists, who lived on lakeshores and riverbanks, or aboard boats. Fisherfolk tended to be poor, but their way of life was highly adapted to their perilous environment.[119]

---

[110] The foreign hunter William Spencer Percival remarked that waterfowl 'swarm all over the river in the winter months.' Spencer Percival, *Land of the Dragon*, p. 76. See also Blakiston, *Five Months*, p. 98.

[111] Blakiston, *Five Months*, pp. 61, 73, 119. On later extinction see Turvey, *Witness to Extinction*.

[112] Wang et al., 'Terrestrial Contributions'; Rowe, 'Water Control'.

[113] Shuiye, *Hankou*, pp. 139–140.   [114] Worcester, *Junks and Sampans*, p. 136.

[115] Upward, *Sons of Han*, p. 56; Blakiston, *Five Months*, pp. 30, 137; Worcester, *Junks and Sampans*, p. 138.

[116] *Special Catalogue of the Chinese Collection of Exhibits for the International Fisheries Exhibition*, p. 46; Laufer, *Domestication of the Cormorant*. For a description of comorant fishing in Hubei see Cornaby, *String of Chinese Peach-Stones*, pp. 4–5.

[117] *Special Catalogue of the Chinese Collection of Exhibits for the International Fisheries Exhibition*, p. 6.

[118] On the fishing season see Shuiye, *Foreign*; Zhang, *Coping with Calamity*.

[119] Rowe, 'Water Control'.

CANGUE USED IN DUCK CATCHING.

Figure 1.1. A fowler in the middle Yangzi region in the late nineteenth century. (Ayean Kum, 'Some Chinese Methods of Shooting and Trapping Game', in *With a Boat and Gun in the Yangtze Valley*. Shanghai: Shanghai Mercury, 1910. Reproduced courtesy of the Cambridge University Library)

In addition to fish, people exploited many other natural endowments of the wetlands. They foraged for edible plants such as lotus, water chestnuts and wild rice, and marketable varieties, such as duck weed, hemp and indigo.[120] They hunted terrestrial mammals such wild pigs, deer, badgers and weasels in forested upper catchments. The most important sources of wild protein, besides fish, were the eggs and meat of birds. Hunters used dragnets, bamboo cages, traps and guns to catch pheasants and snipe and a large selection of waterfowl, including geese, ducks, teal, swans, pelicans and cranes.[121] Figure 1.1 gives an impression of the innovative nature of wetland culture. Fowlers wore oilskins and camouflaged themselves with grass, before floating over to flocks of waterfowl on large

---

[120] Zhang, *Coping with Calamity*; Rowe, 'Water Control'.
[121] Wade, *With Boat and Gun in the Yangtze Valley*, pp. 19, 24, 29; Kum, 'Some Chinese Methods of Shooting and Trapping Game'; Jernigan, *Shooting in China*, p. 212; Worcester, *Junkman Smiles*, p. 48.

wooden boards attached to their necks. Using tame ducks as decoys, they caught their unsuspecting quarries with their hands.[122] Hunting was a profitable enough business to support a specialised market for the meat and feathers of game birds in Wuhan.[123] These reservoirs of wild food may not have been sufficient to support a large population on a permanent basis, yet they helped bolster nutritional intake in normal years and offered a vital resource during floods.

If managed correctly, flooding did not have to be a problem for farmers. In Bangladesh, rural communities distinguish between *borsha* floods, which they depend on for regular agricultural production, from *bonna* floods, which cause widespread loss of crops and life.[124] Those cultivating the lowlands of Hubei drew similar distinctions. They were drawn to areas such as lakeshores precisely because they were flood-prone, as they knew that the regular rise and fall of water deposited rich halos of fertility.[125] In the 1910s the poet Luo Han 罗汉 described how those who cultivated lakes to the north of Wuhan reaped great fortunes from the nutrient-rich soil.[126] This agricultural strategy was not without risks, as entire harvests could be destroyed if water was overabundant. Yet with considerable skill and a little good fortune, the profits accrued during good years easily made up for occasional losses.[127]

For those unable to maintain this delicate balance, lakeshore agriculture could become a poverty trap. The regular loss of crops meant that some communities subsisted on little more than wild plants. Local histories relate descriptions of lakeshore communities who were so poor that their residents became infertile.[128] While travelling through rural Hubei in the 1880s, Archibald Little was confronted with this stark poverty. 'Nothing could be more wretched than the appearance of the few villages we passed – collections of ten to twenty reed-huts perched on the top of a steep mound, which is covered to the water's edge with

---

[122] For description of waterfowl see Little, *Through the Yang-tse Gorges*, p. 22; Blakiston, *Five Months*, p. 93.

[123] Shuiye, *Hankou*, p. 141.   [124] Zaman, *Rivers of Life*.

[125] Del Moral and Walker, *Environmental Disasters*, p. 130.

[126] Luo, *Minchu Hankou*, p. 8.   [127] Zhang, *Coping with Calamity*.

[128] Pi, *Wuhan Tongshi: Minguo Juan (Shang)*, p. 222. Such claims may well have been apocryphal, speaking to a cultural idiom in which an inability to produce descendants considered a highly pitiable fate. Yet severe malnutrition, coupled with the effects of endemic diseases such as snail fever, can cause a dramatic decline in fertility rates. Ó Gráda, *Famine*, p. 108. Gross, *Farewell to the God of Plague*.

buffalo dung.'[129] Flooding was often both a cause and a consequence of economic distress. The only places that people could afford to live were the same places that kept them poor.[130] This was not unique to Hubei. In flood-prone regions of northern India members of lower castes can often be found in disproportionately high numbers in littoral areas around the edges of elevated settlements, their social marginality consolidating them in a position of geographic vulnerability.[131]

Chronic water control problems had serious health effects, which cascaded into further economic problems. By the early twentieth century snail fever was so rife that it infected around 10 million people nationwide, killing around 400,000 annually.[132] People living in infectious zones could do nothing but leave, meaning that large tracts of fertile land remained uncultivated. In Hanyang County, snail fever wiped several dozen villages off the map. Those who refused to be pushed off their land by molluscs soon developed debilitating symptoms, which further hindered their economic productivity. Late-stage snail fever sufferers developed hugely distended stomachs, a symptom so notorious that locals named the condition 'big belly disease'大肚子病 (da duzi bing). Snail fever was particularly prevalent in the villages around Dongxi Lake 东西湖, where eight out of ten people were infected. Residents of this area, so it was said, could be easily identified, as their stomachs entered the room before the rest of their bodies.[133] For those living in such conditions, floods merely amplified ongoing problems – they caused epidemic outbreaks of endemic poverty.

Few epidemics of poverty surpassed that caused by the catastrophic 1849 flood. In some ways this disaster adhered to the typical pattern found in the region, having been caused by heavy summer rains in Hubei, Hunan and Sichuan. Yet the flood also coincided with – and was perhaps precipitated by – a highly unusual period of cold weather in June. The residents of Wuhan, who would ordinarily be sweating in the oppressive humidity of the early summer, instead found themselves wearing furs and skins.[134] Curiously, at the same time, their counterparts in the southern United States were experiencing similar conditions, with a cold and wet

[129] Little, *Through the Yang-tse Gorges*, p. 53.
[130] In some areas there was a direct correspondence between the elevation of land and its value. Zhang, *Coping with Calamity*, p. 153.
[131] Wisner et al., *At Risk*, p. 136.   [132] Gross, *Farewell to the God of Plague*, p. 17.
[133] Pi, *Wuhan tongshi: Minguo juan (shang)*, pp. 220–3.
[134] Oxenham, 'History of Han Yang,' p. 175.

spring in the tributaries of the Mississippi helping one of the worst floods in the history of New Orleans.[135]

As rural communities across Hubei descended into famine, in Wuhan another deadly secondary effect of flooding seemed to be raising its head. The geographer Edward Oxenham suggests that the 1849 flood precipitated an outbreak of cholera.[136] Reconstructing the history of this disease in China is fraught with difficulties. The term *huoluan* 霍乱, which in the modern era came to signify a specific condition caused by cholera vibrio, had been used for millennia as a generic term for any kind of acute gastrointestinal distress.[137] Believing that China was the fountainhead of all things infectious, foreigners often assumed that references to *huoluan* in ancient medical texts were evidence that modern cholera had been present in the country since time immemorial.[138] This was not the case. It is likely that foreigners themselves imported cholera into China during in 1820s, with the vibrio travelling along shipping routes from their home in deltaic India.[139]

Cholera quickly found a niche in the cities of the middle Yangzi, and thrived when humans were pushed into contact with infected water in the summer months. Along with other enteric conditions, it proved particularly lethal to overcrowded settlements of flood refugees who lacked any sanitary provisions. Thus established, cholera became a defining component of the modern disaster regime. It was already exacerbating the effects of flooding in the Yellow River in 1821.[140] Alongside typhus, malaria and dysentery, it would become one of the leading causes of death during nineteenth century famines.[141] Historians have paid relatively little attention to the role that modern diseases played in modern disasters. The epidemiological transitions of this era had a profound influence on the nosological profile of hazards. Populous yet unsanitary cities linked by rapid transportation created new possibilities for transmission of pathogens.[142] These new disease ecologies proved lethal to

---

[135] On the Red River see Blair and Rannie, 'Wading to Pembina'. On the New Orleans floods see Morris, *Big Muddy*.

[136] Oxenham, 'On the Inundations', p. 175.

[137] On traditional Chinese medical conceptions of cholera see Rogaski, *Hygienic Modernity*, esp. p. 96.

[138] For example, in the 1890s, J. C. Thompson published an article stating 'Cholera has been known in China since time immemorial', noting its appearance in records as early as 2,000 years earlier. Quoted in *The China Medical Journal* XLI, no. 7 (July 1927).

[139] MacPherson, 'Cholera in China'; Marks, *China*, p. 227.

[140] Li, *Fighting Famine*, p. 264.   [141] Ó Gráda, *Eating People Is Wrong*, p. 145.

[142] Crawford, *Deadly Companions*; Harrison, *Disease and the Modern World*.

large populations of refugees, thus greatly exacerbating the humanitarian consequences of the disaster regime.

Even by the standards of the nineteenth century, the 1849 flood seems to have had been particularly devastating. The poet Ye Diaoyuan 叶调元 wrote of a million homes washed away by water, impoverished refugees starving to death on the streets and women forced to sell themselves into prostitution. A prevalent theme in his poems was the inequality of disaster outcomes. Wealthy people had fled for safety while poor people had simply died. The rich transported their dead for burial on local hillsides, while the poor were forced to abandon corpses to floodwater. Those who lived in large houses moved to higher storeys, while the lowly houses of the poor were reduced to rubble.[143] While residents of Wuhan were experiencing the inequality of disaster outcomes, their counterparts in New Orleans were also discovering the profound influence that household income has during floods. When the city was inundated, wealthy people 'vertically evacuated' into the upper storeys of their homes, while their poorer neighbours were forced to flee from single-storey shacks to higher ground.[144]

The cultural historian Andreas Bernard has linked the desire of modern urbanites to live in upper storeys to the invention of the lift. In modern cities such as Paris and New York, mechanical lifts helped to transform inconvenient garrets into desirable penthouses.[145] Yet in flood-prone cities such as Wuhan and New Orleans, height had always been a premium commodity, demonstrating that there was more than one form of architectural modernity. In Hubei, there was a distinct convergence between the literal and figurative stratification of the urban landscape. Wealthier citizens built large timber-framed buildings on strong stone or earth foundations, with walls constructed from a variety of materials including brick, stone, timber and bamboo.[146] Those with fewer resources constructed housing frames from cheap timber or bamboo and made walls from tamped earth, thatch or woven reeds. During floods, humble houses dissolved in water or were torn from the landscape, leaving nothing but skeletal wooden frames.[147] At the literal and figurative bottom of the urban landscape people lived in huts

[143] Ye, *Hankou zhuzhici*. The aftermath of this disaster offered little respite for the population, as receding water gave way to invading Taiping armies. Rowe, *Hankow: Conflict and Community* p. 151.
[144] Morris, *Big Muddy*, pp. 71, 106–7.   [145] Bernard, *Lifted*.
[146] Knapp, *China's Old Dwellings*, p. 79.
[147] Ibid.; Buck, *Chinese Farm Economy*, p. 401. Upward, *Sons of Han*, p. 73

Figure 1.2. The Wuhan riverbank in the early twentieth century. (Author's personal collection)

棚子 (pengzi) or low houses 矮屋 (aiwu), which offered virtually no protection from flooding.[148]

Nowhere was the convergence of literal and social stratification more evident than on the riverbanks of cities. Here river merchants lived in stilt houses that would remain above rivers even during the wet summer months. On the banks below people lived in shacks and huts, where they had to contend not only with unpredictable watercourses, but also with sewage and rubbish being thrown down from stilt houses.[149] Some shacks were constructed from urban detritus – discarded planks, pieces of broken metal or anything that could be gleaned from the city above.[150] Other huts were knitted together from reeds, which grew in thick stands on riverbanks and lakeshores often reaching a height of four or five metres.[151] The reed huts that stood on the riverbanks of Wuhan (Figure 1.2) were known colloquially as duck eggs鸭蛋 (yadan).[152]

Huts offered little protection from the elements, and could easily be washed away by flash floods, yet had the advantage of being cheap and

[148] Xie, *Yi jiu san yi nian Hankou dashui ji*, p. 141.

[149] Bird, *Yangtze Valley and Beyond*, p. 67.   [150] Li 'Matou gongren'.

[151] Rensselaer, *A Legacy of Historical Gleanings*, p. 341; Little, *Through the Yang-tse Gorges*, pp. 21–2.

[152] Li, 'Fuhe rensheng', pp. 55–7; or a contemporary description of life in this area see Jie, *Hankou zhi kuli*.

portable. Their occupants could cope with the threat of flooding using one of the most venerable of techniques – evacuation. The occupants of duck egg shacks lived a semi-nomadic existence, moving their homes to high-ground refugia when rivers rose in the summer. Living in a hut, though hardly desirable, was a pragmatic adaptation to a hazardous environment, which allowed people to survive on the littoral and economic margins of the city. To survive this life, one had to be keenly attuned to minor environmental changes. Riverbank communities knew that when the Yangzi assumed a copper hue it was time to move, as there must have been heavy rain upstream in the red sandstone basin of Sichuan.[153] Such signals served as natural early warning systems for the poor, and were a key component of the wetland culture that helped them to live with floods.

There was also a city beyond the riverbanks – one that floated. The Yangzi and Han did not form a hard border; their surfaces extended crowded streets and alleyways out onto the water. Many people worked, slept and ate in floating neighbourhoods. The customs official G. R. G. Worcester estimated that by the twentieth century there were 25,000 junks engaged in traffic between the Wuhan cities. 'They lie 10 or 12 abreast on both the banks of the Han River for a distance of 5 miles back and are packed so close that the Chinese expression "like scales on a fish" is not inappropriate.'[154] These vessels came in all shapes and sizes, from the humble sampans that darted about the harbour unloading larger junks to opulent floating brothels known as flower boats 花船 (huachuan).[155] Just as riverbank neighbourhoods advanced and retreated with the rise and fall of water, so too did this floating city. When Wuhan was inundated, those who lived and worked on the water often encroached beyond the riverbanks; their sampans became water taxis and floating markets. For those habituated to a life on water, flooding was not just a disaster. It was also an opportunity.

A Water-Plagued Land

During the late nineteenth century, a new wave of migrants began to colonise the riverbanks of Wuhan. Under the terms of the 1858 Treaty of Tianjin, the British had been granted the right to navigate the river and build a settlement in the newly designated treaty port of Hankou.

---

[153] Oxenham, 'On the Inundations,' p. 177.
[154] Worcester, *Junks and Sampans*, p. 354.   [155] Ye, *Hankou zhuzhici*, p. 193.

Many new arrivals believed the devastating floods that they witnessed in their new home were simply a pathological feature of the local environment. The geographer Edward Oxenham claimed that the natural sloping of the earth coupled with incessant rainfall had conspired to turn Hubei into a 'water-plagued land'.[156] What foreign observers mistook for environmentally determined inundations were in fact the symptoms of a hydraulic crisis. The decline of Qing infrastructure had been greatly exacerbated during the Taiping Civil War (1850–1864), when Hubei had endured waves of invasion and counter-invasion. This caused the already ailing hydraulic network to spiral into complete decay. Dyke breaches went unrepaired for years on end, and in 1856 Qing commanders militarised a tributary of the Han River, opening the sluice gates to drown their Taiping enemies.[157] Such strategies may have helped to quell the insurgency, yet they came at a huge humanitarian cost. Some 20 million people lost their lives before the Taiping Heavenly Kingdom was defeated, making this probably the most lethal civil conflict in history.[158] The war helped to turn much of China into a water-plagued land. Communities living in the Huai and Yellow River basins faced a series of calamitous floods, which were second only to droughts in their humanitarian cost.[159] By crippling infrastructure and draining resources, warfare had helped to forge a lethal disaster regime. It would continue to do so over the next century.

The Taiping Civil War was not the only conflict raging in the mid-twentieth century. Foreign powers, led initially by the British, launched a series of attacks upon the sovereignty of the Qing Empire. Lying well beyond the coast, Hubei was rarely at the centre of these conflicts. It was influenced by these wars, nonetheless, particularly when Hankou was designated as a treaty port. British High Commissioner James Elgin, who sailed his gunboat up the Yangzi to reconnoitre Hankou, was sorely disappointed. Having read tantalising descriptions of the great commercial entrepôt, he found a city 'almost completely destroyed' by the Taiping invasion. Wuchang was little better. Though there were the 'remains of some buildings of pretension', most areas had been 'sadly mistreated by the Rebels'.[160] As Wuhan recovered over the next few decades, it continued to be plagued by both urban inundations and devastating provincial

---

[156] Ibid., p. 183.   [157] Gao, 'Transformation of the Water Regime', p. 244.
[158] Spence, *God's Chinese Son*, p. 17.
[159] Pietz, *Engineering the State*; Dodgen, *Controlling the Dragon*; Ball, *Water Kingdom*.
[160] Elgin, *Letters and Journals*, p. 294.

floods. Between 1869 and 1872, almost all of Hubei was subsumed under water three times.

These floods proved so serious that administrators finally decided to heed the advice of non-interventionists such as Wei Yuan, and allow two natural breaches in the river dyke network to remain unrepaired.[161] Flood peaks would now flow south towards Dongting Lake. This eased the pressure on the Great Jingjiang Dyke, which would not collapse again until 1931.[162] Yet many of those living around Dongting Lake were not impressed with this solution. The population of Hubei had discovered one of the most effective means of preventing inundation – drown your neighbour's land. The zero-sum nature of water control ensured that hydraulic systems remained a perennial source of political conflicts, not only prompting tensions with neighbouring provinces, but also generating bitter inter-village disputes. This was not unusual. In Ottoman Egypt, neighbours often took to the courts to settle disputes over irrigation channels, while in Louisiana plantation owners became embroiled in prolonged feuds over levees.[163] Most disputes in Hubei centred on issues of dam and sluice construction. They were known to precipitate violent altercations between whole communities, which could last for decades. On some occasions the government was forced to send troops to demolish illegally constructed dams and quell popular unrest.[164]

Among the many communities struggling for hydraulic security during this period were the Britons of treaty port Hankou. Eschewing the insecurity of what they referred to as the native city, they built a segregated concession on the banks of the Yangzi. For the first few decades, this concession failed to live up to their grand expectations. When Archibald Little visited in the 1880s, he noted that the place had 'the lifeless depressing aspect' much like that of 'a seaside watering-place, in the off season'.[165] Things changed dramatically in 1895 with the signing of the Treaty of Shimonoseki. This allowed the French, Germans, Russians and Japanese to build their own concessions. Eventually these formed a contiguous strip, fronted by an embanked riverbank known as a bund. In practical terms, this prevented the river from rising into the concessions and served as a convenient location for wharfs and warehouses.

[161] Will, 'State Intervention,' p. 343.   [162] Zhang, *Coping with Calamity*, p. 123.
[163] Mikhail, *Nature and Empire*; Morris, *Big Muddy*, pp. 61–2.
[164] Rowe, 'Water Control', pp. 353–87; Gao, 'Transformation of the Water Regime', esp. pp. 279–85.
[165] Little, *Through the Yang-tse Gorges*, p. 44.

Yet the bund also allowed foreigners to stamp their alien physical sig-nature upon the city.[166] Travellers arriving in Wuhan were confronted by an imposing skyline of consulates and banks, behind manicured gar-dens and avenues of trees. The bund was central to the founding myth of the Britons of Hankou. They pictured themselves wrestling a tiny sliver of stability and civilisation from a malaria-ridden swamp on the fringes of an exotic city.[167] This bore an uncanny resemblance to the story that Britons liked to tell about the founding of Shanghai, in which ingenious foreign engineering was pictured civilising a watery Chinese wasteland. While this narrative bent the truth in Shanghai, in Hankou it broke it altogether.[168] The riverbank area had been populated for centuries and the bund was built on the same kind of platform that people in Hubei had been employing for millennia to avoid water.[169]

The bund made a rather minor contribution to the hydraulic safety of Wuhan. Floodwater did not generally enter the city from the rivers, but from the lakes and wetlands to the northwest. Every summer these filled with water, and in wet years this ran into the city streets. The wetlands reclaimed Wuhan three times between 1887 and 1889, finally prompt-ing the local government to take definitive action.[170] The renowned Qing statesman Zhang Zhidong 张之洞, then serving as governor of Hubei, ordered the construction of a large dyke network to surround the city.[171] Wuhan would continue to suffer waterlogging, yet these urban flood defences offered several decades of respite from major inundations. The dykes also changed the perception of risk. In the aftermath of the 1931 flood, the missionary H. Owen Chapman would observe that the defences had been built so well that much of the urban population had forgot-ten that they were 'living under Dutch conditions, several feet below the average and twelve feet below the maximum summer level of the great river'.[172]

Flood defences lulled people into a false sense of security. Soon they began to build a dry land city in the middle of the wetlands. Vernacu-lar architecture, which used materials such as wood and reed that could be repaired easily following floods, gave way to more rigid architectural

---

[166] Taylor, 'Bund'.   [167] Upward, *Sons of Han*, pp. 34–8.
[168] On the myth of the Shanghai foreign settlement see Bickers, *Empire Made Me*. On bunds more generally see Bickers, *Britain in China*, p. 141.
[169] Dean, 'Sino-British Diplomacy'.
[170] On these floods see *Wuhan shi zhi: Minzheng zhi*, p. 141.
[171] Rowe, *Hankow: Conflict and Community*, p. 92.
[172] Chapman, 'Fighting Floods and Famine in China', SOAS Archives 10/7/15.

styles, wrought in brick and stone. These new materials allowed Wuhan to cloak itself in the garb of modernity. The brick shopping malls, banks and tenements that sprang up around the city soon dwarfed the timber shop houses and guild temples that had once dominated the skyline. The brickification of Wuhan was the ultimate expression of sedentism – an architecture of permanence created by a culture confident in its abilities to keep itself dry. With the new dyke preventing the north from turning into a giant lake during the summer months, Wuhan sprawled ever further out into the wetlands. By the 1920s it formed the vast conurbation that can be seen in Figure 1.3. The new land created opportunities for novel forms of urban space, such as the large private garden that the businessman Liu Xinsheng 刘歆生 constructed in the north of the city, which the city government would later transform into Sun Yat-sen Park.[173] The foreign population turned their stretch of marshland into a playground for the leisured elite, complete with a racecourse, golf links and swimming pool.[174] Easily the most important development in this newly reclaimed area was the railway line that linked Hankou to Beijing. The embankment elevated trains above the plains and also acted as an extra barrier against flooding.[175]

This urban sprawl had a dramatic effect upon the local environment. In 1910, a foreign hunter named E. G. Bryrne described how the ecological shadow cast by the modern city was already beginning to deplete the wildlife found in the surrounding hinterland. Although the new dykes had helped to prevent summer floods, he noted that they had also

> ... brought about the ploughing up of considerable areas of grass lands, and so limiting the snipe grounds ... One can no longer make a big bag near the French Consulate, now in the centre of the Settlement, nor around the walls of Hankow, while further out, the railway depot, oil installations and factories occupy the ground that used to be the haunts of the pintail ... One unfortunately cannot take any hopeful view of the future of shooting round Hankow.[176]

These oil installations and factories formed part of a wave of industrialisation that had begun to sweep over Wuhan in the 1890s. Once again, Zhang Zhidong had played the principal role in precipitating this seismic change. Although there were already some small-scale foreign

---

[173] Liu, 'Hankou Zhongshan gongyuan'. On Liu see MacKinnon, Wuhan.
[174] The atmosphere of this club is captured in C. S. Archer's fictional account of life in wartime Wuhan. Archer, *Hankow Return*.
[175] MacKinnon, *Wuhan*, 1938, pp. 10–11.   [176] Bryrne, 'Yangtze Notes', pp. 199–200.

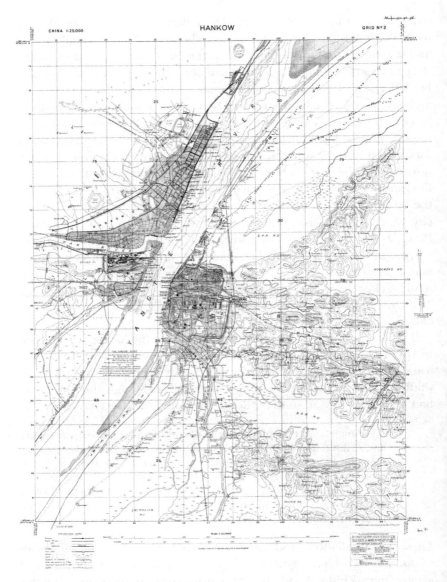

Figure 1.3. A map of the three Wuhan cities in the late 1920s. (British War Office, *General Geological Map of Hankow*, 1946 [1927]. Reproduced courtesy of the Cambridge University Library)

enterprises in Wuhan, most notably a Russia brick tea factory, it was the state-sponsored iron and steel works and the arsenal in Hanyang that initiated urban industrial transition.[177] Factory chimneys were soon rising across the urban landscape. They manufactured a vast array of products, ranging from matches and cigarettes to machinery parts and powdered egg.[178] These new industrial products were sold alongside local agricultural goods, such as rice, sesame, tobacco and sugar; more exotic items from upstream provinces, such as medicinal plants, furs, musk and opium; and also foreign imports, such as kerosene, petroleum and milled flour.[179] Shanghai may have been the Paris of the Orient, but Hankou was Chicago of the East 东方芝加哥 (Dongfang Zhijiage) – a port city with thriving docks through which people and produce never stopped flowing.[180]

Industrialisation would eventually revolutionise the relationship between humans and rivers, as concrete and steel replaced tamped earth and stone. The Nationalist leader Sun Yat-sen had a clear vision of how China could use these new materials to exploit its hydraulic potentials. In the late 1910s, he promulgated a plan to prevent floods and extend electrification by damming the Yangzi.[181] Although these ambitious objectives would finally be fulfilled a century later, at the time they were distinctly unrealistic. While politicians dreamed about damming rivers, they were incapable of maintaining the simple tamped earth dykes that they had inherited from their imperial predecessors. In 1910, the dykes along the Han broke, leaving thousands living in huts throughout the winter.[182] The fall of the Qing the next year brought no respite. The dawn of the new Republic was marked by serious flooding along the Yangzi and Huai basins in 1912.[183]

The collapse of imperial prohibitions against land reclamation precipitated a renewed assault on the wetlands. Farmers could now colonise rivers and lakeshores in exchange for certificates of ownership.[184] The

---

[177] Pi, *Wuhan tongshi: Wan Qing juan (xia)*, p. 16; Tian, *Wusi Yundong shi*.

[178] For a list of foreign industries see Yuan *Hankou zujie*; Shuiye, *Hankou*, pp. 93–132; Wright, *Twentieth Century Impressions*, pp. 701–23.

[179] Richards, *Comprehensive Geography*, p. 127.

[180] Quite where this epithet originated is unclear. Mizuno Kokichi used the phrase in 1907. Shuiye, *Hankou*, p. 1. The first English language reference I have found is Weyl, 'Chicago of China', pp. 716–24. The comparison is often invoked in local histories of Wuhan today. See for example Pi, *Wuhan tongshi: Wan Qing juan (shang)*, p. 315.

[181] Sun, *International Development*.   [182] *North China Herald*, 17 March, 1911.

[183] Will, 'Un cycle hydraulique', p. 286.

[184] Will, 'State Intervention', p. 347 [note 126].

Department of Agriculture and Forestry established by the Beiyang government was dismissed by many contemporary critics as an entirely cosmetic gesture. The historian Deng Tuo 邓拓 remarked on the irony of politicians holding special tree planting events while elsewhere forests were being driven to the point of extinction.[185] The militarists who ruled Hubei in the early Republic were not totally inactive. Xiao Yaonan 蕭耀南 commissioned a far-reaching survey of the hydraulic network with the intention of addressing the deteriorating conditions of flood prevention.[186] Yet incessant warfare prevented any meaningful rehabilitation. In 1921 Wu Peifu 吴佩孚 demonstrated his priorities, blowing up one of the most important dykes in eastern Hubei in order to drown an invading army led by the rival militarist Xia Douyin 夏斗寅.[187]

More serious than these individual acts of sabotage was the unsustainable burden that the economics of war placed on the local environment. This was a symptom of what Edward McCord has described as the 'predatory warlordism', a parasitic mode of governance that blighted Hubei in the 1910s and 1920s.[188] To fund their military adventurism, and often also to line their pockets, warlords embezzled funds earmarked for hydraulic maintenance. They also cut down trees that were planted in dykes to prevent erosion so they could sell the timber.[189] The hydraulic network was left in such a perilous state that by the time that the Nationalists began to advance on Wuhan in 1927, dykes throughout Hubei began to collapse. Only a herculean effort on the part of the local workforce prevented floodwater from bursting through the dykes surrounding Wuhan.[190] Disaster was averted this time. Five years later the city was not so lucky.

Weathering the Storm

The 1931 flood was not an isolated incident. During the late 1920s and early 1930s the world witnessed a succession of weather-induced catastrophes. When the rains failed in eastern Rwanda between 1928 and 1930, as many as 40,000 people died.[191] At approximately the same

---

[185] Deng, *Zhongguo jiuhuang shi*, pp. 388–93; Tao, 'Yi jiu san yi nian'.
[186] Xiao, *Hubei difang jiyao.*   [187] Rowe, *Crimson Rain*, p. 236.
[188] McCord, *Military Force*, pp. 16–49.
[189] Tao, *Yi jiu san yi nian*; Zhang, *Coping with Calamity*.
[190] Todd, *Two Decades in China*, p. 51.   [191] Pedersen, *Guardians*, pp. 243–50.

time, a severe drought struck northern China, killing 10 million.[192] In 1930, French Indochina succumbed to a drought-induced famine, which proved particularly lethal in Vietnam. The desiccation of the Southern Plains of the United States helped to create the Dust Bowl, one of the most iconic images of this troubled era.[193] Meanwhile in the Soviet Union, between 1932 and 1933 drought and crop diseases contributed to the horrific humanitarian catastrophe that may have killed as many as 6 million people in the Ukraine.

The role that the climate played in each of these disasters remains as confusing as it is contentious. Unlike the 1780s or 1870s, when we can be confident in tracing links between disasters and El Niño events, the teleconnections that existed in the 1920s and 1930s were complex and fragmented. Though some climatologists have detected an alternating succession of El Niño and La Niña events between 1928 and 1933, this was not a period of coherent ENSO activity.[194] Even if it were possible to reconstruct the climatic history of this period with any degree of accuracy, we would still need to exercise caution when drawing causal links between climatic anomalies and humanitarian catastrophes. Historians are often seduced by the allure of ENSO, which offers a neat explanation for disasters while also binding them to a climatic process with a distinct celebrity status. What we sometimes forget is that temporal correlations do not necessarily imply teleconnections – just because a climatic hazard coincided with an ENSO event does not mean it was caused by it.

More importantly, none of the foregoing catastrophes were entirely natural disasters. Drought may have may have destroyed harvests in Rwanda and Vietnam, yet the subsequent famine was also caused by Belgian and French colonial policies, which were themselves influenced by the general economic malaise of the Great Depression.[195] Likewise, a dearth of rain killed crops in northern China, yet it was internecine warfare that drove millions into starvation, while broader processes

---

[192] Janku, 'From Natural to National Disaster'. On the El Niño link see Marks, *China*, pp. 254–6.

[193] On recent theories linking the Dust Bowl to La Niña see Schubert et al., 'On the Cause'.

[194] Per Quinn and Neal's classic analysis, there were moderate and strong El Niño events in 1930 and 1931 respectively. See Quinn and Neal, *Historical Record*. Diaz and Kiladis suggest that 1928 and 1931 were La Niña years, and 1930 and 1932 were El Niño years. See Diaz and Kiladis, 'Atmospheric Teleconnections', p. 18. This alternating pattern is supported by the amalgamated dataset offered at www.el-nino.com (Accessed 7 October 2015).

[195] On Rwanda see Pedersen, *Guardians*, pp. 243–50; on Vietnam see Scott, *Moral Economy*, p. 128.

of systemic decline, similar to those detailed in this chapter, had left them chronically vulnerable.[196] Stalinist agricultural collectivisation, rather than drought and wheat rust alone, helped to plunge the Soviet Union into famine.[197] Finally, although an acute water shortage may have helped to whip up dust storms, the calamity suffered by American farmers had been incubated by decades of unsustainable agricultural expansion.[198] In each instance, the climate was a proximate cause but not the sole determinant of disaster. This was also the case during the 1931 Central China Flood.

The cold winter of 1930 caused a heavy build-up of snow in the upper Yangzi. This may possibly have been influenced by the El Niño event of the year.[199] Similarly, the heavy rains that fell throughout 1931 may have been caused by the onset of a La Niña event.[200] Whatever the climatic cause, we know that 1931 was incredibly wet. Early in the year, melting snow and ice flowed downstream from Tibet, arriving in the middle Yangzi at the same time as a period of heavy spring rain. Ordinarily the region experienced three waves of high water, during the spring, summer and autumn; in 1931, there was just one continuous deluge. By June those living in low-lying areas had already been forced to abandon their homes.[201] In an average year this region might expect to experience two cyclonic storms; in 1931 seven occurred in July alone.[202] The water flowing through the Yangzi had soon reached the highest level since records were first kept in the mid-nineteenth century.[203] There was no possibility that the rivers of Hubei could drain this huge volume of water through their artificially restricted channels. Neither could the ailing flood defence system withstand the extreme pressure of water. In the early summer the Great Jingjiang Dyke failed for the first time in sixty years. The water that flowed through multiple breaches went on to

[196] Conflict played such an important role in inducing this famine that some foreign aid agencies argued that no relief should be provided, as giving food would prevent warring parties from reaching a political solution. See Nathan, *History of the China International Famine Relief Commission.*

[197] The extent to which the environment played a role in precipitating the Soviet famines remains highly contested. For a summary of the debates see Wheatcroft, 'Towards Explaining Soviet Famine'.

[198] On the environmental history of the Southern Plains see Worster, *Dust Bowl.*

[199] On the cold winter see Barrett, *Red Lacquered Gate*, p. 265. On the 1930 El Niño see Diaz and Kiladis, 'Atmospheric Teleconnections', p. 18; www.el-nino.com (Accessed 7 October 2015).

[200] Diaz and Kiladis, 'Atmospheric Teleconnections', p. 18; www.el-nino.com (Accessed 7 October 2015).

[201] RNFRC, p. 1.   [202] Buck, *1931 Flood*, p. 8.   [203] Stroebe, 'General Problem'.

compromise 90 per cent of the dykes on the Jianghan Plain.[204] Still the rain did not stop. It continued throughout the summer, culminating in another series of storms in the early autumn. High winds swept across the inundated landscape, whipping floodwater into a series of devastating waves.[205] Water began to recede only in the midautumn, yet even then large tracts of land remained inundated, as the polders that had been built to keep water out now turned into reservoirs.

This flood would not have occurred were it not for nature. Yet the rain that fell drained through a landscape that had been modified by thousands of years of human action. It flowed over denuded slopes and reclaimed wetlands into channelised rivers. Its force was amplified by the constructed landscape that people had built to keep themselves dry. Having domesticated the natural resistance out of plants and animals, and placed them in areas vulnerable to inundation, farmers had created a subsistence system that relied on predictable meteorology, all the while living under unpredictable skies. Agriculture, urbanisation and trade had cultivated diseases that rose to epidemic proportions during floods. The cumulative effect of all these dynamic interactions had established a lethal disaster regime. Long before rain began to fall, all the ingredients for a catastrophe were already in place.

[204] Zhang, *Coping with Calamity*, p. 123.
[205] F. G. Onley, 'Letter Extract', SOAS Archives 10/7/15.

2

THE FLOOD PULSE

> Disturbances are paradoxical. What we see and fear is their
> destructive power, yet these same disturbances help create and
> maintain the biodiversity that benefits both the ecosystem and
> ourselves.
>
> Seth Reice[1]

By August 1931 a gigantic flood lake had swallowed much of Hubei. In
urban areas, a noxious cocktail of water was running through the streets,
contaminated with animal carcasses, industrial chemicals and human
waste. Outside of cities the situation was quite different. The plains to the
north of Wuhan were covered with a vast expanse of clear green water, its
surface broken by the treetops and the roofs of houses. Between the ves-
tiges of this submerged terrestrial world, shoals of small fish now darted
around, exploiting ordinarily inaccessible prey, while green water snakes
swam about on the surface of the lake.[2] For water-resistant species, the
flood was larger than normal, but it was not a disaster. Millions of organisms had died as the erosive force of water had torn them away from
riverbeds and plains, buried them in thick layers of sediment or starved
them of oxygen. Yet for those that survived, through luck or adaptation,
the pulse of water that surged along the rivers had distinct benefits.

The organisms killed by large flood pulses merge together with other
forms of biomass to send ripples of nutrition through both aquatic
and terrestrial food webs.[3] The resultant burst of fertility benefits those
plants that have not been crushed or uprooted by the force of water.

---

[1] Reice, *Silver Lining*, p. ix.
[2] H. Owen Chapman 'Fighting Floods and Famine in China', SOAS Archives 10/7/15.
[3] The following section draws upon insights from a range of ecologists. The flood pulse
concept was first advanced in Junk, Bayley and Sparks, 'The Flood Pulse Concept'. See
also Bayley, 'Understanding Large River-Floodplain Ecosystems'. Recents studies suggest
this model is most applicable to the middle Yangzi; see Wang et al., 'Terrestrial Contributions'. For a discussion of the debates among fluvial ecologists regarding this concept see

Herbivorous fish, molluscs and amphibians consume flourishing vegetation, and, in turn, provide a nutritional windfall for predatory species, including many birds, reptiles and mammals. The redistribution of nutrients is not the only beneficial effect of the flood pulse. As water recedes, empty patches of territory that have been scoured of biota offer new habitats for opportunistic flora and fauna. The seeds and fruits of plants that have been disbursed across the river basin by currents now colonise these patches, as do animals returning from their refugia. The frequent stripping and repopulating of habitats helps to prevent certain species from becoming dominant and purges harmful invasive species. Regular flood pulsing helps to promote biodiversity. Given these numerous beneficial effects, the ecologist Peter Bayley has argued that we should stop describing floods as disturbances. Riverine ecosystems suffer far more when people build structures that cause 'significant departures from the average hydrological regimen'.[4] For nature, it is often the human attempt to control flooding that proves disastrous.

When historians study floods they tend to focus on a single ecological dimension. They examine the effect of inundation on the edible plants consumed by human communities.[5] This approach is, to a great extent, dictated by the limitations of the documentary record. Literate observers who described floods tended to be concerned primarily with their economic effects on the agricultural system. The picture of past deluges that we inherit from these sources is influenced by the nutritional paradigm that defined their priorities. Yet the fact that edible plants continue to dominate historical analyses is not because their absence was the sole determinant of human mortality. It is, rather, because these species possessed the greatest economic value and cultural significance. The nutritional paradigm not only diminishes our understanding of what happened to the ecosystems during historic floods, but also distorts our view of what happened to people. It perpetuates an erroneous assumption that the primary challenge facing disaster-stricken populations was an absence of food. In reality, starvation was just one of many harmful effects of flooding, and was usually not the most lethal.

Arthington, *Environmental Flows*; Likens, *River Ecosystem Ecology*, esp. p. 209. For an analysis of disturbance ecology more generally see Reice, *Silver Lining*; Del Moral and Walker, *Environmental Disasters*. For an interesting historical application of some of the ecological models discussed in the foregoing see Morris, *Big Muddy*, esp. p. 205.

4 Bayley, 'Understanding Large River-Floodplain Ecosystems', p. 154.
5 Two studies that do not do this are Muscolino, *Ecology of War*; Morris, *Big Muddy*.

This chapter offers a more holistic ecological history of the 1931 flood. Though still bound by the limitations of the documentary record, it uses the evidence available to examine how a huge pulse of water affected a range of species that inhabited the ecosystem. It then demonstrates how this biotic response helped to condition the disaster regime. Some of the ecological effects of flooding had positive effects for humans. The aquatic plants and fish that survived and thrived provided vital sources of food. This was not sufficient to make up for the loss of millions of domestic plants and animals, which helped push many areas into famine. Harmful though the loss of nutrition was, its impact on the human population paled in comparison to that of the lethal epidemiological environment. Contrary to the notion that inundation is a destructive event, this chapter suggests that one of the reasons that floods are so lethal for human beings is precisely because they are so ecologically productive. Mosquitoes and molluscs thrived in the new wetlands, and flies gorged themselves on untreated human waste. The pathogenic microbes carried by these vectors soon colonised malnourished human bodies. Before long, the subsistence and health crises had become indistinguishable, as human communities succumbed to a deadly synergy of hunger and disease. A socioecological perspective reveals that the flood pulse was dangerous not only because it destroyed useful species but also because it allowed harmful species to flourish.

Water

The erosive force of floodwater is deadly to many kinds of organism. Strong currents scour algae, plants, fish and aquatic insects from riverbeds, leaving nothing but desolate and lifeless patches in their wake.[6] As water rises onto floodplains, terrestrial flora and fauna are swept into rivers, drowned or buried in sediment. When rivers burst into the human world they prove equally destructive. A witness to a Han River flood in the nineteenth century, described seeing 'an immense rush of water . . . carrying with it numbers of junks, boats, houses, trees, cattle, and I should be afraid to say how many human beings, all mixed up in the most inextricable confusion'.[7] The floodwater that pulsed across Hubei in 1931 had similarly catastrophic effects. It scoured away houses, huts, granaries and shops almost as easily as it washed away topsoil and loose

---

[6] Lake, 'Flow-generated Disturbances', pp. 75–92.78; Death, 'Effect of Floods'.
[7] Captain Todd quoted in Percival, *Land of the Dragon*, p. 59.

rocks. Fast currents swept people under water never to be seen again, or turned their homes into sediment, burying them alive. Around 150,000 people were killed by these initial flood waves.[8] Water did not discriminate between its victims. It followed a path determined by gravity, sweeping away anyone who got in its way. Given the indiscriminate nature of this destruction, it might tempting to assume that those who drowned were simply victims of misfortune, people who happened to be in the wrong place at the wrong time. Yet in a region that suffered recurrent water hazards, being in the wrong place was hardly a matter of chance. The distinctions created by the long-term interplay of water, earth and people, described in Chapter 1, now helped to determine patterns of vulnerability.

The generic term *flood* actually comprises a wide variety of different kinds of water hazard. China experienced numerous floods in 1931. The first were highly destructive mountain floods 山洪 (shanhong).[9] Powerful thunderstorms had been rumbling across the highlands throughout much of the spring. When the heavens opened in July, powerful freshets swept along the courses of the hillside tributaries, wiping away those living adjacent to rivers.[10] In the valleys below, the disaster began not with dramatic flash floods, but with the slow onset of waterlogging disasters 渍灾 (zizai). These may not have been as destructive as flash floods, but were nevertheless catastrophic for agricultural communities. The most lethal form of flooding was yet to come. This occurred when the pressure of water caused dykes to suffer breaches 溃口 (kuikou), the aftermath of which can be seen in Figure 2.1. The proximate cause of hydraulic failures was excessive rainfall, yet the floods they unleashed had an anthropogenic dimension. The constructed landscape amplified the erosive force of water, funnelling it through narrow breach points at high velocity. In late August, water cascading through the dykes of the Grand Canal wrought terrible destruction on Yangzhou 扬州 in Jiangsu. The nearby city of Gaoyou 高邮 seemed initially to have been saved by its walls which acted as a dyke. Unfortunately, the walls collapsed in the dead of night, unleashing a wall of water that killed around 2,000 people, many of whom were still sleeping in their beds.[11] Similarly, in southern Sichuan, water poured over the flood defences of Fushun 富顺,

[8] Buck, *1931 Flood in China*, p. 35.
[9] The typology of flooding used in this paragraph is borrowed from disaster investigations conducted during the 1954 floods. See 'Hubei sheng zaiqing jiankuang, 6 September 1954', *HFKDX*, pp. 225–7.
[10] Yan. *Macheng xian zhi*, p. 44.   [11] RNFRC, p. 8; *Hankow Herald*, 30 August 1931.

Figure 2.1. An aerial view of a dyke breach during the 1931 flood. (The Charles Lindbergh Collection. Reproduced courtesy of the Missouri History Museum)

sweeping an estimated 10,000 residents into the river.[12] These were just a few examples of the numerous localised tragedies nested within the larger disaster.

The location of a community and its capacity to maintain its flood defences played a critical role in determining vulnerability. It was no coincidence that the last area of Hankou to be flooded was the Japanese Concession. Those who ruled this thin strip of land were able to marshal considerable resources, constructing sandbag barriers and pumping the streets dry.[13] The situation was very different for those living near Dongxi Lake, who had very few funds to invest in defences. When the flood struck this area forty families were killed.[14] One particularly impoverished community located next to the Yangzi in Wuchang found itself in a similar predicament. Though this was a highly precarious area, the local cottage industry of chopstick making did not provide enough income for locals

[12] *Hankow Herald*, 23 August 1931.
[13] Tao, *Yi jiu san yi nian da shuizai*; Clubb, 'Floods of China'.
[14] Pi, *Wuhan tongshi: Minguo juan (Shang)*, pp. 220–23.

to invest in a flood wall. When Wuchang's outer dykes collapsed they were submerged beneath 3 metres of water.[15]

Architecture was another area in which economic marginality translated into physcial insecurity. Many people lived in low-standing dwellings built from cheap and flimsy materials. Even if their homes survived the initial flood waves, they would often collapse as water ate away at their foundations.[16] In the wake of the flood, the Nationalist government commissioned academics from the University of Nanjing, headed by the renowned agricultural economist John Lossing Buck, to conduct an extensive survey into the effects of the disaster – referred to hereafter as the Nanjing Survey. The report detailed how almost half of the homes in the flood zone had been completely destroyed, with more than a third of villages wiped off the map. Although the formidable force of water had played a critical role, the report noted that inadequate building standards had left many homes chronically insecure.[17] In Wuhan, those occupying small huts were the most seriously affected by the initial flood waves.[18] This reflected not only architectural vulnerability of these communities, but also the fact that their members were squatting on the cheapest, most flood-prone land.

Even within impoverished neighbourhoods, there were gradations of vulnerability. The least settled – those who lived in huts constructed of reeds, bamboo and salvaged materials – enjoyed something of an advantage, as they were so habituated to being moved on, either by water or by the police, and so were adept at disassembling their homes at speed. When floodwater advanced they simply carried their huts to higher ground. The earthen homes occupied by slightly more established households were much less portable, yet were hardly less vulnerable. Whole neighbourhoods simply melted into the flood, their occupants drowning in a cocktail of mud and water.[19]

Those who lived in taller houses fared much better. The journalist Chen Bing 陈兵 occupied a second-storey room in Wuhan. While

---

[15] Xie, 'Hankou shuizai', *Xinminbao*, HSSDX; *Hankow Herald*, 18 August 1931.

[16] *Hankow Herald*, 23 August 1931.

[17] Forty-five per cent of homes collapsed, 37 per cent of villages were completed destroyed and a further 15 per cent were partially damaged. See Buck, *1931 Flood*, p. 15.

[18] There were numerous reports describing the inundation of hut-dwellers. See Xie, 'Hankou shuizai', *Xinminbao*, HSSDX; *North China Herald*, 11 August 1931; F. G. Onley (Letter Extract), 28 August 1931, SOAS Archives 10/7/15.

[19] On the vulnerability of earth housing see Buck, *1931 Flood*, p. 15. On the effect of the flood on earthen sections of Wuhan see *North China Herald*, 1 September 1931; *Time Magazine*, 31 August 1931.

his flooded downstairs neighbours had to live on wooden boards, his home remained a dry sanctuary above the destruction.[20] Those wealthy enough to occupy multi-storey housing could vertically evacuate to the top of their homes.[21] Life above the water could be surprisingly comfortable. A medical missionary described 'balancing on rafts and planks over unspeakable filth, climbing over banisters in the pitch dark, and finally coming up for air into marvellously kept top floors with electric fans and every comfort one could wish'.[22] In another instance, residents of an alleyway tenement were able to survive the flood by blocking their doors with wooden boards to prevent water coming up stairs.[23] Even within inundated areas, it was possible to forge enclaves of security.

Flood risk cannot be explained by crude socioeconomic determinism. Not all wealthy households were immune from inundation in 1931. The residents of the Jardine Matheson Estate, who were rich even by foreign standards, were among the first flood refugees in Wuhan, having to flee to the city centre when their seculded suburban neighbourhood was inundated.[24] For the most part, however, impoverished people living in insecure areas and insubstantial homes felt the worst effects of the flood. The challenges facing this vulnerable stratum of social landscape did not end with the collapsing of dykes. The geographers Michael Watts and Hans Bohle have cautioned scholars not to think of vulnerability just as a pre-existing condition – new forms of vulnerability are generated continually throughout the disaster process.[25] Such was the case in 1931. Those who had become homeless due to inadequate or poorly located housing later found themselves vulnerable to exposure, with the incessant rainfall and heat in the summer giving way to a bitterly cold winter. They had lost their granaries and other food stores, meaning that they were more vulnerable to famine.[26] Worst of all, being displaced from their homes and corralled into overcrowded and unsanitary camps, they were vulnerable to a range of diseases.

The risks associated with homelessness could be ameliorated by money or social connections. Many wealthy Chinese citizens of Wuhan simply left the city, packing into the steamships for areas such as Shanghai. Their Japanese counterparts sent women and children away from

[20] Chen, 'Wuchang zaiqu', *Yaxi Yabao*, HSSDX.
[21] On vertical evacuation see Godschalk, Brower and Beatley, *Catastrophic Coastal Storms*, p. 38.
[22] *The Chinese Recorder*, January 1932.
[23] Xie, *Yi jiu san yi nian*, p. 144.   [24] *North China Herald*, 1 September 1931.
[25] Watts and Bohle, 'Space of Vulnerability'.   [26] Buck, *1931 Flood*, p. 15.

the city, while the British departed for their summer residences in the mountains of Jiangxi.[27] Those who remained had to find alternative lodgings. Soon the cost of dry ground began soaring, with some landlords and hoteliers even doubling the price.[28] Unscrupulous property owners sought to maximise their profits by packing in as many tenants as possible. Overcrowded buildings with inundated lower floors quickly became structurally compromised. In mid-August, a hotel collapsed near the railway station in Wuhan, killing many people sheltering therein.[29] After a string of similar events the municipal government commandeered some local hotels, so that refugees might have somewhere to shelter.[30] For the journalist Xie Qianmao 谢茜茂, himself homeless during the flood, the economic calculations of his fellow citizens were simply intolerable. 'If our hearts have become this cruel', he mused, 'there is little wonder that a disaster has befallen us.'[31]

Cultivated Plants

Rapid river currents killed millions of plants, scouring them off the surface of the earth, burying them in silt or drowning them. This was the leading cause of the subsistence crisis that struck in the summer of 1931, lasting for at least a year. By the early autumn, many areas had descended into full-blown famine. Across the entire Yangzi Valley, the yield of rice and wheat was reduced by 15 per cent.[32] In flood-stricken areas these losses were much higher. The Nanjing Survey estimated that the total economic cost incurred by each family was equal to one and a half year's net income.[33] Millions of people lost their entire summer harvests and all the grain that they had stored for the future.[34] In monsoon regions such as China, North India and Bangladesh, it is not only the size of a flood but also its timing that determines its humanitarian consequences. Inundations that occur in the lean season – the point furthest away from

[27] *Hankow Herald,* 18 August 1931; *North China Herald,* 1 September 1931.
[28] Xie, *Yi jiu san yi nian,* p. 54.
[29] Ibid., p. 105; *North China Herald,* 11 August 1931; *Hankow Herald,* 20 August 1931. Estimated fatalities varied from 15 to 1000.
[30] *North China Herald,* 11 August 1931.
[31] Xie, *Yi jiu san yi nian,* p. 55.
[32] Kueh, *Agricultural Instability,* p. 178. For a contemporary discussion of the impact of the losses on the economy see 'Shuizai hou zhi liangshi wenti', *Nanjing Shi Zhengfu Gongbao,* 95 (1931).
[33] Buck, *1931 Flood.*
[34] An estimated $79.6 million of stored food was lost. Ibid., pp. 10–12.

the main harvest of the previous year – are by far the most destructive. It is then that farmers are most eager to replenish their food stocks.[35] The late spring and early summer floods of 1931 deprived Chinese farmers of their main harvest, meaning many households had to stretch food stocks harvested in the summer of 1930 until the summer of 1932. Unsurprisingly, many struggled to do so.

Flooding did not destroy plants completeley. When water began to rise in central Jiangsu, villagers quickly rushed to their fields and cut as much rice as they could, regardless of whether it was ripe. As it rose again, reaching to more than a metre in depth, they rowed boats across their inundated fields, gathering more of their crops using rakes.[36] The Nanjing Survey estimated that the agricultural population was able to salvage as much as 17 per cent of its harvest using such techniques.[37] To supplement salvaged grain rural communities consumed semi-edible agricultural by-products, such as rice husks and chaff.[38] To these meagre supplies they added foraged plants, such as lotus and wild rice.[39] Others found ways to access the minimal nutrition available from terrestrial flora, stripping the bark and leaves from trees and digging up grass shoots.[40] Even this sophisticated repertoire of coping strategies could not make up for the huge nutritional shortfall. By the mid-summer many areas had slipped below the minimum subsistence level.[41] Over the following year much of central China was struck by a famine, which was particular severe in Henan, Anhui and Hubei.[42] Even in relatively

---

[35] Wisner et al. *At Risk*, p. 129.

[36] Li, *Village China*, pp. 12–13.   [37] Buck, *1931 Flood*, p. 12.

[38] *Wuhan Ribao*, 15 January 1932.   [39] Clubb, *Communism in* China, p. 105.

[40] 'Wuhan yi cheng canghai', *Guowen Zhoukan*, 8 (1931); RNFRC, p. 62; extracts from letter of Sir J. Hope-Simpson to Mr. F. B. Bourdillon, 16 January 1932, SOAS Archives 10/7/15; Clubb, 'The Floods of China.'

[41] Buck, *1931 Flood in China*, p. 45.

[42] In her brief discussion of the 1931 flood Lillian Li asserts that there were no major food shortages. Li, *Fighting Famine*, p. 306. Her assessment – a brief aside in an otherwise masterful and superbly researched book – is based exclusively on literature published by relief workers. This relatively positive assessment is contradicted even within the sources she herself cites, which attest to the existence of famine in several areas. See RNFRC, p. 68. Several other studies of the flood suggest there was a famine including Yue and Dong, 'Zai lun 1931 nian; Li et al., *Zhongguo jindai shi da zaihuang*; Pietz, *Engineering the State*. The descriptions of widespread malnutrition, an increase in moneylending, the divesting of assets, crime and rioting, the sale of children and, most tellingly of all, homicidal cannibalism, described in this current book all represent classic famine symptoms. Using the qualitative index designed by Howe and Devereux to determine the intensity of subsistence crises, this behaviour would seem to indicate a fairly severe famine. See Howe and Devereux, 'Famine Intensity'.

well-provisioned areas such as Wuhan, many refugees seemed to be in a state of near starvation.[43] Those who reached camps were often so weakened by hunger that they were unable to survive on the rice rations provided.[44]

In some rural areas hunger became so acute that people resorted to the ultimate act of famine survival – cannibalism. In Anhui, a missionary named Reverend Bostock claimed to have witnessed members of flood-stricken communities consuming human flesh.[45] The historian Ouyang Tieguang has found evidence of homicidal cannibalism in government reports, with one elderly woman in Hubei killing and consuming her own son. When her crime was discovered, the legs were all that remained. Elsewhere a farmer killed his youngest son for food, and admitted that he was later planning to consume his eldest.[46] Kathryn Edgerton-Tarpley has cautioned historians not necessarily to accept reports of cannibalism in Chinese documentary records at face value, arguing that they were sometimes figurative illustrations rather than literal accounts.[47] The fact that reports of cannibalism in 1931 came from multiple witnesses – including government officials, relief workers and missionaries – suggests that, in this instance at least, people really had consumed human flesh. Famine had revealed a brutal ecological reality, disavowed in the ordinary course of social relations; in extremis, human beings can sometimes reduce one another to edible biomass.

Although the physical destruction of cultivated plants played a vital role in depleting the nutritional intake of inundated households, the famine had an important economic component. Amartya Sen has argued, famously, that famines do not occur simply because food is unavailable, but also because certain groups cannot access available food.[48] This lack of access to nutrition is described as an entitlement failure. The flood precipitated a collapse of both production-based and exchange entitlements – with their crops destroyed people were unable to access food they had cultivated themselves, and were also unable to

[43] 'Wuhan yi cheng canghai', *Guowen Zhoukan*, 8 (1931); *North China Herald*, 4 August 1931; *North China Herald*, 25 August 1931; Dwight Edwards, 'The CIFRC Report' 1932, DEP 12/14/153.

[44] Edith S. Wills, 'Hanyang 1931', SOAS Archives 10/7/15.

[45] Cited in Clubb, *Communism in China*, p. 105; David Pietz also cites evidence provided by relief workers who personally witnessed people eating their own children. Pietz, *Engineering the State*, p. 68.

[46] Ouyang, 'Zaihuang yu nongmin'.

[47] Edgerton-Tarpley, *Tears from Iron*.   [48] Sen, *Poverty and Famines*.

Table 2.1. *Index of changes to the prices of important commodities during the first three months of the flood*

81 Counties in the 1931 flood area in the Yangzi and Huai Valleys Period just before the flood = 100

Province	Commodities rising in price				Commodities falling in price					
	Grain	Fuel and fodder	Interest rates	Building materials	Land value	Draft animals	Other animals	Farm year wages	Farm day wages	Tools
Hunan	138	146	152	114	68	84	90	81	80	100
Hubei	117	125	111	98	74	82	101	85	82	97
Jiangxi	117	118	101	123	74	74	106	86	77	104
S. Anhui	121	148	128	127	67	75	79	77	81	119
S. Jiangsu	104	126	112	105	79	83	92	89	81	103
N. Anhui	124	142	149	112	51	49	70	80	86	80
N. Jiangsu	117	133	161	106	61	59	98	70	71	88
Average[a]	120	130	133	113	63	70	88	80	80	99

[a] Average by county 县 (xian), not province.

use the market economy to purchase the available food that had been grown by others. Table 2.1 captures the economic quandary facing flood-stricken households. Everything they needed to survive had become prohibitively expensive, while the few commodities that they still possessed were rapidly becoming worthless. Probably the most devastating blow was the steep decline in the value of labour. This meant that, even where work was available, people struggled to earn enough to purchase food.

Even in the absence of a large crisis, the balance of rural employment was already stacked firmly in favour of those purchasing labour. During the flood, the already precarious position of agricultural workers was weakened as the labour market became saturated with refugees. Wages dropped by 20 per cent while grain prices rose by 20 per cent. This 40 per cent difference meant that soon agricultural labourers had to work an entire day for a small meal. With much arable land remaining inundated, even these minimal opportunities were quickly exhausted.[49] The economic shock caused by the flood lasted long after water receded,

[49] Buck, *1931 Flood in China*.

with the price of rice remaining inflated for at least a year.[50] The famine
that ensued is best understood as a dual-pronged attack upon the subsistence of certain sections of society; an ecological shock caused rapid
food availability decline and an economic shock caused acute entitlement failure. This has been the pattern found during most historic
famines.[51]

As is so often the case during famines, some people found ways
to profit from the hunger of others. Inundation had created what
economists describe – appropriately in this context – as a liquidity crisis,
as millions of people were unable to actualise the value of their commodities. In this economic climate, those who controlled the flow of
assets accrued financial rewards, either directly or through credit markets. Debt was an endemic feature of economic life in rural China. With
cash incomes seasonal, credit as a form of deferred payment played a
vital role in sustaining production.[52] Credit arrangements had long been
a mainstay of the rural economy, but, as Prasenjit Duara has argued,
the consequences of debt worsened in the twentieth century. Unscrupulous entrepreneurs took control of rural credit markets, replacing the
village elites who had tended to adopt a more paternalistic approach to
lending.[53] In Jiangsu, for example, between 60 and 70 per cent of rural
households were in debt in the 1930s.[54] Disasters increased the necessity
for credit while decreasing the capacity for repayment.[55] This allowed
creditors to acquire the land and property of impoverished people at
extremely low prices.

Pawnbrokers were another common source of credit for the rural
poor. Many relinquished vital assets, including tools, clothes, furniture
and even roof beams, on an annual basis.[56] Owing to their tendency
to capitalise on catastrophes, moneylenders and pawnbrokers were a
common target for progressive reformers of all political stripes.[57] Yet

---

[50] Shiroyama, *China During the Great Depression*, p. 94.
[51] Dyson and Ó Gráda, *Famine Demography*, p. 14.
[52] Shiroyama, *China During the Great Depression*, p. 103.
[53] Duara, *Culture, Power and the State*.
[54] Shiroyama, *China During the Great Depression*, p. 103.
[55] Will, *Bureaucracy and Famine*, p. 53.
[56] 'They pawn their crops in summer, their farm implements in winter and their household
belongings throughout the whole twelve months.' See Tawney, *The Attack*, pp. 44–5; see
also Shiroyama, *China During the Great Depression*.
[57] See Zanasi, *Saving the Nation*, p. 151. Richard Tawney noted the terrible rates of interest charged by Chinese moneylenders; 'twenty-five to fifty per cent is common; interest at fifty to one hundred per cent is not unknown. As far as the poorer peasants are

while credit markets undoudtedly accentuated long-term inequalities, they could help to diminish the immediate impact of crises.[58] In rural areas, where other forms of credit were conspicuously absent, it was the much-derided moneylender or pawnbroker who often prevented acute starvation.[59] This is not to suggest that credit speculators were misunderstood philanthropists. The exploitative debt arrangements they created not only contributed to the immediate poverty of disaster-stricken people, but also helped to accentuate the underlying destitution that made people vulnerable to disasters in the first place.

Both moneylending and pawning were rife during the flood. The increased demand for money allowed creditors to raise interest rates by as much as 50 per cent. At the same time, the value of land, the most commonly used form of collateral, declined by as much as 50 per cent. As prolonged inundation delayed agricultural recovery, many farmers who had taken out loans were unable to maintain interest payments. This resulted in high levels of land foreclosure.[60] Meanwhile, the crisis terms offered by pawnshops meant that flood-stricken households often surrendered possessions for very little remuneration.[61] In the aftermath of the flood, if they had not managed to secure other forms of credit, they could not redeem vital assets, most notably farm tools, without which reconstruction was impossible.[62] The flood pulse itself may have lasted only a few months, yet the effect of water would continue to ripple through the economy for years to come. The Nanjing Survey summarised the situation succinctly, noting that during the disaster the 'rich got richer, and the poor, poorer.'[63]

Domestic Animals

Animals are often credited with having uncanny instincts that alert them to hazards and allow them to survive. Greg Bankoff has criticised this somewhat sentimental notion, observing that animals tend to perish in far greater numbers than their humans during disasters.[64] There is a key distinction in this regard, between domesticated and wild animals. The

concerned, permanent indebtedness is the rule rather than the exception.' See Tawney, *The Attack*, pp. 44–5; see also Tao, *Yi jiu san yi nian*.

[58] Ó Gráda, *Famine*, pp. 78–81.

[59] On the condition of the rural credit market in early 1930s China see Rajchman, *Report of the Technical Agent of the Council*.

[60] Buck, *1931 Flood*, p. 38.   [61] Shiroyama, *China during the Great Depression*, p. 36.

[62] Xie, *Yi jiu san yi nian*, p. 124.   [63] Buck, *1931 Flood*, p. 38.

[64] Bankoff, 'Learning About Disasters'.

disaster vulnerability of domestic animals depends to a certain extent upon their relationship with the human population. Both horses and dogs, for example, benefitted from their social association with people in 1931, as we will see in a later chapter. Animal vulnerability also depends on the nature of the hazard and the resilience of the particularly species. For obvious reasons, the flood was not as serious a problem for domesticated ducks and geese as it was for pigs and chickens. Thousands of these latter species drowned during the initial flood waves, and later millions starved, succumbed to disease or fell victim to human predation.[65] More than a third of households in Hubei lost pigs and hogs and half lost poultry.[66] The fate of chickens, in particular, reveals the extent to which an association with the humans could increase vulnerability, as the undomesticated junglefowl that were the ancestors of domesticated chickens could simply have flown away from the flood.

Undoubtedly the heaviest blow for farmers was the loss of labour animals. In non-mechanised agricultural societies, animals such as oxen, buffalo, donkeys and cows form the backbone of what John McNeill has described as the 'somatic energy regime'. They convert the solar energy captured by plants into muscular force that could be harnessed for a variety of agricultural tasks.[67] Ruminants were particularly valuable, as they were able to access energy stored in inedible phytomass, such as grass and crop residues, which is otherwise inaccessible for human beings.[68] Bovine labour animals were so important in rural China that they were accorded a high social and even religious status, as Vincent Goossaert has observed. To mistreat such animals was considered deeply immoral (Figure 2.2). Although not as well-known as its Indian equivalent, there was a strong taboo surrounding the consumption of beef, which lasted well into the twentieth century.[69] The value that a culture attributes to animals should not be reduced to a naïve form of functionalism – religious injunctions are never simply expressions of material necessity – and the Chinese beef taboo had numerous influences, not least the Buddhist vegetarian tradition imported from India. Nevertheless, culture cannot be divorced entirely from its ecological and economic contexts. The anthropologist Marvin Harris argued that those who characterise Hindus

---

[65] Xie, *Yi jiu san yi nian*, p. 41.
[66] In Hubei households losing productive animals were as follows – chickens 52 per cent, pigs 34 per cent, ducks 10 per cent, geese 1 per cent. Buck, *1931 Flood*, p. 23.
[67] McNeill, *Something New*. See also Muscolino, *Ecology of War*.
[68] Smil, *China's Past*.
[69] Goossaert, 'Beef Taboo'; Simoons, *Eat Not This Flesh*, pp. 122–4.

Figure 2.2. A moral injunction against the mistreatment of labour animals. Collected in Hubei at the turn of the twentieth century, it gives a clear indication of the high cultural and moral value attributed to such creatures. The characters form the shape of an ox, narrating its imagined autobiography. They describe a life of constant toil, pulling a heavy plough with only a little grass to eat. The passage also serves to warn people that if they mistreat cattle they can expect grave spiritual, economic and social consequences.[70] (William Arthur Cornaby, *A String of Chinese Peach-Stones*. London: Charles H. Kelly, 1895, p. 9. Reproduced courtesy of the Cambridge University Library)

as victims of 'Oriental mysticism' for worshipping cattle fail to appreciate the dreadful fate that would await a 'poor farmer unable to replace a bullock lost through disease, old age, or accident'.[71] In 1931, millions of farmers were forced to contend with just such a fate.

Almost 2 million draught animals were lost during the flood, which was around half the total population. This included water buffalo, oxen, yellow cows, donkeys and mules. After the destruction of crops and housing, this was the greatest economic expense incurred.[72] Many of these creatures drowned, others starved and some were consumed. For rural households, slaughtering cattle meant sacrificing a vital source of energy

---

[70] Cornaby was given this illustration by a watermelon seller in Hankou around the turn of the twentieth century.
[71] Harris, 'Cultural Ecology', p. 56.   [72] Buck, *1931 Flood*, pp. 15–17.

and prestige. Alex de Waal has observed that famine-stricken farmers in Sudan in the 1980s were often willing to endure months of starvation rather than part with cattle.[73] The situation was similar in 1930s China. In a short story written to raise money for the flood relief effort, the American novelist Pearl Buck captured the painful loss suffered by a farmer forced to kill his precious buffalo.

> If any one had told him that he would eat his water-buffalo that had ploughed the good land for him, and year after year pulled the stone roller over the grain and threshed it at harvest he would have called the man an idiot. Yet it is what he had done...But what else could they do on that dark winter's day when the last of their store of grain was gone, when the trees were cut and sold, when he had sold everything...Besides, the beast was starving, also, since the water had covered even the grass lands...When he did it, even in his despair, he groaned, for it was as though he killed his own brother. To him it was the last sacrifice.[74]

Buck was raised in China and had a profound knowledge of the problems facing rural populations. Even so, it might be tempting to dismiss her description as somewhat sentimental. Yet it is corroborated by evidence from other disasters. Even in the depths of the hunger caused by the famine of the late 1950s, Yang Jisheng's stepfather could not bring himself to eat his ox, being simply too close to the animal.[75]

Labour animals that survived inundation now faced an economic crisis alongside their human owners. With vast tracts of pasture under water, they were forced to rely on stored fodder. Unfortunately, the price of these plant residues was subject to the same rapid inflation as human food, rising in some areas by as much as 46 per cent. Soon oxen and buffalo were suffering their own form of entitlement failure; the value of their labour was no longer sufficient to guarantee their endowments. The resultant bovine famine was compounded by the fact that humans were now prepared to consume animal food such as rice husks, cattle feed, and chaff.[76] As the economic crisis worsened, rather than slaughtering their labour animals, many farmers tried to sell them. The simultaneous decision of thousands of people to bring their creatures to market caused the value of cattle to plummet. Government attempts to introduce legislation designed to control the slaughter and sale of oxen had little

[73] De Waal, *Famine That Kills*.   [74] Buck, *First Wife*, pp. 235–6.
[75] Yang, *Tombstone*.   [76] 'Wuhan yi cheng canghai', *Guowen Zhoukan*, 8 (1931).

impact.[77] In Northern Anhui, where famine was at its most intense, cattle sold for less than half of their ordinary price.[78] Once again, economic calculation amplified the crisis.

Wild Animals

In comparison to domesticated species, the wild animals of the wetlands tended to have a far greater tolerance for flooding. Those that survived the initial waves of water could exploit newly expanded habitats and sources of food. These creatures offered a nutritional windfall for those with the requisite knowledge to catch and prepare them. Along with wild vegetation, these animals offered what we might describe as the *ecological endowments* of the flood pulse. It is impossible to quantify the value of these endowments to the human population. While administrators and philanthropists left detailed records enumerating the tonnage of grain distributed to refugees, those who hunted and foraged left precious few traces of their activities. Worse still, as the use of wild food was governed by a complex regime of property and usufructuary rights, in many cases they were positively motivated to conceal their activities.[79] The only knowledge we have of their use of wild food comes from accounts of outside observers, who tended to record such behaviour largely as an index to measure the suffering of the population. Venerable coping strategies based on a profound vernacular knowledge of the environment were usually seen simply as acts of desperation. Though witness descriptions can offer little more than a glimpse, they are the best evidence that we have to

---

[77] Xie, *Yi jiu san yi nian*, p. 76. Cattle speculation remained a problem during the 1954 Yangzi floods, even though the Communist government by then exerted far stricter control over the rural economy. 'Yue xiaxun kuikou fenhong diqu qingkuang', *HFKDX*, pp. 239–40.

[78] *North China Herald*, 11 August 1931.

[79] Historians discussing the use of famine foods in China often refer to botanical encyclopaedias written by scholars from at least as early the Ming dynasty, such as the *Roots and Herbs for Famine Relief* 救荒本草 (*Jiuhuang Bencao*). Such official knowledge was sometimes presented on wall posters pasted up in famine zones. The extent to which ordinary members of the public referred to such texts is unclear. Given the relatively low levels of literacy among the rural poor at the highest risk of famine, it would seem more likely that for most people knowledge of famine foods was transmitted through oral instruction, forming part of what E. N. Anderson has described as the 'foodways' of Chinese culture. See Anderson, *Food of China*. On botanical encyclopaedias see Needham, Lu and Huang, *Science and Civilisation*, Vol. 6 Pt. 1, pp. 331–3; Needham, Robinson and Huang, *Science and Civilisation*, Vol. 7, p. 192.

determine how local communities used knowledge and skills to exploit the ecological endowments of flooding.

Undoubtedly the most useful skill was fishing. Rapid currents would have scoured away countless millions of incubating fish eggs and young spawn, but those that survived would have gorged themselves on aquatic plants and invertebrates, and exploited ordinarily inaccessible sources of terrestrial prey.[80] There are numerous witness accounts describing people fishing in 1931, even in urban areas.[81] Stranded householders in Wuhan leaned from their sagging roofs using small nets to catch the fish that had 'invaded the city from the river'.[82] It is possible that the natural survival behaviour of fish may have made them easier to catch, causing them to seek out the hyporheic zone at the edge of the stream where the current is weakest.[83] Fish sheltering from the flood would have found themselves in close proximity to people living at the edge of the water. Soon there were reports of bumper catches in the flood zone.[84] In some areas the reliability of fishing prompted people to change their professions permanently. In the Hubei district of Songzi 松滋 the number of registered fisherfolk rose from hundreds to thousands in the aftermath of the flood.[85]

Humans were not the only ones who exploited fish. Wetland birds are among the greatest net beneficiaries of inundation. Being able to fly, they can escape the worst effects of flooding with ease and are free to scour the landscape searching for mud banks and shallow pools, where they can exploit stranded fish and invertebrates. Residents of Hubei were certainly adept at hunting such birds, as we have seen, yet there are only a few accounts of them doing so in 1931. A nurse in Wuhan, for example, described how her local colleagues caught and cooked two geese that had been nesting in the grounds of the missionary hospital.[86] We know from other witness accounts that waterfowl were swimming near the human world.[87] As with fishing, the winter was the optimum season to

[80] On the effects of floods on fish populations see Reice, *Silver Lining*, p. 120; Ross, *Ecology of North American*, p. 320; Bayley, 'Understanding Large River-Floodplain Ecosystems', p. 155.

[81] *Wuhan Ribao*, 15 January 1932; Chen, 'Wuchang zaiqu'; H. Owen Chapman 'Fighting Floods and Famine in China', SOAS Archives 10/7/15; Edith S. Wills, 'Hanyang 1931', SOAS Archives 10/7/15.

[82] *Hankow Herald*, 28 August 1931.   [83] Death, 'Effect of Floods'.

[84] *North China Herald*, 22 September 1931.   [85] Zhang, *Coping with Calamity*, p. 178.

[86] 'Letter from Miss Stephenson' SOAS Archives 10/7/15.

[87] Xie, *Yi jiu san yi nian*, p. 341.

catch game birds such as pheasants and snipe.[88] This would have proved timely for famished communities, whose food stocks had run perilously low by late autumn.[89] Other birds, such as snipe, teal, ducks and cranes, made their homes in Hubei in the wet months of the spring and summer. It is likely that hungry people exploited these ecological endowments, yet the extent to which they did so remains unclear.

While the evidence is frustratingly patchy, it certainly suggests that the use of wild food remained quite important to flood-stricken populations. The availability such ecological endowments may help to explain why, throughout Chinese history, floods have tended to kill fewer people than droughts, in spite of the greater physical destruction that they cause.[90] Historians have offered various explanations for this disparity, including the geographic spread and duration of floods, and also the relative poverty of drought-prone areas.[91] Surprisingly little attention has been paid to the ecological differences between inundation and aridity. Droughts cause a great deal of stress for flora and fauna, which are able to survive only by becoming dormant.[92] As the land dries out, insects seek

---

[88] Bryrne, 'Yangtze Notes', pp. 199–200.

[89] Buck, *1931 Flood.*   [90] Pietz, *Yellow River*, p. 74.

[91] The Qing scholar Wang Fengsheng 王凤生 explained this in terms of the differential geographical impact: 'Famine caused by flooding stretches like a thread; famine caused by drought spreads like a sheet.' As Pierre-Étienne Will has noted, this was a gross oversimplification. Will, *Bureaucracy and Famine*, p. 25. There was certainly nothing narrow and thread-like about the 1931 inundation, which spread hundreds of miles beyond rivers. Statistical evidence from the twentieth century does not support the theory that the major difference is one of relative impact on areas of cultivation. Since the 1930s floods in the south have tended to cause a *greater* absolute loss of agricultural produce than droughts in the north. Kueh, *Agricultural Instability*, p. 31. A more convincing explanation lies in the longer relative duration of droughts, which often span several years. See Li, *Fighting Famine*, pp. 131–4; Cohen, *History in Three Keys*, pp. 71–2. Although this theory is persuasive up to a point, it does not account for the prolonged effect that waterlogging and flood deposits can have on arable land after floods. See for example Muscolino, *Ecology of War*. One of the most convincing explanations can be found in the underlying poverty that exists in drought-prone regions, which leaves people highly vulnerable to instability in the food supply. Each of these factors goes some way to explaining why droughts have proved more catastrophic than floods. Yet none account for the numerous harmful effects that inundation has on human communities that are entirely absent during droughts. The desiccation of the landscape does not physically injure or kill people directly, nor does it destroy their homes and granaries. Droughts do not deprive agriculturalists of their tools directly or ruin transportation networks and market infrastructure. In short, the comparison of droughts and floods still needs a good deal of research.

[92] Hardy plants survive by remaining dormant until water returns, while others develop complex taproot systems to access deeper reserves of groundwater. See Lambers, Chapin III, and Pons, *Plant Physiological Ecology*.

refugia, reducing the food available to birds and amphibians. Aquatic species suffer, as the quantity and quality of water recedes and its temperature rises. Fish experience a loss of habitat and become stranded in isolated pools. Their supply of food diminishes as the aquatic faunal assemblage is depleted.[93] The extensive pressure that droughts place on biota within affected ecosystems limits the nutritional opportunities available for human beings – there are few ecological endowments.[94] By the twentieth century, drought-stricken communities in China tended to subsist on agricultural by-products, such as corncobs, peanut hulls, straw roots and cottonseed. The only edible plants hardy enough to survive were trees, which offered scant nutrition, and tuber crops such as sweet potatoes.[95]

The biotic response to flooding was dramatically different. It provided a range of ecological endowments, including fish, aquatic plants and waterfowl. This basic ecological difference may help to explain the varying human experience of inundation and aridity. The literature on flood coping strategies is not as well developed as that describing behaviour during droughts. We know that during the Yellow River floods of 1938 refugees ate wild food and supplemented their incomes by smuggling.[96] Historically, flood-stricken communities in Bangladesh fished and consumed jute leaves.[97] Marine produce may also have helped Irish coastal communities to survive the catastrophic famine of the 1840s.[98] It is important neither to romanticise nor overemphasise the role played by wild food during disasters. Hunting and foraging was almost always a supplementary tactic, used in concert with a range of other coping strategies. For example, in 1931 some fisherfolk left women and children in urban areas, while the men sought to survive on the rivers, relying on a mixture of wild food and charity.[99] Ecological endowments were clearly not a total solution for the problem of famine, yet

[93] Lake, *Drought and Aquatic Ecosystems*; Lake, 'Flow-generated Disturbances', pp. 82–85; Matthews, *Patterns in Freshwater Fish Ecology*, pp. 341–4.
[94] Another way to conceptualise this distinction would be to examine the effect on flows of nitrogen, the adequate supply of which, as Vaclav Smil observes, 'is an irreplaceable condition of human existence.' Smil, *China's Past*, p. 110. Nitrogen is dispersed throughout river valleys by the erosion of minerals in upper catchments, and is fixed by aquatic and riparian plants within the fluvial ecosystem. The impact of floods and droughts on the nitrogen cycle is, then, extremely different. See Arthington, *Environmental Flows*, pp. 65–9.
[95] Mallory, *China*; Thaxton, *Catastrophe and Contention*, p. 27.
[96] Muscolino, *Ecology of War*.   [97] Del Ninno et al., *1998 Floods*, p. 81.
[98] Ó Gráda, *Black '47*.   [99] *Wuhan Ribao*, 15 January 1932.

their use demonstrates that the population of the middle Yangzi still possessed formidable environmental knowledge. Their vernacular skills went almost entirely unrecognised in the official accounts of the flood, as politicians and relief workers posited their own charitable efforts as the only variables preventing starvation.

Microbial Environments

Despite severe food shortages, the major driver of disaster mortality was not starvation. This is clear from the Nanjing Survey statistics, which reveal that during the first 100 days of the flood, only 1 per cent of rural communities starved to death, and in refugee camps there were no cases of starvation. Later, the government would use these statistics to claim that famine had been successfully averted.[100] The health minister Liu Ruiheng 刘瑞恒 observed that people in Wuhan were 'dying of diseases, mainly malaria, typhoid fever and dysentery, instead of starvation'.[101] Such claims were predicated upon a pervasive misunderstanding – or perhaps a convenient misinterpretation – of the nature of disaster mortality. They assumed that deaths could be attributed *either* to hunger *or* to disease. Indeed, this assumption is embedded deep within the popular understanding of disasters, in which the English term *famine* and its Chinese equivalent *jihuang* 饥荒 are taken to imply events in which whole populations starve to death.[102] Very few people literally starve to death during famines. Most fall victim to infectious diseases, at least as their proximate cause of death.[103] Cormac Ó Gráda and Joel Mokyr have observed that during famines hunger and disease 'interact in complicated ways, some of which operate through the human body and some through the fabric of human society.'[104] Malnutrition suppresses both individual and collective immune systems – making human bodies more susceptible to disease and human communities more susceptible to epidemics.[105] Rather than separating hunger from disease, then, we should try to understand the deadly synergy that they form. Disease was certainly the leading proximate cause of death during the 1931 flood. It caused 70 per cent of deaths in rural areas and 87 per cent of deaths in relief camps. Yet those who succumbed to infections had been significantly weakened by malnutrition. It is highly probable that disease

[100] RNFRC.   [101] *Hankow Herald*, 10 September 1931.
[102] On the history of the English concept of famine see De Waal, *Famine That Kills*.
[103] Ó Gráda and Mokyr, 'Famine Disease'.   [104] Ibid., p. 20.   [105] Ibid., p. 20.

Table 2.2. *Causes of flood mortality*

	Information from	
	11,791 farm families in 245 localities in 87 counties 县 (xian)	3796 farm families in refugee camps in Wuchang, Shanghai and Nanjing
Per cent of deaths caused by		
Drowning	24	10
Disease	70	87
Starvation	1	0
Others	1	–
No information	4	3
Number of deaths (in the first 100 days of the flood)		
Deaths per 100	2.2	6.3

masked the true scale of the famine. In the lethal microbial environment created by the flood, people simply did not live long enough to starve to death.

The most dangerous aspect of any famine is usually mass displacement. This pushes malnourished people with weakened immune systems into contact with deadly pathogens, while depriving them of their customary defences against infection. It is for this reason that migration, which is one of the most widely adopted reactions to disasters, is often a spectacularly unsuccessful survival strategy. Table 2.2 demonstrates that the mortality rates suffered in urban refugee camps were almost *three times* higher than those found in rural areas. The sample used was probably too limited to determine whether this pattern applied throughout the flood zone, yet it certainly suggests that those who stayed in the countryside, eking out salvaged crops, fish and aquatic weeds, survived better than those who headed to relatively well-provisioned cities. Of course, many people had little choice but to relocate, as their homes had been inundated. Others simply could not tolerate the lack of food. Hunger may not have been the most lethal of maladies, but it was certainly one of the most persuasive. Politics also played a role. The conflict raging across the flood zone forced many people to become refugees while encouraging local governments to corral homeless people into large camps. Whatever their reason for leaving their homes, refugees were by far the most vulnerable members of the population.

Even in the absence of a disaster, infectious diseases remained the leading cause of death, accounting for more than half of all fatalities in 1930s China.[106] The public health campaigns and medical advances that had helped to bring down infection rates in some urban areas were largely absent in the countryside and in the more deprived quarters of cities.[107] As wealthier populations heightened their defences against infection, susceptibility to disease came increasingly to correlate with poverty.[108] Such differences were amplified during times of disaster. From a global perspective, medical and health improvements tended to intensify the link between disaster mortality and economic inequality, by selectively reducing the vulnerability of elites.[109] This goes some way to explain why certain sections of the population seem to have been relatively immune to flood-related diseases in 1931.

The relative invulnerability of the foreign community in Wuhan provides a particularly visible example of this dynamic at work. Although there were few isolated cases of dysentery and measles, for the most part foreigners survived the flood relatively unscathed, despite the catastrophic health crisis that was unfolding all around them. Even seemingly high-risk groups, such as medical missionaries, do not seem to have suffered substantial fatalities.[110] The reasons for this included their relatively hygienic living conditions, greater access to chemicals to purify drinking water and, most importantly of all, prophylactic inoculations against conditions such as cholera and smallpox.[111] Elites could not be protected from all infections. There were still some diseases, most notably typhus, that killed relief workers and refugees indiscriminately. Though one might assume that the socioecological conditions created by the

---

[106] Lee and Wang, *One Quarter*, p. 44.

[107] On the creation of new public hygiene in urban areas see Rogaski, *Hygienic Modernity*; on prevalence of disease in rural areas see Notestein, 'A Demographic Study'. On the history of public health in the Nanjing Decade see Yip, *Health and National Reconstruction*.

[108] By the 1930s the hygienic deficit suffered by the rural majority meant that male children reaching the age of five in urban areas lived on average fourteen years more than their rural counterparts, and young urban girls ten years more. See Campbell, 'Public Health Efforts', p. 199.

[109] Ó Gráda, *Famine*, pp. 113–15.

[110] A medical missionary named Dr. Hadden contracted dysentery but seems to have survived. 'Handwritten notes in diary format by an unknown individual relating to the flood of Hankow', SOAS Archives 5/1201. Rewi Alley caught malaria while working on the flood relief effort. Airey, *Learner in China*, p. 106. The only foreign fatalities reported in Wuhan during the flood were five Franciscan missionaries who drowned when their boat overturned in the French concession *North China Herald*, 22 September 1931.

[111] Practically all foreigners had been inoculated against cholera and typhoid. *North China Herald*, 22 September 1931.

flood would have been conducive for the lice that spread typhus, mercifully this was one disease that did not make an appearance in 1931.[112]

At the other end of the spectrum, rural refugees arriving in cities were often pushed into lethal microbial environments. Their situation was particularly precarious in Wuhan, which itself succumbed to inundation. Refugees were forced to survive as best they could on an archipelago of flood islands formed on dyke tops, hillsides and railway embankments. The overcrowded conditions on such islands offered a perfect habitat for the measles virus – a perennial enemy of refugees.[113] In one camp, measles infected 1,491 in December alone, resulting in 682 deaths, mostly among children.[114] Measles outbreaks exemplified the complex synergy between hunger and disease. Individuals whose immune systems had been compromised by vitamin deficiencies were more susceptible to viral infections, while communities whose collective immune systems had been compromised by overcrowding were much more susceptible to epidemics. The same dynamic contributed to the smallpox epidemic, which dispatched thousands of undernourished and overcrowded refugees.[115] Most people had yet to be vaccinated against this highly destructive disease, which remained one of the leading causes of death.[116]

The almost total absence of sanitation amplified the risk of disease greatly. With little dry fuel for boiling, those stranded in the oppressive heat of the summer were forced to drink river water contaminated with human and animal faeces. Gastrointestinal infections such as dysentery and typhoid soon ranked among the most prominent causes of death.[117] As rivers emptied sewers into the city streets, coprophagous insects such as flies gorged themselves on human waste. Small fragments became caught on their stiff hairs and were later deposited on human food, helping to extend the range of gastrointestinal diseases.[118] As the flood pulse

---

[112] E. C. Lobenstine, 'The Work of Missionaries and Other Westerners in Flood Relief', SOAS Archives 10/7/15; H. Owen Chapman 'Fighting Floods and Famine in China', SOAS Archives 10/7/15. On typhus in the 1938 Henan flood see Muscolino, *Ecology of War*, p. 63.

[113] On the history of these conditions see Toole, 'Refugees and Migrants', p. 117; Curtin, *Disease and Empire*.

[114] RNFRC, p. 169.

[115] 'Handwritten notes in diary format by an unknown individual relating to the flood of Hankow', SOAS Archives 5/1201; H. Owen Chapman 'Fighting Floods and Famine in China', SOAS Archives 10/7/15.

[116] Notestein, 'A Demographic Study', p. 77.

[117] H. Owen Chapman 'Fighting Floods and Famine in China', SOAS Archives 10/7/15; Xie, *Yi jiu san yi nian*.

[118] Aldrete, *Floods of the Tiber*, p. 149.

interacted with the built environment it created excellent ecological conditions for flies. They were drawn in great swarms to large concentrations of human beings who were unable to dispose of faeces and corpses. The population of Wuhan was soon being plagued by large swarms, which would land on food that was left uncovered for more than a moment.[119] Winged insects are, theoretically, democratic vectors of infection. They can fly between the physical and social barriers that separate human populations, infecting rich and poor alike.[120] Yet homeless refugees lacked walls and fires, the two most basic repellent technologies that people can use to ward off insects, and so there was little they could do to avoid the unwanted attention of these pests.[121] One Irish missionary reported a particular gruesome scene in which an elderly woman living in a hut was 'literally black with flies of the worm generating, blue headed type'.[122]

Flood-stricken communities may have possessed an impressive range of techniques to alleviate starvation, yet they were relatively defenceless in the face of epidemics of gastrointestinal disease.[123] With the flood easily overwhelming the capacities of medical practitioners, most people had to rely on vernacular treatments and dietetic techniques. Some rural communities mixed a form of white clay known as Goddess of Mercy Earth 观音土 (Guanyin Tu) with flour and bran to make cakes.[124] This was a common practice during famines.[125] Historians have tended to characterise the consumption of earth as the ultimate symbol of hopeless desperation – famished people are pictured consuming such materials in order to delude their stomachs into a fleeting feeling of satiation. Yet earth eating, known technically as geophagy, has been found in a wide variety of cultural contexts throughout human history.[126] It is doubtful that it offers valuable nutrition, but coating the gastrointestinal tract with clay may offer protection from toxins and pathogens, and may also ease the pain of hunger.[127] Earth, in other words, may have been consumed more as medicine than as food.

---

[119] *North China Herald*, 22 September 1931; *Hankow Herald*, 13 September 1931.
[120] Biehler, *Pests in the City*.
[121] Webb, *Humanity's Burden*, pp. 44–5.   [122] Barrett, *Red Lacquered Gate*, p. 276.
[123] 'Jizhenhui ling', HSSDX, pp. 166–7.   [124] JHS 10, p. 161.
[125] Mallory, *China*, p. 2; Will, *Bureaucracy and Famine*, p. 33; Li, *Fighting Famine*, p. 361.
[126] Young, *Craving Earth*. Although geophagy has been documented worldwide as a response to hunger, it is not limited to situations of food insecurity. Today, pregnant women and children are among the most enthusiastic geophagists, consuming earth to satiate cravings, known as pica.
[127] For a detailed analysis of the literature see Young, *Craving Earth*; also Hooda and Jeya, 'Geophagia and Human Nutrition', pp. 89–98.

The health properties of earth were well known in China, and had been extolled by medical theorists since at least the Ming dynasty.[128] Famished communities were known to consume earth specifically for its medicinal properties.[129] Certain types of earth even found there way into modern biomedical practice. In 1934 a team of physicians led by Chen Yonghan 陈永汉 experimented with using kaolin clay 高岭 (gaoling) to treat the symptoms of cholera.[130] This must have proved efficacious, because kaolin became a key ingredient in anti-nausea and diarrhea medicines.[131] It is doubtful that the Goddess of Mercy Earth consumed by famished populations was always pure kaolin. Even if it was, excessive consumption would still have caused dangerous gastrointestinal complaints. Yet recognising that geophagy may have had some medical efficacy helps to complicate our image of the behaviour of disaster-stricken communities. Rather than being an act of desperation, eating earth may have been a dietetic technique, which allowed people to treat common symptoms of disaster. Unfortunately, such techniques were at best palliative. When major epidemics of gastrointestinal disease struck, as they did in 1931, most people were largely defenceless.

Refugees could also do little to protect themselves against mosquitoes. These parasitic insects benefited not only from the ready supply of human blood available in overcrowded camps, but also from the huge increase in available surface water in which to breed. The swarms that flew over Wuhan were 'like armies of locusts... attacking the miserable unclothed population'.[132] These mosquitoes soon gave rise to an epidemic of malaria.[133] The League of Nations malariologist Mihai Ciuca reported that of the 711 persons he examined during the flood, 166 were infected with the disease.[134] It was later estimated that 60 per cent of the population contracted malaria due to the flood, causing as many as 300,000 fatalities.[135] Malaria did not affect all members of the population equally. Biology afforded some people natural immunity. Socioeconomic advantages also played a role. Hungry refugees living without repellent technologies near standing water were highly vulnerable. In

---

[128] Young, *Craving Earth*, p. 41.   [129] Will, *Bureaucracy and Famine*, p. 33.
[130] Known as John Wing-hon Chun Wu et al., *Cholera*, pp. 128–9.
[131] Young, *Craving Earth*.   [132] *Hankow Herald*, 28 August 1931.
[133] *North China Herald*, 22 August 1931; 'Handwritten notes in diary format by an unknown individual relating to the flood of Hankow', SOAS Archives 5/1201.
[134] RNFRC, p. 182; for more on League of Nations anti-epidemic measures during the flood see Borowy, 'Thinking Big'.
[135] Yip, 'Disease, Society and the State'.

Wuhan malaria quickly became one of the leading causes of death.[136]
Thankfully, the dominant local species of the parasite causing malaria
was *Plasmodium vivax*. In other areas communities were infected with the
even deadlier strain of *Plasmodium falciparum*.[137] For the population of
Wuhan, there were at least some small mercies.

Succession and Reconstruction

Ecologists refer to the process of natural recovery that occurs in the aftermath of disturbances as succession. Under natural conditions, biological colonisation and weathering repair much of the damage inflicted
by extreme climatic and geophysical events.[138] Had the middle Yangzi
been left to recover naturally in 1932, with the passage of time, succession would have encouraged wetland flora and fauna to recolonise
the basin. Instead, through the human process of reconstruction communities established their favoured anthropogenic environments once
again. Some chose to adapt themselves to the new hydrographic realities. One community in Mianyang 沔阳 converted its flooded polder
into a fishing lake.[139] In most cases dykes were repaired and polders
drained. This allowed people to dominate the process of succession, cap-
turing the biomass deposited by rivers and colonising empty patches with
crops.

Floods have variable effects on soil fertility. They sometimes leave
deposits of sand and rock that make cultivation virtually impossible. This
became a major problem for residents of Henan following the 1938
floods.[140] In other cases the alluvium deposited during inundations
helps to stimulate the growth of vegetation. Such natural fertility had
long been prized by flood recession agriculturalists.[141] By all accounts,
Chinese farmers enjoyed a bumper harvest in 1932, suggesting that
the flood had, in aggregate, helped to improve soil quality.[142] Unfortunately, the economic afterlife of the disaster prevented many farmers
from capitalising on this sedimentary windfall. Having sought credit

[136] H. Owen Chapman, 'Fighting Floods and Famine in China', SOAS Archives 10/7/15;
Xie, *Yi jiu san yi nian*, p. 74.
[137] RNFRC, p. 301.
[138] Del Moral and Walker, *Environmental Disasters, Natural Recovery and Human Responses*.
[139] Zhang, *Coping with Calamity*, p. 123.   [140] Muscolino, *Ecology of War*.
[141] Reice, *Silver Lining*, pp. 114–15. On the role of rivers in the nitrogen cycle see Arthington, *Environmental Flows*, pp. 65–9.
[142] Kueh, *Agricultural Instability*, p. 144; RNFRC, p. 193.

from moneylenders to survive the flood, many households had to hand over a large proportion of their harvests in debt repayments. A similar pattern occurred with those employed in labour relief, who sometimes had to pay 60 per cent of their already paltry wages to creditors, who waited at grain depots.[143] While millions were struggling to rebuild their lives, creditors now profited from the ecological endowment offered by the bumper harvest. Even if they had managed to retain full rights to their land, there was no guarantee that households could cultivate the land, as many had lost labour animals and farm tools. One of the most evocative images that emerged during the period of reconstruction was that of farmers forced to harness ploughs to their own backs, using their bodies to till their land.[144]

Urban populations were not immune from the economic hangover of the flood. The export market in Wuhan was long in disarray. The flood had destroyed huge quantities of cash crops such as cotton. In the year after the flood exports of this commodity were down by as much as 70 per cent.[145] Urban mills that had been flooded in 1931 faced a cotton famine in 1932.[146] The loss of domestic animals was also a serious economic blow, decimating the powdered egg and leather industries.[147] For urban workers, many of whom had lost their jobs when factories were flooded, it was the hike in food prices that proved most devastating.[148] This continued for at least a year. Staple goods remained prohibitively expensive despite the deflationary effect of a large wheat loan from the United States, discussed later in this book. Table 2.3 gives some sense of the prolonged effect that the flood had upon the urban economy. In comparison to Nanjing, which was only lightly inundated, Hankou continued to suffer for at least two years.

When tallying the cost of floods, people seldom think of the loss of trees. Yet this had serious implications during the reconstruction phase. The flood had uprooted and drowned a third of the trees in the disaster zone. A fifth more had been used as fuel or sold as lumber. As timber was the major building material, these losses seriously prolonged the housing crisis. Buildings that had survived the flood were often structurally compromised. Whole neighbourhoods in Wuhan leant precariously, ready to collapse at any moment.[149] When members of the community set about

[143] Yorke, *China Changes*, p. 72. [144] JHS 10, p. 163. [145] Hou, *Shuizai hou Wuhan.*
[146] On the flooding of urban mills see *Hankow Herald*, 18 August 1931.
[147] Hou, *Shuizai hou Wuhan.* [148] *Hankow Herald*, 28 August 1931.
[149] *Hankow Herald*, 28 August 1931.

Table 2.3. *Comparison of prices in Hankou and Nanjing, 1930–1933*

	Food	Clothing	Fuel and light	Building materials	Misc.	General index
Index of wholesale prices in Hankou[a]						
1930	100	100	100	100	100	100
1931	109.6	114.1	121.7	126.7	109.2	114.5
1932	108.5	109.4	120.9	125.7	103.9	112.4
1933	94.0	95.9	101.8	116.2	95.5	98.7
Index of wholesale prices in Nanjing[a]						
1930	100	100	100	100	100	100
1931	99.0	109.6	112.9	108.9	112.4	106.1
1932	93.0	102.5	104.8	109.3	115.7	100.8
1933	85.9	83.3	95.7	102.8	96.7	92.1

[a] Simple geometric averages.

reconstructing their homes, they found that timber prices had become prohibitively expensive.[150] Unlike quick growing grasses such as rice and wheat, the succession of woodlands took years, if not decades. Although one of the key recommendations of the Nanjing Survey had been that all homes should be constructed upon sturdy foundations, given the chronic lack of trees, many people had little choice but to reconstruct their own vulnerability, relying once again on cheap materials with low water resistance.[151] The dearth of trees also meant that farmers struggled to replace essential tools, such as ploughs, carts, and wheelbarrows, and lacked even the most basic furniture such as beds and chairs.[152] The silk industry was devastated by the loss of mulberry trees, which left sericulturalists with nothing to feed their silkworms.[153] This blow came at the same time that they were facing a steep depreciation of the value of silk exports caused by the Great Depression. With meteorology and economics conspiring against them, many converted their mulberry groves into rice paddies.[154]

Agricultural reconstruction usually outpaced ecological succession. In most areas, wild flora and fauna did not have a chance to exploit the rich alluvial deposits of the flood. One exception to this was the plains to the

[150] Buck, *1931 Flood*, p. 38.   [151] Ibid., p. 46.
[152] 18 per cent of ploughs, 4 per cent of carts and 4 per cent of wheelbarrows had been lost among numerous other items of farmyard equipment. Ibid., pp. 18, 22.
[153] Ibid., p. 19; Zhongguo jingji xue she', Jiuzai yijian shu', *Dongfang Zazhi*, 28 (1931).
[154] Shiroyama, *China during the Great Depression*, pp. 122–4.

north of Wuhan. Here the foreign traveller Gerald Yorke described vast tracts of untilled land, where wild grasses and brushwood thrived.[155] The reason was not that the local population had discovered some latent form of ecological consciousness. It was, rather, because the ongoing conflict between the Nationalists and Communists that had prevented them from returning their land to the plough. The succession of the local ecosystem was, in this instance, an evocative reminder of the extent of human suffering. Micah Muscolino has argued that war should be understood as an ecological process, in which militaries metabolise vast energy inputs extracted in the form of human labour and natural resources.[156] This ecological model certainly helps to explain how human conflict and environmental disaster conspired against the population of northern Hubei.

Long before the flood struck, the subsistence system was already straining as a result of the ravages of war. In early 1931 the Nationalists launched the latest of their encirclement campaigns designed to dislodge the Communists from their Soviet at E-Yu-Wan 鄂豫皖, a mountainous borderland region between Hubei, Henan and Anhui.[157] With supply lines cut, the dwindling sources nutrition and energy upon which the three and a half million residents relied were quickly metabolised by the Red Army. Then, in the late spring, flash floods coursed down the mountain slopes, washing away a huge quantity of crops.[158] Starvation and disease followed soon after.[159] With the resources of this region exhausted, Zhang Guotao 张国焘 ordered his half-starved troops to march south and commandeer supplies from market towns, expanding the metabolic reach of the Red Army.[160] Draining as it must have been, the effects of Communist parasitism paled in comparison to the destruction caused by the brutal scorched earth policies launched by the Nationalists. In 1932, with much of Hubei still struggling to cope with hunger and disease, the provincial governor Xia Douyin ordered his troops to commandeer grain supplies and poison drinking wells, making life around the Communist stronghold unliveable.[161] Soon many areas of northern Hubei had been reduced to 'districts of the dead' 死人区 (siren qu).[162] Yorke estimated that as much as a third of the population had been killed, with most

---

[155] Yorke, *China Changes*, p. 61.   [156] Muscolino, *Ecology of War.*
[157] Benton, *Mountain Fires.*   [158] Yan, *Macheng xian zhi*, p. 44.
[159] Rowe, *Crimson Rain*, pp. 240, 316.   [160] Ibid., p. 317.   [161] Benton, *Mountain Fires.*
[162] NB: Huang'an is now known as Hong'an. See Tang, *Hong'an xian zhi*, p. 4. This gazetteer, which offers a typically pro-Communist interpretation, attributes most of this destruction to the Nationalists.

survivors fleeing to urban areas.[163] According to the head of the government relief efforts John Hope Simpson, the majority of the refugees in Wuhan were actually escaping war rather than water.[164] In reality, these two maladies were inextricably linked. The grass and brushwood that flourished in northern Hubei owed its existence to a deadly combination of flooding and conflict.

These were not the only species that thrived in the post-disaster environment. *Cholera vibrio* also found a beneficial niche among starving and overcrowded refugees. Rumours of cholera outbreaks had been circulating since the earliest stages of the flood. Having investigated conditions in Wuhan on behalf of the quarantine service, Wu Liande 伍连德 reported in September that the cholera situation had been 'much exaggerated'.[165] This renowned Malayan-Chinese epidemiologist may have correctly diagnosed a case of collective paranoia at this time, but by the winter cholera really had begun to colonise the city.[166] It dispatched undernourished people at terrifying speeds. As one nurse put it, 'they start with diarrhoea in the evening and are dead the next day.'[167] Doctors, who had little but saline injections to counter these symptoms, were easily overwhelmed by the scale of the epidemic.[168] The quarantine service later estimated that flood-related cholera had killed more than 800 people in Wuhan, with infected refugees then spreading the condition throughout the region.[169] Cholera later climbed the mountains of north Hubei, carrying away thousands of Red Army soldiers.[170] It would seem that the environment was also capable of metabolising armies.

---

[163] Yorke, *China Changes*, p. 61.

[164] Extracts from letter of Sir J. Hope-Simpson to Mr. F. B. Bourdillon, 16 January 1932, SOAS Archives 10/7/15. It should be noted that this picture adhered to the Nationalist representation of the disaster, which tended to blame Communists for displacement. See 'Wei daishou gongfei qu nei nanmin zaikuan qishi', *Jiuguo Zhoukan* 1 (1932).

[165] *North China Herald*, 13 October 1931. Wu Liande was known as Wu Lien-teh.

[166] H. Owen Chapman 'Fighting Floods and Famine in China' SOAS Archives 10/7/15; Xie, *Yi jiu san yi nian*, p. 74; 'Handwritten notes in diary format by an unknown individual relating to the flood of Hankow', SOAS Archives 5/1201.

[167] 'Handwritten notes in diary format by an unknown individual relating to the flood of Hankow', SOAS Archives 5/1201.

[168] H. Owen Chapman 'Fighting Floods and Famine in China', SOAS Archives 10/7/15.

[169] Wu and Wu, *Haigang jianyi*.

[170] Yan, *Machengxian zhi*, p. 498. During earlier stages of the flood the Communists had kidnapped government relief workers to demand autonomy over the reconstruction effort. Tellingly, when they later ransomed Captain Charles Baker their primary demand was for medicine. See George Andrews, 'Letter to John Hope Simpson', 6 June 1932, JHS 6i.

In the summer of 1932, China experienced probably its most deadly cholera outbreak of the twentieth century. Spreading over 300 cities in 20 provinces, the epidemic infected more than 100,000 people, killing around 30,000.[171] Caution should be adopted before reducing the outbreak of epidemics to any single factor. As David Arnold has noted, cholera and famine may have frequently coincided, but there is no automatic correlation between the two.[172] The Nationalist government was certainly keen to downplay the links between the flood and the epidemic.[173] There is little doubt, however, that inundation had created a comfortable habitat for cholera. It had lowered collective immunity by destroying sanitation systems and disrupting the water supply. Cities such as Yichang and Wuhan, which were still struggling to recover from inundation, suffered among the worst levels of infection.[174] By causing widespread food shortages, inundation diminished individual immunity, as *Vibrio* thrived in malnourished bodies.[175] The flood may not have caused the cholera epidemic, but it had certainly helped to forge a conducive epidemiological environment.

The complex links between the flood and the subsequent cholera epidemic illustrate how a socioecological perspective can help to broaden our understanding of the dynamics of humanitarian catastrophes. By moving away from a narrow nutrition-centred approach, we can begin to unpick the tangled knot of causes that helped to form the disaster regime. This shift forces us to confront many of the assumptions that still permeate historiography. Rather than asking only how well the state and society managed to nourish the people, we must also examine how a range of socioecological interactions helped to nourish pathogens. Recognising the impact of water on non-human species also forces us to reframe our understanding of the temporality of disasters. The effect that inundation had on cattle, trees and *Cholera vibrio* demonstrates that acute climatic shocks can have prolonged consequences. This, in turn, raises questions about how we quantify the effects of catastrophes. The convention of determining excess mortality within a limited time frame fails to appreciate that humanitarian catastrophes are never discrete events – they are complex processes that unfold on a variety of

---

[171] RNFRC, p. 17; Poon, 'Cholera'; Zhang, *Minguo shiqi*, pp. 143–5.
[172] Arnold, *Colonizing the Body*, p. 167.   [173] RNFRC; compare p. 132 and p. 149.
[174] RNFRC, p. 17; Poon, 'Cholera'.; For statistics on the Wuhan outbreak see Zhang, *Minguo shiqi*, p. 144.
[175] Thomas, *Lambeth Cholera Outbreak*, p. 38.

temporal scales.[176] Our insatiable urge to count and compare disaster mortality conjures an illusory order out of messy, fragmented and prolonged processes.

If we were to draw temporal boundaries around the flood, limiting the period in which its effects could be examined, we could never hope to understand the role played by endemic diseases such as snail fever. Local histories claim that there was a sharp spike in cases of this water-borne complaint in the aftermath of the flood.[177] But what does this really imply? Inundation certainly seemed to have created an excellent habitat for both pathogens and vectors. Large refugee populations were pushed into proximity with polluted water, in which both schistosome cercariae and freshwater snails thrived. Yet unlike conditions such as dysentery or cholera, which rip through the body at a terrifying pace, snail fever unfolds in prolonged and complicated stages. The acute phase is extremely dangerous, having symptoms much like malaria. Those who survive enter a chronic stage, during which they can remain asymptomatic often for years. Eventually some develop late-stage snail fever, which gives rise to the characteristic distended stomach and other debilitating symptoms.[178] A snail fever sufferer may be pushed from chronic to late-stage disease by various forms of physical stress, including malnutrition.[179]

Given the complex and prolonged nature of snail fever, it is quite possible, likely in fact, that many people who became symptomatic in 1931 may have already been infected, and that malnutrition and other stresses pushed them into late-state schistosomiasis. Conversely, the blood flukes that burrowed into the skin of refugees would have left many in an infectious yet asymptomatic state. Many may have died from a condition they contracted because of the flood, years or perhaps even decades later. Snail fever played a fiendishly complex role in the disaster regime, involving dynamic interactions among hydrology, ecology, epidemiology and biology. This is before we even consider the economic complications caused by snail fever infecting oxen and buffalo. The complexity of this one single condition reveals quite how difficult it is to capture the effects of a disaster using the blunt instrument of excess mortality – a mode of quantification that takes insufficient account of both pre-existing

---

[176] An argument well established in the social science literature dealing with disasters. See Wisner et al., *At Risk*; Oliver-Smith, 'Anthropological Research'.
[177] Pi. *Wuhan tongshi: Minguo juan (shang)*, p. 222.
[178] Gross, *Farewell to the God of Plague*, p. 4.   [179] Gross, *Chasing Snails*, pp. 19–20.

vulnerabilities and long-term implications. It also shows that if we are to view flooding from a socioecological perspective, we must think about how individual events fit into the broader life of both communities and their environments. Long after rivers receded to their courses and refugees returned to their homes, the effects of the flood pulse lingered within human gastrointestinal ecosystems.

3

THE DRAGON KING 龙王

> We heard lots of ridiculous superstitions and legends during
> the flood. Some people said that the inundation had been
> caused by the destruction of a Dragon King Temple... We
> must smash these superstitions.
>
> Xie Qianmao, 1931[1]

One wetland creature inspired more fear than any other in Wuhan. As
rivers crept ominously up around the city's flood defences, a rumour
began to circulate suggesting that a local Dragon King was controlling the
rain. The flood was his act of vengeance against the municipal government for demolishing his temple the previous year. Crowds soon began to
gather at the riverside area that had once been home to the Dragon King
Temple. People fashioned paper effigies of prawns and crabs, declaring
them to be the army of the Dragon King, before instructing him to depart
with his soldiers to the ocean. Daoist priests prayed and shamans chanted
incantations.[2] A Buddhist monk proclaimed that if the deluge had not
receded within a week, he would plunge into river to reason with the
Dragon King.[3] The religious outpouring culminated in a large parade
that weaved its way through the city streets to the site of the former temple, erected an altar where local officials provided ritual offerings and
kowtowed to the Dragon King, beseeching him to forgive Wuhan and
put an end to the flood.[4]

The Dragon King had good reason to be angry. Once a respected
deity, worshipped for his ability to control rainfall, for decades he had
been suffering a sustained attack, launched by those who insisted that
he did not exist. This was part of a broader campaign designed to eradicate an assemblage of beliefs and practices that critics categorised as

---

[1] Xie, *Yi jiu san yi nian*, p. 6.   [2] Ibid., p. 149.   [3] Xu 'Fangxun xianduan', p. 288.
[4] Ouyang, 'Xia siling'; Xu 'Fangxun xianduan'; Tu and Yang, 'Wuhan Longwang Miao'.

superstitions. Eschewing such pejorative labels, historians prefer to describe the many rituals and festivals that gave meaning to the lives of ordinary people variously as folk, local or popular religion. This chapter is concerned with one particular aspect of this loose system – namely the *ethnometeorological* system that residents of Wuhan employed to explain the weather and mediate their relationship with nature.[5] There were numerous systems of ethnometeorology in Republican China. These included those espoused by organised religions, such as Buddhism, Daoism, Islam, Christianity and also, as we shall see, those promulgated by people who saw themselves as advocates of rational science.[6] Popular religious ethnometeorology was not bound to any set of canonical texts or any particular liturgical tradition. It formed part of a practised religion, found in temples, shrines and homes, and involved a vast array of deities and spirits, blended with figures from local historical and cultural traditions. As a living tradition practised by ordinary citizens, popular religion is harder to examine than those forms of belief that attracted more literate adherents. The cult of the Dragon King is a case in point. Adherents do not seem to have been affiliated with any pre-existing institutional apparatus, and left no accounts of their activities. The only records left for posterity were those written by critics, who believed that the Dragon King was a superstitious myth.

There was certainly no shortage of sceptics. Eyewitness descriptions of Wuhan's folly travelled the globe at a remarkable speed. The Britons of Shanghai read that the people of the city believed that the flood had been caused by a dragon that was infuriated by the killing of three snakes.[7] American audiences learnt of a distant population who were committing mass suicide to escape a dragon god.[8] Newspapers in Singapore reported the government of Wuhan would not allow its people to slaughter animals as it believed this would anger some form of river deity.[9] Such reports allowed journalists to add a little cultural flavour to otherwise relentlessly grim articles about the flood. Yet for citizens of Wuhan on

---

[5] See for example Clarke, *Australian Aboriginal Ethnometeorology*.

[6] This chapter does not use the prefix *ethno* as a marker of alterity – to distinguish colourful (and by implication erroneous) local beliefs from the theories of a supposedly cultureless realm of science. Just as everyone has an ethnicity, so too every group has its own form of ethnometeorology.

[7] *North China Herald*, 20 October 1931.

[8] *New York Times*, 22 August 1931; *Washington Post* 24 August 1931.

[9] *The Singapore Free Press and Mercantile Advertiser*, 14 September 1931.

both sides of the religious divide, the Dragon King cult was deadly serious. To understand the passions that inflamed their debates, this chapter delves deep into the history of dragons.

Today dragons remain so closely associated with China that they serve as a metonym for the nation. They stand alongside Russia bears, American eagles, and Indian tigers in the symbolic menagerie of international relations. For much of Chinese history, however, dragons were not just symbols – they were real creatures. They formed a key link within an integrated system of ethnozoology and ethnometeorology, being sentient animals that could control rainfall. The ceremonies that people performed to dragons represented a cultural response to the disaster regime – they helped them to explain hazards and provided a sense of agency in otherwise hopeless situations.

Secular critics were fond of depicting popular religious ethnometeorology as a tragic expression of the ignorance of the common people. Those who had little control over their environment put their faith in false beliefs and inanimate idols. Historically, however, the system of ethnometeorology espoused by literate elites had existed within a moral and conceptual realm similar to that promulgated by popular religion. Indeed, ethnometeorology was embedded within the very structure of the state in the form of the famous Mandate of Heaven 天命 (Tianming). This drew a direct causal link between the stability of environment and official legitimacy, with floods and droughts often being interpreted as signs that Heaven did not approve of the rule of an emperor. Given the profound political implications, it is unsurprising that state officials often tried to promote countervailing explanations for disasters. Among the most popular were the various theories that Mark Elvin has described as 'moral meteorology'. Adherents of such theories understood hazards to be punishments for the misdeeds of affected communities.[10] At the level of elite discourse, moral meteorology can be read as a cynical attempt to evade accusations that the Mandate of Heaven had been violated. Yet such beliefs also formed an important component of local systems of ethnometeorology. They not only provided communities with meaningful interpretive framework for disasters, but also furnished them with a blueprint for action. If climatic hazards were caused by excessive sexual intercourse, the mistreatment of people or animals or the violation of ritual propriety, then prohibiting such activities would surely restore harmony with nature. As we shall see in this chapter, despite

[10] Elvin, 'Who Was Responsible'.

the fall of the Qing dynasty and the rise of scientific meteorology, many observers of the 1931 flood continued to search for political and moral messages in the rainclouds, even some who claimed to have rejected religion.

In recent years, several historical studies have described the clash between popular religion and secularising forces in early twentieth century China. Building upon the pioneering work of Prasenjit Duara, scholars such as Shuk-wah Poon and Rebecca Nedostup have detailed how radical activists sought to eradicate a the corpus of temples, deities and rituals in an attempt to create a modern secular state.[11] What appeared on the surface to be abstract disputes about theological issues often masked hidden political agendas. Such was the case during the 1931 flood. The Dragon King cult unearthed the religious and political fault lines that had emerged in Wuhan during the recent years of turbulent change. Disasters have often served as catalysts for political and cultural disputes. The 1755 Lisbon earthquake initiated one of the most influential debates of the Enlightenment era, with philosophers disagreeing fundamentally about whether seismic activity should be considered a form of divine judgement.[12] Similarly, Rabindranath Tagore accused Mohandas Gandhi of ignoring scientific rationality when the latter claimed that the 1934 Bihar earthquake was a 'divine chastisement' for the sin of untouchability.[13]

Disasters can also inspire debates among ordinary people, although their everyday philosophising is rarely recorded for posterity. The Dragon King cult offers a glimpse of how ordinary people tried to understand the flood, and to explain it to one another. Unfortunately, our knowledge of these events relies solely on the testimony of hostile witnesses. This is an all too common problem. David Arnold has noted that although British descriptions of religion in India were often designed 'to show the absurdity and naïve credulity of the masses', they nevertheless 'take us closer to popular perceptions and responses than other sources allow.'[14] This chapter uses problematic sources in the same spirit, mining them for details of how communities used religion to negotiate with the environment.

[11] Duara, 'Knowledge and Power'; Nedostup, *Superstitious Regimes*; Poon, *Negotiating Religion*; Goossaert and Palmer, *Religious Question*.
[12] Rozario, *Culture of Calamity*, pp. 14–20.
[13] Paranjape, 'Natural Supernaturalism?' I am grateful to Matthew Pritchard for drawing my attention to this comparison.
[14] Arnold, *Colonizing the Body*, pp. 218–19.

Domesticating Dragons

The people of the middle Yangzi had been living with dragons for thousands of years. Though doubtless creatures of great antiquity, nobody is sure quite where they originated. One theory that was popular in the early twentieth century was that dragons were mythologised versions of the alligators that once thrived in this wetland region. Indeed, these alligators were known at one time as *tulong* 土龙 or 'earth dragons'.[15] Recently, the ecologists John Thorbjarnarson and Xiaoming Wang have breathed new life into this old naturalistic theory, noting that the behaviour of alligators mirrors many of the characteristics attributed to dragons. Their seasonal migration pattern brought them to the middle Yangzi in the late spring, just as the rains were engorging the wetlands with water. They then disappeared again in the autumn, just as rivers were beginning to recede. It is certainly not implausible that early human communities may have drawn causal associations between the arrival of these alligators and the coming of the rains. The alligator skin drums that archaeologists have found may have been beaten to imitate the sonorous mating call of these alligators which people attributed with the power of summoning rainclouds.[16] This naturalistic theory helps to embed cultural beliefs in their ecological context, while also explaining the evolution of many aspects of local dragon lore. Yet we should not forget that there have been numerous other theories used to explain the origin of dragons that at one time seemed plausible, yet now have been disproven. One of the most fanciful was L. Newton Hayes's belief that dragons represented a cultural memory of dinosaurs, which had become etched into the human psyche when 'some early member of the human race . . . met with one of these monstrous creatures.'[17] Fortunately, for our purposes, identifying the origins of dragon beliefs is less important than examining how they evolved over time. In Hubei, the gradual domestication of

---

[15] Worcester, *Junks and Sampans*, p. 468.   [16] Thorbjarnarson and Wang, *Chinese Alligator*.
[17] Hayes, *Chinese Dragon*, p. 37. This is just the most implausible of the many theories advanced about the origins of Chinese dragons in the early twentieth century. The Sinologist M. W. De Visser sought to demonstrate that Chinese dragons were distinct from their fire-breathing European counterparts, searching Buddhist and Confucian texts for early references. See De Visser, *Dragon in China*. The folklorist Donald Mackenzie argued that the similarity between Chinese dragon lore and motifs found in areas as diverse as India, Babylon and Polynesia demonstrated a high degree of historical cultural interchange. See Mackenzie, *Myths of China*. The anatomist and evolutionary theorist Grafton Elliot Smith took this even further, suggesting that the ancient Egyptian symbol of the dragons travelled through the world through a process of cultural diffusion. See Elliot Smith, *Evolution of the Dragon*.

dragons – from wild creatures to symbols of the state – mirrored the evolution of the disaster regime.

Dragons were ubiquitous symbols in the religious life of the rice farmers of the Chu State, which occupied an area including Hubei for much of the first millennium BCE.[18] At this stage they remained wild creatures, feared and revered for their capacity to control rainfall. Chu dragons, like all Chinese dragons thereafter, were quite unlike their European fire-breathing cousins. They lived in rivers and and lakes, and flew up into the sky creating rainclouds with their breath. Chu communities continued to beat drums in the late spring – or the fifth lunar month – as their ancestors had before them. By now they were probably not trying to encourage the amorous calls of alligators, but were more likely, as Göran Aijmer has argued, to have been trying to entice dragons to bring rain to water transplanted rice shoots.[19] For farmers, dragons had become key symbols of fertility. Though similar creatures can be found in various cultural traditions throughout the world, the specific association that serpents and dragons have with water seems to be particularly prevalent in rice-growing cultures of monsoon Asia. This possibly reflected a common socioecological context and the associations that people drew between reptilian behaviour and the phases of the agricultural cycle. A more concrete explanation is that culture and technology travelled the same paths, linking the ancient rice-growing world in custom and knowledge. This helps to explain how the Nāga, a serpent-like deity found in both Hindu and Buddhist traditions, managed to make its way to China. Having arrived, it crossbred with local dragons, bestowing a few of its Indian cultural characteristics upon the creatures.[20]

Dragons were not simply mythical figures. They were rare animals that inhabited the hidden recesses of the natural world, accorded credence within the local system of ethnozoology. There was so little doubt that they existed that dragon bones were a prized medicine used to treat a range of ailments. Dragons were not simply figments of the overactive imaginations of uneducated people. Some of the wisest minds in China believed in them. They described their anatomies in precise detail in encyclopaedias and recorded their sightings assiduously in local gazetteers. Timothy Brook has argued that dragon sightings can help us reconstruct climate history, providing evidence of storms and other meteorological events.[21] Dragons were not the only creatures that lurked

---

[18] Major, 'Characteristics of Late Chu Religion'.
[19] Aijmer, *Dragon Boat Festival*, pp. 21–7.   [20] De Visser, *Dragon in China*.
[21] Brook, *Troubled Empire*, pp. 6–24; See also Cohen, 'Coercing the Rain Deities'; Pomeranz, 'Water to Iron'; Overmyer, *Local Religion*.

hidden in the shadows. The world beyond the village boundaries was home to a range of forces, including ghosts, fox spirits and drought demons. With every rocky outcrop and shady pool having its own numinous inhabitant, the natural environment was embroidered in a tapestry of local history. Sinologists often marvelled at the poetry of the Chinese environmental imagination, but for ordinary people the strange and unpredictable forces that occupied the landscape were all too real.

The rise of hydraulic agriculture changed the nature of dragons. No longer simply symbols of fertility, they became avatars of environmental uncertainty. As humans insinuated themselves into the hydrological system by building dykes and polders, legendary hydraulic masters became a new form of deity, worshipped as much for their capacity to domesticate flood dragons as they were for the grand engineering schemes they employed to tame rivers. When a catastrophic flood overran ancient China, Yu the Great 大禹 (Dayu) was said to have dredged channels so that rivers could flow to the sea. Though possibly a highly mythologised version of an actual historical figure, Yu's story was embellished with an array of flood dragons, magical turtles and several other numinous creatures.[22] Dragons also found their way into the legends of Li Bing 李冰, whose remarkable hydraulic system on Min River 岷江 has irrigated the Chengdu Plain for more than two millennia.[23] The legends that pictured hydraulic masters dominating dragons betrayed a key conceptual shift in the understanding of flooding. No longer entirely the product of hydrological fluctuations, inundation was now in part mediated by human agency. To remain safe within an increasingly anthropogenic disaster regime, communities courted the patronage of hydraulic masters who could dominate local dragons.

In the water control temples that sprung up throughout the middle Yangzi, dragons often stood side by side with hydraulic masters. The latter included generic figures such as Yu the Great and also members of the local community who had been deified for building dykes or otherwise making contributions to hydraulic security.[24] Such temples became

[22] Birrell, *Chinese Mythology*, pp. 132–4; Sautman, 'Myths of Descent'; Pietz, *Yellow River*, pp. 29–31.
[23] Worcester, *Junks and Sampans*, p. 588.
[24] There was a Yu the Great tablet in the Hankou Dragon King Temple. See Tu and Yang, 'Wuhan Longwang Miao', p. 1. A late Qing salt merchant who financed an important flood wall near Wuhan in the 1840s was deified posthumously and given his own temple, from which he was expected to continue to maintain the hydraulic security of his community. See Rowe, *Hankow: Conflict and Community*, p. 151. Similar practices occurred in the Yellow River basin; see Dodgen, *Controlling the Dragon*, p. 157.

the most important religious institutions in the polders that dotted the Hubei plains.[25] They helped to foster the communal solidarity that was vital for collective flood prevention. They also served as venues for the rainmaking rituals performed by local priests or shamans. Within the local ethnozoological system, dragons were categorised as 'scaly' 鱗 (lin) animals, alongside reptiles such as snakes and lizards.[26] If ritual specialists wished to enlist a dragon to control rain, they often used scaly reptiles in ceremonies of sympathetic magic. Another approach involved throwing tiger bones into water pools. As tigers were the only creatures that dragons feared, then the hope was that these bones would scare them into flight, thereby causing them to make rain.[27] These rituals were not limited to male-dominated sphere of temple worship. On the second day of the second lunar month – a date known as the 'Raising of the Dragon's Head' 龙抬头 (Long Taitou) – women performed an important water rite, tracing chalk lines to water vessels in their homes.[28] As rain dragons represented the fecundity of nature, women who were trying to conceive children sometimes used candles from dragon processions as part of fertility rituals.[29]

The potency of the dragon as a symbol of local religion was not lost on the state. Rather than suppressing dragon worship, officials employed various means to redirect the spiritual authority of these creatures towards the state. Prasenjit Duara described this mode of official domestication as the 'superscription of symbols'. By bestowing official legitimacy, the state sought to co-opt deities, creating an authoritative image 'with which rural elites could identify, and which peasants and other social groups could acknowledge without renouncing the dimensions . . . that were more immediately relevant to them.'[30] The superscription of the dragon happened in several ways. Most obviously, the creatures were adopted as the official symbol of the regent.[31] From the Song dynasty onwards, dragons adorned the clothes, flags and throne of the imperial family. It became hard for local communities to worship dragons without also worshipping the emperor. The state also inserted itself into the local dragon rituals conducted in the fifth lunar month. No longer a rain-regulating ceremony, this became an occasion to commemorate the death of the scholar official Qu Yuan 屈原. Having been wrongly exiled

---

[25] Gao, 'Transformation of the Water Regime', pp. 69–93.
[26] Sterckx, *Animal and the Daemon.*　　[27] Snyder-Reinke, *Dry Spells*, pp. 15–16; 103–4.
[28] *Wuhan shi zhi: shehui zhi*, p. 106.　　[29] Worcester, *Junks and Sampans*, p. 468.
[30] Duara, *Global and Regional*, p. 95.
[31] Thorbjarnarson and Wang, *Chinese Alligator*, p. 60.

from court, Qu had thrown himself to his death in a river in Hunan. His tragic life came to exemplify official rectitude. When communities beat drums, as they had been doing for thousands of years, they were now said to be stopping fish from devouring Qu's corpse. When they took to the water in special boats adorned with dragons on their prows, they were re-creating the desperate search for the martyred exemplar.[32] The rituals and practices on the Dragon Boat Festival 端午节 (Duanwu Jie) long predated the life and death of Qu Yuan, yet the dragons worshipped on this occasion were now woven into a story of the state.

The process of superscription also helps to explain the emergence of the specific figures known as Dragon Kings. Unlike the wild and unruly dragons that were cajoled into controlling the weather with occult rituals, Dragon Kings were so fully domesticated that they could be enthroned in temples, and venerated with sombre ritual decorum. Their emergence formed part of the broader bureaucratisation of the popular religious pantheon. By the second millennium the gods lived in a world that closely mirrored that of their human counterparts. The Jade Emperor 玉皇 (Yu Huang) presided over a spiritual state, in which deities each had their own obligations and were ranked according to a strict hierarchy. City Gods 城隍 (Chenghuang) ruled urban areas, Earth Gods 土地公 (Tudigong) protected villages and farms, and Dragon Kings governed rivers and rainclouds.[33] Though their true form was that of a dragon, they could shape-shift into snakes or old men, so that they could walk or sliver unnoticed through the human world. This iteration of the dragon arose in a context in which environmental stability had become inextricably linked to the issue of governance. The Dragon King was essentially an environmental bureaucrat, his job being to administer rainfall within his specific jurisdiction.[34]

The link between governance and disasters was solidified by rituals. Dragon King ceremonies had, at least theoretically, to be conducted by figures of equivalent rank within the human bureaucracy, most often the local magistrates.[35] The right to conduct rituals conferred considerable power upon officials, yet if hazards occurred this could threaten their legitimacy. The integration of the state into the religious life of local

---

[32] Aijmer, *Dragon Boat Festival*; Ball, *Water Kingdom*, p. 260.

[33] On City Gods see Zito, 'City Gods'.

[34] Zhao describes Dragon Kings as 'hydraulic magistrates'. See Zhao, 'Chinese Mythology', p. 239.

[35] This did not stop local shamans from also conducting rituals in Dragon King temples. See Sutton, 'Shamanism'.

communities was not simply a means for rulers to assert their authority. It also provided communities with a symbolic forum in which to express dissatisfaction with governance failures. In his fascinating study of late imperial ethnometeorological rituals, Jeffrey Snyder-Reinke highlights the extent to which local governors remained beholden to their constituents, sometimes even performing officially prohibited rituals in order to placate the demands of local communities.[36] When rituals failed, deities were sometimes subjected to humiliations; their effigies were paraded through the street, whipped and exposed to the elements.[37] On such occasions, governors were no doubt acutely aware of their own precarious positions relative to their angered constituents, not to mention their symbolic affinity with the tortured god. Reprimanding tutelary deities such as Dragon Kings and City Gods was a powerful demonstration of public anger, which reminded governors that if disasters were not successfully ameliorated, popular dissatisfaction could easily be redirected from the deity to the state.

As a chronically flood-prone city, late imperial Wuhan formed an excellent habitat for dragons. The local population venerated several water deities. There were numerous religious institutions dedicated to Yu the Great, and also a temple in which locals could petition the minister who had been appointed by the Jade Emperor to preside over issues of water control.[38] Those who wished to take a less bureaucratic approach could attend one of the eight temples dedicated to the god of thunder Lei Gong 雷公, who also had the power to control rainfall.[39] The Dragon King was not, then, the only ruler of the water, but he was probably the most popular.[40] Exactly when his temple in Hankou was first constructed is unclear, although it had already been there for some time when a wharf was built in 1739.[41] Being surrounded by teahouses and a popular local market, and operating its own ferry service, the Dragon King Temple was an important social hub.[42] It was constructed on top of a dyke in an extremely flood-prone area, near the confluence of the Yangzi and

[36] Snyder-Reinke, *Dry Spells.*   [37] Doolittle, *Social Life*, p. 122; Snyder-Reinke, *Dry Spells.*
[38] Fan, *Hankou congtan*, pp. 138–209; Shuiye, *Hankou*, p. 485; Liu, *Tianxia diyi*, p. 180.
[39] A full list of late Qing temples can be found in Fan, *Hankou congtan*, pp. 38–209;. See also Liu, *Tianxia diyi jie*, p. 180; Rowe, *Hankow: Conflict and Community*, p. 21.
[40] In addition to the Dragon King Temple in Hankou, there was also a temple to the East Ocean Dragon King 东海龙王 (Donghai Longwang) in Wuchang. See *Wuchang xian zhi*, p. 584.
[41] Liu, *Tianxia diyi jie*, p. 180.
[42] Tu and Yang, 'Wuhan Longwang Miao', p. 1; Rowe, *Hankow: Conflict and Community*, p. 32.

Figure 3.1. The Dragon Boat Festival in early twentieth century Wuhan. (Bernard Upward, *The Sons of Han: Stories of Chinese Life and Mission Work*. London: London Missionary Society, 1908, p. 131. Reproduced courtesy of the Cambridge University Library)

Han Rivers.[43] This strategic combination of religion and hydraulic engineering is highly revealing. Contrary to the arguments advanced later by secular critics, ritual and practical solutions were not mutually exclusive. Both formed part of a holistic response to the problem of flooding.[44]

For the people of late-imperial Wuhan, the dragon remained a potent symbol of local religion. G. R. G. Worcester captured the raucous nature of the dragon parades that were held on the fifth day of the lunar New Year: 'Undulating and rocking high above the crowd, the monster proceeds slowly forward, until at a signal it is galvanized into an absolute frenzy of activity.' This culminated with the dragon taking a bow amidst 'a perfect fusillade of crackers...leaving the air thick with the smoke and the pungent smell of black powder'.[45] The Dragon Boat Festival (Figure 3.1) was a similarly boisterous occasion. Crowds congregated on the banks of the Yangzi, where they gathered the roots of a local variety of

---

[43] Ye, *Hankou zhuzhici*, p. 2; Xu, 'Fangxun xianduan'.
[44] Snyder-Reinke, *Dry Spells*, p. 73; Overmyer, *Local Religion*, p. 18.
[45] Worcester, *Junks and Sampans*, p. 125.

bulrush 菖蒲 (changpu). This was mixed with spirits and drunk as a remedy against summer epidemics.[46] Enlivened by this medicinal cocktail, they carried the effigies of dragons and other deities through the streets, while they shouted and banged gongs and drums. With great ceremony, the dragon heads were placed upon the prow of competing boats, which were then raced by rival gangs of labourers from each of the major wharfs in Hankou.[47]

For William Rowe, the Dragon Boat Festival was a key expression of the solidarity of the working population in nineteenth century Hankou.[48] It was also an occasion on which intergroup tensions bubbled to the surface. Violent altercations often broke out between different regional and ethnic groups during the festivities. Many members of the Confucian elite disliked this festival intensely, seeing it as an occasion on which unruly workers and vagrants wrought havoc upon the city.[49] The various attempts that they made to ban the Dragon Boat Festival reveal that disputes about popular religion were hardly unique to the twentieth century.[50] Dragons remained a contested symbol. Despite various attempts at domestication, these ancient wetland creatures retained their wild subversive potential, being a vital expression of local identity and religion.

Doubting Dragons

The Dragon King Temple was demolished in 1930. On the surface, this was a routine decision made by town planners who wished to construct a new road. Yet it also betrayed the extent to which popular religious ethnometeorology had been devalued in the eyes of municipal administrators. The religious landscape of Wuhan had never been static, as was demonstrated by the wide variety of religious institutions, including temples, monasteries, mosques and churches.[51] The iconoclasm of the twentieth century was also not entirely novel. When the forces of the

---

[46] Fan, *Hankou congtan*, pp. 193–4; Upward, *Sons of Han*, p. 130. These bulrush roots, known to botanists as *acorus calamus*, and is also sometimes known as sweet flag. Some residents of the middle Yangzi have told me that they still use these roots during this festival. Now they do not ingest them but use them as soap or shampoo.
[47] Worcester, *Junks and Sampans*, pp. 534–5; Rowe, *Hankow: Conflict and Community.*
[48] *Hankow: Conflict and Community*, pp. 201–6.   [49] Fan, *Hankou congtan*, pp. 193–4.
[50] Rowe, *Hankow: Conflict and Community*, pp. 201–6.
[51] On Buddhist and Daoist temples see Fan, *Hankou congtan*, pp. 38–209; on Mosques see 'Rev. Claude L. Pickens, Jr. collection on Muslims in China', Album 3, ca. 1932–1947 (Harvard-Yenching Library).

Taiping Heavenly Kingdom invaded Wuhan in the 1850s, they too had desecrated temples, hoping to impose their idiosyncratic theology upon the local populace.[52] This humiliation of the deities coupled with the profound physical destruction of the city plunged Wuhan into a state of spiritual disequilibrium. During the latter half of the nineteenth century, some turned to millenarian sects such as the Green Lotus 青莲教 (Qing Lianjiao), which offered spiritual salvation for those who accepted a lifestyle of abnegation and vegetarianism.[53] Others explored the faiths that were being proselytised by the foreign residents of the city. Following the opening of Hankou as a treaty port, Wuhan gained several Catholic and Protestant missions, and a rather grand church built by the Russian Orthodox community.[54] There was even a gurdwara to serve members of the local Sikh community who worked as policemen and factory guards in the concessions.[55]

Foreign Christians tended to be hostile to popular religion. In the 1860s, the Protestant missionary Justus Doolittle wrote a scathing denunciation of a Dragon King parade he had witnessed as part of a rain-making ceremony in northern China. Unlike critics in the 1930s, who tended to couch their objections to popular religion in terms of scientific scepticism, Doolittle had no objection to the general principle of deities exercising agency over the weather. His major grievance was that the villagers seemed to be beseeching the wrong deity. They were, he lamented, 'deplorably ignorant [of] Him who gives us rain from heaven!'[56] Missionaries believed their own faith was substantively different from Chinese popular religion, which they saw as overly functional and even instrumental. The Christian journalist Clarence Burton Day argued that deities such as Dragon Kings, Fire Spirits, and Thunder Gods were indicative of a crude form of 'peasant religion' that had developed

---

[52] On the destruction of temples see Elgin, *Letters and Journals*, p. 292. On Taiping Christianity see Kilcourse, *Taiping Theology*.

[53] Rowe, *Hankow: Conflict and Community*, pp. 21, 257–61.

[54] Catholic missionaries had been active for at least a century. There was a Franciscan church in Wuchang and a Columban order in Hanyang. By the late nineteenth century Protestantism had become the largest denomination, and was proselytised by representatives of the London Missionary Society and Wesleyan Methodist Missionary Society. See Walsh, *Observations in the Orient*, pp. 131–42; Barrett, *Red Lacquered Gate*. Wuhan even had its own Catholic matryr, John Perboyre, who was strangled on a cross in 1839. See Fiat, *Life of Blessed John Gabriel Perboyre*; Upward, *Sons of Han*; Chang, 'Tension within the Church'. On the Russian Orthodox church see Fang, 'Zhudong songhuan huilai de zujie'.

[55] Yuan. *Hankou zujie zhi*, p. 391.   [56] Doolittle, *Social Life of the Chinese*, p. 122.

in a hazard-prone region.[57] This was religion not as moral code but a passive reflex – a bargain that local communities made purely for material protection.

These critics were correct in one sense. Hazardous conditions probably had played a role in the evolution of environmental customs. What they failed to acknowledge was that their own faith appealed to local converts for the same reasons. One pamphlet that missionaries used in Hubei depicted Noah alongside sinful communities being engulfed by water. The accompanying caption read: 'Those who oppose Heaven court disaster' 逆天招灾 (nitian zhaozai).[58] Those reading this message could be forgiven for assuming that the Heaven that purportedly spared Christians from calamities was the same Heaven to which they prayed for deliverance. In Figure 3.2, from another pamphlet used in 1930s Hubei, a Sinicised Jesus Christ is depicted miraculously controlling water to rescue fishermen from a storm. Even if missionaries had not explicitly sought to suggest that their faith held the key to avoiding disasters, such images, and the extent to which the miraculous elements of Christianity seem to have been emphasised, would have been highly suggestive to communities living in a disaster-prone region. The image of Jesus Christ that missionaries were presenting bore more than a passing resemblance to a hydraulic deity – he was somewhere between Yu the Great and a Dragon King.

Christians were not alone in their disdain for popular religion. Chinese elites had often been critical of what they saw as heterodox practices of the common people. From the late nineteenth century this perennial distaste took a new form, as intellectuals and politicians began an assault upon the institutional foundations of popular religion. Zhang Zhidong played a prominent role in these campaigns, proposing that 70 per cent of temples should be transformed into schools. Zhang should not be confused with a modern secularist, as his dislike for popular religion has as much to do with his orthodox Confucianism. Furthermore, his campaigning was motivated to a large extent by economic imperatives. Temples possessed huge reserves of wealth and land that he wished to expropriate to fund the development of a modern education system.[59] Neither Zhang nor the state he served survived long enough to witness

57 *The Chinese Recorder*, July 1932.
58 William Wilson, 'Eye-Gate or the Value of Native Art in the Mission-Field with Special Reference to the Evangelization of China', SOAS Archives 6/107a.
59 Poon, *Negotiating Religion'*, p. 24.

Figure 3.2. 'And he saith unto them, Why are ye fearful, O ye of little faith? Then he arose, and rebuked the winds and the sea.' (*The Life of the Chinese Christ by Chinese Artists*. The Society for the Propagation of the Gospel, London. Reproduced courtesy of The United Society)

these reforms fully enacted. Yet his proposals set the precedent for the denuding of the religious landscape over the subsequent century.

In 1911, Wuhan found itself at the centre of the Xinhai Revolution, which precipitated the final collapse of the Qing dynasty. The Republican governors who assumed power were tasked with the difficult job of decoupling religious and political authority.[60] When Li Yuanhong 黎元洪 sought to establish himself as the new ruler of city shortly after the revolution, he chose to emulate the ritual practice of the deposed empire, dedicating sacrifices to Heaven, Earth and the Yellow Emperor.[61] Just one year later, local governors were no longer content with imitation. Instead they sought to create new rituals, which reflected the priorities of the modern nation. They seized one of the most prominent official temples in Wuchang, and redecorated it from imperial red to sombre grey. They replaced the tablet of the emperor with portraits of fallen revolutionaries, and provided them with sacrificial offerings of meat, fish, wine and tea.[62] The spiritual authority of the Qing state was not denied but rather usurped. Revolutionary martyrs – the hungry ghosts of the new state – were accorded the ritual courtesy once reserved for the emperor himself.

This repurposing of imperial temples marked the beginning of a sustained attack on institutional and conceptual foundations of popular religion in Wuhan. In his 1915 gazetteer, the local garrison commander Xu Huandou 徐焕斗 argued that temple rituals and geomantic theories 风水 (fengshui) designed to control the weather were highly anachronistic, having developed to 'comfort the hearts' 按人心 (an ren xin) of ignorant people who had little control over their environments.[63] Unlike previous generations of scholars, who often chose to attack popular religious practices as heterodox deviations from sound cosmological theories, Xu described these beliefs instead as 'superstitions' 迷信 (mixin), denying the very cosmological foundations upon which they stood. This was a neologism that had entered the lexicon only a few decades earlier alongside the less pejorative term 'religion' 宗教 (zongjiao).[64] Together this new theological terminology armed intellectuals with powerful new conceptual weapons in their campaign against popular beliefs. While many

---

[60] Nedostup, *Superstitious Regimes.*
[61] Harrison, *Making of the Republican Citizen,* pp. 17–18.
[62] 'Emily Rattenbury (née Ewins) to Anon (Letter)', 1912, *Methodist Archives,* GB-135 DDHBR; Zhe, Yu and Di, *Wan Qing–MinchuWuhan yingxiang,* p. 217. The original name of this temple is not provided in either source.
[63] Xu, *Hankou xiaozhi.* [64] Poon, *Negotiating Religion.*

who sought to lambast superstition still held a degree of reverence for religion, many others, including the Communists, saw no substantive difference between the two. In the 1920s the radical intellectual Yun Daiying 恽代英 was one of the most prominent atheist campaigners in Wuhan.[65] Not content merely to criticise the relatively soft target of popular religion, he also launched a scathing attack upon what he described as 'Christian superstitious rubbish' 基督教迷信的一派鬼话 (Jidujiao mixin de yi pai guihua).[66]

Intellectuals such as Yun were not simply nihilists. In place of an enchanted world of deities and rituals they hoped to build a new scientific culture, which would provide a more cogent response to the problem of disasters. The hydrologist Zhang Hanying 张含英 believed that when the common people were educated sufficiently to understand the physical processes that governed the environment, they would learn to reject their superstitions about the weather. The historian Deng Tuo concurred, arguing that religious ethnometeorology had its roots in the ancient past, when the agricultural population had little agency over the natural world. The fact that traces of this 'fatalistic ideology' 天命主义 (tianming zhuyi) still permeated Chinese culture in the early twentieth century, was, Deng argued, a bitter indictment of contemporary socioeconomic conditions.[67]

Although it did not lack passion, the intellectual assault on popular religion seems to have had relatively little political impact in the early 1920s. The militarist governors who ruled Wuhan continued to perform temple rituals just like their imperial predecessors. When the spring rains failed in 1924 the provincial superintendent proclaimed a three-day prohibition against the slaughtering of pigs and cattle. This was a common tactic used to demonstrate the moral credentials of the local community, thereby eliciting sympathy from Heaven.[68] Sure enough, a few days later

---

[65] The May Fourth Movement was a moment of intellectual awakening. It has most often been narrated from the perspective of Beijing and Shanghai. Recently Shakhar Rahav has demonstrated the important role that intellectual networks based in the universities and bookshops of Wuhan played in mobilising these new ideas as a form of mass political action. See Rahav, *Rise of Political Intellectuals*.

[66] Yun, *Yun Daiying wenji*, p. 371. On Yun's campaigns against religion see Kuhlmann, 'Negotiating Cultural and Religious Identities', p. 356.

[67] Deng, *Zhongguo jiuhuang shi*, pp. 161–6.

[68] During this period, the British press in China recorded the religious activities of local administrations assiduously. Although their interpretation of events was coloured by cultural prejudice, their reports offer a valuable insight into realm of ethnometeorology. The following account is based on *North China Herald*, 23 May 1924. No figure is referred

rain began to fall. To give thanks for delivering his province from disaster, the superintendent travelled with a retinue of senior politicians to the Dragon King Temple, where he ordered the city magistrate and the chief of the municipal government to erect a special altar to give thanks to the benevolent deity. To the chagrin of secularists, rituals continued to play a role in the governance of Hubei. This was all about to change. Following their rise to power in 1927, the Nationalists would launch a comprehensive campaign to destroy the foundations of popular religion. Things looked bleak for the Dragon King.

Dethroning the Dragon King

On 1 January 1927, jubilant crowds gathered on the streets of Wuhan to celebrate the announcement that the city had been declared the provisional capital of a new regime. The previous autumn a coalition of Nationalists, Communists and allied militarists marched the Northern Expedition into Hubei, deposing the warlord leader Wu Peifu.[69] Over the next few months a new radical regime presided over the region, known as the Wuhan Government. A Soviet translator named Vera Vladimirovna Vishnyakova described the heady atmosphere on the streets of city, with crowds partly celebrating the new government and partly a demonstrating against the presence of British imperialists in the city. At the centre of the crowd an effigy of a dragon was held aloft and danced through the streets: 'His terrible head with a wide-open mouth and protruding eyes soared over the crowd, bending right and left.'[70] Unlike the Xinhai Revolutionaries, who had consciously co-opted the sombre rituals of the Qing state, these anti-imperialist protestors were drawing upon the symbolic power of popular religion, their procession recreating the highly charged atmosphere of a festival parade. Over the next few days everlarger crowds gathered, and on 3 January protestors marched to the borders of the British Concession.[71]

Accounts of the ensuing events diverge along predictable ideological lines. An Australian physician named H. Owen Chapman described

---

to by name, but Xiao Yaonan 蕭耀南 was the provincial superintendent 督办 (duban) around this time. See *Wuhan shi zhi: Junshi zhi*, p. 52. It is unclear from this account whether the ceremonies were conducted at the Dragon King Temple in Hankou or the East Ocean Dragon King Temple in Wuchang.

[69] Van de Ven, *War and Nationalism;* Wilbur, *Nationalist Revolution.*
[70] Vishnyakova, *Two Years in Revolutionary China,* p. 276.
[71] Ibid.; Yang, 'Yisan can'an'.

how an angry mob began pelting the concession with rocks. The British marines posted as guards acted with admirable restraint, yet were eventually forced to engage in hand-to-hand combat to prevent rioters from entering the concession.[72] A Chinese student named Yang Chunbo 杨春波, present on the other side of the barbed wire blockade, suggested that the protestors were entirely peaceful until the British marines decided to launch a spontaneous attack. Soon a Chinese sailor lay dead, alongside several severely injured wharf workers.[73] As the news spread, enraged protestors stormed the concession and occupied British territory. Such violent episodes occurred frequently during the anti-imperialist movement of the mid-1920s China. What was remarkable about the storming of the Hankou concession was that the British were forced to capitulate. Under the terms of the subsequent Chen–O'Malley Agreement, they surrendered all territorial claims in Hankou. For British leaders, this was a tactical retreat, allowing them to cling to their far more important territory in Shanghai. For the new Wuhan Government, it was a significant symbolic victory, marking what Robert Bickers has described as 'the first unavenged defeat of the British empire in Asia',[74]

The seizure of the British Concession would later enter the canon of revolutionary history as a key moment of national and class awakening.[75] Yet neither the Communist trade union movement under Li Lisan 李立三, nor the Nationalist politicians under figures such as the foreign minister Chen Youren 陈友人, could claim any responsibility for the event.[76] One Soviet official present in Wuhan argued that it has occurred 'spontaneously, without any leadership'.[77] This was not quite true. The events had followed an established script of popular protest, just not one comprehensible to modern political activists. Since the late nineteenth century, anti-foreign protests had become a regular feature of the Dragon Boat Festival in Wuhan. Indeed, this was not even the first time that wharf labourers had attacked the British Concession. In 1872, they had attempted to storm the police station inside the concession.[78] The

---

[72] Chapman, *Chinese Revolution 1926–1927*, pp. 32–5.
[73] Yang 'Yisan can'an'. See also HSSI, *Hankou Jiujiang shouhui Ying zujie*, pp. 5–8.
[74] Bickers, *Britain in China*, p. 142; see also Yuan, *Hankou zujie zhi*, p. 391.
[75] These events are often described as the January 3rd Massacre (*Yi san Can'an* 一三惨案). See HSSI, *Hankou Jiujiang shouhui Ying zujie*.
[76] Known as Eugene Chen. For an account of these events from the perspective of Li Lisan see Lescot, *Before Mao*. For an account of these events from the perspective of Chen see Chen, *Return to the Middle Kingdom*.
[77] Quoted in Isaacs, *Tragedy of the Chinese Revolution*, p. 124.
[78] *North China Herald*, 29 June 1872.

tensions that had once caused wharf labourers to fight with one another now spilled out in popular anger at the foreigners who built a secluded space within their city. The timing of the protests, in January 1927, did not correspond with the date on which the Dragon Boat Festival fell, yet the symbolism employed by protesters certainly evoked the traditions of the festival.

The semiotics of protest – chanting, firecrackers, drumming and dragons – all drew heavily on established ritual practices. Over the following months, as Wuhan became the capital of radical China, the streets were filled time and again with political demonstrations. As Owen Chapman observed, these bore an uncanny resemblance to 'processions for worship or prayer at temples, processions for rain, dragon processions'.[79] Popular religion had always contained a political subtext, with processions serving as symbolic expressions of collective dissatisfaction and communal power. Now popular protest seemed to be utilising the aura and atmosphere of religious parades, appealing to local populations on a recognisable and affective level. The similarities between religious precessions and political demonstrations shed light on why the government took the Dragon King cult in 1931 so seriously. Popular anger could easily erupt from the exuberance of collective worship. The overlaps also help to explain why, when the government started to suppress political radicalism in late 1927, they also launched a vociferous attack on popular religion.

In April 1927 Chiang Kai-shek began a violent campaign to suppress Communists in Shanghai and the lower Yangzi region. The Wuhan Government initially condemned this purge, yet as it became clear in which direction the political wind was blowing prominent left-wing Nationalists fled for the sanctuary of Moscow.[80] Meanwhile the pacification of the countryside had begun, led by none other than Xia Douyin, whom we last met inflicting scorched earth policies on rural Hubei in the wake of the flood. Following a few years of warlordism in the early 1920s, Xia had made a timely alliance with the forces of the Northern Expedition, and was now stationed as a division commander near Changsha. Aghast at the radicalism in Wuhan, and even more so about the movement against rural landowners, Xia mutinied and began a march on the city, leaving a trail of brutality in his wake.[81] Having been repulsed by troops loyal to

---

[79] Chapman, *Chinese Revolution*, pp. 24–5.
[80] Chen, *Return to the Middle Kingdom.*   [81] Rowe, *Crimson Rain*, pp. 271–5.

the regime, Xia contented himself with purging the countryside of radicals. As William Rowe has observed, this conflict was as much a gender war as it was a political dispute. Xia took ghoulish pleasure in inflicting horrific vengeance on women who had had the temerity to bob their hair in a modern style, divorce their husbands or defy other precepts of rural gender relations. With counterrevolution sweeping the countryside, Wang Jingwei 汪精卫 and the other remaining Nationalists in Wuhan severed their ties with the Communists. In mid-July, the military authorities seized the labour union headquarters and began executing suspected Communists.[82] Once again, violence against women was rife, with one leading feminist being executed and having her severed head displayed on the city walls.[83] This penchant for misogynistic violence was indicative of the deep social conservatism that would form one of the strongest undercurrents in Wuhan politics over the next few years. Amidst the technocrats who sought to reform the city, many 'party warlords', as Edward McCord has characterised them, would continue to exert considerable power and promote socially conservative policies in Hubei.[84]

Whether by accident or design, this conservative clampdown coincided with an amplification of the official campaigns against popular religion. New legislation was introduced in 1928, which allowed secular activists to launch vicious attacks against popular religion. Rebecca Nedostup and Shuk-wah Poon have described the impact of this legislation in the Nationalist heartlands of Jiangnan.[85] In Wuhan, a far more contested territory, the clampdown appears to have been even more vicious. Other municipal administrations contented themselves with issuing edicts outlawing fortune-tellers. In Wuhan, the authorities ordered them to find a new profession within three months.[86] The annual pilgrimages to temples that took place during Mid-Autumn Festival were banned, and soldiers were posted to prevent worshippers from entering.[87] Earth God shrines were closed, and religious adherents were prohibited from burning spirit money and incense. Some particularly unfortunate Earth Gods had their temples turned into

---

[82] Wilbur, *Cambridge History of China*, p. 671; Isaacs, *Tragedy of the Chinese Revolution*, p. 270.
[83] On the gender war see Rowe, Crimson Rain, pp. 276–85.   [84] McCord, *Military Force*.
[85] Nedostup, *Superstitious Regimes*; Poon, *Negotiating Religion*.
[86] *North China Herald*, 27 October 1928.
[87] *North China Herald*, 6 October 1928; *Religious Tract Society in China 1928–1929*, Vol. 54 (Hankow: Religious Tract Society Press, 1929), pp. 2–3.

public toilets.[88] When this failed to have the desired effect, the authorities decided to arrest the Earth God idols. They carried these wooden statues to the local police stations, and executed them by decapitation.[89] This highly ritualistic mode of iconoclasm seemed to bear an indelible trace of the very religiosity it sought to eradicate. Not all deities suffered this ignoble fate. Yu the Great survived as an exemplar of Chinese engineering prowess.[90] The flood dragons and magic turtles that added colour to his myths were conveniently overlooked. The Dragon King was not granted the same latitude. In 1928, he was officially classified as a superstition.[91]

It was in this context that municipal planners took the decision to demolish the Dragon King Temple. This lack of consideration for local sentiments was entirely in keeping with the new political direction taken by the urban administration. After the collapse of the radical Wuhan Government, Chiang Kai-shek had appointed a loyalist named Liu Wendao 刘文岛 as mayor. An army of young technocrats was parachuted in from other regions and tasked with transforming Wuhan into a modern metropolis, to rival Paris, Tokyo or London.[92] A renewal the transportation infrastructure was central to this urban renaissance. Wuhan had bad roads. There were only around 700 automobiles in the city in the early 1930s, fewer than half of those found in Nanjing or Guangdong, and a fraction of those driving through the ultra-modern streets of Shanghai.[93] The labyrinthine alleyways of Hankou were notorious for being narrow and uneven, cluttered with shop signs and perpetually muddy.[94] Wuhan needed a new road to run along the riverbank, and no temple was going to stop this development.[95] In the spring of 1931, with the Dragon

---

[88] *North China Herald*, 2 November 1929.   [89] *North China Herald*, 30 November 1929.

[90] Contemporary articles praising Yu include Fang, 'Da Yu zan'.; 'Kongzi dachen yu shuizai', *Guowen Zhoukan*, 8 (1931). On the numinous elements of the Yu myth see Birrell, 'Four Flood Myth Traditions'. On the fate of Yu during anti-superstition campaigns see Nedostup, *Superstitious Regimes*, p. 82; Poon, *Negotiating Religion*, p. 68.

[91] Worcester, *Junks and Sampans*, p. 467.

[92] On urban redevelopment see *Wuhan Shizheng Gongbao*, Vol. 5, 1929, 17; 'Liu Wendao tan Hankou shi muqian jianshe gaikuan, *Daolu Yuekan*, 1931. For an interesting analysis of these plans see Ye, 'Big Is Modern', pp. 116–19.

[93] Rajchman, *Report of the Technical Agent*, pp. 54–5.   [94] Shuiye, *Hankou*, p. 75.

[95] The renaissance of the riverside area where the Dragon King Temple stood had originally been suggested by Sun Yat-sen as part of his ambitious development plan for China. See Sun, *International Development of China*. Sun did not live to see this plan to fruition, but his heir Sun Ke 孙科 – known as Sun Fo – worked closely with the Wuhan administration to ensure that this ambition was fulfilled. See Fang, 'Difang bizhi'.

King evicted and the new road under construction, all of the ambitious plans of the municipal planners seemed to be coming to fulfilment. A missionary returning to Wuhan after a two-year absence was amazed to see 'great new streets driven right through the old, dark, crowded, narrow, dirty, unhealthy native city. These new streets have smooth tarred surface, side walks, drains underground.' Local businesspeople embraced these reforms, filling the new area with 'shop fronts with plate glass, profusion of the latest neon-light advertising and sky signs, and motors and garages are in every street.'[96] Material modernity had arrived in Wuhan and was unceremoniously trammelling its way through the religious landscape. Overhead, storm clouds gathered.

A Great Flood Inundates the Dragon King Temple 大水冲了龙王庙

By July 1931, with rivers rising all around, people in Wuhan were desperate for an explanation for the terrible weather. A local benevolent hall hired a mystic 仙 (xian) to glean some insight into events. He used a divining instrument known as a fuji 扶乩 to conduct a spirit-writing ritual.[97] The results read *laohan wuyou* 老汉无忧, a message so esoteric that nobody had a clue what it meant. It was finally decided that 'laohan' did not refer to an old individual, which was one possible interpretation, but rather to 'old Hankou'. The message meant that 'old Hankou need not worry', suggesting that the historic centre of the city would escape inundation.[98] Any comfort derived from this prediction was short-lived. Soon after, floodwater engulfed the entire city, new and old alike. For some, this disaster was a sign that Heaven was displeased with local citizens.[99] One observer suggested that the flood was a way of 'getting rid of bad people' living in Wuhan.[100] Clearly, moral meteorology continued to have an influence on local interpretations of disaster causation. For other people there was a much simpler explanation – the Dragon King was expressing his anger through incessant rainfall.

The flood had come at an inconvenient time for opponents of popular religion. The fact that the deluge occurred just one year after the temple demolition seemed more than sufficient evidence to convince many people that the rainclouds were the work of a vengeful deity. The population of Wuhan were not alone in identifying a religious origin for the flood. Citizens of Gaoyou were convinced that their local City God

[96] A. J. McFarlane 'Report of the Year 1931', 14 January 1932, 65/10.
[97] Cf. Meyer-Fong, *What Remains*, p. 23.   [98] Xie, *Yi jiu san yi nian*, p. 76.
[99] Ibid., p. 6.   [100] *North China Herald*, 20 October 1931.

would never have permitted the disastrous inundation of their homes. Unfortunately, reckless secular activists had destroyed his temple shortly before the flood.[101] Shanghai residents were more fortunate. In the early summer a room-service attendant discovered that three elderly people staying in a hotel had transformed into snakes. Local citizens quickly deduced that these were no ordinary reptiles – they were Dragon Kings who had shape-shifted into serpent form. Crowds descended upon the hotel, burned incense and provided offerings, imploring the Dragon Kings not to inundate their city.[102] Shanghai experienced only relatively light flooding.

This proliferation of rumours demonstrates the limited impact that the anti-superstition campaigns seem to have had on ethnometeorology. Government legislation had not simply passed by unnoticed; it had been incorporated into the fabric of religious narratives. The flood seemed to threaten the mandate of scientific reform, with angry deities using rain to wreak vengeance on arrogant secularists. Religious rumours often contained a degree of nostalgia for past modes of governance. One refugee in Wuhan suggested that in the past administrators would merely have had to kowtow to the floodwater and it would have receded. The problem was that these governors 'do not believe in spirits' 不信神 (buxin shen).[103] During floods in Hubei in 1935 refugees expressed similar sentiments, criticising officials for preventing them from singing spirit operas 神戏 (shenxi) that they ordinarily performed to assuage flood dragons.[104]

Some local governors seem to have been sympathetic to religious explanations. The military commander Fang Benren 方本仁 was said to have kowtowed to a snake he saw swimming in the floodwater, declaring it to be the Great Serpent King 蛇大王 (She Dawang), a preternatural reptile intimately associated with the Dragon King.[105] The provincial authorities also became involved in ritual responses to inundation. Having initially resisted calls to institute a slaughter prohibition, they eventually capitulated, banning the practice for five days and sticking up posters to encourage encouraging moral behaviour.[106] Soon foreigners were complaining that it was impossible to buy meat in the markets.[107] Other officials became even more directly involved. The unfortunate mayor He

[101] Sha, 'Xinyang yu quanzheng'; Nedostup, *Superstitious Regimes*, p. 111.
[102] *Da Gongbao*, 18 September 1931.   [103] Xie, *Yi jiu san yi nian*, p. 149.
[104] Chen, *Jianghe shuizai*, p. 233.   [105] Li, 'San shi nian dai shuizai'.
[106] Xie, *Yi jiu san yi nian*, p. 125; *North China Herald*, 25 August 1931.
[107] *Hankow Herald*, 24 August 1931.

Baohua 何葆华, who had succeeded Liu Wendao just months before the flood, travelled to the former site of the Dragon King Temple and partook in rituals designed to placate the deity.[108] Xia Douyin played an even bigger role, leading the procession through the streets and presiding over the altar rituals.[109]

For the historian Liu Fudao 刘富道, the involvement of municipal governors in religious rituals epitomised the irrationality and inertia of the local regime.[110] This assessment underestimates the political capital that stood to be gained by such a manoeuvre. It is entirely possible that Xia and his counterparts believed that the angry Dragon King was posing an existential threat to Wuhan. It is equally plausible that they were using rituals to assuage public anger. Just as Qing administrators had ignored state proscriptions on heterodox practice so that they might dampen the anger of their local constituents, these leaders may have been willing to defy anti-superstition legislation to perform obeisance to a powerful local deity. An even clearer example of this dynamic was reported during a drought in 1934, when the residents of a rural district on the border of Anhui and Henan forced their reluctant magistrate to undertake a rainmaking ritual to the local Dragon King. When seven days elapsed and there was still no rain, the magistrate had the deity executed by firing squad.[111] Given the political subtext of religious rituals, granting credence to deities could be an eminently sensible way of diffusing public anger. It is impossible to know whether governors took part in such rituals because they believed them to be efficacious, or whether they were merely using religion as a strategic political performance – perhaps both were true. What is clear is that Xia Douyin did not suffer politically because of his veneration of the Dragon King. He was promoted to provincial governor in 1932.[112] In this post he seems to have made no effort to reconstruct the Dragon King Temple.

[108] Tu and Yang, 'Wuhan Longwang Miao'; Fang, 'Difang bizhi'. According to one media report, the former mayor Liu Wendao himself claimed to have seen a dragon in the floodwater. If true, this would be particularly remarkable, given that he headed the very administration that was responsible for the destruction of the Dragon King Temple. The British-owned *North China Herald* was not known, however, for the highest standards of journalistic impartiality. See *North China Herald*, 15 September 1931.

[109] There is an oral history account of this recorded in Ouyang, 'Xia siling'. Other local histories describing Xia Douyin's pariticipation include Xu, 'Fangxun xianduan I'; Yan, 'Dashui chongle Longwangmiao'; Tu and Yang, 'Wuhan Longwang Miao'; Pi, *Wuhan tongshi: Mingguo juan (shang)*, p. 215; Liu, *Tianxia diyi jie*, pp. 181–2.

[110] Liu, *Tianxia diyi jie*, p. 181.

[111] *The Straits Times*, 11 August 1931.   [112] Rowe, *Crimson Rain*, p. 306.

Embracing the Feet of the Buddha

Not everyone was convinced by the popular religious interpretations of the flood. Many of the journalists who reported from the inundated streets of Wuhan offered scathing criticisms. Guan Xuezhai was bemused to see people rescuing effigies from temples during the flood. He asked his readers why people were putting their faith in wooden figurines that had not even be able to save themselves. Chen Hesong 陈鹤松 considered the religious reaction to the flood to be an act of arch hypocrisy. He ridiculed those who ordinarily demonstrated little piety, yet seemed to have suddenly found faith when disaster threatened. To Chen these people were merely 'embracing the feet of the Buddha in their hour of need' 临时抱佛脚 (linshi bao fojiao).[113] Xie Qianmao was undoubtedly the most vociferous critic of religion during the flood. A local journalist who became a refugee, we know relatively little about Xie. He seems to have been broadly supportive of the Nationalist regime. The monograph he wrote about his flood experience includes a manifesto written by Chiang Kai-shek and endorsements from other party luminaries. Yet he was by no means a slavish propagandist, and he was keen to document the injustices suffered by refugees at the hands of the military. Like many journalists from this era, he employed a highly didactic style, particularly when lambasting the beliefs of his fellow citizens. For Xie, religion was not just foolish but also dangerous, as it fostered a fatalistic outlook that stopped people from fighting disasters.[114] In one passage that seemed to anticipate the religious and environmental policies of the Maoist state, he argued that to prevent future catastrophes the Chinese people needed to 'smash' 打破 (dapo) superstition and realise that 'humans must conquer nature' 人定胜天 (rending shengtian).[115]

Local journalists were not alone in their criticisms of the popular religious reaction to the flood. Foreign observers were both amused and appalled by what they witnessed. For O. Edmund Clubb, an American consulate worker, the Dragon King cult revealed the apathy and fatalism of the local governors, who, he argued, had simply capitulated in the face of inundation. They 'understood that the Dragon King, Ruler

---

[113] Chen, 'Wuchang zaiqu shidi shichaji' *Yaxi Yabao*, HSSDX.

[114] Xie, *Yi jiu san yi nian*, p. 6.

[115] Shapiro, *Mao's War against Nature*, pp. 66–7. Xie was not unique in his use of combative rhetoric. The military commander Jiang Jianren 蒋坚忍, who wrote a foreword for Xie's monograph, called on his compatriots to draw on their ancient heritage to 'win a victory over the environment' 战胜环境 (zhansheng huanjing) and defeat floods. Xie, *Yi jiu san yi nian* [Foreword].

of the River, was displeased with the destruction of his temple that had taken place some time previously in the city, and would take toll despite all puny efforts toward protection.'[116] The British press in Shanghai reported that the population of Wuhan was 'strongly under the conviction that the floods have been caused by the Dragon God' and so had become helplessly apathetic.[117] The tone of these criticisms bore superficial similarities to the denunciations found in the Chinese press. Yet there was a substantive difference between introspective analysis and external critique. British journalists made no effort to scrutinise the religious response of members of their own culture during the flood. Nobody mocked missionaries for engaging in Christian ethnometeorology.[118] One medical missionary remarked that it was miraculous that neither he nor any of his fellow relief workers had fallen sick in spite of constant contact with infected refugees, attributing their survival to 'God's protection', and rather overlooking the role played by inoculation.[119] When heavy snow fell in the winter Edith Wills feared for the lives of homeless refugees in her charge, but was relieved when her God 'sent the warm spring sun' demonstrating that these unfortunate people were 'very near His heart'.[120] Willis was not alone in attributing the weather to God. A notoriously racist journalist named William Bruce Lockhart suggested that the flooding of Wuhan had been 'the answer of the Infinite to the corruption and violence of the people of that region during the past years'.[121] Employing an Old Testament variant of moral meteorology, Lockhart argued that the flood was divine retribution for the insubordination the population of Wuhan had displayed towards the British community.

Few expressed themselves using quite so strong a religious idiom, yet many Britons seemed to agree that the flood was in some way linked to their humiliating loss of status that had occurred following the events of 1927. One commentator noted that after the Chinese had taken over the British Concession, they had adopted a '*laissez faire* attitude' to flood defence. Worse still, corrupt politicians had embezzled the taxes paid by honest British residents for the upkeep of the city dykes.[122] The clamour

---

[116] Clubb, 'Floods of China'.   [117] *North China Herald*, 15 September 1931.
[118] See for example 'Letter from Miss Stephenson', SOAS Archives 10/7/15.
[119] *The Chinese Recorder*, November 1931.
[120] She also wrote that 'God has been very good and the weather has been marvellous.' Edith S. Wills, 'Hanyang 1931', SOAS Archives 10/7/15. 'Letter from Miss Stephenson', SOAS Archives 10/7/15.
[121] *North China Herald*, 25 August 1931.   [122] *North China Herald*, 18 August 1931.

of protests eventually reached such a fever pitch that Frederick Maze, the Inspector General of Chinese Maritime Customs Service, travelled to Wuhan to investigate the situation personally. He dismissed the accusations as mischievous propaganda, noting that the flood defences at the back of the former concession had not collapsed until weeks after the river had already inundated the area.[123] Proving that the British loss of sovereignty had played no role in the flooding of Wuhan did nothing to diminish the volley of criticisms launched by foreigners. Secular rumours often proved just as invulnerable to evidence as their religious equivalents. People tended to see their own parochial concerns reflected in the floodwater. Bruce Lockhart believed that his countrymen were innocent victims of petulant nationalist aggression; Xie Qianmao believed that were it not for the character flaws of fatalism and superstition, the Chinese people would surely be able to resist disasters. It would seem that even secularists had their own forms of ethnometeorology.

Dragons at the Breach

'There are real dragons living in China to-day', L. Newton Hayes wrote in 1926, 'They possess marvellous powers and they occasionally permit themselves to be seen by mortal eyes. Such is the belief of at least seven out of every ten Chinese.'[124] The persistence of such beliefs amused foreign observers as much as it infuriated local reformers. Yet it was hardly surprising. Dragons had been a consistent feature of the ethnozoological system for millennia, their charismatic appeal and symbolic flexibility allowing them to survive the exigencies of political and environmental change. This tenacity was due in part to the consistent challenges posed by living in a chronically hazard-prone region. For as long as floods and droughts continued to plague communities, they would need to negotiate with the dragons that controlled the rain. Chinese ethnometeorology functioned as a key component of what Greg Bankoff has described as a 'culture of disasters'.[125] Deities and rituals allowed people 'to come to terms with the chronic threat of hazard and to mitigate the worst effects of disaster.'[126] This helps to explain why the nature of

---

[123] Maze, *Documents Illustrative*, p. 555. This assessment was overly generous, as the provincial government itself had censured several officials for neglecting the dykes. See *Hankow Herald*, 19 August 1931. It should be noted that Maze had a very close working relationship with the Nationalist regime. See Van de Ven, *Breaking with the Past*.

[124] Hayes, *Chinese Dragon*, p. 3.

[125] Bankoff, *Cultures of Disaster: Society and Natural Hazard*.

[126] Bankoff, 'Cultures of Disaster, Cultures of Coping', p. 266.

dragons changed over time; as configurations of risk evolved, so too did the deities implored for protection. The history of dragons can be read as a history of the disaster regime.

Those who railed against popular religion were loath to admit that it had any functional utility. Instead they saw it as a malign force, which encouraged fatalism and apathy. This view was predicated on a fundamental misunderstanding of the nature of popular religion, which assumed that those who resorted to rituals took no practical measures to protect themselves. Yet the people of Hubei had always built temples and dykes together, using rituals and engineering in concert. Religion had many positive functions. It fostered the communal bonds that helped people to build hydraulic networks, and inspired the philanthropy that was required to support refugees when these networks collapsed. Monks and priests were in the front line of the disaster relief effort in 1931, distributing food and turning their temples into refugee camps. They could be accused neither of apathy nor inaction.

This is not to suggest that religion was entirely benign, or that secularists were simply intolerant. Though they often harmed marginal and impoverished people, not all victims of secular campaigns were blind fortune-tellers and itinerant priests. Some reformers sought to expose unscrupulous political leaders who exploited the religious sentiments to evade responsibility for social problems.[127] These included people like the Hubei magistrate who left his people to starve in 1925 while he prayed for rain in a local temple, or the warlord Zhang Zongchang 张宗昌 who fired artillery shells into the sky during a drought[128] Criticising such people was not simply an act of elitist intolerance. It was courageous, given that outspoken journalists in 1930s China were often known to pay with their lives. The governors who became involved in the religious response to the flood were not beleaguered victims of intolerant modernity. They imposed their will and policed their streets with extreme brutality, as we shall see later in this book. This repressive context may help to explain why Xie Qianmao made only vague allusions to senior figures involved in religious rituals, noting that members of the 'self-proclaimed intellectual class' 自命为知识阶级 (ziming wei zhishi jieji)

---

[127] On the role religion played in supporting blind fortune-tellers see Nedostup, *Superstitious Regimes*, pp. 191–3; one questionable and arguably exploitative practice was the sale of spirit water during cholera epidemics. See Rogaski, *Hygienic Modernity*, pp. 98–9.

[128] Rowe, *Crimson Rain*, pp. 239–40. De Bary, *Sources of Chinese Tradition*, pp. 316–29; Ebrey, *Chinese Civilization*, pp. 373–7.

had worshipped the Dragon King alongside the masses.[129] It is impossible to ascertain to whom this oblique description referred, but powerful members of the local regime such as Xia Douyin would certainly seem likely candidates.

By early August 1931, the floodwater that had been besieging Hankou finally broke through the last lines of defence and poured into the streets. At this stage, the Dragon King cult seems to have disbanded, or, at least, it is then that it disappears from the documentary record. Historians have attributed this final collapse of Wuhan's flood defences to several different factors. One local legend has it that senior figures in the administration, including the provincial governor He Chengjun 何成濬, failed to act promptly as they did not want to disturb their game of mah-jong.[130] The historian Fang Qiumei 方秋梅 has offered a somewhat more prosaic explanation. She traces the origin of the flood to several years of neglect by the municipal administrators, claiming that they failed to maintain dykes because they had funnelled all their money into building roads.[131] Ye Zhiguo claimed that the demolition of the city walls around Wuchang and the northward expansion of Hankou both vastly exacerbated the consequences of the flood.[132] The suggestion that road building and urban renewal schemes might have exacerbated the inundation of Wuhan further complicates the religious debates that raged in the city. The broad portfolio of urban reforms which had included the destruction of the Dragon King Temple, it would seem, really might have had an influence on the flooding of the city.

Dragons may have played an even more direct role in the genesis of disaster. The flooding of Wuhan unfolded in stages, as we shall see in the next chapter. By late July the only thing standing between Hankou and destruction was the railway embankment in the north of the city. On 1 August the work team responsible for the defence of the embankment decided to down tools. In the next few hours a small hole developed which eventually became a full-scale breach. The next morning water rushed into the city streets. Why the workers chose to stop repairing the embankment at this critical moment remains a mystery. Chinese journalists in Shanghai blamed a government engineer for abandoning his post.[133] The British press suggested that a coolie gang had called a

---

[129] Xie, *Yi jiu san yi nian*, p. 6.   [130] Tu and Yang, 'Wuhan Longwang Miao', p. 3.
[131] Fang, 'Difang bizhi'.   [132] Ye, 'Big Is Modern', p. 137.
[133] *Shenghuo* 1931. 6, Issue 37, 1931. This account came from a letter written to the editor Zou Taofen 邹韬奋. Although it described the specific conditions in Wuhan, the picture

spontaneous strike to demand higher wages.[134] Xie Qianmao offered a quite different explanation. He reported that eyewitnesses claimed that there had not been a strike, but that the stoppage was part of a nefarious plot by the embankment supervisor to embezzle the wages of his workers. So that he might effect an escape with the cash, he decided to frighten the labourers into leaving their posts by claiming that dragons were about the attack.[135] When the terrified workers returned they found that the embankment had suffered irreparable damage. After all was said and done, it would seem that dragons really were responsible for the flooding of Wuhan.

of official incompetence and inaction bore an uncanny resemblance to the campaign of criticism that *Shenghuo* was propagating at the time to lambast the supposed capitulation of the national government in the face of Japanese aggression. See Yeh, *Shanghai Splendor*, pp. 123–5.

[134] *North China Herald*, 11 August 1931.   [135] Xie, *Yi jiu san yi nian*, p. 148.

4

A SENSE OF DISASTER

> Words can hardly depict the feelings of oppression and
> poignant agony which filled me when I witnessed with my own
> eyes the scenes of death and desolation, of the excruciating
> sufferings of the injured and famished, and of those living torn
> asunder from their friends and relatives.
>
> Chiang Kai-shek[1]

Several weeks after the collapse of the railway embankment, 100-ton
junks were able sail through the streets of Wuhan. The local population
could do little but watch as these large boats negotiated a path between
the inundated electric pylons and lamp posts that were jutting out from
the water. In late August, a sampan drifted into a petroleum and oil repository owned by Texaco. The cooking stove burst into flames, sending
burning kerosene pouring along the top of the water into the repository.
In the ensuing inferno oil drums were thrown 60 metres into the air,
where they exploded before falling back down into the water. The fire
sent noxious plumes of black smoke spewing out into the atmosphere.
Burning petroleum and oil spewed out of the repository, confronting
those in the surrounding area with an apocalyptic vision of water on
fire. The heat was so intense that the fire service was unable to get any-
where near the blaze, and could do little more than wait until the inferno
burned itself out a few days later.[2] As darkness descended upon a city
starved of electricity, the fire provided a rare source of illumination. It
shed its flickering light on a world subverted by water, in which families

---

[1] From Chiang Kai-shek's manifesto to the flood-stricken population, reprinted in *Hankow
Herald*, 6 September 1931.
[2] This event was widely reported in the media at the time. See *Zhongyang Ribao*, 13 September 1931; 'Changjiang yidai zhi shuizai canzhuang', *Dongfang Huabao*, 28 (1931); *North
China Herald*, 1 September 1931; *Hankow Herald*, 4 September 1931. For a more in-depth
discussion see Worcester, *Junks and Sampans*, p. 382.

were living in trees, dogs and cats were starving on rooftops and the dead and living floated side by side.

A raging fire was hardly the most predictable outcome of a torrential flood. Yet the counterintuitive and bizarre had become common currency on the inundated streets of Wuhan. The experience of living through a catastrophe of this magnitude rarely makes sense. Disasters unfold as a succession of horrifying sights, strange sounds, painful sensations and repellent odours. They elicit a complex range of emotions that are impossible to fully convey and often highly traumatic to recall. In the epigraph that opens this chapter, Chiang Kai-shek remarks upon his inability to articulate the suffering he witnessed during the flood. If this was merely a rhetorical flourish, then it was one often repeated in 1931. The journalist Guo Jingrong 郭镜蓉 described a terror so vivid that it could never be committed to the page.[3] Bishop Galvin observed that, 'No pen can give an adequate picture of this frightful disaster.'[4] Faced with the task of explaining the inexplicable, observers often fell back upon describing their immediate sensations, offering disjointed accounts littered with vivid images and emotional vignettes. Later, when the flood came to be translated from lived experience to academic prose, these immediate sensations and feelings were largely expunged. They were replaced by neat equations of physical causes and statistical consequences. The flood began to make sense.

This chapter seeks to rescue some of the adjectives that were purged from the history of the flood, giving readers an impression of the immediate sensory and emotional impact of the disaster. Recreating the internal world of those living in bygone eras is an impossible task. Lucien Febvre was one of the first to argue that neither sensory perception nor emotional experiences are transhistorical or transcultural.[5] The feelings and sensations elicited during the flood can never be translated to contemporary readers, who live their lives in a vastly different sensory epoch. Yet witness descriptions bring us as close as we can get to the immediate experience of disaster. There are methodological as well as philosophical problems in attempting to re-create the feelings of past

---

[3] Guo Jingrong, 'Wuhan zaihou pian pian lu', *Guowen Zhoukan* 8, no. 36 (1931).

[4] Barrett, *Red Lacquered Gate*, p. 274.

[5] On the evolution of sensory history see Smith, *Sensing the Past*. For exemplary sensory histories see Corbin, *Foul and the Fragrant;* Smith, *Sensory History;* Classen, Howes and Synnott, *Aroma*. On the history of the emotions see Matt and Stearns, *Doing Emotions History*. Sensory approaches also form an important component of the affective turn in anthropology; see Massumi, *Parables of the Virtual;* Seigworth and Gregg, *Affect Theory Reader*.

peoples. Historians generally rely on a limited palette of visual traces, bequeathed by a narrow range of observers. It is impossible to know to what extent the experiences recorded in written sources were representative of the millions of disaster-stricken people who left no records. The cosmopolitan nature of Wuhan offers some assistance in this regard, as different witness accounts can be compared to highlight shared and contrasting experiences. Yet the very act of recording was a luxury not afforded to the majority. Close attention must be paid, therefore, both to what is recorded and what is omitted from the documentary record.

Detailing the sensory dimensions of disaster is not merely a novel descriptive device. It offers a valuable insight into the way that communities respond to catastrophes. Human behaviour is a critical variable within the disaster regime. Only when we attempt to appreciate how people felt during the flood can we begin to explain why they acted as they did. Historians of disasters tend to focus upon a narrow range of behaviours. Typically, they examine survival-orientated activities and coping strategies employed by members of affected communities. Recognising such behaviour is vitally important, as it is only through highlighting autonomous agency that we can debunk pervasive stereotypes that characterise disaster-stricken communities as helpless victims. Yet fixating on survival privileges certain forms of agency, and leads historians to fail to account for the full range of reactions that people display when faced with disaster. By asking how the flood made people feel, both physically and emotionally, this chapter builds a more comprehensive picture of the agency exhibited by people in Wuhan. It highlights activities that may not have enhanced immediate chances of survival, but offered other ways to overcome the experience of disaster.

The Lake

The experience of the flood began long before water crashed through dykes. It started with residents of Wuhan watching dark clouds gather in the sky, listening to the sounds of storms sweeping down the river, feeling strong winds buffeting their bodies and struggling to remain dry as incessant rain drenched their homes. The early summer in Hubei is damp and uncomfortable. Evaporating water creates extremely high levels of humidity, giving the impression that rivers and lakes have risen from their beds to envelope the landscape.[6] Isabella Bird described the

[6] The dankness that pervades the atmosphere during this period has led some to suggest that the 'plum rains' 梅雨 (meiyu), named as their arrival coincides with ripening of this

local climate as 'not an agreeable one. The summers, lasting from May till the middle of September, are hot and damp... The atmosphere is thick and stagnant, and there are swarms of mosquitoes.'[7] In 1931, the oppressive humidity of the early summer was accompanied by continuous rainfall and a succession of spectacular storms.[8] As rivers and lakes began to rise, many residents of Wuhan were gripped by a palpable sense of fear. One refugee described being so distraught that he was unable to eat for several days.[9]

The urban poor had the greatest to fear. Many had little more than knitted reed walls and thatched roofs to protect them from the rain and wind. Hut dwellers enjoyed few of the amenities of the modern city. Most were employed in low-income professions. Some worked as rag pickers, gleaning from the refuse dumps on the outskirts of the city; others pulled rickshaws or worked as coolies, carrying produce between warehouses and wharfs.[10] The urban poor were the first to experience the discomforts of the flood. When the wind began to howl, the loose frames that held these huts together groaned ominously, and the loose organic material that formed their walls began to come away.[11] Next floodwater began to rise around their feet. Long before dykes collapsed, gathering rainwater and rising rivers left whole neighbourhoods waterlogged and uninhabitable. The ditches that ran through the city began to overflow, filling low-standing areas with a foul brew of floodwater and sewage.[12] Inured to a life of chronic instability, hut dwellers knew how to evacuate with relative ease. They disassembled their simple homes and carried them to higher ground. Here they vied for space with a gathering population of rural refugees, who had been displaced over the previous months by a deadly combination of water and warfare.

On 22 July, a section of the outer dyke network to the north of Hankou collapsed.[13] The area that had been reclaimed over the course of the early twentieth century was swallowed back into the wetlands. Water swept over the communities of market gardeners who lived on the northern

fruit in the late spring might be described more accurately using a close homophone as the 'mould rains' 霉雨 (meiyu). See Knapp, *China's Vernacular Architecture*, p. 33.

[7] Bird, *Yangtze Valley*, p. 62.

[8] On the rain preceding the flood see *Shenghuo*, 6, Issue 37, 1931.

[9] Xie, *Yi jiu san yi nian*, pp. 148–9.   [10] On rag-picking see Cornaby, 'Morning Walks'.

[11] Edith S. Wills 'Hanyang 1931', SOAS Archives 10/7/15; Clubb, *Communism in China*.

[12] Chen, *Wuhan Wenshi Ziliao*.

[13] This occurred at a place called Red Pool 丹水池 (Dan Shuichi). *Shenghuo*, 6, Issue 37, 1931.

fringe of Wuhan. It was at this stage that Sun Yat-sen Park was destroyed, alongside the surrounding residential neighbourhoods.[14] Of the 4,000 to 5,000 homes in this area, a mere 80 were left standing.[15] Backwater flooding caused water to stream into the exclusive recreational facilities of the foreign residents of the city. The race club, golf links, tennis court and swimming pool located in northern Wuhan formed an enclave of wealth, juxtaposed in stark relief against the thick neighbourhoods of huts in the immediate vicinity.[16] Now a giant flood lake had swallowed both the grand houses and humble dwellings alike.

Those whose homes had survived had much to fear from the stormy weather. In 1849 Ye Diaoyuan described how flood-threatened residents of northern Wuhan were terrified by the sound of the howling north wind.[17] The gales that blew over the vast flood lake in 1931 caused large waves to sweep across the water. These rollers easily destroyed buildings that had been structurally compromised by inundation. For H. Owen Chapman the noise of waves pounding against walls 'wasn't pleasant music to sleep to.' The nurses in his hospital 'spent the night with white faces glued to the windows listening to the howling of the storm, trembling at the dull thuds of floating wreckage banging against their walls.'[18] This sense of chronic insecurity would continue to pervade the atmosphere in Wuhan for months.

The full force of water had yet to be unleashed upon Wuhan-proper. The embankment for the railway that linked the city to Beiping 北平 had formed an ersatz dyke protecting the city centre.[19] Belatedly realising the extent of the threat, the municipal authorities sent hundreds of workers to bolster this final line of defence. They laboured against the water for days, blocking the gates in the embankment with sandbags and rocks.[20] On the night of 1 August, under the mysterious circumstances described in Chapter 3, a small hole developed between the sandbags blocking one of these gates.[21] This rapidly developed into a full-scale breach.

---

[14] *Wuhan Ribao*, 13 January 1932; Liu, 'Hankou Zhongshan gongyuan'.

[15] Xie, *Yi jiu san yi nian*, p. 56.

[16] See Mae Fitkin, *Great River*, pp. 59–60. For a fictionalised representation of life in the clubs of Hankou in the 1930s see Archer, *Hankow Return*.

[17] Ye, *Hankou zhuzhici*, p. 177.

[18] H. Owen Chapman, 'Fighting Floods and Famine in China', SOAS Archives 10/7/15.

[19] Beiping was the name given to Beijing during the Nanjing Decade.

[20] Xie, *Yi jiu san yi nian*, pp. 39–40.

[21] The Single Passage Gate 单洞门 (Dandong Men) in northern Hankou. See *Shenghuo* (1931). 6, Issue 37; 'Wuhan yi cheng canghai', *Guowen Zhoukan*, 8 (1931).

The first sensory experience many people had of the flood was not visual but auditory. Just as church bells signalled imminent disaster in Europe, in China people beat gongs to warn of oncoming fires or floods.[22] Such auditory warnings came too late for many of those living beneath the railway embankment in Wuhan. The flood lake poured through the embankment into the city like a 'galloping horse' 奔马 (ben ma).[23] Whole communities of hut dwellers were washed away in an instant. Occurring in the dead of night, this flash flood killed many people in their sleep. Those who survived this initial bombardment now began a desperate struggle to find a patch of dry land. A Dong 阿栋 described how the immense current swept three children from the hands of their father, who was desperately trying to take them to safety.[24] Wealthy people fleeing on horses or in cars knocked down elderly pedestrians. Where the water was too deep, people clung to lampposts crying for assistance.[25] The flooding of Wuchang was not quite as dramatic, but it occasioned a similar mass exodus. When the dykes on the outskirts of the city collapsed, 100,000 people gathered their possessions and rushed to the city centre.[26]

Those whose houses survived now began vertically evacuating into their upper floors, salvaging what they could from the rising water.[27] Others gathered what they could and fled to high ground. What people chose to save during this initial stage of the disaster revealed much about the value they attributed to the material world.[28] Many of the objects had practical uses, some were economically important, while others were rescued for sentimental reasons. Families assembled the basic supplies of furniture, straw matting and cooking utensils that would help them to survive displacement. Others took domestic animals.[29] Buoyancy became a highly desirable property. People detached doors from frames and gathered possessions in the wooden washing tubs. Not all salvaged objects had practical value. Some people saved religious effigies, perhaps with the intention of conferring merit during a period of catastrophe.[30] Others carried family treasures, such as Confucian tracts and other

---

[22] See for example Cornaby, 'Morning Walks'. On Europe see Corbin, *Village Bells*.
[23] 'Wuhan yi cheng canghai', *Guowen Zhoukan*, 8 (1931).
[24] *Shenghuo*, 6, Issue 37, 1931.   [25] Xie, *Yi jiu san yi nian*, p. 40.
[26] *Hankow Herald*, 2 September 1931.
[27] See for example 'Letter from Miss Stephenson', SOAS Archives 10/7/15.
[28] I am grateful to Adam Yuet Chau for directing my attention to this line of inquiry.
[29] A list of some of the items taken by refugees is provided in Clubb, 'Floods of China'.
[30] Chen, 'Wuchang zaiqu shidi shichaji', *Yaxi Yabao*, HSSDX.

books.[31] These objects had little immediate utility yet a high social and
emotional value. Together the salvaged objects formed the vital prereq-
uisites for rebuilding homes as economic, social and emotional units.

Sound and Vision

As the cacophony of rushing water and collapsing buildings subsided,
a grim soundscape of misery and pain was revealed. Witness accounts
are filled with highly evocative descriptions of the auditory environment.
Sound plays an important role in the way people understand and remember disasters. One can close one's eyes to visual destruction, yet noises
are harder to escape. A year after a colliery spoil tip collapsed onto
the Welsh village of Aberfan in 1966, members of the local community
still recalled with dread the swishing and rumbling of coal and slurry
seeping downhill. This was replaced by a terrible nothingness, with the
voices of the children in the village school having been permanently
silenced.[32] Kai Erikson, a pioneer of the sociopsychological approach to
disasters, described how survivors of a catastrophic flash flood that swept
through the town of Buffalo Creek in 1972 continued to be haunted
by sounds. Loud noises caused community members to relive their
traumatic experiences, taking them straight back into the heart of the
storm.[33]

Sound played a similarly important role in the experience of the 1931
flood. One of the most pervasive descriptions is of cries of pain or grief.
A Dong described the constant sound of wailing that could be heard following the collapse of the railway embankment.[34] For Bishop Galvin, the
sound of babies crying in the dead of night was one of the most dreadful
experiences he suffered during flood.[35] Another observer remarked on
how the 'moans and groans of the aged and pitiful cries of children added
the final touch to the bedlam which prevailed.'[36] When the American
consulate worker Edmund Clubb witnessed a dyke collapse, he remarked
that the deathly silence that followed was even more ominous than the
shrieking beforehand.[37] As the visual landscape was transformed sound
became a vital tool to negotiate the inundated city. Sometimes the ears
were alerted to horrors the eyes could not see. Chen Hesong discovered

[31] Clubb, 'Floods of China'. [32] Lee, *I Can't Stay Long*, p. 87.
[33] Erikson, *In the Wake*, pp. 93–111. [34] A Dong, 'Hankou shuizai zhenxiang'.
[35] Quoted in Barrett, *Red Lacquered Gate*, p. 274. [36] *Hankow Herald*, 30 August 1931.
[37] Clubb, 'Floods of China', p. 203.

100 women trapped in the upper stories of a church after hearing their cries and moans while passing in a boat.[38] The volume and variety of auditory accounts suggests that the sound of the flood had a profound effect on flood survivors, lasting long after water had receded. Even five decades later, Hu Xuehan 胡学汉 could still recall the cries of terrified and grief-stricken refugees.[39]

Those who survived the initial flood wave were confronted not only by the terrible sounds of suffering but also the gruesome spectacle of death. In less populated areas river currents washed away corpses. In the city centre human bodies lingered, floating amidst the carcasses of domestic livestock and the debris of smashed furniture and collapsed buildings.[40] The sight of death would not have been particularly unusual for most citizens of Wuhan. Although a proper burial was considered vital to Confucian ritual norms, it was a luxury often denied to the poor. In the 1910s corpses were dumped indiscriminately on waste ground to the north of the city, some in coffins and others exposed to the elements.[41] The vicious conflicts that raged in Hubei during the 1920s often left corpses scattered in the streets.[42] The warlords who governed Wuhan used public executions as warnings to their political opponents.[43] Such experiences had no doubt inured the local population to the sight of death. Nevertheless, the sheer scale of the mortality crisis during the flood seems to have left a lasting impression. Witness accounts returned time and again to the grisly spectacle of corpses floating in the water. When the rain stopped and intense humidity took hold, the visual signature of disaster became even more horrifying. Descriptions of putrefying and swelling corpses bursting through their clothes were ubiquitous.[44]

As if these grim visions of disaster were not traumatic enough, the flood also deprived the population of both practical and cultural methods for coping with death. The absence of dry ground made it impossible to bury human remains, while a lack of fuel prevented cremation. When the population had faced this problem in the nineteenth century, the relatively wealthy had paid for the remains of family members to be

---

[38] Chen, 'Wuchang zaiqu shidi shichaji', *Yaxi Yabao*, HSSDX.
[39] Hu, *Wuhan Wenshi Ziliao*, p. 145.   [40] Xie, *Yi jiu san yi nian*, p. 41.
[41] Shu, 'Some Attempts at Sanitary Reforms'.
[42] For a description of violence in Wuchang see Mae Fitkin, *Great River*.
[43] For a discussion of the intense violence and public spectacle of death in Hubei in the 1920s and 1930s. See Rowe, *Crimson Rain*.
[44] Examples include Guan, 'Shuishang san dian zhong', *Yaxi Yabao*, HSSDX; Xie, *Yi jiu san yi nian*, p. 41; Chen, 'Wuchang zaiqu shidi shichaji', *Yaxi Yabao*, HSSDX.

transported to high ground for burial, while the poor had been forced
to abandon their kin to the floodwater.[45] Government sanitation teams
briefly contemplated this latter option in 1931, eventually dismissing the
mass sinking of corpses as a hygienic risk.[46] Benevolent halls did their
best to provide impoverished citizens with a means to bury their dead, as
did the Red Cross Society.[47] Even with this assistance, countless corpses
were left to pile up in mounds. In one refugee camp, the living and dead
were side by side, with those close to the end often being carried to the
outskirts, stripped of clothing and left to die.[48] Bodies that made it into
coffins did not necessarily remain interred. Fast-flowing currents caused
coffins to collide and burst open, depositing their contents into the
water.[49] The presence of death had soon become practically unavoidable.

While the municipal authorities and local charities were attempting
to cope with the biological remains of human beings, bereaved people
found themselves struggling to fulfil their moral and religious obligations
to deceased kin. A proper burial was an obligation that the living owed
to the dead.[50] Failing to fulfil this might result in the spirit of a loved
one becoming a hungry ghost 饿鬼 (egui), wandering the earth causing
misfortunes for the living. One of the most important occasions for hon-
ouring the dead was the annual Ghost Festival 鬼节 (Gui Jie), which fell
in the seventh lunar month.[51] On this occasion, a portal opened to the
world of the dead, allowing religious adherents to provide offerings of
food and spirit money to their relatives, and to give gifts to untended spirits to prevent them from becoming hungry ghosts.[52] In 1931, the Ghost
Festival fell in late August at the very height of the flood. With temples
flooded, monks scattered, and supplies of spirit money destroyed, most
religious adherents were unable to fulfil their spiritual duties. This led
one foreign observer to remark wryly that like so many others the 'spirits must go hungry and penniless'.[53] This was not quite accurate. Guan
Xuezhai witnessed religious adherents performing funerary rituals, having somehow managed to find dry spirit money and candles. He saw this

[45] Ye, *Hankou zhuzhici*, p. 85.   [46] RNFRC, p. 162.
[47] Hsu, 'Some Attempts at Sanitary Reform'; Xie, *Yi jiu san yi nian*, p. 64; 'Buxing de tianzai, Wenhua*, 24 (1931).
[48] *North China Herald*, 15 September 1931 and *North China Herald*, 13 October 1931.
[49] Xie, *Yi jiu san yi nian*, p. 78.
[50] For a discussion of traditional Chinese funerary norms see Rogaski, *Hygienic Modernity*, p. 70; Meyer-Fong, *What Remains*, p. 100.
[51] On Ghost Festival in Republican Hankou see Xu, *Hankou xiaozhi*, p. 80.
[52] Wolf, 'Gods, Ghosts, and Ancestors'.   [53] *North China Herald*, 15 September 1931.

as a lamentable waste of effort and resources, claiming that the desire to burn spirit money was indicative of an ancient clan mentality that still possessed the common people.[54] Yet this seemingly unproductive activity offered a form of psychological coping strategy – a means by which the local population attempted to ameliorate the traumatic effects of inundation. Rituals served to comfort those left with little choice but to live alongside the decomposing remains of friends and family.

Under the Qing, dealing with neglected spirits had come under the purview of local magistrates, who conducted mass rituals to placate the untended dead.[55] In 1931 the government not only failed to conduct such rituals but also attempted to prohibit the local community from employing its own weapons against malevolent spirits. With official anxiety about the threat of Communist insurgency being massively amplified by the refugee crisis, the municipal authorities issued a ban on the use firecrackers, claiming that their sound was too similar to gunfire. Together with drums and gongs, firecrackers were an essential feature of the cacophonous rituals conducted by religious practitioners.[56] They had a variety of symbolic and practical functions, often being used to ward off dangerous forces such as ghosts. Banning firecrackers represented one of the many ways in which government officials allowed their own anxieties to supersede the fears and desires of the local population. Sounds that to official ears signalled danger had the capacity to reassure a grief- and terror-stricken community.

The Aquatic City

The aquatic city that emerged in 1931 was not just horrifying but also bizarre. As the screams and moans that had shattered the atmosphere following the immediate outbreak of the flood subsided, the urban soundscape became eerily peaceful. In the initial stages of the flood, people had still able to wade through the streets. Cyclists fought their way through water and automobiles drove rapidly, sending off huge bow waves.[57] As the water became deeper automobiles and rickshaws could no longer negotiate the streets. This made the city centre noticeably quieter. One resident reported 'the stillness is almost uncanny, and the relief from hooting of horns is delightful.'[58] In this new calm it was

---

[54] Guan, 'Shuishang san dian zhong', *Yaxi Yabao*, HSSDX.
[55] See Meyer-Fong, *What Remains.*   [56] Chau, *Miraculous Response*, p. 133.
[57] Worcester, *Junks and Sampans*, p. 381.   [58] *North China Herald*, 11 August 1931.

possible to discern subtle sounds of the flood. Chen Hesong described hearing utensils clinking against one another.[59] Xie Chuheng described a stillness in which one could discern the subtle sound of oars clattering and people chatting in passing boats.[60] This was an eerie calm – merely the eye of the storm. The strange auditory environment formed the backdrop for a weird new visual landscape. The familiar sights of the city had been subverted. When Chen Bing went to sleep one evening the ditches in his neighbourhood were beginning to overflow; while he was 'still in his dreams' the water rose suddenly, and when he looked out of his window the familiar landmarks of his neighbourhood were submerged beneath metres of water, with only few elevated objects projecting out.[61]

The watery landscape confused the body in subtle, almost imperceptible ways. One resident of Shanghai, returning from a trip to the Wuhan, remarked on the curious feeling of 'taking the first walk on dry land, real, hard firm ground' for two weeks'.[62] People now lived in an unstable and precarious world. They sheltered on roofs, perched on mud walls and balanced on tree branches.[63] In the city centre, pedestrians bobbed and wobbled along on bamboo walkways, which strained under the weight of thousands of bodies.[64] This new landscape disrupted the expectations of the vestibular system – the portion of the inner ear that governs the human sense of motion. People may be less aware of this sixth sense than they are of its five more famous counterparts, yet they become acutely affected when their vestibular inputs are at odds with the physical expectations of their bodies. Sensations such as vertigo and motion sickness result from such disturbances.[65] Those living in the inundated city were subject to numerous such discombobulating effects. The pitch and roll of water subverted the expectations of bodies habituated to solid earth, forming a subtle yet constant sense of disorientation.

Those who wished to travel beyond the wooden walkways made use of the diverse range of vessels that now floated through the inundated streets. Even in the absence of a flood, a large section of the urban population lived on the water. The Yangzi and Han teemed with a wide variety of boats, creating a 'forest of masts' that spread for several miles around

[59] Chen, 'Wuchang zaiqu shidi shichaji', *Yaxi Yabao*, HSSDX.
[60] Xie, 'Hankou shuizai shidi shicha ji', *Xinminbao*, HSSDX.
[61] Chen *Wuhan Wenshi Ziliao*.   [62] *North China Herald*, 8 September 1931.
[63] *Time Magazine*, 8 August 1931; Clubb, 'Floods of China'., p. 205.
[64] Xie, *Yi jiu san yi nian*. p. 22. *Hankow Herald*, 9 September 1931.
[65] Goldberg, Wilson and Cullen, *Vestibular System*, p. 12.

Figure 4.1. Hankou city centre under water, August 1931. (*Illustrated London News*, 19 September, 1931)

the confluence.[66] As Wuhan became an aquatic city, the floating subculture that thrived in the harbours was able to colonise new areas. Like the fish that swam into the city, they rowed their ways through canal-like streets in search of new opportunities, as can be seen in Figure 4.1.

---

[66] 'Forest of masts' had long been a cliché used by foreigners to describe the Wuhan harbours. Examples include Huc, *A Journey*, p. 143; Weyl, 'Chicago of China'.

Before long, rich businesspeople were vying to see who could sport the most stylish sampan. Some even imported boats from other cities.[67]

Poorer people were forced to improvise, taking to the water on a bizarre armada of makeshift vessels. They made rafts from doors and bedsteads, canoes from coffins, boats from wooden tubs and boxes and even lifejackets from inflated goatskins.[68] Before long 'big boats were floating like frogs on the water, while small ant-like boats drifted all around them.'[69] This creative adaptation to the new aquatic environment was a major headache for the local traffic police, who struggled to maintain order on the new canals. With no rickshaws, cars or buses to direct, they busied themselves policing sampans, making sure they remained in the correct lanes. Initially balancing upon piles of wooden boxes, as the floodwater rose they were forced onto their pillar-boxes. Eventually they were reduced to directing the traffic from the branches of trees. When large junks began to sail through the city streets the traffic police could do little but sit back and watch.[70]

Water had created a palpable sense of subversion. Scenes of policemen nesting in trees and people rowing coffins provided great copy for journalists, who peppered tragic reports with light-hearted vignettes, highlighting the triumph of ingenuity over adversity. This was a particularly prevalent theme in foreign accounts, with observers often expressing admiration for the high spirits of the local population – 'the wonderful stamina of the Chinese masses, who refused to remain cast down'.[71] A propensity for high physical and emotional resilience was one of the many Orientalist stereotypes that foreigners developed to describe Chinese people. Stoicism was the discursive mirror image of fatalism, also a trait that supposedly permeated Eastern cultures. Famously, the missionary Arthur Henderson Smith remarked on the 'absence of nerves' in the Chinese body, which enabled people to withstand the severe privation of hunger and pain with relative ease.[72] Both physiognomy and culture, it would seem, had inured this inscrutable 'Oriental race' to suffering.

The discourse of resilience cannot simply be dismissed wholly as racial stereotyping. Studies from disasters in other regions suggest that those

---

[67] Worcester, *Junks and Sampans*, p. 381.

[68] *Time Magazine*, 8 August 1931; Guo Jingrong, 'Wuhan zaihou pian pian lu', *Guowen Zhoukan* 8, no. 36 (1931).

[69] Quoted in Li et al., *Zhongguo jindai shi da zaihuang*, p. 209.

[70] *North China Herald*, 25 August 1931; *North China Herald*, 1 September 1931.

[71] *North China Herald*, 1 September 1931.   [72] Smith, *Chinese Characteristics*, p. 96.

who experience regular hazards often do develop great psychological reserves, which allow them to mitigate physical and emotional traumas.[73] Greg Bankoff has argued that in the Philippines – an unusually hazard-prone region – people have developed various cultural traits that helped them to cope. These include a form of gallows humour that serves as 'an important means of dealing with angst, relieving stress, and overcoming anguish'.[74] Psychological coping strategies were deeply embedded in the culture of Hubei. Owen Chapman was impressed with the extent to which people in Wuhan were 'trained and inured to calamities, their ways of life and work so developed that they can be adapted to any circumstances'. Even in the depths of a catastrophic flood they had 'a cheerful and self-reliant will to survive that is indomitable'.[75] Emotional resilience and practical adaptability were not racial attributes. They had become embedded within the culture of a people who too often had to cope with disastrous situations.

It is important not over-rationalise psychological reactions to catastrophes. Kevin Rozario has described how extremely different the emotional responses that people display during disasters can be from what one might be expect. In some instances, people have even reported enjoying their experiences of catastrophes. Some survivors of the 1906 San Francisco earthquake described it as the most exciting experience of their lives.[76] Scholars have long been aware of this phenomenon. Robert Kutak described a form of 'crisis intoxication' that gripped the flood-stricken population of Louisville in 1937, with locals deriving a kind of 'masochistic pleasure' from the destruction of their city.[77] Similarly, the geographer Gilbert White observed that floods offered 'a refreshing sense of release from humdrum obligations and tasks'.[78] While there is little evidence to suggest that people found the 1931 to be an overwhelmingly enjoyable experience, some groups certainly found ways to derive pleasure from adversity. Chief among the revellers were the children of Wuhan, who turned the inundated streets into a watery playground. Much to the chagrin of the local police, who were doing their best to pull people out of the fetid water, youngsters swam and floated

---

[73] Aldrete, *Floods of the Tiber*, p. 157.

[74] Bankoff, 'Cultures of Disaster, Cultures of Coping', p. 270.

[75] H. Owen Chapman 'Fighting Floods and Famine in China', SOAS Archives 10/7/15.

[76] Rozario, *Culture of Calamity*.   [77] Kutak, 'Sociology of Crises', p. 67.

[78] White, 'Human Adjustment to Floods', pp. 92–3.

about in wooden buckets, seemingly oblivious to the dangers.[79] In the north of the city, where the water was less polluted, adults dived, swam and took trips out to explore the flood lake, devouring picnics of fish along the way.[80]

Humans were not the only creatures swimming through the floodwater. The aquatic city was soon colonised by an eclectic array of wetland creatures. Fish, frogs and waterfowl began subverting the distinction between domestic and wild spaces. Local cinemagoers found themselves sharing the auditorium with flocks of ducks. Servants had to chase fish out of the lobby of an exclusive club.[81] This invasion of wild creatures added to the sense of subversion. A city that had emerged from marshes and rivers centuries earlier seemed to be returning, albeit temporarily, to its wetland origins. Some species proved less able to adapt to the new aquatic conditions. Thousands of chickens, pigs, dogs and cats drowned during the initial flood waves. Those that survived were left stranded on rooftops or floating on debris.[82] Many would eventually succumb to hunger and disease, yet a few were able to benefit from the largesse of their human counterparts. Chen Hesong was amazed to see people rescuing stranded dogs at the height of the flood. When he asked them why they were taking the trouble to save animals when so many humans were suffering, they replied that it was in part a hygienic consideration; they did not want to share the floodwater with any more animal carcasses. Yet they also spoke of their emotional affinity with animals – 'dogs are also living creatures,' and were now 'in the same pitiful state as humans'.[83] The practice of rescuing animals was a cultural tradition in China that stretched back over a millennium. Freeing creatures from captivity or the butcher was a charitable act imbued with much religious and moral significance.[84] Whether those who rescued dogs during the flood did so to accrue merit is impossible to determine. What is clear is that they couched their actions in explicitly affective terms, bringing non-humans into the orbit of their social and emotional world.

---

[79] Guo, 'Wuhan zaihou pian pian lu', *Guowen Zhoukan* 8, no. 36 (1931); Xie, *Yi jiu san yi nian*, p. 75.

[80] H. Owen Chapman, 'Fighting Floods and Famine in China', SOAS Archives 10/7/15.

[81] Worcester, *Junkman Smiles.*   [82] Xie, *Yi jiu san yi nian*, p. 141.

[83] Chen, 'Wuchang zaiqu shidi shichaji', *Yaxi Yabao*, HSSDX.

[84] Smith, *Art of Doing Good*, pp. 15–42.

Dysfunctional Modernity

Unfortunately, this outpouring of interspecies compassion was not always reciprocated. With their regular food sources under water, starving dogs soon began to consume human corpses.[85] The aquatic city had become a frighteningly wild place. With animals reclaiming the streets and consuming human bodies, locals could be forgiven for believing that their city was regressing to a primitive state. In many respects, however, the disaster was a thoroughly modern affair. Wuhan was probably the most technologically advanced city in the Chinese interior. Over the past few decades, urban space had become interlinked by a complex infrastructure of roads, wires and pipes, which had transformed the physical and sensory environment. The luxuries of urban modernity may not have been available to all citizens, but for the relatively wealthy, the city offered a promise of comfort and an escape from unpredictable environmental forces. The flood shattered this illusion. It demonstrated just how easily nature could impose itself upon the bodies of the urban population. While many of the risks experienced in 1931 had been perennial features of flooding, others were products of the new industrial landscape. Water removed the benefits of new technology, leaving only hazardous remnants, such as industrial chemicals and corrupted machinery, in its wake. It created a form of dysfunctional modernity.

Inundation destroyed modern conveniences to which members of the urban community had only relatively recently become accustomed. The telegraph office and telephone exchange quickly became inoperable. Soon the only way to communicate was by using the makeshift post offices that had been formed on small boats throughout the city. The airport was closed and the railway inundated, meaning that transportation was limited to boat journeys.[86] One of the biggest blows was the loss of the electrical infrastructure. Most communities in China continued to rely on oil lamps and candles for illumination. Not so in Wuhan, where locals had been habituated to electrical lighting for decades. Originally limited to use in the foreign concessions, citywide electrification had been initiated in the 1890s as part of the urban modernisation scheme

---

[85] The *North China Herald* reported on 'One recent corpse of a girl about twelve, which apparently had been uncovered by the dogs'. See *North China Herald*, 15 September 1931. Elsewhere a relief worker talked about 'scaly pariah dogs' gathering around human beings. See *North China Daily News*, 24 October 1931.

[86] *North China Herald*, 11 August 1931.

initiated by Zhang Zhidong.[87] By the early 1930s this novel source of energy had become a key signifier of urban life. It flowed through the commercial district of Jianghan Road 江汉路, illuminating bright neon signs on swish shopping malls. It coursed into the thousands of small bulbs that lit the lively night markets, casting light on acrobats and opera singers and powering cinema screens showing the latest local and foreign films.[88] There were limits to electrification. Most people continued to live, as Lu Hanchao has put it, 'beyond the neon lights'.[89] Factory workers, teachers and other moderately well-off members of the urban population resided in narrow alleyway tenements, where they still relied primarily on kerosene – the revolutionary nineteenth century technology that had only recently been usurped by electricity as the most reliable source of illumination.

Floodwater plunged Wuhan into darkness. Electricity suppliers struggled valiantly to maintain their operations, but eventually power stations and cables were destroyed.[90] The authorities reacted to the blackout by requesting that local citizens prepare kerosene lamps and candles.[91] But stocks could not meet the demand. For many people, the night hours of the flood were lived in almost total darkness.

Jeffrey Jackson has described how when Paris was deprived of electrical and gas lighting by the catastrophic floods of 1910, citizens were so afraid of dangers lurking in the dark that the municipal authorities had had to post armed guards.[92] Residents of Wuhan were probably more habituated than Parisians to living with little illumination. This did not mean that they were comfortable in the dark. Throughout history and across cultures, darkness has often been a harbinger of fear. Craig Koslofsky has described how centuries before electrification, residents of early modern Europe believed that the night was filled with terrifying forces such as ghosts and witches.[93] As Piero Camporesi puts it, the 'night realm belonged to ruffians, low-lives, and those in a bad way; to the dubious presences that the darkness covered in its deep, faceless anonymity; to ghosts, spirits of the dead returned

[87] Pi, *Wuhan Tongshi: Minguo juan (shang)*; Wright, *Twentieth Century Impressions*, p. 708.
[88] Luo, *Minchu Hankou zhuzhici*, p. 9; Yorke, *China Changes*, p. 59.
[89] Lu, *Beyond the Neon Lights*.
[90] On power cuts see 'Wuhan yi cheng canghai', *Guowen Zhoukan*, 8 (1931); 'Zaizhen zhong zhi Zhi'an' HSSDX; Li et al., *Zhongguo jindai shi da zaihuang*, p. 210; *The Chinese Recorder*, September 1931.
[91] Xie, *Yi jiu san yi nian*, p. 28.   [92] Jackson, *Paris Under Water*.
[93] Koslofsky, *Evening's Empire*.

amongst the living.'[94] In China darkness held similarly terrifying associations.[95]

Electricity, the harbinger of enlightenment and exorcist of numinous forces, had failed Wuhan in its hour of need. In a final cruel twist, the technology of progress turned against its human masters. As pylons collapsed and wires flailed into the water, electric shocks killed as many as fifty people.[96] Electrocution was just one of several modern hazards generated by the inundation of a modern city. As an industrial city, Wuhan held large repositories of dangerous chemicals. In late August, several barrels of benzene floated off into the flood, posing a serious risk to those sailing through the city.[97] Chemical fires, such as the blaze at the Texaco repository described earlier, were another major risk. In one case a labourer discarded a cigarette into a large store of paint and matches, causing a spectacular blaze.[98] The threat of fires became so great that the municipal authorities established fixed quotas on the sale of kerosene, further limiting the illumination of the city.[99] The fire service tried its best to put out blazes. Deprived of their usual equipment, they painted a boat red and mounted a portable hand pump on its stern.[100] Fire was by no means a novel hazard in Wuhan. Narrow lanes of tall wooden buildings often gave rise to highly destructive conflagrations.[101] During the flood, highly flammable makeshift buildings were packed in ever-denser encampments. Cramped refugee huts built from straw and reeds made excellent kindling. A group of Chinese doctors living among the refugees had a narrow escape when their hut caught alight. Though they were not injured, they lost all their possessions, money and even their shoes.[102] For the authorities, fire held another fear, with many convinced that the Communists were intent on setting Wuhan ablaze.[103]

[94] Camporesi, *Bread of Dreams*, p. 95.

[95] On this theme see Dikötter, *Exotic Commodities*, pp.140–1.

[96] Xie, *Yi jiu san yi nian*, p. 105; see also *North China Herald*, 25 August 1931.

[97] *Hankow Herald*, 26 August 1931.   [98] Xie, *Yi jiu san yi nian*, p. 127.

[99] 'Zaizhen zhong zhi Zhi'an' HSSDX. Elsewhere during the flood, a fire destroyed twenty thousand piculs of relief grain. In Jiujiang a refugee camp burned to the ground, killing at least sixteen residents. See *North China Herald*, 12 January 1932.

[100] Worcester, *Junks and Sampans*, p. 381.

[101] Ye, *Hankou zhuzhici*; Rowe, *Hankow: Conflict and Community*, p. 159. Hankou had been set aflame during the Xinhai Revolution, and few buildings outside the foreign concessions had managed to survive. See MacKinnon, 'Wuhan's Search', p. 164.

[102] Edith S. Wills, 'Hanyang 1931', SOAS Archives 10/7/15.

[103] *North China Herald*, 11 August 1931.

Even without fires, Wuhan was interminably hot. Together with Chongqing and Nanjing, the city is known as one of the 'three great furnaces' 三大火炉 (san da huolu) of China. The foreign traveller Gretchen Mae Fitkin remarked that even 'the mosquitoes themselves die from heat' in the oppressive Wuhan summers.[104] By the 1930s, wealthier citizens possessed a range of technologies to help them ameliorate this intense humidity. They used electric fans and drank beverages chilled by ice from several local factories. Some even indulged in the exotic luxury of ice cream.[105] Most people continued to rely on vernacular technologies and techniques of heat alleviation. They used hand fans, kept in the shade during the hottest hours of the day and slept outside on reed mats.[106] The flood disrupted both high- and low-tech heat solutions. As electricity failed and factories were inundated, the rich had to cope without their fans and ice. The situation was much worse for the vast army of homeless people, who had little more than a few cloths stretched over their heads to protect them from the intense sun. By mid-August the temperature had soared to 35 degrees Celsius.[107] Even for those inured to such a climate would have struggled to cope with the heat, as their bodies were weakened by hunger and disease.

Wuhan may have been at the heart of a vast lake, yet it was very difficult to find sufficient potable water to slake the intense thirst prompted by the hot summer sun.[108] In recent decades piped water had become another key signifier of urban modernity. Wuhan had been the first in inland China to benefit from this vital material advance. Until the early twentieth century even rich citizens had had to rely on water from rivers, springs or wells, which was often a source of gastrointestinal infections.[109] The water supply system was fuelled by muscles, forming part of an urban somatic energy regime, in which hundreds of coolies formed human chains, passing buckets up and down the steep steps that led down to the rivers.[110] In 1907 a water tower was constructed in Hankou. This led to a dramatic reduction in the rate of infection for dysentery and

---

[104] Mae Fitkin, *Great River*, p. ii.   [105] Dikötter, *Exotic Commodities*, p. 221.
[106] These remained popular practices into the late twentieth century, but have been eclipsed in the last few decades by the inexorable rise of air conditioning. In the late nineteenth century, even some foreign residents also slept outside to avoid the heat. See Bird, *Yangtze Valley*, p. 62.
[107] Xie, *Yi jiu san yi nian*, p. 205.   [108] A, 'Hankou shuizai zhenxiang'.
[109] Pi, *Wuhan tongshi: Minguo juan-shang*, p. 324.
[110] Orchard, 'Man-Power in China', p. 568.

cholera.[111] Over the next few decades, access to clean water became a marker of socioeconomic distinction. Those living in modern houses enjoyed the benefits of piped water. The foreign club in the north of the city even invested in a special ultraviolet ray purification unit for its pool, and had its water tested microscopically by physicians.[112] The water in which foreigners bathed was probably cleaner than that which was drunk by the poorer residents of Wuhan, who continued to rely on rivers and wells, making water more palatable and hygienic by boiling, filtering and adding chemical clarifying agents.[113]

The piped water system in Wuhan ceased to function early on during the flood.[114] Potable water was now a scarce resource. Those who could access alum used it to purify water.[115] Most were unable to practice even such rudimentary methods. Local charities organised boats to distribute boiled water, yet they struggled to meet the demand.[116] Those stranded in oppressive heat were left with little choice but to drink foul floodwater.[117] Even before considering the dire health implications, this was a disgusting prospect. The term floodwater is something of a misnomer, as the liquid that flowed through Wuhan was actually a muddy concoction of earth, debris, rotting material, industrial chemicals and sewage. Eventually relief organisations began to treat floodwater with chloride of lime to make it safer to drink.[118] Unpleasant as the taste of this chemical may have been, it was no doubt more palatable than the polluted cocktail that people had been drinking before.

Chemicals may have masked the foul flavour of water but they could do little about its horrific stench. If there was any sensory aspect that unified all witnesses to the flood, irrespective of social or cultural background, it was their reaction to the repellent smell. This was caused by two universal sources of disgust: death and faeces. The foul and ominous odour emitted by piles of corpses was compounded by a total breakdown in the urban sanitation system. The problems began in the early stages of inundation when sewers could no longer discharge their contents into swollen rivers. As most people did not possess piped facilities, this problem was not as serious as the disruption of the night soil industry, which most people relied on to dispose of their household wooden buckets of

[111] Shu, 'Some Attempts at Sanitary Reform'.
[112] Mae Fitkin, *Great River*, p. 60.   [113] Jahn, 'Drinking Water'.
[114] 'Wuhan yi cheng canghai', *Guowen Zhoukan*, 8 (1931).
[115] Chen, *Wuhan Wenshi Ziliao*, p. 146.
[116] Chen, 'Wuchang zaiqu shidi shichaji' *Yaxi Yabao*, HSSDX.
[117] Barrett, *Red Lacquered Gate*, p. 205.   [118] RNFRC, p. 162.

effluent.[119] With waste gathering in ever-greater quantities, those who possessed sufficient resources organised sewage boats to carry it away to a safe distance.[120] Most people did not have this luxury. They simply emptied their buckets into the floodwater. The bowels of the city spewed out into the streets, bringing waves of infectious disease, which would eventually kill tens of thousands of refugees and pervade Wuhan with a truly horrific stench.

Attitudes towards odour are by no means universal. They have changed profoundly over time and between cultures.[121] Alain Corbin has argued that the advent of modernity in France ushered in a period of increased olfactory sensitivity. Emphasis gradually shifted from the masking of individual smells to the deodorisation of public space – perfume gave way to sanitation.[122] China followed its own path to olfactory modernity, yet there were many similarities with the European experience. In both areas malodour had traditionally been understood to be a pathogenic force. The miasmas that were once central to European diagnostic traditions had their equivalents in the various forms of pathogenic *qi* 气 found in Chinese medicine.[123] There was also a shared assumption that malodour indicated an absence of individual or collective civilisation.[124] By the twentieth century the creation of a deodorised body became a key prerequisite of the modern citizen. Meanwhile, the removal of oppressive smells from public spaces became a marker of what Ruth Rogaski has described as 'hygienic modernity'.[125] Wuhan was, once again, at the forefront of this olfactory revolution, being the first inland city to receive a piped sewage system in the early decades of the twentieth century.[126] As well as improving public health, this reduced the odour of human effluent considerably.

Floods had unleashed foul odours on urban spaces from time immemorial, yet the olfactory crisis that occurred in 1931 was the product of a specific form of dysfunctional modernity. The sewage system acted as a conduit pumping effluent out onto the streets at far greater volumes than ever before. The result was an unavoidable stink that united the whole city in disgust. Even more than the horrifying visual and

---

[119] Wu et al., *Cholera*, p. 170.
[120] H. Owen Chapman 'Fighting Floods and Famine in China', SOAS Archives 10/7/15.
[121] Classen, Howes and Synnott, *Aroma*.   [122] Corbin, *Foul and the Fragrant*.
[123] Rogaski, *Hygienic Modernity*, p. 114.   [124] Dikötter, *Sex Culture*, p. 160.
[125] Rogaski, *Hygienic Modernity*, p. 114.
[126] Pi, *Wuhan Tongshi: Minguo juan (shang)*, p. 324. Similar processes were occurring in Guangzhou. See Poon, 'Cholera, Public Health, and the Politics of Water'.

auditory atmosphere, the smell of disaster was utterly inescapable. As one foreign journalist noted, it was impossible to avoid 'offensive odours created by rotting food, floating bodies and disruption of all normal sewage facilities'.[127] Even when the stink abated, its visceral memory was slow to fade. Decades later, Hu Xuehan still recalled the horrific smell of people defecating freely throughout the city.[128] The stench invaded bodies, eliciting involuntary physical reactions. Xie Qianmao spoke of an 'oppressively stinking air' 臭气逼人 (chouqi biren). Chen Hesong described how the odour of corpses had been so bad that it made him want to vomit.[129] The extremity of the malodorous environment had cut through layers of socialisation and acculturation and found the common biological bodies of those living in Wuhan. Olfaction was functioning, as G. Neil Martin has put it, as a 'chemosensory custodian of survival'.[130] This most ancient of senses was now alerting humans to the very real dangers that had been unleashed by the dysfunctional infrastructure of this modern city.

A Tale of Two Floods

Given the universality of disgust elicited by the overwhelming stench of the flood, it might be tempting to conceive of olfaction as a kind of sensory leveller. The stink paid no heed to social, economic or cultural boundaries. It insulted the nostrils of impoverished refugees, foreign traders and local businessmen alike. Yet while everyone was exposed to malodour, not everyone was forced into intimate contact with its source. 'Abhorrence of smell', Corbin has argued, 'creates its own form of social power.'[131] During the flood one manifestation of this power was the right to decide who was responsible for malodour. Refugees and homeless people were often singled out in this regard, described defecating freely and pouring effluent into the water. Virtually nobody who described the smell of the flood admitted that their effluent had contributed. Power also had a physical manifestation. Some people could ensconce themselves in hygienic enclaves, mounting armchairs on the backs of sampans so that they might travel through the inundated streets in style. Meanwhile, rickshaw pullers and coolies waded waste deep amidst the corpses

---

[127] *North China Herald*, 25 August 1931; *North China Herald*, 1 September 1931.
[128] Hu, *Wuhan Wenshi Ziliao*, p. 145.
[129] Chen, 'Wuchang zaiqu shidi shichaji', *Yaxi Yabao*, HSSDX.
[130] Martin, *Neuropsychology of Smell and Taste*, p. 3.
[131] Corbin, *Foul and the Fragrant*, p. 5.

and effluent.[132] They returned home to cramped and unsanitary conditions, where it was virtually impossible to maintain any form of personal hygiene regime. This was just one of the many ways in which stark disparities of income were translated into vastly differing disaster experiences.

Homeless refugees had to compete for limited dry space with hundreds of thousands of other people. They soon found themselves living in the most abject conditions. One journalist described visiting a warehouse that was housing an estimated 5,000 refugees. Overcrowding made it 'almost impossible to walk about without treading on somebody's body or limbs.' Living in such cramped and unsanitary conditions had serious health implications. 'Every other person appeared to be suffering from some grave illness: filth lay everywhere.'[133] People who were wet for weeks developed the symptoms of trench foot and other conditions. Sometimes their limbs swelled so much that they looked like they were suffering from elephantiasis.[134] As if these conditions were not tough enough, those living in refugee enclaves often had no information about the progress of the flood, or whether assistance was on its way. A month after the initial flood wave had struck Wuhan, the authorities were alerted to an isolated island formed by a mountain near the city, on which as many as 16,000 people were sheltering. Dead and dying people were apparently strewn around indiscriminately throughout the camp and there was no sanitation of any kind.[135] Hunger exacerbated the discomfort. The experience of starvation is lingering and painful. Blood vessels and decomposing tissues leak fluid that collects under the skin, causing swelling in the abdomen, legs, feet and face. Starving bodies soon begin to suffer skeletisation, and become listless and lethargic.[136] Most people were spared the full effects of literal starvation in 1931 by the dubious mercy of disease.

The chronic vomiting and diarrhoea caused by gastrointestinal diseases made collective conditions worse, and soon marked infected people out as objects of fear and disgust. Cormac Ó Gráda has noted famines lead not only to a disintegration of public sanitation, but also to a decline

---

[132] *North China Herald*, 15 September 1931; Guo, 'Wuhan zaihou pian pian lu', *Guowen Zhoukan* 8, no. 36 (1931).

[133] *North China Herald*, 1 September 1931.

[134] *Hankow Herald*, 28 August 1931. Xie Qianmao also refers to some people suffering from *jiaobing* 脚病 – literally 'foot diseases' – possibly describing a trench foot-like complaint, or maybe demonstrating that some refugees had succumbed to the micronutrient deficiency beriberi for which the Chinese terminology is very similar 脚气病 (jiaoqibing). See Xie, *Yi jiu san yi nian*, p. 74.

[135] *North China Herald*, 15 September 1931.

[136] Tyner, *Genocide and the Geographical Imagination*, p. 82.

in personal hygiene, which is caused by physical exhaustion and the absence of washing facilities.[137] Ye Diaoyuan noted this problem in 1849, with flood-stricken people being unable to clean themselves for weeks on end.[138] In 1931 the sight of people struggling to survive, eating unsavoury food, with unwashed clothes, caked in the filth and debris of the flood and being forced to defecate wherever they could, would have done little to dispel prejudices held by both Chinese and foreign elites about the 'uncivilised' and 'backward' nature of the poor. One missionary described the experience of seeing 'a wretched mother, with empty shrunken breasts' as 'nauseating'.[139] Another spoke of discovering 'some poor, old and ugly witch-like creatures' living 'under some evil-smelling matting'.[140] The overt sentiment may have been compassion, yet the revulsion was barely concealed. As was so often the case, the symptoms of poverty were essentialised as inherent cultural characteristics. Unwashed bodies seemed to reflect an innate inability to attain modern hygiene standards. Many witnesses failed to recognise that it was the extreme conditions of the flood, or the poverty that had preceded it, which had reduced people to such desperate states. For those observing from afar, the bodies of the poor seemed mired in filth of their own creation.

The experience of the flood was vastly different for members of the foreign elite. Even in non-crisis periods, this population resided in a world largely removed from the ordinary population. Since the first concession had been established in the 1860s, foreigners considered their territory to be entirely separate from the so-called native city. They had attempted to exclude China by erecting walls and barbed wire fences and prohibiting entry to all but a select few locals. The American traveller William Edgar Geil justified this exclusion by noting that there were so many Chinese that 'if they took a notion to have a promenade, the walk and everything else would be appropriated, for if you give a Chinese an inch he will take a thousand miles.'[141] The racial apartheid broke down somewhat in the early twentieth century, as foreigners realised how much money could be made by renting properties to local residents and businesses, who were attracted by the favourable taxation regime within concessions. The spatial divisions declined further when the Germans lost their concession during the First World War, becoming the first

---

[137] Ó Gráda, *Famine*, p. 100.   [138] Ye, *Hankou zhuzhici*, p. 186.
[139] H. Owen Chapman 'Fighting Floods and Famine in China', SOAS Archives 10/7/15.
[140] *North China Daily News*, 24 October 1931.   [141] Geil, *Yankee on the Yangtze*, p. 46.

of three special administrative zones. The second was formed shortly after, as the Soviet Government surrendered the Russian Concession voluntarily. The third was created following the successful reacquisition of the British Concession by the Wuhan Government in 1927.

Despite this slow transition of territorial power, the foreign section of Wuhan remained a tightly regulated and exclusive zone. It provided foreign visitors with a retreat from the alien sensory experience of life in China. Gretchen Mae Fitkin spoke of how the concessions offered 'a kind of peace and rest that might come with a visit to a clean homeland, a relaxation from a habit of tensing the muscles against the sights and smells of China'.[142] The American journalist Walter Weyl contrasted the 'modern and cheerful' concessions with the 'dense and swarming native city'.[143] Not all foreign visitors were as enamoured. Gerald Yorke preferred 'the full-blooded enjoyment' of the Chinese portion of the city to the 'effete boredom' of the concessions where 'white women toy with their tiffin'.[144] Later in the 1930s, the foreign student Innes Jackson echoed this sentiment, describing the concessions as 'a second Shanghai though smaller, shoddier, and even more appallingly late-Victorian'.[145] Chinese residents of Wuhan, for their part, were variously bemused and infuriated by the concessions. The poet Luo Han 罗汉 remarked on the curious fact that residents of Wuhan were often prevented from crossing borders delineated by foreigners within their own city.[146] Nevertheless, he enjoyed the exoticism of the concessions, particularly that owned by the Japanese, with its picturesque song houses lit by red lanterns.[147]

The concessions offered locals a window onto a world of sensory experiences. Rogaski has described treaty ports as 'hypercolonies,' which were 'at once not a colony, yet still the site of multiple colonialisms'.[148] Nowhere was this more apparent than Hankou, with its contiguous series of five concessions – British, German, Russian, French and Japanese. It was possible to experience a dizzying array of cultures condensed within a few minutes – pedestrians could walk down Rue de Paris and then turn onto Huangpi Lu 黄陂路 before taking a right onto Lockerbie Road.[149] Within these streets, visitors could taste a wide range of international cuisine in several restaurants and hotels. If they had arrived in summer, they might choose to alleviate the stifling heat by downing a few iced drinks

---

[142] Mae Fitkin, *Great River*, pp. 58–9.   [143] Weyl, 'Chicago of China'.
[144] Yorke, *China Changes*, pp. 59–60.   [145] Jackson, *China Only Yesterday*, p. 211.
[146] Luo, *Minchu Hankou zhuzhici*, p. 2.   [147] Ibid., p. 3.
[148] Rogaski, *Hygienic Modernity*, p. 3.
[149] Yuan, *Hankou zujie zhi*. See maps in unnumbered section at the front.

at one of the city's clubs or by eating an ice cream.[150] As evening drew in, they could take in a cabaret, with Chinese and White Russian dancers entertaining visitors with energetic displays.

The concessions were the last area of Hankou to be inundated. They were protected by floodwalls at the rear and the elevated riverside bund at the front.[151] Even these formidable defences eventually proved inadequate. For about a week after the rest of the city was flooded, the Japanese Concession remained dry, as the authorities pumped water desperately back into the river. Foreign observers made much of this valiant defence, contrasting it with the supposed apathy of the Chinese authorities.[152] Yet by mid-August even the Japanese Concession was under water. The flood was not the only danger encroaching into foreign territory. Homeless refugees were soon squatting in godowns and other properties owned by the expatriate population. Five thousand people were granted refuge in the Japanese barracks.[153]

As water broke down the social and cultural boundaries of the city, members of the foreign community tried to continue their ordinary lives as best they could. The United States consulate continued to hoist its national flag every morning in accordance with State Department regulations, even though now they had to row out to their flagpole.[154] Others entertained themselves by riding their horses through the flooded streets or playing tennis on the roofs of godowns.[155] Before long, a regular ferry service had been established to transport foreigners from the city centre to the race club to the north.[156] The concessions may have been the centre of the commercial and political life, but this club was the beating heart of foreign social life. As Mae Fitkin had remarked, without the club 'the foreign women of the community would find no relief from the excessive heat of the summer; without it the men would grow fat and lazy and the city would resolve itself into gossiping and gossip creating circles.'[157] A staggering array of entertainments were available to the exclusive patrons of the club, including polo, horse racing, clay pigeon shooting, swimming, tennis, bowling, golf, cricket and baseball; there was also an orchestra which played concerts and accompanied dances.[158]

[150] Auden and Isherwood, *Journey to a War*.   [151] Maze, *Documents Illustrative*, p. 557.
[152] Clubb, 'The Floods of China'.   [153] *North China Herald*, 11 August 1931.
[154] *North China Herald*, 8 September 1931.   [155] *North China Herald*, 18 August 1931.
[156] Worcester, *Junks and Sampans*, p. 382.   [157] Mae Fitkin, *Great River*, p. 59.
[158] Ibid., p. 60. The refined luxury of the club was off limits not only to Chinese citizens of Wuhan, of course, working class foreigners who travelled to the city – as sailors or soldiers, for example – were equally unwelcome. Britain in China was, as Robert Bickers

Though the grounds of the club were inundated early on, its buildings continued to serve as the social and recreational centre of foreign life. There was, as one correspondent noted, 'nothing much doing at the Race Club, but people still go there for a change and gaze at an unbroken sheet of water instead of at the canals that are the streets.' The horror and disgust that was gripping much of Wuhan seems to have had relatively little impact on the sedate life of club members, who complained only of a shortage of ice and soda water, meaning that the 'friendly drink in the evening or at Saturday noon is now often taken neat.'[159] Just a short distance away, a burgeoning population of refugees was gathering on the racecourse grandstand. Here they vied for space with cattle that had been housed on the clubhouse veranda. The stables were also home to club racehorses. Of all the species caught in the flood, these equestrians were among the least well equipped to cope with inundation. Centuries earlier, Qing military commanders had found it extremely difficult to keep horses in the wetlands of Hubei, meaning they struggled to garrison cavalry divisions.[160] What horses lacked in terms of natural resilience, they made up for through their unrivalled social and economic relationships with human beings. When water poured into the club some horses were moved onto the roofs of riverside warehouses, others were even evacuated to Shanghai.[161] Like those who rescued dogs, foreign horse owners couched their actions in distinctly affective language, claiming that they were worried about the suffering of their beloved horses. The financial investment they had made in these precious animals no doubt also played a role.

Very few provisions were made for the human refugees who were sheltering just metres from these horses. They were only eventually evacuated when club members, concerned about the hygienic risk they posed, petitioned the local authorities to have them removed.[162] Those whiling away their time in the clubhouse and those sheltering in the grandstand were separated by little physical distance, yet their

---

has argued forcefully, divided almost as much by class as by race. See Bickers, *Empire Made Me*.

[159] *North China Herald*, 1 September 1931. The flood had prevented the Hankow Dispensary from producing aerated water, but it was still able to offer 'silent water' and a range of 'silent fruit drinks' with 'every drop' sterilised. *Hankow Herald*, 22 August 1931.

[160] Gao, 'Retreat of The Horses'.

[161] *North China Herald*, 11 August 1931; *North China Herald*, 25 August 1931.

[162] *North China Herald*, 1 September 1931.

experiences of disaster could hardly have been more different. It was as if they were living through two different floods. One occasioned mild inconvenience and boredom, while the other destroyed and ended lives. One left people drinking neat whisky and complaining about a lack of vegetables, while the other left people drinking dirty river water and scavenging for wild plants. The border between these two floods was not defined by culture or nationality. Wealthy Chinese residents of Wuhan, who hiked up their rent and gouged rice prices, also lived in a world far removed from that of most refugees.[163] We have focussed here on a certain section of the foreign community not because they were uniquely invulnerable, but because their invulnerability was relatively visible, delineated, as it was, by ethnicity as well as economics. There were many foreigners who experienced extreme discomfort, just as there were many locals who remained relatively unaffected.

The existential chasm between the two floods goes some way to explaining the dismissive attitude that many literate witnesses had regarding the behaviour of refugees. Piero Camporesi has suggested that the perpetually hungry poor in early modern Europe lived in a world that was incomprehensible to their wealthier counterparts. There, prolonged malnutrition and habitual consumption of narcotic substitute foods consigned them to a realm of terrifying visions and vivid sensations. Enlightened intellectuals condemned the beliefs of these people without appreciating that they lived in a vastly different experiential dimension.[164] For outside observers of the 1931 flood, the sensory and emotional realm occupied by impoverished refugees was similarly inaccessible. Those with vaccinated and nourished bodies passed judgement on the behaviour of people beset by hunger and disease. Those who prided themselves on having a rational and modern view were unable to appreciate the spectres that haunted people living in a liminal zone of extended possibilities. The ghosts and dragons that haunted the refugees and homeless were the product not only of their cultural context, but also of a suggestible psychological state engendered by extreme physical and mental trauma. This was a mode of being that was not available to casual observers. It had to be experienced to be believed.

---

[163] Rewi Alley would later claim that local politicians held champagne dinners while refugees starved, though his account is not borne out by contemporary evidence. See Airey, *Learner in China*, p. 100.

[164] Camporesi, *Bread of Dreams*.

Escaping the Body

As conditions in Wuhan became ever more desperate, some people responded by doing nothing. There were reports of refugees sitting 'apathetic and stunned, waiting for they know not what.'[165] As one Chinese journalist remarked, with no food or shelter, these people could 'only wait to die' 惟有待斃 (weiyou daibi).[166] We cannot say with any degree of certainty why people responded in this manner. Many contemporary observers were convinced that the answer lay in their inherent passivity and fatalism. There were several theories circulating at the time that suggested that such negative attributes were part of the cultural or perhaps even racial inheritance of the Chinese people. The environmental determinist Ellsworth Huntington suggested that passivity was both a cause and consequence of disasters in China. When catastrophe struck, he reasoned, the 'brainy' and 'skilful' men in the affected area, together with the 'brightest, prettiest girls', emigrated out of the disaster zone.[167] Those who remained in famished areas transmitted passivity to their children as a heritable trait. Over time, disaster-prone regions were left populated by physically inferior and mentally 'subnormal' people' who were 'little more than morons'.[168] Such ideas may have been extreme, but they were by no means considered unacceptable. They formed part of a wider discourse, explored in Chapter 5, which cast disaster-stricken communities in the role of hapless victims who needed to be cajoled and coerced into productive responses. Chinese scholars analysing disasters often cited the work of foreign experts such as Huntington, sharing his assumption that the apathy of the common people acted to exacerbate disasters.[169]

We cannot access the interior worlds of flood refugees, most of whom are now long deceased. Any explanation of their behaviour can only ever be speculative. It should be noted, however, that there is nothing inherently irrational about doing nothing. Indeed, as we saw in Chapter 3, those who sat and waited out the flood may have survived better than those who sought to improve their conditions by taking to the road. Many people may have been simply incapable of activity, owing to the debilitating effects of disease and hunger. Limiting physical movement can

---

[165] *North China Herald*, 25 August 1931.
[166] 'Wuhan yi cheng canghai', *Guowen Zhoukan*, 8 (1931).
[167] Huntington, *Character of Races*, p. 193.   [168] Ibid., p. 175.
[169] Examples include Chen, 'Zaihuang yu Zhongguo nongcun renkou wenti'; Deng, *Zhongguo jiuhuang shi*.

also be an efficient means of maximising the benefits of limited nutritional intake. Managing the body in this way has been recognised as a coping mechanism often employed by Chinese populations faced with famine.[170] It may seem absurd to talk about inactivity as a survival strategy, yet in some situations reserving energy by waiting patiently until conditions have improved can be an expression of agency. In Sudan in the 1980s, Alex de Waal noted that people were often prepared to cope with long periods without food through binding their stomachs to relieve the pain of hunger pangs, and then simply waiting until drought abated so that they could plant their seeds.[171] An inability to see strategy in passivity perfectly encapsulates why the everyday tactics employed by disaster survivors are so often overlooked. Those who were understood to be stoically awaiting death in 1931 may have been patiently waiting to survive.

The close examination of the phenomenological dimensions of the disaster provided in this chapter can also help to contextualise the activities of refugees – or in this case their inactivity. Given the overwhelming and disorientating experiences to which they had been subjected, it is certainly not unreasonable to suggest that people who sat stunned and unmoving were suffering from the effects of trauma. Today, disasters are recognised to cause major psychological and neurological damage. In addition to the organic brain disorders that result from physical injury and disease, catastrophes cause a range of trauma-related psychiatric conditions.[172] Little attention was paid to the psychological effects of flooding in the 1930s. Studies conducted in the aftermath of the 1998 Yangzi floods suggest that that many people experienced serious psychological problems.[173] One symptom of such traumas can be inactivity and a sense of dissociation. Andrew Crabtree has described how survivors of Kosi River Floods of 2008 in India spoke of being in a state of 'numbness' and 'helplessness' in the immediate aftermath. Others suggested that their 'senses were not working'.[174] The seeming apathy and inactivity of flood survivors in 1931 seems to speak to a similar form of traumatic immobility. This does not preclude the role of culture, which may have influenced the specific understanding of the unfolding trauma, yet it certainly refutes the notion that passivity was somehow culturally specific.

In some cases, the traumatic effect of the flood may have had even more profound consequences. There were numerous descriptions of

---

[170] Smil, *China's Past*, p. 75.   [171] De Waal, *Famine That Kills*, p. 112.
[172] Fullerton and Ursano, 'Psychological and Psychopathological'.
[173] Feng et al., 'Social Support'.   [174] Crabtree, 'Deep Roots of Nightmares', p. 169.

people committing suicide during the flood. A Dong described how a husband and wife who had lost all their children to the current became so distraught that they drowned themselves.[175] A foreign correspondent wrote that, despite cultural prohibitions, 'everywhere one saw [people] hopelessly, apathetically killing themselves.'[176] While this was no doubt something of an exaggeration, epidemics of suicide were not unknown in China. During the Taiping Civil War, canals in some districts of the Jiangnan region were clogged with the corpses of those who felt that taking their own lives was preferable to facing the trauma of war.[177] The historian Li Qin 李勤 has described how families in Hubei sometimes tied themselves together and plunged into the floodwater to escape the dire consequences of inundation in the 1930s.[178] Following catastrophic floods in the region 1954, more than 2,000 people were reported to have taken their lives. On this occasion, the psychological effect of inundation was more disastrous than the nutritional effects, with the number of people dying by their own hands far exceeding those who starved to death.[179]

In recent decades, historians have done much to complicate the image of passive disaster victims waiting for the assistance of generous outside benefactors. They have stressed the agency of survivors, detailing the sophisticated strategies they employ. This approach has done much to enhance our understanding of disasters. In 1931, communities displayed a formidable capacity to cope with a disaster. Yet in focussing solely on survival, there is a risk that we might reduce members of disaster-stricken communities to simple rational actors. Catastrophes become obstacles to be overcome by survival-oriented people, who are little more than nutrition-seeking organisms. This leaves little room for the subjective and traumatic reactions that go beyond survival. How do we account for those who sat motionless, or ended their lives so that they might blot out the physical and emotional pain? Where, in the literature on coping strategies, is there space to consider those who simply could not cope?

Understanding how people behave during crises is vital to the analysis of disaster regimes. It helps to illuminate patterns of collective action,

---

[175] A 'Hankou shuizai'.   [176] *Time Magazine,* 31 August 1931.
[177] Meyer-Fong, *What Remains,* pp. 119–20.
[178] Li, 'San shi nian dai shuizai dui zaimin shehui xinli de yingxiang'.
[179] 'Hubei sheng yi jiu wu si nian shuizai qingkuang ji zaihou huifu qingkuang tongji', HSD (Wuhan, 1954). Of course, the veracity of statistical evidence compiled during the Maoist era cannot be trusted. In this instance it is possible that the category of 'suicides' 自杀 (zisha) was used to mask more politically sensitive causes of mortality. For more on the 1954 flood see the epilogue.

and can offer insights into how famines and epidemics operate in populations. The urge to congregate with fellow survivors is a pattern of behaviour that often increases risk, yet the desire for company is entirely understandable on an affective level, when considering the often terrifying and traumatic experience of living through a catastrophe. By paying close attention to the sensory dimensions of experience, this chapter has presented readers with a vast array of human reactions to the 1931 flood. Not all were directed towards survival. People responded to traumatic and bizarre situations by engaging in seemingly unproductive activities, including displays of grief, religious rituals and acts of compassion for animals. These activities did not necessarily enhance their chances, but were nevertheless expressions of agency and humanity – complex reactions of a community confronted by an overwhelming sensory experience.

5

DISASTER EXPERTS

When the workmen chant the Inspector's Song,
Hearts break, tears fall like rain,
Ten thousand slave in the quarries,
But who will haul the stone to the river bank?

Li Bai 李白 (701–762)[1]

They said, 'Work fight or go to jail',
I said, 'I ain't totin' no sacks'.
I won't drown on that levee,
And you ain't gonna break my back.

Lonnie Johnson, 1928[2]

On 21 September 1931 a large crowd of refugees were gathered in sampans on the outskirts of the city of Xinghua 兴化 in Jiangsu, when all of a sudden a Lockheed–Sirius monoplane appeared in the skies above their heads, before coming to land on its pontoons in the river nearby. Their curiosity piqued, the sampan owners sailed over to this incongruous aircraft, to see what mysteries it contained. Three men emerged, led by the pilot, who snapped some photographs of the unfolding scene, including the one reproduced in Figure 5.1. The assembled crowd soon began to wonder whether the plane might contain relief supplies, and began to beg the crew for food. Two of the men appeared to be foreigners, so the refugees intimated their desires by using simple sign language – fashioning rice bowls with one hand and clasping imaginary chopsticks with the other. At first it seemed as if their entreaties had been successful. The pilot leaned into the cockpit and brought out a large white packet. Quick as a flash, one of the refugees snatched this from his hands. Before

---

[1] In Lynn, *Yangtze River*, p. 48.
[2] Johnson, *Broken Levee Blues*. A song inspired by the experiences of African Americans during the 1927 Mississippi flood. In some versions the last lines are, 'I ain't drilling no levee; the planks is on the ground, and I ain't drivin' no nails.'

Figure 5.1. Sampans gathered around the monoplane at Xinghua. (The Charles Lindbergh Collection. Reproduced courtesy of the Missouri History Museum)

he had the opportunity to open it, other members of the crowd had torn it away. To their disappointment, the package contained not food but medicine. Undeterred, the famished refugees began to clamber onto the pontoons that were keeping the monoplane afloat. Worried that his aircraft would be dragged down by their weight into the floodwater, the pilot reached into his cockpit and pulled out a Smith and Wesson pistol. He fired a warning shot into the air, and then pointed his gun at the crowd. Fearing for their lives, the refugees jumped back onto their sampans and quickly poled away. The pilot and crew jumped into their now unencumbered monoplane and flew off into the distance, never to return.[3]

As the refugees watched the monoplane disappear over the horizon it is unlikely that any of them realised that they had just received a visit from one of the most famous men in the world. The aviator Charles Lindbergh had arrived in China with his wife Anne on the final leg of a tour of East Asia. Witnessing the destruction caused by the flood, the couple had

---

[3] This passage is adapted from an account described by Anne Lindbergh. She was not present at the time, and based her description on her husband's recollections. See Lindbergh, *North to the Orient*, p. 140.

offered their assistance to the Nationalist government. They were commissioned alongside pilots from the British Royal Air Force to chart the extent of the flood, creating one of the first aerial surveys of a disaster. Later Lindbergh was persuaded to undertake 'a new experiment in flood relief', flying to the heart of the disaster zone and delivering packages of serum and vaccine.[4]

This experiment was, in many ways, illustrative of the broader official relief effort. It was ostentatiously modern, deploying the new science of aviation to assist otherwise inaccessible refugees, and thoroughly international, with the Nationalist health minister Liu Ruiheng 刘瑞恒 and his friend the Rockefeller Foundation public health worker John Grant accompanying Lindbergh on his flight.[5] The crew of this plane carried an impressive cargo of knowledge and skills, and were backed by considerable political and financial resources. Despite this, their experiment was not a success. They did not manage to inoculate a single refugee, and instead ended up involved in an unfortunate confrontation. What appeared to be a feasible relief plan had failed to account for the behaviour of disaster-stricken people. Epidemics may have been the most pressing physical threat to their survival, yet the psychology of starvation was a far more powerful motivator. What famished refugees desired was food, not an abstract and alien biomedical procedure without discernible immediate benefits.

The Xinghua incident was one of the few instances in which the elite cadre of disaster experts met directly with the objects of their expertise. The fact that these two groups ended up in a tense standoff betrayed the profound disjuncture between the image of the flood conjured in the official imagination and the reality of the disaster on the ground. This chapter and the next explore the difficulties in translation that occurred between two groups speaking very different languages of expertise. The first was a language spoken by the technical experts who emerged from the monoplane outside Xinghua. It was peppered with abstract economic concepts, medical theories and scientific terminology. The second was that spoken by those living on sampans. It was a language of vernacular expertise, its grammar inflected with customary knowledge transmitted down through generations as part of a culture of disasters. These two languages proved mutually incomprehensible to such an extent that when their emissaries met in the water outside Xinghua, they could communicate only through basic sign language and threats of violence.

---

[4] *North China Herald*, 29 September 1931.   [5] Known as J. Heng-Liu.

As the history of the flood was recorded for posterity, those who wrote about the disaster almost exclusively employed the language of technical expertise. When described in this authoritative register, the flood became a story dominated by government agencies and relief organisations. Those employing top-down measures emerged as the sole arbiters of refugee survival. Vernacular expertise, when noticed at all, was represented as a symptom of desperation. The vital role played by humble technologies such as sampans was forgotten, while ostentatious yet largely ineffective technologies such as aircraft were heralded for their critical contribution. This was not a deliberate obfuscation on the part of relief institutions. It was the product of the institutional ideology that dominated those working in the realm of disaster governance.

In the aftermath of the Xinghua incident, the crew of the monoplane chose not to mention the unfortunate incident with the gun. The story only came to light a few years later in an account written by Anne Lindbergh. It was decided that the telling the truth might give a 'false impression . . . of the Chinese people'.[6] In place of the somewhat messy reality, a heroic narrative of an adventurous experiment in aviation was born. The press continued to follow the Lindberghs in their journey across China with avid interest.[7] Having been reunited, Anne and Charles flew to Wuhan, where one of the wings of their monoplane was caught by water and they were tipped out into the Yangzi. According to Pearl Buck, local onlookers were amazed they did not drown, and attributed their survival at the hands of the demon river to the fact that they were Americans.[8] The indignity of having to be fished out of the muddy Wuhan harbour did little to diminish the heroic reputation of the Lindberghs. Before they departed from China, the first lady Song Meiling 宋美龄 threw the couple a special tea party, where Chiang Kai-shek presented Charles with the nation's first ever aviation medal as a reward for his service to the flood effort.[9] The fact that his mission had not been quite the spectacular success that many believed was conveniently overlooked. As with so much else during the relief effort, actions were judged by their intentions rather than their results.

---

[6] Berg, *Lindbergh.*

[7] See for example *Zhongyang Ribao*, 18 September 1931; 'Linbai suo she zhi Zhongguo shuizai zhaopian', *Dongfang Zazhi*, 1932, 29; 'Fabiao Linbai kan zai baogao', *Dongbei Wenhua*, 169 (1931); *North China Herald*, 29 September 1931.

[8] Quoted in Lynn, *Yangtze River*, p. 43.

[9] *North China Herald*, 29 September 1931. This medal now resides as part of the Lindbergh collection in the Missouri History Museum.

In the historiography of Chinese disasters, the official response to floods and droughts has often been used to gauge the broader legitimacy of the political system. One problem with viewing disasters through an official prism is that our own vision is clouded by the assumptions of the elite. It is hard to avoid leaning on official sources, as technical experts, be they imperial scholar officials or modern famine activists, spilled far more ink than any other group. Such accounts tend to suggest that the sole variable determining refugee survival is the efficiency and benevolence of governors. This chapter and the next challenge this view. The first examines the limitations of official relief and the second highlights how governance often impinged on autonomous survival. Taken together, these two chapters demonstrate the political and social dimensions of the disaster regime. This chapter examines the actions of the disaster technocracy – the group of governmental and nongovernmental figures who took on the responsibility for managing the relief effort. It argues that their approach to disaster relief, although constrained by the economic climate, was strongly influenced by a powerful institutional ideology, which blinded them to the shortcomings of their policies. This was not a deliberate conspiracy of silence. It was the product of the somewhat insular world inhabited by technocratic experts, which allowed them to fall victim to bias and tautological reasoning. Survivors were counted as government victories, while the dead were blamed on the environment.

The Disaster Technocracy

The Nationalist government could hardly have ignored the flood. By the early summer tens of thousands of refugees had descended upon their capital in Nanjing. Later, some 40,000 local citizens fell victim to the flood, when the city itself succumbed to inundation.[10] As the magnitude of the disaster became clear, the finance minister Song Ziwen 宋子文 was appointed to head the specially created National Flood Relief Commission 救济水灾委员会 (Jiuji Shuizai Weiyuanhui – hereafter the NFRC).[11] As the brother to three famous sisters, each of whom was married to a highly influential politician, Song was deeply embedded within the kinship structure of the Nationalist movement. Yet while he may have been brother-in-law to Chiang Kai-shek, like many fellow party members Song objected to the myopic obsession

---

[10] Lipkin, *Useless to the State*, pp. 72–4.   [11] Known as T. V. Soong.

that the Generalissimo and his military allies had with destroying the Communists.[12] By establishing the NFRC, Song demonstrated his clear preference for a programme of economic reconstruction rather than one of military consolidation.[13] He staffed the executive tier of the commission with several like-minded politicians, who helped Song to recruit some of the most eminent technical experts in China.[14]

Given their formidable list of qualifications, it would be easy to assume that those appointed to the NFRC were chosen solely on meritocratic criteria. Closer inspection reveals a form of elite networking at play. Many were members of an educational elite known as the Returned Students, who had attended university in Europe, America or Japan. A good number were, in fact, Song's own friends and former classmates. Two of his contemporaries from his Harvard University years served on the Medical Advisory Committee, and three friends from the nearby Massachusetts Institute of Technology served on the Engineering and Labour Relief Committee.[15] Two decades before the flood at least six of the members of the NFRC had dined together at a Chinese restaurant in Boston to celebrate the second anniversary of the Republic of China, which had, of course, been established by the most famous of Song's brothers-in–law, Sun Yat-sen.[16] This close-knit alliance politics typified

---

[12] Margherita Zanasi has suggested that the Nationalist administration during this period could be divided into two loose factions. The first was a faction of *militarists* led by Chiang, whose members believed that the annihilation of the Communist threat was the most pressing imperative for nation building. The other comprised a faction of *reconstruction-ists*, loosely aligned around Wang Jingwei, whose members believed that building the economic base of the nation was the highest priority. The alliances and inclinations of senior party members were perhaps more convoluted and changeable than this typology suggests, yet Zanasi's classification remains a useful heuristic device, which helps to capture the divided loyalties and intentions of the government at this stage. See Zanasi, *Saving the Nation.*

[13] In 1933 Song would resign as finance minister to protest Chiang's military spending. See Benton, *New Fourth Army*, p. 140.

[14] These including another of Song's brothers-in-law Kong Xiangxi 孔祥熙 – known as H. H. Kung – a prominent financier and politician, and also the government minister charged with reorganising the disaster relief infrastructure Xu Shiying. On Xu see Janku, 'Internationalization of Disaster Relief'.

[15] For a full list of senior staff in the NFRC see RNFRC, pp. 211–15. Two of the serving physicians, including Health Minister Liu Ruiheng, were Song's Harvard classmates. T. C. Hsi, H. K. Chow and Z. Y. Chow were all at MIT. On the membership of MIT Chinese Club see *The Chinese Students' Monthly*, June 1914, p. 618. The club pages of this periodical show frequent contact between the small Harvard and MIT clubs during this period.

[16] *The Chinese Students' Monthly*, March 1913. In 1914 Harvard and MIT staged a Chinese fete, complete with dragons, ox demons and other traditional characters. One of those

the modus operandi of the Nationalist government. The façade of meritocracy obscured a somewhat insular world of elite networking.

After a brief stint in a New York bank, Song had left the United States to join the Nationalist cause. His Harvard classmate Liu Ruiheng chose a different path, taking positions at the Peking Union Medical College 北京协和医学院 (Beijing Xiehe Yixue Yuan).[17] This organisation would play an integral role in the NFRC's response to the health crisis. Established in 1917 by the Rockefeller Foundation, a global philanthropic empire funded by profits derived from the Standard Oil Company, its objective was to train an elite cadre of professionals to promote biomedicine in China.[18] The NFRC boasted many Peking affiliates, including Niu Huisheng 牛惠生, Jin Baoshan 金宝善, Yan Fuqing 颜福庆 and Brian Dyer.[19] Beyond the medical committee, the fingerprints of the Rockefeller Foundation could be found all over the relief effort. It had provided the seed funding, for example, for the team of agricultural economists led by John Lossing Buck, who compiled the Nanjing Survey.[20] The Rockefeller Foundation also paid the salary of the Canadian public health pioneer John Grant. Born to missionary family in China and educated in the United States, Grant was known as the 'Medical Bolshevik' for his left-leaning views about public health. He used an intimate knowledge of Chinese language and culture to pioneer a strategy in which curative and preventative medicine would be combined.[21] Grant's contribution to the NFRC went far beyond accompanying Liu and Lindbergh on their monoplane trip to Xinghua. He used the relief effort as a springboard to promote his broader public health strategy.

In addition to the Rockefeller Foundation, several other organisations piggybacked their policies onto NFRC, most notably the China International Famine Relief Commission 华洋义赈会 (Hua-Yang Yizhen Hui – hereafter CIFRC), whose members such as John Earl Baker and George

organising the production was a young Song Meiling. See *The Chinese Students' Monthly*, May 1914.

[17] *Who's Who in China*, pp. 192–3.   [18] Bullock, *Oil Prince's Legacy*.

[19] Niu Huisheng was known as New Way-sung; he was a Harvard classmate of Song Ziwen. Jin Baoshan – known as P. Z. King – was a Japanese educated physician involved in early public health work in Beijing; he later joined the Ministry of Health. See *Who's Who in China*, p. 52. See also Yip, *Health and National Reconstruction*, p. 75. Yan Fuqing – known as F. C. Yen – served in the Chinese Labour Corps in the First World War and later went on to be educated at Harvard. See *Who's Who in China*, p. 277. On Brian Dyer see RNFRC, p. 155.

[20] Bullock, *Oil Prince's Legacy*.   [21] Bullock, *American Transplant*, pp. 134–61.

Stroebe were employed in senior positions. Originally formed by an alliance of foreign and Chinese treaty port elite during the North China Famine of 1920–1921, the CIFRC had carved out considerable power over the previous decade.[22] This organisation more than any other would help to shape the NFRC's disaster reconstruction policies.

The foreigners employed by the NFRC were by no means all old China hands. Since the late 1920s the League of Nations had been sending advisors to China to help the Nationalist government establish health policies. The most important of these was the Polish physician and bacteriologist Ludwik Rajchman, who would eventually develop a close working and personal relationship with Song Ziwen.[23] Rajchman and his colleagues were representatives of what Susan Pedersen has described as the 'technical' League, whose members sought to 'combat the proliferating hazards and traffics of an increasingly interconnected world.'[24] Whereas the more politically orientated aspects of the League's activities would eventually founder in the fractious international order of the 1930s, the technical League never really went away. It was reincarnated in various forms, later becoming the bedrock of what is known today as the non-governmental organisation (NGO) sector.[25] The political League was deeply enmeshed in the already declining world of European imperialism. Yet many of the members of the technical League, or at least those involved with NFRC, came from regions that had not played a significant role in the colonial subjugation of East Asia. They included figures such as the Croatian public health specialist Berislav Borcic, the Romanian malariologist Mihai Ciuca and the Spanish fumigation expert Alberto Anguera.[26]

The official report of the NFRC would go on to present a typically Eurocentric picture of the relief effort. Yet digging beneath the surface, it quickly becomes apparent that these international experts were a lot more cosmopolitan than they first appeared. The Egyptian government organised a travelling bacteriological laboratory to be sent to the flood zone.[27] This was negotiated personally between Liu Ruiheng and Muhammad Shahin Pasha, two biomedical physicians turned

[22] Nathan, *History of the China International Famine Relief Commission.*
[23] Borowy, 'Thinking Big'.   [24] Pedersen, *Guardians*, p. 9.   [25] Ibid.
[26] RNFRC, p. 182; Borowy, 'Thinking Big'; Rajchman, *Report of the Technical Agent*, p. 13.
[27] 'Dr. J. Heng Liu to M. (Muhammad) Shahin,', 22 November 1931, *Egyptian National Archives*, File 0078–022795. I am grateful to Shuang Wen for providing me with this reference.

politicians.[28] This resulted in a team of bacteriologists led by Hussein Mohammad Ibrahim travelling to China and distributing a large consignment of vaccines.[29] In another instance, a team of physicians from the Dutch East Indies also travelled to the flood zone. We know little of how this particular medical interaction was initiated, though it may be significant that those who travelled to the flood zone were members of the Indonesian Chinese community.[30] Their involvement may have reflected the rising importance of a transnational Chinese identity in global politics in the early twentieth century.[31] Such complex motivations are not reflected in the official literature, which simply thanked the government of the Dutch East Indies for 'sending' physicians.[32] As we shall see, the Chinese diaspora was quite capable of organising its own forms of humanitarian assistance, independent from colonial overseers. One of the most famous citizens of the diaspora was the Malayan epidemiologist Wu Liande, who had risen to prominence fighting plague in northern China two decades earlier. As the head of the newly established quarantine service, Wu was a vitally important addition to the NFRC.[33]

The figure tasked with corralling this disparate band of experts into some form of coordinated body was the Briton John Hope Simpson. Having spent his youth working for the Indian Civil Service, from the mid-1920s Hope Simpson assumed a succession of posts for the League of Nations. He was first sent to monitor the Greek-Turkish population exchange, before incurring the wrath of the Zionist movement by suggesting that Jewish migration to British Mandate Palestine was placing unsustainable pressure on the Arab population.[34] In his capacity as a kind of expert without portfolio, Hope Simpson had one foot firmly anchored in the imperial past, with the other striding towards a new postcolonial order. Pedersen has observed that much of the writing on the League relies on the simplistic binary of colonised and coloniser, which has long been the paradigm for imperial history.[35] Figures like

---

[28] Muhammad Shahin Pasha was both personal physician and Under Secretary to King Fuad. Lanfranchi, *Casting off the Veil*, p. 184.

[29] RNFRC, p. 155.

[30] They included Sie Boen Lian 施文连 (Shi Wenlian), an eye specialist trained in Jakarta and Prague, who would later act one of the personal physicians of Indonesian President Sukarno. Suryadinata, *Prominent Indonesian Chinese*, p. 148.

[31] See Willmott, *National Status*.   [32] RNFRC, p. 155.   [33] Wu and Wu, *Haigang jianyi*.

[34] Details of John Hope Simpson's fascinating career can be found in JHS 10.

[35] Pedersen, *Guardians*.

Hope Simpson specialised in working in liminal territories that defied this binary, such as Greece, Palestine and China. His career seems to have anticipated a world where Western experts would seek to justify their disproportionate influence by recasting themselves not as rulers but as technical experts. He could, in this respect, be considered an early incarnation of what would later become known as a development professional. Despite his considerable experience, heading up the NFRC would prove to be one of the most intense challenges of his career. Song Ziwen may have remained nominally in control, yet it fell to Hope Simpson, a man who had never before set foot in China, to administer the day-to-day business of a powerful government commission.

The NFRC was, in a sense, a triumph of state building. Bringing government technocrats and private experts under a single umbrella was an efficient way of organising and coordinating the official response to the flood. Lillian Li has argued that this allowed the Nationalists to assert their sovereignty over influential independent organisations, most notably the CIFRC, which had carved out considerable power during the 1920s.[36] Yet bringing nongovernmental experts into the fold was a double-edged sword. It allowed the government to exercise nominal control, but it also allowed nongovernmental experts to exert considerable influence over official policies. For many politicians, this does not seem to have been considered particularly problematic. They shared a technocratic outlook, coming from similar educational backgrounds and often mixing in the same social circles as their foreign counterparts. Government technocrats and private experts spoke the same language, both figuratively and literally, with much of the official literature being published exclusively in English. While this common background eased communication it also limited diversity, creating a rather shallow gene pool of ideas, which meant that the NFRC quickly developed an insular institutional ideology. This would act both as a guide for relief policies and as an impenetrable barrier against criticism.

Practical Humanitarianism

At the heart of the institutional ideology of the NFRC lay shared assumptions about the nature of poverty and the appropriate methods for delivering charity. With a few notable exceptions, the central committee all seemed to be keen adherents to what might be described as the

---

[36] Li, *Fighting Famine*, p. 306.

pauperisation thesis. They believed that if charity were not conducted with appropriate discipline and restraint, recipients would be seduced into a life of parasitic dependency. Such ideas were predicated on the assumption that human beings were inclined to follow the path of least resistance. If the opportunity presented itself, they would be content to live off the largesse of their economic superiors. The pauperisation thesis – at least in its modern iteration – was a relatively recent import to China from Western Europe and North America, where it had long been a guiding principle of charitable activities. The moral dimensions of this theory, which had been largely absent in traditional Chinese philanthropic thinking, had found fertile soil among reforming politicians, penologists and social scientists since the late Qing. Janet Chen has detailed the inexorable rise of the pauperisation thesis, alongside a suite of other compatible theories, demonstrating that they resulted in the virtual criminalisation of the poor in Republican China. Those deemed 'guilty of indigence', to use her evocative phrase, were detained in workhouses, beggar camps and a range of other institutions, where the line between charity and punishment became increasingly blurred. These institutions were designed to remove those who failed to meet the prescriptions of modern citizenship from the generation population, and to inculcate normative attitudes towards life and labour.[37]

The staff of the CIFRC were ardent exponents of the pauperisation thesis. Over the previous decade, several members had published studies setting out their very particular approach to disaster relief. These included Liang Ruhao 梁如浩, a former Beiyang politician who held a senior role in the organisation for much of the 1920s.[38] He contrasted the 'scientific' approach to famine relief employed by the CIFRC, with the 'customary' methods employed by Chinese administrators in the past.[39] Here, science was merely a synonym for a neo-Malthusian interpretation of famine causation, in which demographic pressure became the ultimate culprit of all of China's woes. The most famous exponent of these views was the former CIFRC director Walter Mallory. His study *China: Land of Famine* became one of the most influential treatments of the subject, and is still often cited today. Mallory characterised floods and droughts as proximate triggers for famine, with the ultimate cause being the desperate poverty that resulted from the unparalleled 'fecundity of

---

[37] Chen, *Guilty of Indigence.*   [38] Known as M. T. Liang.
[39] Liang, 'Combating the Famine Dragon'. Liang was appointed Minister of Communications by Yuan Shikai 袁世凱. See Weatherley, *Making China Strong*, p. 72.

the Chinese'.[40] In a less well-known study, the founding director of the CIFRC John Earl Baker presented a very similar assessment. He claimed that Chinese people themselves had a kind of intuitive grasp of demographic determinism, and that they worried about overpopulation while having no knowledge of Malthusian economics.[41] Baker seems to have been unaware of the work of the scholar Hong Liangji 洪亮吉, who had advanced a demographic theory of famine causation before Thomas Malthus. The crux of Hong's theory was that 'after a long peaceful rule, Heaven-and-Earth cannot stop people from reproducing. Yet the resources with which Heaven-and-Earth nourish the people are finite.'[42]

To be fair to Baker, most Chinese intellectuals in the early twentieth century also seem to have been largely unaware of Hong Liangji. They were certainly not, however, as ignorant of Malthusianism as Baker believed. They had been debating the merits of demographic determinism since the late nineteenth century. Sun Yat-sen was one of the staunchest critics, calling Malthusianism a 'poisonous doctrine', and subscribing instead to the theories of Henry George, who argued in favour of increasing populations as a means to guarantee the 'preservation of the race'.[43] While the imperatives of Social Darwinism led Sun to criticise arguments in favour of limiting the population, they led others to the exact opposite conclusions. The sociologist Wu Jingchao 吴景超 praised Mallory for introducing scientific rigour into the study of Chinese famines, seeing the population problem as one of the major inhibiting factors preventing the development of a strong nation. Chen Tinghong 陈汀泓 spoke of the necessity of limiting numbers to improve the 'health of the population' 人口品质 (renkou pinzhi).[44] His analysis demonstrated how easily demographic theory could be combined with eugenics. Mallory himself advocated a rigorous programme of eugenics as one of the solutions to the problem of famine.[45]

Malthusianism not only provided the CIFRC was an explanation for famines but also undergirded their relief methods. Baker described the

---

[40] Mallory, *China*, p. 87.   [41] Baker, *Explaining China*, pp. 231–5.

[42] Hong, 'China's Population Problem'. As William Rowe has observed, Hong's ideas were disputed by the literatus Bao Shichen 包世臣. See Rowe, 'Bao Shichen and Agrarian Reform'.

[43] Trescott, 'Henry George', p. 366.

[44] Wu, 'China-Land of Famine (Walter H. Mallory)'.; Chen, 'Zaihuang yu Zhongguo'.

[45] Mallory, *China*, 184. It should be noted that the kind of eugenics he advocated involved contraceptive solutions rather than the far more sinister practices of regimes such as the German National Socialists.

approach they had developed as 'practical humanitarianism'. Though this was supposedly a scientific approach, it was actually steeped in a combination of Protestant moralisation and utilitarian calculation. At the heart of practical humanitarianism was a rather stark conviction that human life was not worth preserving if in doing so the underlying threat to collective well-being was not ameliorated.[46] Baker argued that it was pointless – even counterproductive – to feed famished people merely to preserve population numbers. A dole of free relief rations could only delay the inevitable positive check of famine, ensuring that recipients were 'spared to suffer and beg again another day.'[47] What was required instead was a disciplined programme, in which relief was provided strictly as remuneration for labour. Put simply, you only ate if you worked. This would help to prevent the pauperisation of refugees, ensuring that they were not 'supported in their idleness', as Mallory put it.[48] Malthusianism, which was presented as rational and scientific, was used to buttress a highly moral interpretation of poverty and labour.

Labour relief also appealed to practical humanitarians on technical grounds. It offered an opportunity to mould the minds and bodies of refugees while also providing a ready supply of cheap labour. This allowed engineers such as Oliver Todd to conduct ambitious hydraulic schemes.[49] The use of refugees to conduct infrastructural improvements was hardly novel in China. Imperial administrators had been using famished populations to construct dykes and dredge rivers for centuries. What differed now was the ideological context. Organisations such as the CIFRC and the American Red Cross, which Baker also headed for a time, saw labour relief not only as a practical solution to the technical problem of famine, but also as a moral solution to the problem of pauperism.[50]

---

[46] This was logic was common among those who subscribed to Malthusianism. The demographer Frank Notestein, for example, argued that even if the preventable diseases that cut short millions of Chinese lives could be cured, 'sober students might ponder long before utilizing this power,', due to the supposedly dire demographic consequences. See Notestein, 'Demographic Study', p. 77.

[47] Baker, *Explaining China*, p. 244.   [48] Mallory, *China*, p. 172.

[49] For Todd's own account of his activities see Todd, *Two Decades*. For an account of the figure known for his talents and ego as 'Todd Almighty' see Li, *Fighting Famine*, p. 330.

[50] During the North China Famine 1920–1921, which marked an escalation of foreign involvement in famine relief, there had been considerable debate about whether relief should be provided as a dole or as remuneration for labour. Ultimately it appears the latter argument won out, with foreign Red Cross workers believing that labour relief would restore an 'ability to organise' and 'pride' which would lift China 'out of the category of international "poor relation" to the status of a self reliant, progressive power'. American Red Cross, *Report of the China Famine Relief*.

They were, in fact, simply continuing the venerable tradition of pressing poor people into labour service, only now they relied solely on the compulsion of hunger, rather than a system of corvée, in which labour service functioned as a form of taxation. When the Nationalists rose to power, this approach to labour relief became the guiding principle for their response to disasters. The minister in charge of disaster relief, Xu Shiying 许世英, issued regulations stipulating that rations should be distributed only in remuneration for work.[51] This approach appealed to a government that was committed both to inculcating normative attitudes to labour and promoting technical solutions to the problem of famine. The NFRC proved the perfect vehicle to expand this approach.

Not all NFRC members were committed practical humanitarians. Hope Simpson complained about frequent conflicts with a 'notorious philanthropist, a Buddhist, and a man of very old fashion', who believed that it was 'almost a crime to demand that flood sufferers should do something in order to justify their relief'.[52] The unnamed object of his ire was most likely Zhu Qinglan 朱庆澜, a military leader and prominent philanthropist. Zhu did not leave any record of his activities in the NFRC, though as an ardent Buddhist he likely saw the provision of relief as a moral and religious obligation.[53] This clash demonstrates how the fault lines running through the NFRC were as much theological as they were ideological. Many Chinese members, including Song Ziwen, were practicing Protestants.[54] Their religio-ethical approach to charity was another form of common language that they shared with many of their foreign counterparts. Figures such as Zhu Qinglan, who came from an alternative philanthropic and linguistic tradition, struggled to have their voices heard.

These theological fault lines did not stop in the upper echelons of the NFRC. The language of pauperisation filtered through the organisations down to the ground. Protestant missionaries working directly with refugees were convinced 'of the desirability, wherever possible, of giving relief in return for work', and dismayed at Buddhist charities that collected vast funds but then gave them out to anyone who looked like they needed help.[55] Such an approach, it was reasoned, possessed no

[51] Janku, 'Internationalization of Disaster Relief'.
[52] 'John Hope Simpson to K. Zillacus', 29 June 1932, JHS 6i.
[53] Carter, *Heart of Buddha*, pp. 111–12, 126.
[54] Goossaert and Palmer, *Religious Question*, p. 69.
[55] E. C. Lobenstine 'The Work of Missionaries and Other Westerners in Flood Relief,', SOAS Archives 10/7/15.

mechanism to 'exclude malingerers'.[56] Allusions to the pauperisation
thesis were notably absent in accounts of relief work written by Catholic
missionaries. Like their Buddhist counterparts, the Irish Columban
order, who tended to refugees in Hanyang, seem to have seen charity as
a sacred obligation.[57] Bishop Galvin donated almost the entire savings
of his church, claiming that 'God gave us that money . . . and God gave us
these people on the hills. We are going to give the money back to Him.'[58]
Practical humanitarianism may have been an infectious ideology, but it
by no means enjoyed complete hegemony.

The Globalisation of Disasters

Ideology may have been an important factor, but the most powerful
force shaping the methodology of the NFRC was the inclement financial
climate. Before leaving for China, Hope Simpson had been promised
$30 million with which to organise the relief effort. When he arrived, he
found that he had only a small fraction of this sum.[59] Having discovered
the truth about his shoestring budget, he wrote a private letter to Song
expressing his fear that the whole NFRC venture would be 'a colossal
failure'.[60] Writing to his family he was even more candid, admitting that
he had taken on 'a dreadful job'.[61] Song's response to this pessimistic
assessment has not survived. It is likely that he was somewhat more
sanguine. After all, he had spent most of his political career peering
over the edge of a financial precipice. During the previous few years
he had been tasked with constructing modern economic institutions
while simultaneously attempting to prevent his entire fiscal base from
being squandered by profligate militarists. The flood was only the latest
in a long list of severe economic setbacks he had been required to
overcome.

Song's first instinct was to fall back on the bond market. The Qing
government had first introduced bonds in the 1890s, and the domestic

[56] 'Report of the Work of Rev. F. G. Onley', 1931, SOAS Archives 65/10.
[57] Such theological distinctions regarding the morality of labour would come as no surprise
to Weberian sociologists. See Weber, *Protestant Ethic.*
[58] In Barrett, *Red Lacquered Gate*, p. 281. On internal debates about charity within Western
Christianity see also See Fuller, 'Struggling with Famine', pp. 344–5.
[59] John Hope Simpson, 'Extracts from letter of Sir J. Hope-Simpson to Mr. F. B. Bourdillon',
16 January 1932, SOAS Archives 10/7/15.
[60] 'John Hope Simpson Confidential Letter to T. V. Soong', 23 November 1931, JHS 6i.
[61] 'John Hope Simpson to Maddie', 23 November 1931, JHS 6ii.

market had grown steadily in the early Republic, increasing dramatically in the late 1920s as banks began to invest heavily in government bonds.[62] Given these recent successes, salt bonds appeared to be a sound means of funding flood relief. Unfortunately, the Japanese invasion of Manchuria in the autumn had caused the bond market to collapse.[63] When the Japanese launched a further attack against Shanghai in early 1932, the value of government bonds plummeted by 50 per cent.[64] Song attempted to make up for the revenue shortfall by imposing a surtax on customs duties, and by negotiating a loan from the Hong Kong Shanghai Banking Corporation. Yet these added revenue streams were insufficient to make up for the losses.[65] Given these severe financial constraints, it is little wonder that Hope Simpson's first weeks in China were marred by doubts.

Charitable donations provided welcome financial respite. By the 1930s disasters were already becoming global charity events. As domestic and international audiences read descriptions of the flood in their morning papers, many were moved to send money for relief effort. By far the greatest proportion of the charitable relief came from within China itself. Much of this was dispensed through the remnants of the traditional philanthropic infrastructure, which operated through religious charities, native place associations and benevolent halls. Others chose to donate directly to the NFRC. The commission praised the generosity of local citizens for subscribing sums ranging from 'from $300,000 to $1, the latter being donated by a prisoner under sentence of death'.[66] The relief effort also utilised the charitable infrastructure of organisations such as the Chinese Red Cross Society 中国红十字会 (Zhongguo Hongshizi Hui). Formed in Shanghai in the dying days of the Qing dynasty, by the early 1920s this charity boasted a membership of more than 40,000.[67] Its success inspired members of a syncretistic religious movement known as the Daoyuan 道院 to establish the World Red Swastika Society 世界红卍字会 (Shijie Hongwanzi Hui). By emulating certain functions of the Red Cross, but placing them under the banner of a recognisable Buddhist symbol, this charity infused a traditional religious philanthropic ethic with a modern methodology.[68] Both the Red Cross and Red Swastika were involved

---

[62] Boecking and Scholz, 'Did the Nationalist Government', p. 132.
[63] RNFRC, pp. 17–18.
[64] Boecking and Scholz, 'Did the Nationalist Government', p. 132.
[65] RNFRC, pp. 18–19.   [66] Figures in Chinese dollars. RNFRC, p. 14.
[67] Reeves, 'Red Cross Society of China'.   [68] Duara, 'Transnationalism'.

in the organisation of relief throughout many areas of the flood zone in 1931.[69]

The national press also played an important role in the charity drive. In her study of the 1870s famine, Kathryn Edgerton-Tarpley described how the nascent print media helped to motivate new forms of national consciousness, inspiring urban readers to donate to far distant regions in the north of the empire.[70] By the 1930s both the national consciousness of the Chinese people and the techniques used by the media had developed significantly. Half a century before Western popular musicians began to release charity singles for famine victims, Wang Renlu 王人路 penned the *Disaster Relief Song* 赈灾歌 (Zhenzai Ge).[71] Beginning with a rallying cry to all 'comrades' 同志们 (tongzhimen), the song details the terrible situation unfolding in the flood zone. In addition to eliciting empathy – asking listeners to put themselves in the place of flood victims 将心来比心 (jiangxin lai bixin) – it also mobilised sentiments of shame, asking how listeners might live with their consciences if they failed to help refugees. It concludes by encouraging listeners to donate expediently and generously to the relief effort. The sheet music for this song appeared on the children's page of the official Nationalist newspaper *Zhongyang Ribao* 中央日报. It seems to have been part of a concerted effort to involve young people in the charity effort. The paper also printed cartoons depicting scenes of devastation, and photographs of young people using collecting tins to gather funds for the relief effort. Children may not have had significant economic resources of their own, but they still played an important role as emotional labourers, encouraging their elders to give generously.[72]

The Disaster Relief Song – Wang Renlu

Comrades, listen to my song,
The calamitous flood this year, has left rivers and lakes overflowing,

[69] The Chinese Red Cross was active in Wuhan. See 'Zhongguo Hongshizihui Hankou fenhui cheng yanmai gongzuo wen,', HSSDX; 'Buxing de tianzai, *Wenhua*, 24 (1931). The World Red Swastika Society took an active role dealing with the refugee crisis in Shanghai. See Zheng, 'Shijie hongwanzi hui si xian fen hui', 12 December 1931, Q120-4-302, 1931 (SMA). They were also involved in the relief effort in Hankou; see Xie, *Yi jiu san yi nian*, p. 23. On occasion the Red Cross and Red Swastika worked together; see *Zhongyang Ribao* October n.d. 1931 (p. 1046 of compiled edition available in Bodleian Library Oxford and Shanghai Municipal Library).
[70] Edgerton-Tarpley, *Tears from Iron*.   [71] *Zhongyang Ribao*, 12 September 1931.
[72] This is somewhat similar to efforts made by Catholic missionary societies who in the nineteenth century encouraged French children to donate money to their Chinese counterparts. See Harrison, 'Penny for the Little Chinese'.

Humans and animals suffer, houses are destroyed, fields flooded.
Refugees are scattered over ten thousand miles, with nowhere to hide,
Our poor compatriots are anxious to escape,
Yet they can think of nowhere to turn, except for their temples.
Their stomachs are hungry, yet they have no food to eat,
Night falls, yet they have no bedding to sleep,
If they are not relieved, they will certainly perish.
We must all donate quickly, to alleviate their suffering,
These pitiful refugees, who weep and wail night and day,
It fills one with sadness.
I put myself in their place – for we are all the same,
And ask how it would be if it were I, and my family,
Who suffered in this flood?
I know I would certainly be nervous,
Searching for shelter from the east to the west,
I think once more of myself, now drowning in the water,
I would cry and wail, uncontrollably panicked.
There are so many refugees,
Now wandering aimlessly,
With no clothes to keep out the cold,
No rice when they are hungry,
So many lives that depend upon relief.
If you do not help now, could you live with your conscience?
Comrades, come quickly,
Everyone must work together,
Everyone must work diligently,
Be frugal with your food and clothes,
So that we might save the common people.

The charity effort was not limited to the Chinese press. The scale of the flood proved so dramatic that it even stirred the charitable sensibilities of the editors of the *North China Herald.* Serving as the mouthpiece of the more conservative Britons of treaty port society, this newspaper was not usually known for excessive sympathy for Chinese people. At the height of the disaster, however, its editors appealed to their readership to donate generously, putting away any sense of 'racial or national prejudice'.[73] This did not go down well with all readers. The letters page was soon filled with angry denunciations of the 'sickly sentiment' expressed by this uncharacteristically sympathetic editorial line.[74] William Bruce Lockhart, whom we encountered earlier invoking divine retribution as the cause of the flood, penned an angry missive in which he declared that foreigners should not deplete their 'dwindling

[73] *North China Herald*, 18 August 1931.   [74] Ibid.

resources on the shifting human quicksands of this ever hostile race of people', and should not even 'concern themselves with the holocausts of miseries that periodically occur in this land'.[75] Bruce Lockhart's unsympathetic views provoked fiery debate on the letters page, with some correspondents denouncing him and others praising his 'sane and refreshing common sense'.[76] This debate revealed a somewhat unsavoury aspect of the British experience of Chinese disasters – one that is not usually reflected in a literature dominated by sympathetic missionary accounts. While many Britons in China displayed compassion and generosity during the flood, a vocal minority, stung by their loss of prestige in recent years, seemed to have revelled in Chinese suffering.

As news of the flood spread beyond China, charity began to stream in from other world regions. Religious organisations proved to be among the most generous. The Panchen Lama donated on behalf of the Tibetan Buddhists, while Pope Pius XI offered the financial support of the Vatican.[77] As they heard descriptions of the flood relayed from their missionaries in the field, Christian congregants dutifully emptied their wallets and purses onto church collection plates. The author Pearl Buck, whose novel *The Good Earth* published earlier in the year had presented English readers with one of the most sympathetic portraits of the Chinese poor to date, now wrote a series of short stories describing the flood to be broadcast on the radio.[78] She was not the only celebrity to endorse the relief effort. Following their flights over the flood zone, Charles and Anne Lindbergh gave lectures about their experiences.[79] Meanwhile, in China, the renowned Beijing Opera artist Mei Lanfang 梅兰芳 not only donated personally to the relief effort, but also performed several benefit concerts.[80] Today, endorsing charitable efforts is an integral aspect of celebrity culture. Some historians trace the origins of this practice to the 1960s, when Western popular music stars became involved in relief

---

[75] Ibid.
[76] Ibid. The correspondence continued until *North China Herald*, 25 August 1931. Even Wu Liande was moved to write to the paper, lamenting 'the mentality of Mr. Bruce Lockhart and his kind'. *North China Herald*, 18 August 1931.
[77] Ibid.; *North China Herald*, 22 September 1931.
[78] Buck, *Good Earth*. A selection of the flood stories can be found in Buck, *First Wife*.
[79] Berg, *Lindbergh*.
[80] *Hankow Herald*, 5 September 1931. A virtuoso of the *nandan* 男旦 style, in which male actors perform as perform as female characters, Mei was not only a prominent figure on the Chinese national stage, but had also become something of an emissary of Chinese culture, touring countries as diverse as Japan, the United States and the Soviet Union. See Tian, *Mei Lanfang*.

campaigns during the Biafran famine.[81] The involvement of figures such as the Lindberghs and Mei Lanfang in the 1931 relief effort suggests a much longer history. Already by the 1930s, celebrities were using their magical aura to elicit charitable donations from their adoring publics.

Alongside such ultra-modern forms of charity, older methods of patronage persisted. Emperor Hirohito provided a steamship laden with food, medicines and blankets for flood victims.[82] This was a somewhat surprising gesture, given the parlous state of Sino-Japanese relations at the time. In September 1931, the Japanese had invaded Manchuria on the later disproven pretext that Chinese dissidents had attempted to bomb a railway that they operated. This act of international aggression initiated protests and boycotts throughout China. These, in turn, were used by the Japanese military as a justification for launching a punitive attack on Shanghai in January 1932. In what became known as the Battle of Shanghai, the city suffered significant fighting and aerial bombardments, leaving many areas outside the foreign concessions in ruins. Eventually, the League of Nations negotiated a controversial ceasefire. In what was interpreted by many Chinese citizens as a humiliating capitulation, the Nationalist army was forced to withdraw from Shanghai, which became a demilitarised zone.[83] Given the escalating conflict, many Chinese people were ill-disposed to accept charity from the Japanese emperor. Though he had initially accepted the donations, Song later rebuffed what he saw as a hypocritical gift.[84] In Japan, the flood offered further ammunition to those opposed to military adventurism. As one Christian named Motoichiro Takahashi wrote in apologetic poem: 'When your country is overwhelmed with a great flood, and troubled by internal dissention, we do not help you, but rather further the Manchurian aggression!'[85]

The most significant international donations came from overseas Chinese communities, particularly those based in Southeast Asia.[86] As news of the disaster reached diasporic communities in British Malaya and the Dutch East Indies, flood relief committees were quickly organised.[87]

---

[81] Alexander, 'Celebrity Culture'.
[82] *North China Herald*, 15 September 1931; *North China Herald*, 6 October 1931; *Hankow Herald*, 13 September 1931.
[83] Jordan, *China's Trial.*   [84] *North China Herald*, 29 September 1931.
[85] *The Chinese Recorder*, May 1932.
[86] 'John Hope Simpson to Sir John Campbell', 19 March 1932, JHS 6i.
[87] 'Facts in Brief Concerning China's Floods of 1931', SOAS Archives 10/7/15; 'China Flood Relief', *The Straits Times*, 8 September 1931; 'China Flood Relief,', *The Straits Times*, 23 September 1931. On Aw Boon-Haw see Kuo, *Networks beyond Empires*.

In Singapore, community leaders such as the businessman Aw Boon-Haw 胡文虎 (Hu Wenhu) remitted generous individual donations and helped to organise charity drives. Known as the Tiger Balm King due to his popular line of patent medicines, Aw was a colourful figure, fond of driving around the city in a car painted with tiger stripes.[88] According to the Singaporean press, Aw's donation so impressed one elderly Buddhist in Mainland China that he was inspired to donate all of his worldly goods, worth $200,000, before retiring for a life of quiet contemplation in the mountains.[89] For diasporic communities, charity maintained an important symbolic and economic link with Mainland China, and also helped to raise prestige within their own communities. The mobilisation of the overseas communities demonstrated that globalised charity was most certainly not an exclusively Western phenomenon. Members of the diaspora redeployed traditional institutions such as native place associations to create their own pathways of international charitable assistance.[90] Their generosity was unmatched by any other group outside the mainland, though it received only a very brief mention in the official NFRC report.[91]

Quite how much money was raised from charitable subscriptions remains unclear. The official report of the NFRC claimed the princely sum of $7,459,817. In private correspondence, Hope Simpson suggested a more modest figure of $2,000,000.[92] Even if charitable donations had reached the former, more generous, of these sums they would still have been insufficient to finance the relief effort. The situation became so desperate that NFRC staff worked with no pay for months.[93] With all other options exhausted, it was time to turn to the international market.

I Must Not Forget the Name – America!

In one of the short stories that she wrote to raise money for the relief effort, Pearl Buck imagined the plight of a young child stranded together with her family on a small flood island. Having survived by eating shrimp

---

[88] *The Straits Times*, 24 October 1931.

[89] Ibid. It should be noted that the Singaporean inspiration for this gift is not noted in newspapers published outside Singapore. See *North China Herald*, 6 October 1931.

[90] Kuo, *Networks Beyond Empires*.

[91] RNFRC, p. 158. In his correspondence Hope Simpson acknowledged the role of overseas Chinese communities. See 'John Hope Simpson to Sir John Campbell', 19 March 1932, JHS 6i.

[92] 'John Hope Simpson to A. A. Pallis', 13 February 1932, JHS 6i.

[93] 'Extracts from letter of Sir J. Hope-Simpson to Mr. F. B. Bourdillon', 16 January 1932, SOAS Archives 10/7/15.

and other ecological endowments, they found themselves on the verge of starvation, only to be rescued by the arrival of a boat carrying sacks of flour. In the closing lines of the story, the protagonist vows to commit to memory the words printed on the sacks that carried this precious relief: 'I must not forget the name – America!'[94] The grain to which Buck alluded was part of a loan of 450,000 tons of wheat and flour provided by the United States government for flood relief from late 1931 to early 1932. Contrary to the impression created in this fictional representation, the Americans were not motivated solely by the beneficent desire to save starving children. The wheat loan furthered their own economic interests. It offered the United States Farm Board a means to dispose of a large agricultural surplus that had been crippling its rural economy for years.

The global wheat crisis had its roots in the First World War. With vast tracts of European arable land being turned into trenches, farmers in the United States, Canada, Argentina and Australia planted tens of thousands of acres of wheat to meet the increased demand. With the cessation of hostilities and the recovery of European agriculture, the global market was left saturated with wheat. American farmers saw the value of their produce plummet by as much as 80 per cent over the course of the 1920s.[95] A bountiful harvest in 1929 caused the price of wheat to reach an all-time low. As millions of farmers in northern China were starving in droughts, their counterparts in America were facing a crisis of overabundance. Heaps of unsalable grain led to widespread impoverishment and land foreclosures. Favourable weather had ensured that even before the Wall Street Crash in 1929, often seen as the beginning of the Great Depression, many rural communities were already facing economic ruin. Herbert Hoover was eventually forced to swallow his Republican principles and use government tax revenue to purchase huge quantities of wheat.[96] This offered respite to rural families, but left the government in possession of millions of bushels of seemingly unmarketable grain. The global depression caused a further slump in agricultural prices.[97] Just as it seemed that there was no hope of finding an export market for the vast quantities of wheat that were languishing in government stores, news reached the United States of a catastrophic flood across the ocean.

Chinese economists who were familiar with the machinations of the global market were under no illusions as to the true nature of the wheat

[94] Buck, *First Wife*, p. 260.   [95] White, *It's Your Misfortune*, p. 464.
[96] Conkin, *Revolution Down on the Farm*, p. 56.
[97] Shiroyama, *China during the Great Depression*.

loan. Wang Weiyin 王维驷 suggested, somewhat optimistically, that the loan represented a happy convergence of self-interest, offering economic benefits to both nations involved.[98] This positive analysis overlooked the extent to which the United States was willing to exploit the asymmetrical nature of its economic relationship with flood-stricken China. As David Pietz has observed, American negotiators insisted that the wheat was to be valued at the price on the day of sale, rather than the price at the time of negotiation. Because of the inflationary effect that the loan itself had on the value of wheat within the American commodity exchange market, the price paid by the Chinese government was far higher than it would have been on the open market. To prevent further price fluctuations harming their own economic position, the Americans added stipulations prohibiting the sale of wheat by the Nationalist government, although this policy was relaxed somewhat in the aftermath of the Japanese invasion.[99] Negotiators also insisted that preferential treatment be given to American shipping companies, and that half the wheat be milled in the United States.[100] This latter stipulation helped to briefly revive the export market for American flour to China, which had boomed in the late nineteenth century before declining significantly following the rapid growth of the native milling industry.[101] The flood provided American millers with an irresistible advantage while also offering exporters a means to circumvent the import tariffs that had been established in the late 1920s following the Nationalist takeover of the Chinese Maritime Customs Service.[102]

In the latter half of the twentieth century, the United States government would donate huge quantities of food aid to many of those countries that had by then become grouped in the Third World. Often couched in terms of charity, critics argued that food aid allowed the Americans to dispose of agricultural surplus and also to manipulate the policies of nominally independent postcolonial states.[103] Historians usually trace the origin of such policies to the Food for Peace initiatives of

---

[98] Wang, 'Jiuji shuizai'.   [99] Pietz, *Engineering the State*, pp. 65–8.

[100] Chou, '1931 nian Zhong-Mei'.

[101] At the end of the nineteenth century American millers had enjoyed a brief export boom as the demand for their produce soared among wealthy urban consumers in China. This market was stifled in part by the Anti-American Boycott of 1905 during which Chinese patriots shunned American produce in retaliation for discriminatory immigration policies. A far more significant factor was the growth of a local industrialised milling industry. See Meissner, *Chinese Capitalists.*

[102] On these tariffs see Van de Ven, *Breaking with the Past.*

[103] Jachertz and Nützenadel, 'Coping with hunger?'

the early 1950s.[104] The 1931 wheat loans may not have been as politically manipulative as the arrangements that developed during the Cold War, yet they did seem to anticipate the use of aid as a means of surplus dumping, obscured behind the façade of humanitarian assistance. Stipulations favouring the use of American companies were an early instance of what would later become known as aid tying, whereby donor nations determine how recipients spend the financial assistance rendered.[105] The government of Benito Mussolini also engaged in a form of aid tying, using the Italian portion of the Boxer Indemnity Fund to pay for tools donated to the NFRC.[106] What appeared to be an act of charity was a generous subsidy for the Italian tool industry.

The practice of aid tying has been criticised for increasing the cost of goods and undermining local markets. This certainly seems to have been the case with the wheat loan. As flood-stricken communities waited months throughout the summer of 1931 for shiploads of relief to cross the Pacific Ocean, there was surplus grain in China that could have been utilised. In Wuhan, people complained about the smell of rotting rice and grain in godowns, while, just a short distance away, refugees were starving.[107] Meanwhile, in Shanghai there were warehouses full of wheat and flour that could no longer find a market. Had Song secured a capital loan as he had originally requested, he could have bought far greater quantities of cheaper Australian or Canadian wheat, or better still, purchased food going to waste in Wuhan.[108] Wang Weiyin suggested that Song should buy surplus grain from Manchuria, achieving the dual aims of stimulating the war-torn economy while also providing relief.[109]

Flawed as the wheat loan may have been, it had some undeniably positive effects. Not only did grain alleviate hunger directly, but news

[104] Ibid.; Ahlberg, *Transplanting the Great Society*.
[105] Although in this instance the United States government was tying a *loan* rather than aid, essentially paying China to buy its unwanted surplus and then demanding repayment with interest.
[106] RNFRC, p. 17. The Boxer Indemnity was funded by the reparations payments demanded from the Qing dynasty by the eight nations that repressed the rebellion at the turn of the twentieth century. It remains a source of funding for academic research and other ventures to this day.
[107] *Hankow Herald*, 20 August 1931. There is a painful irony in the fact that a headline reading 'Grains Goods Rotting' is followed immediately by another reading 'Urgent Relief Needed'.
[108] The market pages of the *North China Herald* demonstrate that foreign merchants had a keen grasp of the effect that the wheat loans were having on the domestic and international grain prices; see for example *North China Herald*, 28 July 1931.
[109] Wang, 'Jiuji shuizai'.

of the loan also helped to reverse the rapid inflation of prices that was exacerbating the flood-induced entitlements crisis.[110] American wheat probably helped avert famine in some areas. Yet in the longer term, saturating the market with cheap foreign wheat had devastating effects for local producers.[111] Since as early as the Han dynasty (206 BCE–220 CE), administrators had been aware that 'expensive grain hurts the people, cheap grain hurts the farmers'.[112] For years after the flood, farmers paid the price for the cheap grain that had been used to feed refugees. Between 1931 and 1933 the value of wheat across China dropped by a third partly because of the loan.[113] The insistence that half the wheat be milled in America worsened conditions for the already depressed Chinese flour industry. In Wuhan, there was a fourteen-fold increase in foreign flour imports between 1930 and 1932. Local millers had still not fully recovered half a decade later.[114]

The flood could not have happened at a worse time for the fledgling Nationalist economy. As China was one of the few nations operating on the silver standard, it had been shielded from the worst effects of the Great Depression during its first two years.[115] The decision of a succession of major economies, beginning with Great Britain, to abandon the gold standard in 1931, meant that China had lost its cushion against the effects of the global economic downturn. The price of silver, which had been depreciating steadily since the 1870s, suddenly began to increase. This not only harmed the export market but also ensured that domestic products faced increased competition from imports. The Great Depression may have struck China later than most countries, yet the delay did nothing to soften the blow.[116] In considering the downturn of the Chinese economy in the early 1930s, Tomoko Shiroyama and other economic historians assign primary importance to global fluctuations in commodity prices. While this macroeconomic context

---

[110] In Hankou rice rose from $15 to $16.5 per picul by 1 September. In early November, with the arrival of the loan, it dropped to $15. See RNFRC, p. 190. This was still above the non-crisis price of $14.3. See Xie, *Yi jiu san yi nian*, p. 16.

[111] Chou, '1931 nian Zhong-Mei'; Lin, 'Ping 1931 nian Jianghuai shuizai'.

[112] Li, *Fighting Famine*, p. 119.

[113] Shiroyama, *China during the Great Depression*, p. 93. In his otherwise excellent discussion of the rural depression in early 1930s China, Shiroyama fails to consider the economic impact of the 1931 American wheat loan.

[114] Hankou's native flour industry was decimated by the huge rise in imports in the early 1930s. In 1930 imports had accounted for a mere $31,133; in 1931 this rose to a staggering $464,986 and in 1932 $437,921. See Yuan, *Hankou zujie zhi*, pp. 102–4.

[115] Shiroyama, *China during the Great Depression*.   [116] Ibid.

undoubtedly played a primary role, the flood amplified China's financial woes considerably. The relief effort demonstrated the extent to which the global economy had already extended its reach deep into rural subsistence systems. Hans van de Ven has cautioned historians not to view the globalisation of China in the early twentieth century as an exclusively urban phenomenon.[117] The case of the American wheat loan illustrates his point clearly. Chinese farmers had become entangled in a vast network of economic relations, which linked them to their wheat-growing counterparts across the Pacific Ocean. This relationship helped to ameliorate some of the immediate symptoms of Chinese poverty, but it also became one of its underlying causes.

A Perilous Journey

Setting aside the economic debates, the American wheat loan was a hugely impractical affair. The costs involved in transporting massive quantities of food halfway across the world were shockingly high, eventually taking up 14 per cent of the entire operating costs of the NFRC.[118] This was essentially a huge transfer of wealth from flood-stricken China to the American shipping industry. Transporting grain halfway around the world was also extremely time consuming. The wheat and flour did not even begin to arrive in Shanghai until mid-November, four months after the flood started. Later deliveries were significantly delayed by the Japanese attack on the port, during which grain ships were forced to dock amidst 'roar of guns and the droning of hostile aeroplanes'.[119] The Battle for Shanghai also had a direct impact on flood refugees who had fled city. In early February 1932 a camp in the Zhabei 闸北 district, housing 10,000 people displaced by the disaster, was subjected to successive days of Japanese aerial bombardment and machine-gunning, resulting in an estimated fifty casualties[120]. Hope Simpson was furious at this brazen attack on helpless refugees, and wrote a series of angry letters to the Japanese consul before lodging a formal complaint with the League of Nations. The consul denied the deliberate targeting of civilians, attributing the attack to 'a mishap of stray bullets', and blaming it on the fact that the camp was surrounded by barbed wire, and so

[117] Van de Ven, 'Globalizing Chinese History', p. 4.
[118] Chou, '1931 nian Zhong-Mei'.   [119] RNFRC, p. 29.
[120] 'John Hope Simpson to T. V. Soong', 11 February 1932, JHS 6i. For full details of the Japanese assault on Zhabei see Henriot, 'Neighbourhood under Storm'.

had been easily mistaken for a legitimate military target.[121] Hope Simpson countered that this barbed wire did not exist, and pointed out that the camp was marked clearly with a Red Cross flag at its entrance, and a Blue Cross flag over its hospital.[122] This bombing was one of the many ways that war hindered the relief effort.

Having passed through the active conflict zone of Shanghai, the wheat then had to traverse a vast inundated area. With the rail and road infrastructure destroyed by water, and with larger boats struggling to negotiate the uneven submerged terrain, often the only viable means of transport was the humble sampan.[123] Once again, a trusty vernacular technology proved more reliable than its ostentatious modern rivals. The difficulties facing transport crews were further compounded by the fact that many people saw the wheat as an easy source of income. Parasitism ranged from petty pilfering, with boat crews skimming a little flour off each sack, to larger scale acts of criminality, such as when a Shanghai gang murdered a warehouse guard so that they could steal a large quantity of wheat.[124] Relief grain was also an easy target for the estimated 20 million bandits who operated in 1930s China.[125] Bandit attacks on relief boats were so common that the NFRC was forced to hire armed escorts and pay danger money to shipping companies.[126] In one case, an army of bandits brandishing swords stole thirty-one sacks of grain from a train.[127] While commission workers complained bitterly about the effect of banditry, there was little mention of the predation that occurred at the hands of government troops. When two generals supposedly allied to the Nationalists, helped themselves to 2,000 tons of wheat, Song was placed in the invidious position of having to reassure his fellow NFRC members that the government would replace the lost grain.[128]

The Communists were also a significant hindrance. In May 1932, they commandeered a shipment of grain intended for flood victims in Anhui

[121] 'Japanese Consulate to John Hope Simpson', 6 March 1932 JHS 6i.
[122] 'John Hope Simpson to the League of Nations', 17[h] February 1932, JHS 6i. Circumstantial evidence certainly seems to support Hope Simpson's account. Christian Henriot has described how the Japanese forces often inflicted violence upon civilians in Zhabei in 1932. See Henriot, 'Neighbourhood under Storm'.
[123] Lindbergh, *North to the Orient*, p. 139.
[124] 'John Hope Simpson to F. B. Bourdillon', 23 February 1932, JHS 6i.
[125] Billingsley, *Bandits in Republican China*, p. 1.
[126] RNFRC; Yorke, *China Changes*, p. 61.
[127] 'John Hope Simpson to F. B. Bourdillon', 23 February 1932, JHS 6i.
[128] 'John Hope Simpson to F. B. Bourdillon', 23 February 1932, JHS 6i.

and kidnapped the accompanying relief workers.[129] This was one of numerous similar incidents. Although rarely mentioned in official histories of the rise of the party, kidnapping had been a favoured strategy of the Communists since the late 1920s. Missionaries proved to be particularly lucrative targets, as their home congregations would often raise significant funds to have them released. When ransom demands were not met, the Communists were known to torture and kill their hostages.[130] Several NFRC workers met this fate, including Reverend Ferguson and three of his Chinese co-workers.[131] The Irish missionary Father Sands proved more fortunate, eventually being ransomed with funds provided by his Columban mission.[132] Though they had made him live among rats and other vermin, Sands described those who lead his captors as 'perfectly honest men, and really convinced Communists'. However, he claimed that most of the ordinary troops 'were only Communists because otherwise they could not obtain any livelihood.'[133]

Given their predilection for kidnapping and murdering his staff, Hope Simpson took an understandably dim view of the Communists. This did not prevent him from negotiating with their representatives. In his private correspondence, he revealed that he and Song had agreed terms with the leadership of one Soviet about how relief work could be conducted in areas under Communist control. This deal was conducted under strict secrecy, lest Chiang Kai-shek or any of the other aggressive militarists in the Nationalist regime discovered that the NFRC was in effect financing the enemy. Song argued that 'far from it being undesirable for us to work with the Reds, it was highly advantageous at this time that we should do so . . . we should use every endeavour to get into touch with them and work with them'.[134] This conciliatory approach seems to support Margherita Zanasi's characterisation of the Nationalist regime in the early 1930s as a party divided by the conflicted aims of economic

[129] RNFRC, p. 88.
[130] In 1930, for example, the Communists kidnapped two medical missionaries in Fujian named Eleanor Davis and Miss Nettleton. They were tortured and executed when the demanded ransom was not forthcoming. See *North China Herald*, 7 October 1931. I am grateful to Kitty Kavanagh for sharing this family story with me. For other examples of the kidnapping of missionaries and Chinese Christians during this period see Barrett, *Red Lacquered Gate*, pp. 265–85.
[131] Yorke, *China Changes*, p. 61; *Chinese Recorder*, November 1932.
[132] Barrett, *Red Lacquered Gate*, pp. 265–85.
[133] 'John Hope Simpson: Notes on a Meeting with Father MacPolin and Father Sands', 7 December 1932, JHS 6i.
[134] 'John Hope Simpson to K. Zillacus', 29 June 1932, JHS 6i.

consolidation and military conquest. While Chiang and his counterparts sought to starve the Communists out of the hills, Song surreptitiously sent them food, using the olive branch of relief to keep lines of communications open.

Having undergone a tortuous journey through some of the most dangerous terrain on earth, the much-reduced stocks of wheat finally reached flood-stricken communities. In a last bitter twist, it transpired that few refugees truly wanted wheat. Unlike their counterparts in the north, farmers in central China tended to grow wheat for the market rather than personal consumption, and did not have the requisite knowledge and utensils to cook the grain.[135] Many refugees decided to exchange wheat for more familiar foodstuffs. With the market saturated, they often lost as much as 20 per cent of the financial value in this transaction.[136] The antipathy towards wheat was so strong that labour relief organisers found it hard recruit workers from the Yangzi region, who demanded to be paid in rice.[137] Characteristically, the NFRC took this failure as a sign of success – after all, a population willing to sell grain at below the market value could not truly be starving. In reality, this represented yet another deleterious consequence of a relief strategy designed to serve the United States Farm Board not Chinese refugees. The grain merchants who capitalised on a saturated market were the last in a long line of disaster profiteers. In its journey from the American soil to the bowls of Chinese refugees, the wheat had profited bandits, gangsters, Communists, Nationalists, shipping companies, foreign mill owners and even Herbert Hoover.

Emergency and Labour Relief

Having managed to transport grain to the heart of the flood zone, the NFRC began to implement its relief strategy in late autumn. They began with an emergency phase during which refugees were fed with daily rations distributed in camps or through larger allocations within their own villages. Much to the chagrin of the practical humanitarians, the Buddhist philanthropist Zhu Qinglan was placed in charge of this phase of the relief effort.[138] Being an advocate of charity for its own sake, Zhu seems to have expended little effort on monitoring distribution. This was, in any case, a virtually impossible task. Some camp administrators

---

[135] Li, *Fighting Famine*, p. 93.   [136] RNFRC, p. 192.
[137] Ibid., p. 126.   [138] RNFRC, p. 63.

attempted to separate refugees in accordance with a hierarchy of need, hoping to ensure that only the truly destitute received food, and making those deemed wealthy enough pay.[139] Such policies proved impossible to enforce. To avoid unrest, camp administrators were forced to distribute rations to all assembled refugees. Having left his base in Shanghai to visit Wuhan, Hope Simpson complained that in one camp on Black Hill 黑 山 (Heishan) there were 150,000 refugees housed, of whom only 5 per cent were in true danger of starvation, yet to relieve this minority, it was necessary to provide rations for the remaining 95 per cent. Hope Simpson resigned himself to the fact that this was 'in accordance with Chinese principles'.[140] Few people seemed to have considered that this absence of obvious starvation may actually have been a testament to the success of Zhu Qinglan's supposedly irrational relief strategy.

As the relief effort continued, administrators were able to institute greater discipline, excluding those they deemed unworthy from distributions and requiring those who remained to undertake physical labour or to participate in handicraft activities.[141] Lillian Li has described how during the 1935 Yellow River Flood, relief camp administrators used their authority to compel refugees to adhere to a range of new bodily standards expected of modern citizens. To receive food, men were forced to cut off their traditional braided ponytails – known as queues – and women were made to unbind their feet.[142] There is no evidence to suggest that such prescriptions were adopted in 1931, but camps were certainly used as didactic spaces, in which authorities used propaganda to inculcate political and social messages.

While administrators had only limited power to control the distribution of emergency rations in camps, in rural areas, the NFRC was forced to surrender control almost completely, delegating responsibility for distribution to village chief men.[143] There is little evidence to describe how this process worked in practice. Studies from other regions suggest that major principal–agent problems of corruption can develop when local elites are entrusted to distribute relief.[144] The context of rural China in the 1930s would certainly seem conducive to the development of such problems. Prasenjit Duara has described the significant breakdown in

---

[139] *North China Herald*, 1 September 1931.
[140] 'John Hope Simpson: Report on the National Flood Relief Commission', 30 June 1932. JHS 6i.
[141] Kong, 'Minguo Jiangsu', p. 95.   [142] Li, 'Life and Death', p. 474.
[143] RNFRC, p. 78.
[144] On principal–agent problems in relief see Ó Gráda, *Famine*, p. 210.

the structure of village governance during the early twentieth century, as predatory brokers working at the behest of absentee landlords took over from more paternalistic local leaders.[145] In Hubei these structural changes occurred against a backdrop of brutal political violence between impoverished farmers and rural elites, as William Rowe has described.[146] Given this fractious context, it is certainly plausible that local leaders would have taken advantage of their monopoly control over relief in order to advance their own economic and political interests. Yet we cannot assume that this was the case. A traditional paternalistic ethos continued to exist in many rural areas, as Pierre Fuller has argued convincingly.[147] The leaders of the NFRC do not seem to have entertained the possibility that rural elites might fail to deliver relief, and were far more concerned that they would prove *overly generous*. They fretted that village leaders would be unable to say no to their compatriots.[148] This concern revealed much about the bizarre sense of prioritisation that permeated the NFRC, whose members worried more about food reaching too many people than in failing to reach those in need.

While relief was being distributed in camps and villages, Liu Ruiheng and his colleagues were introducing a range of measures designed to tackle the burgeoning health crisis. Police recruits were trained as sanitary inspectors in an effort to establish hygienic discipline within camps. Refugees were employed to dig latrines, dispose of refuse and carry water to tanks for sterilisation with alum and chloride of lime.[149] Emergency hospitals were established to offer medicinal assistance. Those found to be infected with smallpox and cholera were placed in special isolation wards.[150] The government closed medical schools and sent their students to assist the NFRC in its inoculation campaign.[151] Teams set up stalls on streets, visited houses and established travelling clinics, such as the one pictured in Figure 5.2.[152] In total, health workers administered more than 2 million injections, an impressive figure, yet only a small fraction of the flood-affected population. Unfortunately, the majority remained isolated in villages or stranded on flood islands far beyond the reach of needles.

---

[145] Duara, *Culture, Power and the State.*   [146] Rowe, *Crimson Rain.*
[147] Pierre Fuller, 'North China Famine Revisited'.   [148] RNFRC, p. 81.
[149] Ibid., pp. 161–2.   [150] Kong, 'Minguo Jiangsu', p. 98.
[151] E. C. Lobenstine 'The Work of Missionaries and Other Westerners in Flood Relief', SOAS Archives 10/7/15.
[152] RNFRC, pp. 151–61.

Figure 5.2. The inoculation campaign, 1931. (*Report of the National Flood Relief Commission 1931–1932*. Shanghai: National Flood Relief Commission, 1933. Reproduced courtesy of Trinity College Library, Cambridge)

The efforts of NRFC inoculation teams met with resistance from refugees who did not want to be injected. Although the practice of variolation – whereby infected tissue was used to immunise against infection – had actually originated in China, its modern variant had little resonance with local medical practices.[153] In his classic ethnographic study of a cholera epidemic in Yunnan in 1942, the anthropologist Francis Hsu described how many people chose not be inoculated and instead to rely on a combination of traditional medical and ritual techniques, including dietary restrictions, slaughter prohibitions and sexual abstinence.[154] This reflected a religious conceptualisation of disease causation, involving cosmological principles similar to those found in moral meteorology; indeed, we might describe this as a form of moral aetiology. Those who resisted the NFRC inoculation campaign seem to have had similar doubts about the efficacy of foreign medicine. This was no doubt compounded by their distrust of officials, discussed further in the next chapter.

[153] RNFRC, p. 166; 'Zhongguo Hongshizihui Hankou fenhui cheng yanmai gongzuo wen', HSSDX.
[154] Hsu, 'Cholera Epidemic', p. 141.

David Arnold has described how resistance to inoculation in India was inextricable from broader antipathy towards the British imperialist state.[155] For ordinary Chinese citizens, inoculation was freighted with similar associations, albeit that their reticence was directed more towards their own state and its overzealous modernisation policies. The same government that had torn down temples and derided environmental beliefs now called on people to disavow moral aetiology and traditional treatments and submit their bodies to an alien biomedical procedure. It is important not to attribute resistance to inoculation purely to cultural factors. Fear of pain was also an issue, as it was in Europe and India.[156] Although Hsu refused to grant credence to such mundane factors, many of his Yunnan informants claimed that they did not want to be inoculated simply because it hurt.[157] This was probably also a factor in 1931.

The NFRC deployed a comprehensive propaganda campaign to persuade refugees of the benefits of inoculation.[158] The public health worker Wu Zhangyao 伍长耀 later detailed the many techniques used, which included lurid posters, wireless announcements, instructional films shown at cinemas and even leaflets dropped from planes.[159] Some health educators even resorted to the popular techniques used by patent medicine peddlers, standing on street corners and entertaining audiences with rousing speeches peppered with patriotic slogans, before extolling the virtues of inoculation and hospitalisation. One of the most intriguing techniques was the use of processions. Wu observed that a 'properly planned and well executed parade' could be 'an effective weapon' for public health campaigners. 'Steeped as they are in age-old traditions of ceremonial, revelling in dragon festivals, and funeral and marriage processions miles long, the Chinese are particularly susceptible to this type of appeal.'[160] Once again, the symbolic power of popular religion was being repurposed. Innovative and dedicated as they may have been, the message promulgated by public health workers struggled to filter out beyond urban areas. Even when information did manage to reach the countryside, refugees were not always receptive. In some instances,

---

[155] Arnold, *Colonizing the Body*, pp. 219–22.   [156] Harrison, *Disease and the Modern World*.

[157] Hsu insisted that this was mere obfuscation, citing the popularity of acupuncture as evidence to dispute the possibility that Chinese villagers would be afraid of needles. Hsu, 'Cholera Epidemic', p. 144.

[158] RNFRC, p. 177.

[159] Known as C. Y. Wu. These techniques were employed both in 1931 and 1932. In Wu et al. *Cholera*, pp. 145–78.

[160] Ibid., p. 154.

NFRC workers were forced to adopt a more coercive strategy, denying rations to those who refused to be injected.[161] It is doubtful that relying on the compulsion of hunger would have built much trust between refugees and health professionals.

For almost a year, relief policies were constrained by the physical effects of the disaster and inhibited by domestic and international conflicts. It was not until the disaster reconstruction phase in the spring of 1932 that that NFRC was able to implement a strategy that fully reflected its institutional ideology. It was at this stage the CIFRC began exercising a formidable amount of control over government policy. Politicians simply handed this private organisation responsibility for all major reconstruction projects, arguing that the experts employed by the commission had by far the most experience developing 'methods of control of the labourers'.[162] This was partly a matter of expedience. The dyke network needed to be constructed quickly, so that China might avoid being inundated again in the summer of 1932. It was also a matter of politics. With the government distracted by the Japanese invasion, Song and his colleagues were happy to delegate responsibility to an enthusiastic outside party. Accordingly, the Chinese government chose to place the labour and lives of more than 1,100,000 of its citizens in the hands of a foreign-dominated organisation.[163] This was the greatest opportunity that the CIFRC would ever be given to impose its ideas upon the Chinese population. Over the next few months, refugees who were still reeling from the trauma of disaster were subjected to a punishingly hard schedule of labour relief. Work teams such as the one pictured in Figures 5.3 and 5.4 could soon be found toiling throughout the flood zone.

The NFRC paid workers with food. They had little choice but to do so, as the United States government had forbidden them to sell the wheat. Although a matter of necessity, this strategy proved to be an efficient means of ensuring worker compliance. The NFRC had initially complained that news of the wheat loan had had 'a bad psychological effect' upon the workforce.[164] What this meant was that the decline in the price of grain caused by the anticipated arrival of the wheat loan had made workers significantly less insecure. For the first time in months it seemed that the price of food was about to become affordable. Being in a less precarious position, workers were emboldened to negotiate more favourable terms of employment. By replacing their cash wage with a wheat ration, the CIFRC undermined this negotiating position. Workers

---

[161] RNFRC, p. 177.   [162] RNFRC, pp. 114, 124.   [163] Ibid.   [164] Ibid., p. 60.

Figure 5.3. Labour relief workers in central China, 1931–1932. (*Report of the National Flood Relief Commission 1931–1932*. Shanghai: National Flood Relief Commission, 1933. Reproduced courtesy of Trinity College Library, Cambridge)

Figure 5.4. Relief labourers reconstructing dykes in 1932. (*Report of the National Flood Relief Commission 1931–1932*. Shanghai: National Flood Relief Commission, 1933. Reproduced courtesy of Trinity College Library, Cambridge)

had to accept a punishing schedule of labour to earn their allotted rations.

Low wages were, in fact, an important component of the 'scientific' approach to labour relief advocated by the CIFRC. Underpaying was a strategy designed to exclude 'professional mendicants' from relief projects, the logic being, as Mallory surmised, that 'no one who could possibly get along otherwise would toil for less than the usual rate of pay.'[165] This logic echoed the principle of 'less eligibility' that governed British workhouses in the nineteenth century. To ensure that only the truly destitute were accommodated, workhouse administrators sought to ensure that the terms of employment were kept below the standard of the outside labour market.[166] Such techniques had also been used in the test camps that were developed in British India as a diagnostic device for famine.[167] If Indian labourers were willing able to accept starvation wages, administrators could be certain that a subsistence crisis was occurring. The CIFRC did not use low wages as a diagnostic test, but rather as a means to determine whether refugees were morally qualified for assistance.

The wage scheme adopted by the NFRC was justified by the artificial division between relief work and the labour market. Refugees were not understood to be selling their labour as a commodity, as they might in a non-crisis period. Instead, they were being *given* work as a form of charity. This was a convenient fiction which furnished governments with the requisite labour to conduct otherwise prohibitively expensive infrastructural improvements. Flood refugees had to work for eleven hours a day and were paid a piece rate for the quantity of earth they shifted.[168] Deciding this was still too generous, the NFRC later cut rations of salt and fuel and made labourers buy these items, along with any vegetables or meat they might want. Comfort and hygiene were not high on list of priorities for those organising labour relief. Workers often lived in cramped and squalid conditions. In one camp in Jiangsu they slept in long sheds without even the space to turn in their sleep. Soon many workers began suffering from skin diseases.[169]

---

[165] Mallory, *China*, p. 174.   [166] Ó Gráda, *Famine*, p. 212.

[167] Mukherjee, *Hungry Bengal*.

[168] RNFRC, p. 126. Here the NFRC once again overstated the novelty of their practices. Imperial administrators had not only also quantified remuneration by calculating earth moved, but had also paid labour relief workers considerably lower than the usual rate for constructing dykes. See Li, *Fighting Famine in North China*, p. 59.

[169] *North China Herald*, 12 April 1932.

Labourers found creative ways to ameliorate these conditions. Years after the flood, Wang Guowei 王国威 recalled how he and his fellow workers attended multiple grain distributions, duping their employers by pretending to be different people. This allowed them to collect up to three times their stipulated allocation.[170] The CIFRC lived in perpetual fear of such deceptions. Ultimately, however, all their economising proved unwarranted, as the cost of the reconstruction effort actually came in considerably *under budget.*[171] This was taken as a point of pride for the CIFRC, as it demonstrated that they had organised reconstruction with efficiency and economy. Nobody seemed to reflect on the fact that if the wage scheme had been less fanatically frugal, then this budgetary surplus would have been passed on to the impoverished refugees. Such considerations were unthinkable to those who operated from behind an impenetrable ideological barrier of practical humanitarianism.

Not all refugees were employed in labour relief. The NFRC also funded some households to undertake farm rehabilitation. Once again, this built upon CIFRC policies developed over the previous decade.[172] Mutual aid societies and rural cooperatives were used to provide credit to those who would otherwise be compelled to borrow at steep interest rates from moneylenders.[173] The targets for these schemes were diligent and honest farmers – the moral mirror images of paupers and mendicants who haunted the imaginations of many relief workers. Farm rehabilitation seemed to have a fairly positive impact. It allowed rural households to purchase tools and seed to reconstruct their systems of subsistence. This may have contributed to the high yields harvested in 1932.[174] This strategy demonstrated what could be achieved when relief agencies trusted refugees to manage their own recovery.[175] Unfortunately, the 360,000 farm families who received farm rehabilitation loans were a mere drop in the ocean. Hope Simpson later conceded that farm rehabilitation had been the least successful aspect of the relief effort.[176]

---

[170] Wang, *Wuhan Wenshi Ziliao*, pp. 146–7.   [171] RNFRC, p. 115.

[172] Nathan, *History of the China International Famine Relief Commission*, pp. 27–34.

[173] RNFRC, pp. 92–103.

[174] Although the relatively good harvest was also attributable to flood deposits and favourable meteorological conditions. For an analysis of weather patterns see Kueh, *Agricultural Instability in China*.

[175] Critics of existing relief policies suggest that successful relief policies must be used to support the autonomous survival strategies of communities themselves, rather than imposing top-down schemes. See De Waal, *Famine That Kills*; Edkins, *Whose Hunger*.

[176] 'John Hope Simpson: Report on the National Flood Relief Commission', 30 June 1932, JHS 6i.

Although the CIFRC took a great deal of credit for the reconstruction, they had only been responsible for rebuilding larger dykes. The
much greater task of rebuilding village dykes and polders was delegated
to local elites.[177] The same people who had been given the responsibility to allocate emergency rations were now contracted to employ relief
labourers. This strategy had deep implications for the way that China
reconstructed. The NFRC recognised that before the flood the hydraulic
system had been 'piecemeal' because it 'was not originally constructed
according to a modern scientific plan'.[178] The widespread destruction
of dykes provided a unique opportunity to redesign and standardise the
whole system. Yet, with the exception of the Huai River, where extensive
conservancy work had already begun, the NFRC chose to rebuild an exact
replica of what had been destroyed.[179] Though partly a matter of expedience, with all projects having to be finished before the summer rains,
this decision was also a concession to local elites. The rationalisation and
standardisation of the hydraulic network would have been a complicated
business, involving the reorganisation of tenancies and the compensation
of affected landowners. It was far easier just to allow people to reconstruct
a fallible system.

There was one group that was delegated funds that did not make
it into any of the official reports. Song and Hope Simpson used back
channels to pay the Communists to reconstruct hydraulic networks
under their command. They often had little choice in the matter. The
Communists had kidnapped relief workers and stipulated in their ransom demands that they must be granted control of labour relief schemes
in their territory and allowed to complete them free from Nationalist
harassment.[180] The relief methodology employed in Communist areas
was vastly different from that found under the CIFRC. Labourers worked
for six hours a day rather than eleven, their wages were higher and they
were paid per capita rather than piece-rate.[181] At this stage, at least,
the Communists aimed to strengthen the rights and rewards enjoyed by
workers. When Rewi Alley later wrote about the 1931 flood, in his capacity as unofficial foreign spokesman for the Maoist regime, he heaped
praise upon He Long 贺龙 and the Red Army for saving the people by
rebuilding dykes, while all around the government was machine-gunning

[177] RNFRC, p. 82.   [178] RNFRC, p. 189.
[179] On the Huai River see Pietz, *Engineering the State.*
[180] 'John Hope Simpson: Resume of Communist Demands', 7 December 1932, JHS 6i.
[181] Yorke, *China Changes*, p. 74.

villages.[182] This version of history omitted the fact that the Communists had, in fact, been paid by their Nationalist enemies.

The Many Parents of Success

All involved seemed convinced that the NFRC was a resounding success. For the Nationalist government, whose first years in office had been hounded by a succession of disasters and wars, the relief campaign seemed to mark a decisive step forward. Song Ziwen wrote proudly of how an organisation of more than 7,000 staff had recruited and trained millions of workers, and protected them from the predation of Communists and bandits. The success of the NFRC had helped bolster official legitimacy with the result that 'the peasant population now regards the Central Government with more interest and respect.'[183] The freshly reconstructed hydraulic network seemed to objectify the government's commitment its people. A 1,812 km length of dykes had been built along the Yangzi, and 337 km along the Han River. The amount of earthwork conducted in just six months would have been sufficient to construct a dyke 2 metres high and 2 metres broad around the entire length of the equator.[184] Better still, this staggering engineering feat had been achieved under budget!

Each of the non-governmental agencies involved in the relief campaign claimed its own portion of this victory. For the CIFRC, the reconstruction phase seemed to vindicate the scientific approach to the management of labour. Dwight Edwards concluded that it had been 'quite conclusively demonstrated that the spade is the best tool in famine relief and has outdistanced the rice bowl. The latter is still necessary under certain conditions but the indigent are ever with us and will eat free food whenever and as long as offered.'[185] Protestant missionaries rejoiced that they had finally taught this once indifferent Oriental race the value of philanthropy, noting that, while they had once worked for China, now finally they were working under Chinese leadership.[186] Their Catholic counterparts thanked God that the flood

---

[182] Alley, *Man against Flood*, p. 16; Alley would later claim to have played an instrumental role in persuading the NFRC to provision He Long with wheat. Hope Simpson certainly did know Alley, who was then working for the Shanghai Municipal Council, yet Alley is not mentioned in relation to this decision in Hope Simpson's papers. See Airey, *Learner in China*, pp. 103–4.

[183] RNFRC, pp. 193–4.   [184] Ibid., pp. 138–9.

[185] Dwight W. Edwards 'The Engineer and Famine Relief', DEP 12/7/97.

[186] *The Chinese Recorder*, November 1931.

had allowed them to garner 'a landslide of conversions' among the 'pagans'.[187] For the League of Nations, reeling under criticisms about their ineffectual political response to Japanese aggression, the relief campaign pointed to a more successful technical collaboration with the Chinese government.[188] In the United States, the government sought to capitalise on its new relationship with China, negotiating a further US$50 million wheat and cotton loan in 1933.[189] Each of these groups congratulated themselves on a job well done.

These positive assessments were not deliberately misleading. In most cases the authors most likely believed them to be true. There is no reason to doubt that those involved in relief had anything other than compassionate motivations. Even those who subscribed to somewhat stark formulae regarding the correct treatment of impoverished people were, in their own way, attempting to improve the lot of the disaster-stricken population. The problem was that they reached their positive conclusions by using selective criteria that excluded any inconvenient evidence. In all the glowing endorsements of the relief effort any discussion of the issue of flood mortality was conspicuously absent. When the death toll was mentioned, it was used solely to highlight the magnitude of the initial disaster. Fatalities were never used as an index to gauge the success of official policies. While the government claimed the survivors, the dead were nature's victims.

Rather than referencing these most vital of statistics, each group employed indices that reflected their own professional biases. Building on the work of Robert Chambers, Alex de Waal has noted that the assessments provided by disaster experts can be coloured by various forms of professional bias. This occurs when people concentrate solely on the one specific area of prevention or alleviation in which they themselves have expertise. This results in a failure to appreciate the 'closely interconnected and intermeshed nature' of all complex issues surrounding a disaster.[190] The NFRC, which divided the relief effort into a series of separate problems to be solved, proved the perfect incubator for professional bias. The medics judged their effectiveness in terms of the quantity of inoculations administered, charities quantified the donations they received, engineers used an equation of earth moved relative to wheat consumed and missionaries counted their converts. Each group succumbed to a form of circular reasoning, whereby their specific strategic

---

[187] Quoted in Barrett, *Red Lacquered Gate*, p. 284.   [188] Borowy, 'Thinking Big', p. 215.
[189] Zanasi, *Saving the Nation*, p. 98.   [190] De Waal, *Famine That Kills*, p. 21.

objective became the exclusive criterion used to determine success. The millions of people who died fell through the gap between these statistics.

Even when using the index of systemic improvement favoured by technical experts, the NFRC was far from the overwhelming success that was claimed. The fact that the dyke network had survived the 1932 flood season was extremely fortunate. Many of the most lethal floods of the nineteenth century had occurred with the Yangzi had breached dykes for two successive years.[191] Yet the absence of flooding in 1932 was not attributable solely to the actions of the NFRC. It simply had not rained very much that year.[192] When the hydraulic network was severely tested three years later, it once again failed, resulting in the devastating Yangzi floods of 1935.[193] The problem was not that the NFRC had constructed dykes that were too small or weak; it was rather that they had failed to learn any fundamental lessons from the flood. In an analysis of historical reactions to disasters, Christian Pfister has distinguished between 'cumulative learning', which prompts societies to react in accordance with an established pattern, and 'fundamental learning', which prompts them to adopt more holistic solutions aimed at root causes.[194] For the sake of expedience, and not wishing to disturb the regime of rural property rights, the NFRC had reconstructed dykes exactly in accordance with their original design.[195] This was an act of cumulative learning, which failed to appreciate that uncoordinated and piecemeal dyke network had contributed to the disaster. In this sense, the reconstruction effort represented something of a wasted opportunity for more systematic reform.

While the NFRC spoke at great volume about the dykes that had been constructed, whether consciously or unconsciously, they tended to avoid careful analysis of the death toll. There was a political reason for this, as the huge number of corpses rather undermined the positive story they were trying to tell about the flood. The official narrative was triumphalist, describing a progressive trajectory in which the government gradually imposed order on chaos. This disingenuous interpretation illustrates how political considerations can distort the reality of the disaster regime, creating misleading indices to measure success and obscuring the true nature of causality. The mortality statistics actually revealed how irrelevant official policies often were when confronting with the realities of

---

[191] As we saw in Chapter 1 For example, 1592 and 1593, and the three successive flood years of 1869–1870.
[192] Kueh, *Agricultural Instability in China.*   [193] Ibid.
[194] Pfister, 'Learning from Nature-Induced Disasters', pp. 17–40.   [195] RNFRC, p. 189.

the flood. As we have seen in previous chapters, those in camps, who were under the care of the NFRC, seem to have died in far higher numbers than those left to fend for themselves in rural areas. In one camp in Jiangxi, 2,476 of the 20,249 inhabitants died in just three months. The annual mortality rate was a staggering 48.9 per cent.[196] On some occasions the government bore direct responsibility for exacerbating disease, as we shall see in the next chapter. In most cases mortality resulted from practically uncontrollable dynamic of mass displacement and sanitary collapse. Official grain distributions and public health campaigns could do little when faced with such lethal disease ecologies. For all their qualifications, theoretical insights and technical equipment, the experts of the NFRC were often little more than passive witnesses to a history written by microbes.

[196] RNFRC, pp. 74–5.

6

THE FLOATING POPULATION

We are often told that the poor are grateful for charity. Some of them are, no doubt, but the best amongst the poor are never grateful. They are ungrateful, discontented, disobedient, and rebellious. They are quite right to be so. Charity they feel to be a ridiculously inadequate mode of partial restitution, or a sentimental dole, usually accompanied by some impertinent attempt on the part of the sentimentalist to tyrannise over their private lives.

Oscar Wilde[1]

The refugees are not willing to abandon their household goods and so refuse to leave the disaster zone, they would rather make their own shelters on the hillside. We went to consult with them and promised that we would safeguard their property, we told them one hundred times but they still refused to listen.

Police Chief Su Shi'an 苏世安[2]

By early August 1931, tens of thousands of refugees were sheltering on the railway embankment in northern Wuhan. The journalist Xie Qianmao hired a sampan and went to investigate the conditions. As he negotiated a path amidst floating debris and animal carcasses his eyes were drawn to an elderly woman who was weeping desperately and clinging to a corpse. She informed Xie she was a market gardener from the north of the city whose home had been washed away when the dykes had collapsed. She had been separated from all her family members, except for the deceased child she now cradled in her arms. As she was relating her tragic story, a soldier armed with a gun and a sword approached. He informed the refugees gathered on the embankment that the local

[1] Wilde, *Soul of Man*, p. 4.
[2] Su, 'Gong'anju cheng nanmin taoji Guishan ji Binggongchang', in HSSDX, pp. 293–4.

195

government was prepared to offer them assistance, relocating them to an organised camp where they would receive food and shelter. This must have seemed an attractive proposition to those struggling to live in such precarious circumstances, yet the refugees were suspicious. 'You have come to cheat us,' said one, 'you say you will give us three meals a day, I expect we won't even get one.' Another explained that he could not possibly leave his treasured possessions: 'It was only through bitter struggle that we managed to accumulate our belongings. They might not compare to the possessions of the rich, yet we cannot leave them. There would be no point saving our lives if you didn't save our belongings.' His assistance rebuffed, the soldier departed.[3]

This seemingly insignificant incident offers us a rare glimpse of the attitudes that ordinary refugees held towards official assistance. Their words and deeds contradicted many of the key assumptions that underpinned the methodology promoted by relief institutions. Rather than being willing paupers content to follow the path of least resistance to a life of helpless dependency, those gathered on the railway embankment chose to reject charity, believing it to be an ineffective means of guaranteeing their long-term economic well-being. They distrusted assurances offered by uniformed representatives of the state, preferring to rely on their own autonomous coping strategies. This was not the only time that refugees acted in this manner. The local police chief Su Shi'an, quoted at the beginning of this chapter, was tasked with relocating refugees in Hanyang. He was exasperated by their continual refusal to leave a hillside where they were encamped, despite repeated assurances that the lives and property would be safeguarded.[4] In an even more extreme example, a refugee being transported by the military to conduct labour relief chose to throw himself into the floodwater and swim to his escape.[5]

In this final chapter – the last of our six histories – we travel down into the inundated streets of Wuhan to explore the behaviour of ordinary refugees. Rather than characterising displaced people as a problem requiring technical management, as they were so often viewed by relief agencies, we instead examine the vernacular expertise that refugees employed, as they negotiated hostile natural and political environments. One of the reasons that people chose to reject official relief was because they had developed a profound distrust of the state. In as much as this

---

[3] Xie, *Yi jiu san yi nian*, p. 147.
[4] Su, 'Gong'anju cheng nanmin taoji Guishan ji Binggongchang', in HSSDX, pp. 293–4.
[5] Xie, *Yi jiu san yi nian*, p. 78.

distrust had been inspired by repressive refugee management policies enacted during the flood, it had also been fostered over the previous few years by a violent dynamic of state–society relations. Local military leaders, who were trigger happy at the best of times, were committed to using any means necessary to prevent social and political disruption during the flood. The harsh strategies they deployed destroyed the last vestiges of trust that existed between refugees and the state.

The militarisation of the refugee crisis undermined the considerable efforts that civic organisations in Wuhan made to relieve the suffering of displaced people. It also impinged on the coping strategies employed by refugees themselves. The local state inhibited, and on occasions even criminalised, vernacular expertise. As legitimate sources of nutrition and revenue evaporated, many people found themselves having to rely on the illicit economy – a shadow market that commoditised human bodies in a variety of ways. Eventually, as official anxiety reached fever pitch, the military expelled refugees from the streets and instituted a policy of enforced encampment. This was lauded as a beneficent act of state charity. Yet it probably raised the mortality rate suffered by refugees. Displaced people were rehoused hastily in poorly prepared camps, where they were exposed to a lethal array of epidemic diseases. Refugees, who were perceived to be a danger *to the state*, were themselves endangered *by the state*. In a pattern found all too often, violence and repression became critical catalysts within the disaster regime, vastly exacerbating the humanitarian impact of inundation.

Floating and Wandering

Refugee crises were nothing new. Chinese communities had been coping with them for millennia. Imperial administrators described people displaced by social or environmental disasters as the 'floating population' 流民 (liumin).[6] Never has this term been more appropriate than in 1931, when hundreds of thousands of refugees literally floated across the landscape in search of food and security. Even in a country inured to refugee crises, the scale of population displacement was exceptional. Contemporary estimates suggested that maybe 10 million people were

---

[6] Lu, *Street Criers*, pp. 18–19. This should not to be confused with the term 流动人口 (liudong renkou), also translated as the 'floating population', which is used today to describe rural migrants living outside the area of their official household registration 户口 (hukou).

forced to leave their homes.[7] Recent studies suggest that these original figures vastly underestimated the magnitude of the crisis.[8] On average, 40 per cent of flood-affected people had to leave their homes. In Southern Anhui, the proportion reached 61 per cent.[9] To put this in context, the rate of displacement and homelessness during the Sino-Japanese War of 1937–1945 reached a national average of 26 per cent, with the highest provincial total being 43 per cent.[10] War-induced displacement lasted longer and affected greater numbers, yet the proportionate comparison gives some sense of the social impact of the flood.

China has often been caricatured as having a sedentary culture, with a population reluctant to leave its villages.[11] This is not accurate. The state was probably more active than most in arresting population movement, and there was often a strong cultural affiliation with native place, yet mobility remained a vitally important process shaping Chinese history. In late nineteenth and early twentieth centuries, the scale of internal migration to the north-eastern region of Manchuria alone equalled the westward expansion of the United States, and doubled levels of emigration from Ireland, albeit from a much larger starting base.[12] Meanwhile, southern Chinese migrants were populating much of Southeast Asia, forming large ethnic enclaves throughout Malaya, Singapore, the Dutch East Indies and many other areas. In the Yangzi basin, migration was generally directed towards cities. In his peerless study of Hankou during the late Qing, William Rowe described how successive waves of internal migration helped to forge a vibrant city, with regional groups dominating specific occupational guilds, religious organisations and neighbourhoods.[13] Some were pulled to the city by commercial opportunities, while others were pushed from their homes by poverty and disasters. Migrants who made their way to Wuhan in the early twentieth century were often attracted by the opportunities offered by the burgeoning industrial sector. Many ended up in casual forms employment, working as wharf coolies or rickshaw pullers; their bodies fuelling the urban somatic energy regime. A sizable portion ended up in street professions, working

---

[7] Buck, *1931 Flood*, p. 27.   [8] Xia, *Minguo shiqi*, p. 389.   [9] Buck, *1931 Flood*, p. 33.
[10] The destruction caused by the 1931 flood cannot compare to that of the Sino-Japanese War, which was waged over a larger area and a longer period of time. The total numbers of war refugees was 95,448,753, which exceeded the 50–60 million affected by the flood in 1931. See Mackinnon, 'Refugee Flight'.
[11] For a typical analysis of the supposedly sedentary Chinese population see Fei, *From the Soil*.
[12] Gottschang, 'Economic Change'.   [13] Rowe, *Hankow: Commerce and Society*.

as beggars, fortune-tellers, acrobats and opera singers. This latter group formed part of an itinerant subculture, long considered an affront to Confucian sedentary norms, known traditionally as the 'wandering population' 游民 (youmin).[14]

Pierre-Étienne Will has argued that the 'threat of an aimlessly wandering peasantry... [was] one of the government's central preoccupations in times of crisis' during the late imperial period.[15] Almost all disaster alleviation policies were designed to ensure that members of the floating population – who had been cast adrift temporarily from the moorings of native place – were not subsumed among the ranks of the wandering population – who lived a permanently rootless existence. The re-establishment of taxable agricultural production was the overarching imperative. Over time, the state developed a range of ideological and institutional techniques designed to prevent people from leaving home and, if that failed, to repatriate them as quickly as possible in the wake of disasters. Confucianism promoted attachment to natal areas, as did institutions such as lineage organisations and native place associations. The ideological foundations of these organisations helped to persuade people that they should remain rooted to their homes. Meanwhile mechanisms of population registration, most notably the household responsibility system 保甲 (baojia), made it practically more difficult to migrate.[16] During crises, these institutions were often used to regulate relief distributions, meaning that, after the acute phase of emergency relief had finished, refugees would be fed by granaries only if they went home. When persuasion failed, government troops were ordered to exclude refugees from entering cities and expel those who refused to leave.

The capacity of the state to control population mobility declined markedly during the nineteenth century. The deterioration of the disaster alleviation infrastructure coincided with – and helped to precipitate – a rise in the number of refugee crises. As the middle Yangzi descended into hydraulic crisis, mass displacement became a regular feature of life. By the 1880s Hankou was receiving approximately 30,000 refugees on an almost annual basis.[17] This pattern continued during the early

---

[14] Lu, *Street Criers*, pp. 18–19. This is roughly equivalent to the term 'vagrant' in English. In his writing in the 1920s, Mao Zedong used the term 游民物产阶级 (youmin wuchan jieji) which translates literally as vagrant property-less class as an equivalent for the Marxist term 'lumpen-proletariat'. Chen, *Guilty of Indigence*, p. 59.

[15] Will, *Bureaucracy and Famine*, p. 49.　　[16] See Von Glahn, 'Household Registration'.

[17] Rowe, *Hankow: Conflict and Community*, p. 227.

Republic, with the new railway system helping to ensure that Wuhan became a major destination for the destitute. The city experienced a succession of refugee crises during the 1920s. The response of the local community demonstrated a growing tension between charitable and militarised responses. When a severe drought threatened Henan with famine in 1920, 30,000 hungry people boarded trains and fled to Hankou. Local charities provided considerable support, feeding the refugees through the winter with 3 million kilos of rice purchased by a local bureau.[18] By early 1921, with the refugee populations swollen by another 10,000, the local military decided to prevent any more people from entering the urban centre. At this stage refugees were still accommodated for half a year before being subjected to militarised constraints. In 1928 the municipal authorities proved much less patient. When a mere 2,000 refugees descended on Wuhan from drought and locust attacks in Henan, the nascent Nationalist administration barred them from entering the city, placing them aboard ships bound for Nanjing.[19] This tension between benevolence and force would define the local response to the 1931 refugee crisis.

Refugee City

A steady trickle of refugees began to arrive in Wuhan in the late spring. By the early summer this had turned into a deluge. The city was already struggling to find room to shelter rural migrants when the urban dyke networks began to fail. The floodwater that surged into Wuhan affected an estimated 782,189 people. More than 70 per cent were in Hankou.[20] Rural migrants and the urban homeless merged to form a vast refugee city. The few temporary shelters that the municipal authorities had constructed were quickly overrun. Soon spontaneous squatter camps were mushrooming up on any area of dry ground that could be found.

[18] Fuller, 'North China Famine Revisited', p. 22.   [19] Lipkin, *Useless to the State*, pp. 61–3.
[20] As with all statistics provided during the flood, these figures are suggestive rather than exact, and must be treated with a healthy degree of scepticism. They are taken from *Wuhan shi zhi: Minzheng zhi*, p. 145. The closest contemporary figure was from the periodical *Shenbao*, which estimated that throughout the Wuhan cities the flood affected 163,000 households or 780,000 people. See *Shenbao*, 8 August 1931. Xie Qianmao estimated 400,000 homeless people in the three Wuhan cities, with Hankou housing 200,000 in organised refugee camps, Wuchang 50,000 and Hanyang 30,000, and the remaining population scattered throughout the city. See Xie, *Yi jiu san yi nian*, p. 107. John Hope Simpson put the figure at 300,000 homeless in Hankou alone. See 'John Hope Simpson to F. B. Bourdillon', 23 February 1932 JHS 6i.

Thousands of refugees ended up 'cooped sardine-wise' in various build-ings, including schools, temples, churches, hotels and warehouses.[21] Others built their own huts on patches of dry ground, dyke tops and even in the branches of trees. Thirty thousand refugees sought shelter on a six-mile stretch of railway embankment. Some headed for high ground on the outskirts of the city. Twenty thousand sheltered on Black Hill in Hanyang.[22] This was one of numerous refugee islands that formed an archipelago in the vast flood lake.

Understandably, those who reported on the refugee crisis sought to highlight the abject living conditions found in squatter camps. Few reflected on the considerable skill and ingenuity that had been required to construct makeshift neighbourhoods from debris and plants salvaged from the floodwater. Simple huts fashioned from reeds and bamboo were a vital technology of the poor. They may not have offered the best protection from the elements, but they were cheap and portable. Individual families constructed huts that were around a single metre in height and breadth and up to 3 metres long.[23] Later, government relief agencies would exploit the same architectural techniques, com-missioning refugees to construct extensive camps and even hospitals from bamboo, matting and reeds. Like the ability to fish and forage, this architectural knowledge was an important component of the local culture of disasters. As with most forms of vernacular expertise, how-ever, when the history of the flood came to be written the ingenuity of hut-builders was entirely overlooked.

The refugee crisis had soon exceeded anything in living memory. Community leaders formed an Emergency Relief Committee 急赈会 (Jizhen hui) to co-ordinate the activities local philanthropic societies, occupational guilds and native place associations. In the late imperial period, local organisations such as these formed the bedrock of what Susan Mann has described as the 'liturgical governance' system, in which local elites assumed responsibility for key management functions rather than the state.[24] With the collapse of the Qing, and the failure of any coherent government to emerge in the early Republic, the surviving ves-tiges of this liturgical governance system often became the only available

[21] *North China Herald*, 25 August 1931; Rev. F. G. Onley (Letter Extract), 28 August 1931, SOAS Archives 10/7/15.
[22] *North China Herald*, 15 September 1931; Xie, *Yi jiu san yi nian*, p. 19.
[23] Extracts from letter of Sir J. Hope-Simpson to Mr. F. B. Bourdillon, 16 January 1932, SOAS Archives 10/7/15.
[24] Mann, *Local Merchants*.

sources of relief for disaster-stricken communities. In his study of the North China Famine of 1920–1921, Pierre Fuller argues that local charitable networks provided much more effective and timely relief than more celebrated international organisations.[25] China International Famine Relief Commission 华洋义赈会 (Hua-Yang Yizhen Hui, CIFRC) workers such as John Earl Baker and Walter Mallory may have taken most of the credit, yet it had been paternalistic local elites, working 'below the radar' of the news media, who had provided most of the relief.

The violence and disruption of the 1920s had done much to erode traditional systems of liturgical governance, yet local relief continued to play a vitally important role during the Wuhan refugee crisis. Months before the first shipments of American grain had arrived in China, the Emergency Relief Committee was accommodating and feeding hundreds of thousands of displaced people.[26] Within the first month alone, they raised more than a million silver dollars.[27] They used this to open rice porridge kitchens 粥厂 (zhouchang) and distribute steamed bread 馒头 (mantou) to refugees.[28] The Emergency Relief Commission even began to make plans for the aftermath of the flood, suggesting that a large number of permanent houses should be constructed for the poor, and promoting a system of business loans to help them get back on their feet.[29] Religious organisations also played a key role. While they were being traduced as fatalistic and apathetic by iconoclastic journalists, Buddhist monks were taking responsibility for housing and feeding refugees in their temples and monasteries.[30]

Local civic organisations not only provided food but also sought to tackle the emerging health crisis. They distributed boiled water to try and prevent refugees from drinking floodwater and collecting dead bodies. Long before Liu Ruiheng arrived to coordinate the biomedical response to the flood, traditional medicinal practitioners were offering palliative

---

[25] Fuller, 'North China Famine Revisited'.

[26] *The Chinese Recorder*, November, 1932, pp. 667–80.

[27] *Hankow Herald*, 4 September 1931.

[28] Zhang, 'Lun Zhengfu'; *Wuhan shi zhi: Minzheng zhi*, p. 145; 'The Yangtze Valley Floods by a Hankow Missionary', SOAS Archives 10/7/15.

[29] *Hankow Herald*, 8 September 1931.

[30] Hong Hill Pagoda 洪山塔 (Hongshan Ta) in Wuchang was the sight of a major refugee camp. Guiyuan Temple 归元寺 (Guiyuan Si) in Hanyang offered relief to thousands. The Temple of Ancient Virtue 古德寺 (Gude Si) in Hankou provided financial and material assistance in the reconstruction phase. RNFRC, p. 70; Xie, *Yi jiu san yi nian*, p.96; *Wuhan shi zhi: Minzheng zhi*, p. 145; Zhang 'Lun Zhengfu'; 'Shourong' HSSDX, pp. 52–7. Details of the contribution of the Temple of Ancient Virtue can still be found on a display board outside the temple.

care to refugees free of charge.[31] They massaged the stomachs of those suffering from starvation with warm cloths in order to preserve their primordial essence 元气 (yuanqi), and filled the ears and nostrils of those suffering from exposure with preparations of powdered herbal medicine.[32] Those who advocated a scientific approach to relief may have criticised the customary methods employed by local communities, but civic organisations, monks and traditional physicians were shouldering the responsibility of caring for refugees long before the practical humanitarians arrived.[33] They also helped to establish functioning infrastructure on which the National Flood Relief Commission 救济水灾委员会 (Jiuji Shuizai Weiyuanhui, NFRC) would later come to rely heavily. Needless to say, their efforts received little more than a cursory mention in the official literature.

Refugees did not necessarily want to depend on elite philanthropy. The first people they turned to for assistance tended to be their own families. The kinship system functioned as a form of informal credit cooperative, offering those in dire financial straits a viable alternative to relying on moneylenders or pawnbrokers. Traces of this system can still be found today. The anthropologist Yan Yunxiang has argued that an informal economy of gifts and relations still helps rural communities to survive economic hardship, in lieu of formal lines of credit.[34] The existence of such networks was even more important in the Republican era, when most people lived entirely outside the reach of formal banking or state assistance. Mallory, who was critical of many aspects of Chinese traditional society, was extremely impressed by the capacity of the kinship system to function as an informal support network – 'the more prosperous members or branches of the family provide for the poorer members against temporary periods of unemployment, sickness, or loss of crops.'[35] These horizontal channels of relief reflected the existence of a kind of moral economy, operating largely out of sight of the state.[36] This seems to have extended beyond immediate kin. Edith Wills, who volunteered giving out food tickets, expressed great admiration for the solidarity displayed by refugees. 'Often have I marvelled at the goodness of the poor to each other . . . They will draw my attention to a really needy case and do not say a word if I write a ticket for something or even give money sometimes.'[37] Even in the depths of hunger, there remained an

[31] Xie, *Yi jiu san yi nian*, p. 62.   [32] 'Jizhen hui ling', HSSDX, p. 167.
[33] Liang, 'Combating the Famine Dragon'.   [34] Yan, *Flow of Gifts*.
[35] Mallory, *China*, p. 24.   [36] See Scott, *Moral Economy*.
[37] Edith S. Wills, 'Hanyang 1931', SOAS Archives 10/7/15.

ethical code that governed economic relations, even between those not formally related.

This ethical code helps to explain how so many people seem to have been able to survive by begging. During the first 100 days of the disaster, it was estimated that as many as a fifth of displaced people were relying on begging to survive.[38] Even in non-crisis periods, mendicancy was a ubiquitous feature of life in Wuhan. The number of registered beggars in the city rose from hundreds to thousands during the early twentieth century – and this was probably only a fraction of the actual population.[39] The historian Lu Hanchao has described the fascinating subculture of begging that had existed in China since the late imperial period. Mendicancy may have been disreputable, but it was, nevertheless, a recognised profession.[40] In Wuhan, as elsewhere, beggars had their own guild and even managed apprenticeships, where they learnt the tricks of the trade. Some solicited money directly often using real or simulated disabilities to elicit sympathy. Others engaged in acts of degrading self-mutilation, sticking needles through their wrists or holding burning incense on their heads.[41] Begging guilds were certainly not philanthropic institutions, and their members were involved in an array of criminal activities, including prostitution and people trafficking. Yet they did have a strict code of ethics. One of the central rules was that beggars were to stick to their own territories. Anyone not from an established mendicant lineage found in the jurisdiction allotted to another beggar could expect to be banished, beaten or worse.[42] This territorialism meant that professional beggars did not welcome disaster refugees, who encroached upon their patches and disturbed the delicate relationship they had fostered with the local community. Refugees did not abide by the correct etiquette, and sought alms in areas where the locals had already paid off the begging guild. When floods struck the middle Yangzi in 1911, merchants in Hankou berated the local beggar chief for failing to control refugees. He complained, in turn, that the municipal administration had no business allowing displaced people to compete with registered professionals.[43]

The flood precipitated a huge growth in the beggar population throughout China. In Wuhan, the police were soon expressing concern that professional mendicants and other members of the wandering population had infiltrated the ranks of the legitimate refugees.[44] Others

[38] Buck, *1931 Flood*, p. 15.   [39] Shang, '"Gaibang" tanmi'.
[40] Lu, *Street Criers*, p. 17.   [41] Shang, '"Gaibang" tanmi'.
[42] Ibid.   [43] Crow, *Four Hundred Million Customers*, pp. 258–63.
[44] 'Zaizhen zhong zhi Zhi'an' HSSDX, p. 44.

worried about the pauperising effect that relying on charity was having on
ordinarily productive people. One foreign resident of Wuhan noted that
some beggars had 'developed the habit, not of waiting for the food given
them, but of going to the houses of their benefactors, where they make
themselves very much at home, demanding and taking instead of receiving.' He feared that 'after a comparatively easy kind of existence many
are not going to take kindly again to work as a means of livelihood.'[45] In
response to such concerns, the police attempted to drive all the beggars and itinerant entertainers away from Wuhan. Those who resisted
were sent to a special Vagrant Camp 游民收遣所 (Youmin Shouqian-
suo), where they were incarcerated before being forcibly expelled from
the city.[46] There is no evidence to describe how this institution operated,
but it was typical for the time.

Throughout the early twentieth century, the municipal authorities in
Wuhan had established a range of institutions to house impoverished
people. These were not entirely novel. Special shelters providing respite
for impoverished groups such as beggars and widows had existed for
centuries.[47] Yet the ideology and methodology governing these new institutions marked them out as idiosyncratically modern. Janet Chen has
observed that the workhouses that became a common feature of the
urban landscape in early twentieth century China were designed to have
both didactic and punitive functions. They first separated indigent paupers from the ranks of the deserving poor, and then attempted to inculcate normative attitudes towards labour and society.[48] Workhouses in
Wuhan seem to have had economic as well as a sociopolitical function.
Some produced handicrafts, and one even had its own Pauper's Factory
贫民工厂 (Pinmin Gongchang).[49] When the Nationalists took power
in 1927, the police took a much more active role in managing these
institutions, establishing new facilities for impoverished women, children
and beggars.[50] The fact the destitution was now perceived as a policing

---

[45] *North China Herald*, August 1931. [46] 'Zaizhen zhong zhi Zhi'an', HSSDX, p. 44.

[47] In the radical early months of 1927, women's groups had been highly critical of virtuous
widow halls, calling them 'cattle pens'. Rowe, *Crimson Rain*, p. 278.

[48] Chen, *Guilty of Indigence*.

[49] Wuhan got its first modern Vagrant Workhouse 游民习艺所 (Youmin Xiyisuo) in 1910,
employing 200 inmates. *Wuhan shi zhi: Minzheng zhi*, pp. 151–63.

[50] Wang, 'Hankou tebie shi'; Shang, '"Gaibang" tanmi'; *Wuhan shi zhi: Minzheng zhi*,
pp. 151–63. When the left-wing Wuhan Government briefly ran the city in 1927, trade
unions seem to have played a bigger role, opening a special relief institution 收容所
(shourongsuo) for wharf labourers who lived a marginal existence in the city. *Hankou
Minguo Ribao*, 6 January 1927.

problem may help to further explain why some refugees were reluctant to submit themselves to state institutions. It was better to survive on the streets, perhaps, than risk being incarcerated for being poor.

Commerce and Crime

Not all of those who made their way to Wuhan in 1931 were seeking charity. Some wanted to turn the disaster to their advantage by exploiting the new demands for services. The rapid reconfiguration of commodity prices had tended to penalise those in low-income professions. An important exception was the members of the riverine culture who fished, ferried goods or transported people across water. As the streets of Wuhan became canals these people found they could make great profits by renting out their vessels as water taxis.[51] Before long the media was reporting that sampan owners were 'reaping a rich harvest in fares'.[52] Ordinarily the boat journey from Wuhan to the rural seat of Huangpi 黄陂 cost a mere 2 yuan. During the flood, it cost 25 yuan.[53] In the city itself, the cost of hiring a sampan rose to thirty-eight times its normal price.[54] This was particularly frustrating for merchants who relied on sampans to evacuate their goods.[55] As it became apparent quite how much money could be earned working the streets, 2,000 sampans descended on Hankou. Major thoroughfares quickly became virtually impassable, and those living in larger houses stretched barbed wire across their walls to keep boats away.[56] Eventually, fearing that the accumulation of vessels would pose a threat to public order, the authorities issued a proclamation stating that only sampans displaying a shipping bureau flag would be able to work the streets.[57]

While the traffic police fretted about blocked thoroughfares, the military worried that criminals and political miscreants were hiding among the sampan operators. The boat people of the Yangzi were a perennial source of official suspicion. This was not entirely without justification.

---

[51] This was a common strategy during floods. In the nineteenth century sampan owners who arrived in Hankou as refugees stayed on and started commercial ferry services. See Rowe, *Hankow: Conflict and Community*, p. 231.

[52] *North China Herald*, 4 August 1931. In the initial stages of the flood, the journalist Chen Bing could hire a sampan for a day for as little as 5 mao. Later foreign reporters described being charged up to $6 a day. Chen, *Wuhan Wenshi Ziliao*, p. 143.

[53] Xie, *Yi jiu san yi nian*, p. 149.

[54] *Hankow Herald*, 29 August 1931.   [55] *Hankow Herald*, 18 August 1931.

[56] Hu Yu-tsen (Letter Extract), 28 August 1931, SOAS Archives 10/7/15.

[57] Xie, *Yi jiu san yi nian*, pp. 75–6; *Hankow Herald*, 2 September 1931.

Boat people had long been involved in all kinds of nefarious activities, particularly smuggling. The infamous Shanghai crime syndicate known as the Green Gang 青帮 (Qingbang) had its origins in such an organisation.[58] Bandits were also known to use sampans to commit piratical raids on riverside communities.[59] The military were all too aware of this reputation. In mid-July, it seemed as if their worst fears had been realised, when a rumour began to circulate that a flotilla of a thousand bandit boats, armed with guns and bombs, was descending on Wuchang. As panicking garrison troops were preparing themselves for a river battle, it emerged that this deadly armada consisted of ten boats of unarmed refugees, who dispersed voluntarily when the alarm had been raised.[60] The fact that there was no substance to this rumour did little to assuage the official paranoia. Eventually, the provincial government instituted a ban on the use of vessels on several sensitive waterways.[61] In early September, the military seized more than 200 sampans in Wuhan for failing to display the correct flag.[62] These blanket measures did not discriminate between bandits and those using boats for more innocuous purposes, such as fishing and transportation. The irony was that sampan owners were displaying exactly the kind of work ethic and self-sufficiency that was so often lauded by the government and relief agencies. Official anxieties impinged on one of the most viable and innocuous of coping strategies, as well as diminishing the already scarce resources of flood-stricken people. Deprived of their boats, sampan owners became ordinary refugees.

As lawful avenues of survival evaporated, some people turned to crime. The level of hunger in Wuhan was not as intense as in rural areas, where there had already been several grain riots, yet by late August looting had become ubiquitous.[63] Refugees looted rice shops, and in one instance stormed rickshaws containing bread, stopping only when the police beat them back.[64] Amidst these spontaneous acts inspired by hunger, more professional crimes were also taking place. Abandoned houses and shops became easy targets for burglars.[65] Wealthy families paid guards to protect their property, while those with fewer resources took turns standing watch over their neighbourhoods, pelting any boat that failed

---

[58] Rowe, *Hankow: Conflict and Community*, pp. 231–5, 261–2; Wakeman, *Policing Shanghai*, pp. 25–7.
[59] 'Zaizhen zhong zhi Zhi'an' HSSDX, p. 39.
[60] Ibid.   [61] 'Zaizhen zhong zhi Zhi'an', HSSDX, pp. 43–4.
[62] *Hankow Herald*, 4 September 1931.   [63] Ouyang, 'Zaihuang yu nongmin'.
[64] *North China Herald*, 25 August 1931.   [65] 'Zaizhen zhong zhi Zhi'an', HSSDX, p. 42.

to provide an adequate account of its business with rocks.[66] Homeless refugees simply carried all their most valued possessions on their person.[67] Quite who was responsible for these crimes is uncertain. In late imperial Wuhan, criminal gangs had often taken advantage of the chaos caused by disasters to loot the property of their fellow citizens.[68] The local authorities tended to attribute such crimes to 'hooligans' 流氓 (liumang), a vaguely defined group that could encompass anything from petty criminals to organised gangs.[69] Whether the crimes committed in the inundated city were acts of desperation or opportunism – or both – is difficult to determine. Cormac Ó Gráda has observed that famine often gives rise to petty criminality, as hunger fuels desperation and lowers inhibitions.[70] It is worth noting that in the refugee camps, where hunger was often at its most intense, witnessed remarked on the absence of crime. It is possible that refugees had too little to steal and that the city outside had far richer pickings. Yet those who worked among the displaced population attributed this to the solidarity of the poor. Refugees would not prey on one another despite their desperation.[71]

Crimes against property must be viewed within the economic milieu of the flood. While many citizens of Wuhan displayed admirable generosity, there were more than a few who sought to exploit the disaster for profit. Even before the city had succumbed to water, merchants were already hiking food prices.[72] Soon the most commonly eaten vegetables were selling at twice their normal value. On the rare occasions that meat could be procured, it was generally of too dubious quality to eat. Even foreigners complained that their usual diet was becoming prohibitively expensive, with many resorting to eating at the club rather than trying to access food in markets.[73] For the poor, it was the increase in the price of grain staples that proved most devastating. Even the cheapest varieties of rice were soon being sold at hugely inflated prices.[74] As refugees began to suffer the effects of severe malnutrition, stocks of hoarded grain were rotting

---

[66] Xie, *Yi jiu san yi nian*, p. 146.

[67] Clubb, 'Floods of China'; Hu Yu-tsen (Letter Extract), 28 August 1931, SOAS Archives 10/7/15.

[68] Rowe, *Hankow: Conflict and Community*, p. 220.

[69] See for example Xie, *Yi jiu san yi nian*, p. 75; *Wuhan Ribao*, 1 January 1932.

[70] Ó Gráda, *Famine*, pp. 53–6.

[71] H. Owen Chapman 'Fighting Floods and Famine in China', SOAS Archives 10/7/15.

[72] Xie, *Yi jiu san yi nian*, p. 16.

[73] *North China Herald*, 11 August 1931; *Hankow Herald*, 10 September 1931.

[74] Xie, *Yi jiu san yi nian*, p. 16. No normal price of low-grade rice is provided. See also RNFRC, p. 190.

in flooded warehouses.[75] In such circumstances, looting represented an understandable coping strategy – one in which desperate people defied legal sanctions to ameliorate the effects of an avoidable famine.

Those charged with policing the streets had scant regard for the economic context of criminality. To begin with, looters could expect to be imprisoned. Later they risked summary execution. Given the pitiful lack of provisions for the incarcerated population, in some instances the former punishment may have been preferable. With water advancing on Wuhan, the municipal authorities made no attempt to evacuate those trapped in a courthouse jail at Xiakou 夏口. Around 300 inmates were inside the jail when it was inundated. Casualty reports varied widely, with some suggesting only 10 prisoners drowned and others estimating more than 100.[76] As one journalist noted wryly, no matter whether they faced a fixed-term penalty or life imprisonment, all had now been sentenced to death.[77] Perhaps the prison authorities were guilty of a careless oversight, or perhaps this was a callous calculation driven by a desire to maintain public order. Whichever was the case, this incident reveals how incarcerated populations face unique problems during disasters. When Hurricane Katrina struck the United States in 2005, with no evacuation plan in place, those locked in the Orleans Parish Prison were left living in filthy water for days.[78] Just as in Wuhan, those considered the most dangerous were among the most vulnerable.

Water Chickens and Gendered Survival

While some begged, borrowed and stole, others sold their bodies. Prostitution was an ever-present feature of life in Wuhan. Since the late imperial period, there had been a highly variegated market for sexual services, catering to clients of all tastes and economic circumstances. Those with sufficient money could visit luxurious brothels or the extravagant flower boats that plied the harbours. Those with humbler tastes and lighter wallets could head to one of the numerous cheaper establishments, or even pay for a quick assignation in a secluded backstreet.[79] The red-light

---

[75] *North China Herald*, 25 August 1931; *Hankow Herald*, 20 August 1931.

[76] Xie, *Yi jiu san yi nian*, p. 74; *North China Herald*, 11 August 1931.

[77] Quoted in Pi, *Wuhan Tongshi: Minguo Juan (Shang)*, p. 213.

[78] Kotey, 'Judging Under Disaster'.

[79] Rowe, *Hankow: Conflict and Community*, pp. 194–5. For a reference to flower boats see Ye, *Hankou zhuzhici jiaozhu*, p. 193. Some historians have claimed that the French Concession was a major centre of prostitution. See Fei, *Zhongguo zujie shi*, p. 290. Most contemporary descriptions seem to suggest that brothels were actually found in all areas,

district on Shajia Lane 沙家巷 certainly catered for a more frugal cliente. In the 1910s, the poet Luo Han wrote a light-hearted verse extolling the merits of the area, observing that although the women may not have been the most beautiful, they were popular because of their competitive prices.[80] Just a decade later, attitudes had changed considerably, at least in some quarters. For the investigative reporter Ji Xun 芰薰 Shajia Lane was a despicable 'human meat market' 人肉市场 (renrou shichang), controlled by pitiless madams and lecherous pimps. Subjected to a life of violence and sexually transmitted diseases, the women who worked the lane soon became 'young skeletons' 青年的骷髅 (qingnian de kulou).[81] The reality of life for women working as prostitutes was captured neither by Luo's irreverent poetry nor by Ji's didactic journalism. Although undoubtedly an existence defined by frequent hardships and ruthless exploitation, women who worked as prostitutes were more than just hapless victims. They were adept at finding ways to survive on the economic and moral fringes of the city.

The flood may have destroyed Wuhan's brothels but it took more than water to eradicate prostitution. In colloquial Chinese, female prostitutes are often described as 'chickens' 鸡 (ji). At the height of the flood, the journalist Guo Jingrong described how 'water chickens' 水鸡 (shuiji) lined the inundated streets, selling sex from boats.[82] Whether these women could find customers is a different question. Extreme hunger suppresses the libido, as malnutrition lowers testosterone levels and human bodies seek to conserve energy.[83] With thousands of people facing severe dietary limitations, the market for those selling sexual services did not look promising. For this reason, Xie Qianmao argued that women who worked as prostitutes should be sent to camps alongside ordinary refugees.[84] Yet the subsistence crisis did not fall evenly across the urban community. With some still able to secure food, their appetite for sex may not have been diminished. For those who had been working as prostitutes before the flood, the real threat was not the lack of food but the increased competition from refugees. Like professional beggars, they found themselves working in a saturated market – both literally and figuratively.

including the Chinese city. Certainly in Shanghai foreign areas had large numbers of women working as prostitutes. Frederic Wakeman estimated that in 1915 there was one prostitute for every sixteen women. See Wakeman, *Policing Shanghai*, p. 12.

[80] Luo, *Minchu Hankou zhuzhici*, p. 24.   [81] Ji, 'Hankou renrou shichang'.

[82] Guo, 'Wuhan zaihou pian pian lu', *Guowen Zhoukan*.

[83] Ó Gráda, *Famine*, p. 106.   [84] Xie, *Yi jiu san yi nian*, p. 158.

We do not know how many refugees sold sex in Wuhan. Women in neither party were particularly motivated to record details of their encounters. Historically, women in similar situations had often ended up working as prostitutes.[85] Whether they entered the trade of their own volition or were compelled to do so is a different question. At the height of the flood one foreign journalist reported that 'white-slavers' were 'endeavouring to buy up young girls of prepossessing appearance from the refugees. With nothing in the world left but a daughter, some of the poor are falling into this trap.'[86] Although the use of the term 'white slavers' perhaps betrayed this journalist's predisposition towards stereotypes of Oriental sexual deviance, there well may have been some truth in these claims. Abduction and forced prostitution were not unknown. Ji Xun described a shadowy group called the 'chicken callers' 叫鸡子 (jiao jizi), who specialised in kidnapping young girls and selling them to brothels.[87] During the so-called bandit pacification campaigns, the name the Nationalists gave to their Communist eradication policies, government soldiers had abducted thousands of women and children for this purpose.[88] Quite how widespread such practices were remains a matter of debate. Gail Hershatter has observed that Nationalist laws against forced prostitution encouraged women to claim they had been abducted, as they then stood a better chance of winning legal redress from pimps and madams. Many had probably been sold willingly by family members or entered the profession through the compulsion of poverty.[89] Zhao Ma has described how many of those accused of kidnapping women claimed, sometimes with justification, to be helping them to leave economically unviable domestic arrangements.[90] The poor had to make the difficult choices even at the best of times. During the flood thousands of husbands sold their wives so that both might face better prospects.[91] For the media, kidnapping provided an easily digestible narrative, in which the spectre of criminality obscured stark economic realities. By presenting women as victims of deviant male sexuality, journalists could report on such problems while maintaining prevalent gendered expectations about female chastity, spousal obedience and the sanctity of the family.

At the height of the flood an author named Zeng Xianhe 曾宪和 wrote a short story imagining the life of a female refugee entering a city.

[85] Rowe, *Hankow: Conflict and Community*, p. 195.
[86] *North China Herald*, 11 August 1931.   [87] Ji, 'Hankou renrou shichang'.
[88] Benton, *Mountain Fires*, p. 315.   [89] Hershatter, 'Modernizing Sex', p. 167.
[90] Ma, *Runaway Wives*.
[91] *Wuhan Ribao*, 1 January 1932; Li et al., *Zhongguo jindai shi da zaihuang*.

It began with her sitting on a corner, 'her two eyes ashen and her face gaunt; all day she has not had the strength to walk down the street.' We learn how her husband was killed in a battle against bandits and the rest of her kin had perished in the flood. Not wanting to remarry, she hoped with her last breaths to join her husband in death.[92] This fictional account betrayed the tendency of early twentieth century authors to fall back on what Prasenjit Duara has described as a 'patriarchal legacy'.[93] Despite its modern realist style, this fictional account relied on a gendered motif of a virtuous widow that would not have been out of place in a Confucian morality tract. Even in the nineteenth century, when the grip of traditional gender norms was far stronger, not everyone had accepted the validity of such prescriptions. During the 1849 floods, Ye Diaoyuan had castigated his conservative counterparts for stigmatising women who used 'promiscuity to beg for money' 风流好乞钱 (fengliu hao qi qian).[94] Such sympathy was not that common. Many of those who described disasters preferred their women helpless yet morally unimpeachable. This was not unique to China. Images of female suffering have been a common motif used to describe disasters throughout the world.[95]

The link between gender and disasters is somewhat more complex than such narratives suggested. Social scientists have often argued that women suffer disproportionately high rates of disaster risk. They point to the fact that in the impoverished societies where hazards are most dangerous, women tend to be the most economically disadvantaged. This poverty translates into greater disaster vulnerability.[96] Gender norms also inhibit female coping strategies. Indian women in Tamil Nadu, for example, suffered disproportionately during the 2004 Indian Ocean tsunami because most had not been taught how to swim.[97] There were no studies of the effect of gender on vulnerability in 1931. We know that women were poorer than men, and can assume that gendered practices such as foot binding would have placed them at a physical disadvantage. Despite these inhibiting factors, however, the statistical evidence shows that women survived somewhat *better* than men. In relief camps the gender ratio slightly favoured women at 51 per cent to 49 per cent, whereas in the countryside female to male ratios stood at 45 per cent to 55 per cent. Even those who compiled these statistics admitted

---

[92] Zeng, 'Nanmin ku'.
[93] Duara, 'Regime of Authenticity'.   [94] Ye, *Hankou zhuzhici*, p. 189.
[95] Kelleher, *Feminization of Famine*; Edgerton-Tarpley, *Tears from Iron*.
[96] See Enarson, 'Preface'.   [97] Valdés, 'Gender Perspective'.

that they were based on unreliable data, with family members failing to mention all who had perished.[98] Female fatalities were habitually under-reporting in the Republican era, not least because young girls often fell victim to infanticide.[99] Flood-stricken families who wished to avoid moral opprobrium or legal sanctions would have been motivated to conceal the deaths of young girls.[100]

We cannot, however, dismiss the influence of gender as a simple glitch in the statistics. Unlike social scientists, who treat the relative disaster vulnerability of women as a truism, demographers have long recognised that male mortality rates are usually higher than female during famines.[101] There are various explanations for this. As this female survival advantage is both transcultural and transhistorical, it is likely that there is a biological component. Women seem to be physically better able to withstand prolonged starvation than men.[102] Kathryn Edgerton-Tarpley has identified several additional cultural factors, including the fact that women often play a greater role in food preparation, meaning they have better access to nutrition, and are usually cast in caring roles, which are valued much more in crisis situations. Another important factor is the fact that women can sell sex or enter into various forms of contract marriage much more easily than men.[103] This suggests that, although they may have been stigmatised and pitied, those who worked as prostitutes may have had a survival advantage.

Women were not the only ones whose survival was influenced by gender norms. The expectations placed on men during the flood were often onerous. They were expected to conform to a model of masculinity in which they were required to withstand physically punishing conditions while receiving minimal charitable assistance. Relief institutions habitually excluded men, believing that they should be able to survive on their own. In Wuhan there was a special Relief Shelter for Women 妇女救济所 (Funu Jiuji Suo), which issued two meals of rice porridge to 2,000 people every day, and would not allow men to enter no matter their physical condition.[104] Missionary organisations also raised special funds to

[98] Buck, *1931 Flood*, p. 35.

[99] Campbell, 'Public Health Efforts', p. 190.   [100] Li, 'Life and Death'.

[101] Macintyre, 'Famine and the Female Mortality Advantage'; Ó Gráda, *Famine*, pp. 99–100; Edgerton-Tarpley, *Tears from Iron*, esp. p. 179. In Sudan during the 1984–1985 famine houses headed by women not only were less poor than those headed by men, but also became less destitute in the long term. De Waal, *Famine That Kills*, p. 143.

[102] Dyson and Ó Gráda, *Famine Demography*.

[103] Edgerton-Tarpley, *Tears from Iron*.   [104] *Wuhan Ribao*, 7 January 1932.

be spent exclusively on female refugees.[105] Women did not have to participate in the punitive schedule of labour relief, and where they were required to work were usually employed in lighter tasks, such as handicraft production. By contrast, an ability to undertake physically testing labour was central to the gendered morality of relief institutions. Adhering to a prescriptive mode of labouring masculinity became a prerequisite used by those controlling the flow of nutrition to guarantee the compliance of male refugees. Men who failed to fit the image of the diligent worker could expect to starve.

Saving the Children

Prostitution was just one of the ways that refugees engaged with the illicit economy. Those who could not sell sex sometimes sold their children. The very young, along with the very old, are the most vulnerable to disasters. They are unable to withstand the physical force of hazards and the severe malnutrition that follows, and have the lowest immunity to diseases. Historically, when Chinese parents found themselves in desperate situations they had often considered selling children to be a viable option to increase the probability of mutual survival. It was certainly preferable to the grim alternatives, which included committing infanticide or watching children starve. Young girls were sold most frequently, reflecting their generally lowly position within the gendered kinship structure. Some ended up as bonded servants in the homes of the elite, while others worked in brothels, slowly paying the madam or pimp back for the price of their original purchase. With constant fees levied for rent and other charges, this debt obligation could last years.[106] Young boys were also sold, although this was less common. Some probably also ended up working as prostitutes, although male sex workers are less visible in the documentary record. Others became bonded servants or factory workers.[107] Children made up around 8 per cent of the workforce in textile mills, and were also employed in hazardous industries such as match manufacturing, where fire and phosphorus poisoning were ever-present dangers.[108]

The logic behind selling children was stark, but it was logic nonetheless. The money a family received could be used to support the remaining

---

[105] 'The Boone Compound and Flood Relief', 3 October 1931, SOAS Archives 10/7/15.
[106] Ji, 'Hankou renrou shichang'.
[107] JHS 10, p. 165.   [108] Orchard, 'Man-Power in China', pp. 577, 583.

members, while the child faced a better chance of being fed by its new guardians. An eminently practical solution, selling children had nevertheless always been controversial. It had become more so since the late nineteenth century, when foreign missionaries became vocal opponents of the practice, equating it with child slavery.[109] Those purchasing children had a very different view of the morality of bonded servitude, as Rachel Leow has observed. They saw it as a form of charity, which assisted both the child and its impoverished family.[110] Missionaries seem to have rejected this logic out of hand, believing it to be an obfuscation used to gloss over an inherently exploitative arrangement. These moral objections did not stop Christians themselves from becoming involved in the market for children. French Catholics purchased orphans for religious conversion, and the Salvation Army had become embroiled in a scandal when one of its workers bought 100 girls for similar purposes.[111] Purchasing a child was not considered immoral if the purpose was to save its soul. By the 1920s, missionary pressure had helped to achieve a ban on bonded servitude in Chinese communities under British colonial rule.[112] Later in the decade the Nationalist government followed suit, issuing legislation to abolish child slavery. These new laws proved largely ineffective, as those who purchased children simply claimed to have adopted them.[113]

Images of parents – particularly mothers – forced to part with their children proved particularly evocative for outside observers of the flood. In one of her short stories, Pearl Buck imagined the plight of two parents who, having been pushed off their land by water, made the agonising decision to sell their daughter.[114] This fictional representation had roots in reality. Reports of famished people offering children for sale emerged throughout the flood zone.[115] In the refugee camps of Wuhan, both boys and girls were sold for just a few coins. If no buyer could be found, some simply gave children away.[116] Under ordinary circumstances, orphanages offered refuge for children abandoned in the city. During the flood, these

---

[109] In 1880, a missionary named J. A. Davis wrote a novel entitled *The Chinese Slave-Girl*, which told the tale of a family impoverished by the overpopulation of their native land, forced to sell their daughter into a life of drudgery, cruelty and degradation as a bonded servant. See Davis, *Chinese Slave Girl*.

[110] Leow, 'Do You Own Non-Chinese Mui Tsai?'

[111] Harrison, 'A Penny for the Little Chinese'. See Fuller, 'Struggling with Famine', p. 306.

[112] Leow, 'Do You Own Non-Chinese Mui Tsai?'

[113] Ibid., p. 1743; Hershatter, 'Modernizing Sex'.   [114] Buck, *First Wife*.

[115] See for example *Wuhan Ribao*, 8 January 1932; Li et al., *Zhongguo jindai shi da zaihuang*, p. 213; Keith Gillison, 'Report for the Year, 1931', SOAS Archives 65/10.

[116] H. Owen Chapman, 'Fighting Floods and Famine in China', SOAS Archives 10/7/15.

institutions soon ran out of space. In the Black Hill camp alone, around half of the 100,000 refugees were children, with 4,000 estimated to be parentless.[117]

As winter began to set in, local citizens petitioned the municipal government to create an emergency orphanage to house homeless children. Special notices were posted encouraging parents unable to cope with the burden of childcare to place their children in such institutions.[118] Locals clearly did not lack compassion for the suffering of youngsters, as some critics of Chinese culture were wont to suggest. They simply did not have the facilities to care for such overwhelming numbers. Neither were stereotypes about the callous indifference of Chinese parents borne out by the facts. In one case, for example, a widowed father could not bear to leave his speech-impaired child in hospital, as he feared that the nurses would be unable to understand the special signs he made when wanting milk.[119] In spite of such affection, the issue of child selling soon became so acute that it drew the attention of the child welfare activist Wu Weide 吴维德.[120] Having witnessed the scale of the problem, he lobbied the municipal authorities to issue a proclamation against the trade.[121] Officials paid lip service to his overtures, issuing edicts against child selling and the use child labour to pull rickshaws.[122] Yet legal sanctions could not ameliorate the profound want that drove families to resort to such desperate measures.

The problem became so acute that even foreign charities became involved in the market for children. According to John Hope Simpson, funds from the Geneva-based charity Save the Children were used to purchase children from parents who would otherwise 'have sold them to agencies certainly not philanthropic. These children were kept, looked after, and fed, and on the close of the famine were returned to their parents',[123] presuming, of course, that their parents had survived. Elsewhere Hope Simpson revealed that the NFRC itself had bought children, fearing that they might fall into the hands of unscrupulous factory owners.[124] Foreign organisations that became involved in this market realised that the practical necessity of saving children trumped

---

[117] *The Chinese Recorder*, March 1932.   [118] *Wuhan Ribao*, 8 January 1932.

[119] Edith S. Wills, 'Hanyang 1931', SOAS Archives 10/7/15.

[120] Known as Andrew V. Wu. He was secretary of the foreign-funded National Child Welfare Association of China. For a brief biography see *Who's Who in China*, p. 267.

[121] *The Chinese Recorder*, March, 1932.   [122] *Wuhan Ribao*, 13 January 1932.

[123] John Hope Simpson 'Report to the League of Nations', 30 June 1932, JHS 6i.

[124] JHS 10, p. 165.

simplistic moral formulae about the commoditisation of human beings. Yet few seem to have reflected on the fact that the members of the Chinese elite who kept bondservants used the exact same arguments to justify their acts – claiming that they were buying children to save them.

Red Bandits and Martial Law

On 8 August two soldiers were rowing a sampan along an inundated street in the Liujia 刘家 area of Wuhan. Neither was an experienced boatman, and soon they crashed into a small storehouse. The impact knocked a female refugee in her seventies, who was sheltering on the roof, into the floodwater. After a few passers-by had fished her out, she had a few choice words for the careless soldiers. Rather than apologise, the soldiers took umbrage at her temerity, and began to administer a savage beating. Only the intervention of members of the gathering crowd prevented them from drowning the woman. Neither soldier faced any formal reprimand for this unwarranted and brutal attack.[125] Though she may have sustained physical injuries, this septuagenarian was more fortunate than some. When a low-ranking cavalry soldier felt that a street vendor named Li Jinfang 李金芳 had not sweetened his soymilk sufficiently, he demanded that she add some more sugar. Following a brief verbal altercation, the soldier kicked Li into the floodwater. Perhaps she was unable to swim, possibly the current was too strong or maybe the soldier's blow caused an injury. Whichever was the case, a few minutes later Li was dead – drowned over a bowl of soymilk.[126]

Casual brutality such as this made it much more difficult to administer relief. It fostered a deep sense of distrust between the population and authorities. Unfortunately, such incidents were all too common in Hubei at the time. Hans van de Ven has suggested that a 'culture of violence' permeated China during this period. Though incubated by years of warlord conflict, this had emerged particularly during the Northern Expedition, as 'the barriers that had contained violence had crumbled.'[127] Emboldened by an atmosphere of unaccountability, the military chiselled away the already scant civil liberties enjoyed by ordinary citizens. Few localised cultures of violence were nastier than that which developed in Hubei, an epicentre of the civil war that was raging between the Nationalists and

[125] Xie, *Yi jiu san yi nian*, p. 81.
[126] Ibid., p. 128.   [127] Van de Ven, *War and Nationalism*, p. 94.

the Communists.[128] The forms of military repression that developed during the 1931 refugee crisis were symptomatic of a mode of governance marred by violence. As Edward McCord has observed, it was a shared hatred of the Communists, rather than the lofty principles of Sun Yat-sen, that served as the true 'ideological glue' that bound provincial party warlords to the Nationalist regime.[129] This is not to suggest that the fear of Communist insurgency was illusory. Just a few years earlier, the Communist forces led by Li Lisan had launched an ill-fated attempt to retake an urban base in central China.[130] When this failed they temporarily abandoned hopes of establishing power in a city. Nevertheless, at least two of their rural soviets were in easy striking distance of Wuhan, Zhang Guotao to the north and He Long to the west.[131]

Fearing that the Communists would use the refugee crisis to secretly infiltrate Wuhan, the Nationalist military lost no time in establishing a strict surveillance regime. Working alongside Xia Douyin was the military commander Ye Peng 叶蓬, another brutal figure who had earned his stripes during the bandit pacification campaigns.[132] From early on during the flood soldiers from the garrison had been ordered to monitor the squatter camps, on the pretext that they wanted to protect refugees from the predation of hooligans.[133] Ostensibly a paternalistic gesture, this surveillance was clearly targeted at the refugees themselves. Later, this pretence was abandoned, as it became an open secret that the military had spies watching the refugees.[134] The police also monitored the situation carefully, sending plainclothes detectives to mingle among the population, with the hope of rooting out troublemakers.[135] As Hope Simpson would later report, the authorities convinced themselves that the refugees were 'largely composed of Communists'.[136] They enjoyed the support of Chinese Chamber of Commerce, whose members petitioned Nanjing to send more troops.[137] The media did little to quell

---

[128] For an account of the violence in northern Hubei during this period see Rowe, *Crimson Rain*. As Rowe points out, this was not simply a Nationalist versus Communist story. It involved multilayered conflicts between poor farmers' associations, Red Spear defence militias, bandits and warlord armies.

[129] McCord, *Military Force*, p. 120. McCord is here referring to He Jian 何键, who was a key figure in the military response to the flood. See Alley, *Man Against Flood*, p. 12.

[130] Lescot, *Before Mao*.

[131] According to Alley, the army was most concerned about He Long. Alley, *Man against Flood*, p. 12.

[132] Ibid.   [133] Xie, *Yi jiu san yi nian*, p. 75.

[134] *Hankow Herald*, 3 September 1931.   [135] *Hankow Herald*, 8 September 1931.

[136] 'John Hope Simpson to F. B. Bourdillon', 23 February 1932 JHS 6i.

[137] *Hankow Herald*, 26 August 1931.

these fears. Loyalist newspapers carried stories about bands of Communists harassing the refugee population.[138] The British treaty port press followed suit, accusing Communists of all manner of crimes, including arson attacks and deliberate dyke breaches.[139]

In late July, three 'red bandits' 赤匪 (chifei) were caught while allegedly attempting to blow up the railway embankment so that they might unleash floodwater on Wuhan.[140] What the Communists would have had to gain from this act is difficult to determine. Xie Qianmao was content to suggest the oblique motive of 'causing chaos and disturbing the peace' 扰乱治安 (raoluan zhi'an). Acts of sabotage targeting hydraulic defences were certainly not unknown, yet such attacks were generally motivated by water right disputes or an attempt to disrupt enemy troop movements.[141] These purported Communists were accused of pursuing a policy of seemingly meaningless terrorism. Having refused to divulge the identity of their 'bandit chief' 匪首 (feishou), the three were hastily executed.[142] It is unclear whether the military believed this highly questionable account, or whether their leaders were simply using it as an excuse to further their own political aims. Whichever was the case, local troops were soon being ordered to initiate a clamp down. Soldiers constructed a fortified camp on a hill on the outskirts of Wuhan, from where they could monitor those entering the city and launch campaigns against their enemies in the surrounding countryside.[143] This made it harder for genuine refugees to seek relief in the city, including, somewhat ironically, those attempting to escape genuine Communist aggression in northern Hubei.[144]

Even these new stringent measures did not satisfy local military leaders, who soon decided to declare a state of martial law. The police and army were empowered to use lethal force to suppress any form of political or social disorder. Martial law had been a favoured legal instrument

[138] See for example *Wuhan Ribao*, 8 January 1932 and *Wuhan Ribao*, 17 January 1932.
[139] *North China Herald*, 11 August 1931; *North China Herald*, 15 September 1931; *North China Herald*, 25 August 1931.
[140] Communists were always referred to using some variant of the term bandit during this time. In early 1931, Chiang Kai-shek had issued a proclamation ordering that his enemies should henceforth be known as 'red bandits' 赤匪 (chifei). See Clubb, *Communism in China*, p. 27.
[141] Zhang, 'Water Calamities'; Rowe, 'Water Control'.
[142] Xie, *Yi jiu san yi nian*, p. 82. A similar incident, probably the same one, was reported in the *North China Herald*, 28 July 1931.
[143] *North China Herald*, 1 September 1931; Xie, 'Hankou shuizai shidi shicha ji'. *Xinminbao*, HSSDX.
[144] H. Owen Chapman 'Fighting Floods and Famine in China', SOAS Archives 10/7/15.

of governments in China for decades. Warlords had often sent soldiers onto the streets to quell disruptions by establishing curfews and staging summary executions.[145] The Nationalists were equally fond of invoking this legal instrument. The founding violence of their regime had been committed under the cover of martial law, when Chiang Kai-shek had launched a purge of his erstwhile Communists allies in 1927. Later, martial law allowed right wing forces to crush the radical movements in Wuhan.[146] Over the subsequent years the Nationalists had established several laws that extended policing rights. From January 1931, those caught disseminating anti-state propaganda or making subversive speeches risked a custodial sentence.[147] The provincial authorities in Hubei were particularly draconian. If an individual was caught harbouring a Communist or sabotaging state property, his whole village would be held collectively responsible. As the American consulate worker O. Edmund Clubb observed, the 'common punishment for the offenses for which the population is given vicarious responsibility is death.'[148]

The declaration of martial law during the flood removed the last vestiges of restraint on the military. The scenes of casual violence described earlier were a direct consequence. It may have offered comfort to paranoid municipal governors, but martial law was a dangerously blunt instrument, allowing ill-disciplined soldiers to act with virtual impunity.[149] They abused this power not only by inflicting meaningless violence but also by expropriating property. Soldiers who did not want to pay the high rates charged by sampan owners simply took their boats.[150] Xie Qianmao was forced to give up a boat that he had hired for the day after a soldier threatened to beat him with the punting pole.[151] In one instance a boatman refused to relinquish his vessel and was shot dead at point blank range.[152] The military also extorted money and even food rations from refugees.[153] This was not that unusual. Soldiers frequently abused their positions for personal enrichment. One favoured tactic involved

---

[145] See Sapio, *Sovereign Power*, pp. 42–3; Wakeman, *Policing Shanghai*, pp. 10, 24.

[146] Wilbur, *Cambridge History of China*, p. 671.

[147] National Government of the Republic of China, 'Emergency Law for the Suppression of Crimes Against the Safety of the Republic'.

[148] Clubb, *Communism in China*, p. 38.   [149] Van de Ven, *War and Nationalism*, p. 116.

[150] Alley, *Man against Flood*, pp. 12–13. As a Communist sympthasier, Alley's account of the flood is hardly impartial, yet the accounts he gives of soldiers abusing sampan owners is corroborated by several contemporary witnesses cited in the text that follows. For more on Alley's political leanings see Brady, *Friend of China*.

[151] Xie, *Yi jiu san yi nian*, p. 139.

[152] *North China Herald*, 25 August 1931.   [153] Yorke, *China Changes*, p. 72.

planting bullets on travellers and then threatening to execute them as Communists if they failed to pay an exorbitant bribe.[154] Even such obvious ruses were not required during the flood, as soldiers had been granted the right to behave as they pleased.

The mistreatment of refugees was not simply the product of indiscipline. Military commanders used martial law as a pretext to conduct a campaign of political and social repression. Commandeered sampans were mounted with machine guns so that soldiers could patrol the city day and night. The punishments they meted out to criminals ranged from beatings to extrajudicial executions.[155] By late August, soldiers were 'very much in evidence' and the 'execution squad' was conspicuous in its presence.[156] They carried out raids and rounded up those suspected of seditious activities.[157] Students were monitored particularly closely, and a crackdown was launched against those involved in Communist and anti-Japanese activists.[158] Rewi Alley would later claim that Ye Peng had 'scavenged around with his gangsters trying to ferret out anyone who might be accused of being a Communist' before having them executed in batches in front of the Customs House.[159] Although not the most impartial of sources, Alley's description of summary executions is corroborated by other witnesses, including a missionary who saw government troops shooting eleven refugees.[160] Many of those who were executed as Communists were simply trying to organise refugee self-help groups.[161] We do not know how many people fell victim to political repression. Some historians have suggested the number stretched well into the hundreds.[162]

Clearing the Streets

Even martial law could not quell the official anxiety. By the end of August, a vocal faction led by Ye Peng decided that the only viable solution was

---

[154] 'Report of the Work of Rev. F. G. Onley', 1931, SOAS Archives 65/10.
[155] 'Zaizhen zhong zhi Zhi'an' HSSDX, p. 37. *North China Herald*, 11 August 1931; Xie, *Yi jiu san yi nian*, p. 82.
[156] *North China Herald*, 1 September 1931. The foreign correspondent did not disapprove of these activities.
[157] *North China Herald*, 15 September 1931.   [158] *North China Herald*, 8 December 1931.
[159] Alley, *Man Against Flood*, p. 14; Airey, *Learner in China*, p. 100.
[160] 'Report of the Work of Rev. F. G. Onley', SOAS Archives 65/10.
[161] Airey, *Learner in China*, p. 100.
[162] Li and his colleagues cite a contemporary report that claimed several hundred refugees had been killed on the pretext of having committed political crimes. See Li et al., *Zhongguo jindai shi da zaihuang*, p. 211.

the wholesale removal of the refugee population.[163] Squatter settlements were to be demolished and their inhabitants relocated to larger organised camps in the outskirts of Wuhan. Dispersing those on the railway embankment was the highest priority, as they were not only posing a threat to public order but also preventing the reopening of a vital transportation route.[164] Despite their abject conditions, many refugees were reluctant to leave, as we saw at the start of this chapter. Given the context of martial law and casual violence, the popular distrust for official assurances was hardly surprising. Initial attempts at persuasion were followed by a firm policy of forced relocation. The mayor He Baohua ordered the police to compel the refugees to leave, with garrison troops providing eighteen boats to take them to the camps.[165] Still some refugees remained, elevating themselves on platforms or climbing inside partially inundated railway cars.[166] The police eventually resorted to starving the stragglers off the embankment by preventing the delivery of relief rations.[167]

Local citizens of Wuhan proved even harder to dislodge. Many refused to leave their submerged homes no matter how uncomfortable they became. To the annoyance of the military, they proved adept at avoiding eviction. Some stayed in upper stories; others sheltered on their roofs, making small tents from their clothes to keep the sun off their heads.[168] Those whose homes were entirely uninhabitable resorted to building shelters in nearby trees.[169] Resistance to evacuation is not unusual. Such behaviour is often dismissed as irrational, with those who refuse to leave criticised for impinging on the capacity of the state to manage disasters. Yet there are numerous reasons why people resist evacuation. During the floods along the Kosi River in India in 2008 around 15 per cent of the population chose to remain in their villages, fearing the loss of property more than the risk of inundation.[170] In 1991 residents of Santa Rita in the Philippines threatened by mudflows from the eruption of Mount Pinatubo chose to place their faith in prayer rather than abandon their

[163] Alley attributes this action to Ye Peng. The fact that Alley was pro-Communist and Ye later joined the Japanese collaborationist regime may also have influenced his recollection of these events. See Alley, *Man against Flood*, p. 14.
[164] Xie, *Yi jiu san yi nian*, p. 67.   [165] Ibid.
[166] 'The Yangtze Valley Floods by a Hankow Missionary', SOAS Archives 10/7/15; *Hankow Herald*, 19 August 1931
[167] Xie, *Yi jiu san yi nian*, p. 67.   [168] *North China Herald*, 25 August 1931.
[169] A Dong 'Hankou shuizai zhenxiang'; *North China Herald*, 1 September 1931; Clubb, 'The Floods of China', p. 205.
[170] Crabtree, 'Deep Roots of Nightmares'.

homes.[171] As Hurricane Katrina was blowing its way to New Orleans in 2005, many elderly people refused to leave because they did not want to abandon their pets.[172]

Those who resisted evacuation in Wuhan seem to have been motivated primarily by material considerations, not wanting to abandon their homes to water or looters. Their behaviour demonstrated a degree of strategic long-term planning, nestling amidst the emotional appeal of remaining close to home. Xie Qianmao reported one conversation with a refugee from Huangpi who explained that he simply did not trust military assurances. 'They are giving us food for free now,' he noted, 'but how long will it last?'[173] This question betrayed the profound lack of trust that this refugee had for the authorities. It also demonstrated that when forming a survival strategy, he was looking beyond the immediate requirements of food and shelter. In his study of the Sudanese famines of the mid-1980s, Alex de Waal observed that agriculturalists resisted the temptation to consume seeds, knowing that if they did so they would have nothing to plant the next season. Some even went so far as to mix millet seed with sand, so that it would be inedible.[174] Those who resisted evacuation in Wuhan were motivated, at least in part, by a similar desire to preserve economic capacity. They sacrificed the opportunity for comfort in the short term to retain their property and economic capacity.

Unfortunately, military commanders were not prepared to accommodate these strategies. At the end of August they ordered the forced evacuation of refugees from Wuhan 'at the point of the bayonet'.[175] These clearances offered another chance to dispose of politically dubious people, with those suspected of Communism being separated from the refugee population and executed.[176] Hope Simpson concluded that the 'removal of this enormous mass of humanity from the towns' had resulted in 'great misery'.[177] Later, the official report on the flood made no mention of the violent coercion involved in forced evacuation and encampment of refugees. Instead its authors presented a positive narrative, in which relief camps became spaces of benevolent assistance, which

---

[171] Bankoff, *Cultures of Disaster: Society and Natural Hazard*, p. 168.
[172] Hartman and Squires, 'Pre-Katrina'.
[173] Xie, *Yi jiu san yi nian*, p. 149.   [174] De Waal, *Famine That Kills*.
[175] 'Hope Simpson to F. B. Bourdillon', 23 February 1932 JHS 6i. One journalist reported that the military 'forcibly removed thousands of refugees'. See *North China Herald*, 25 August 1931.
[176] 'Report of the Work of Rev. F. G. Onley', 1931, SOAS Archives 65/10.
[177] 'John Hope Simpson to F. B. Bourdillon', 23 February 1932 JHS 6i.

members of the displaced population entered of their own volition. In reality, the evacuation policy had been instituted before adequate accommodation had been made. The NFRC had enjoined military commanders not to clear the streets until the camps had been prepared. Health professionals echoed these sentiments, recognising that while it was important to remove refugees, emergency measures were necessary to prevent the spread of epidemics.[178] These pleas fell on deaf ears. The imperative to secure the city would supersede any other consideration of refugee well-being.[179] The results would prove catastrophic.

Rushed resettlement made it extremely difficult to impose hygienic discipline. Although the epidemics that swept through the camps cannot be explained by a single causal factor, it is instructive to note that there was a precipitous increase in disease mortality following the policy of forced encampment. Dysentery struck the Black Hill camp in mid-September, just as refugees were pushed from the city streets. It was soon taking the lives of forty to fifty people every day.[180] Around this time, the health minister Liu Ruiheng noted that thousands of people 'having been removed by rescue ships to places of safety, have died of disease.'[181] A Chinese Red Cross report described the upsurge in mortality in the camp at He Mountain 赫山, where 656 people died in 15 days in mid-September.[182] A medical missionary described the same camp as being in a 'dreadful state' at that time.[183] The problem was not that there were too many refugees, but the fact that the camps were not ready. The numbers housed continued to increase, rising even more dramatically in November. Critically, however, by this time the hygienic discipline and organisation of the camps had improved so much that incoming refugees did not precipitate a similar upsurge in disease mortality.[184] We can only wonder

[178] *Hankow Herald*, 23 August 1931.
[179] Well, not quite deaf ears, apparently, these moderate voices managed to persuade the military against the favoured strategy of scattering the refugees to camps thirty miles away from Wuhan. With no arrangements for feeding or housing such a vast population, Hope Simpson estimated that this would have resulted in tens of thousands of deaths. Quoted in Airey, *Learner in China*, p. 102.
[180] 'Handwritten notes in diary format by an unknown individual relating to the flood of Hankow', SOAS Archives 5/1201.
[181] *Hankow Herald*, 10 August 1931.
[182] 'Zhongguo Hongshizihui Hankou fenhui cheng yanmai gongzuo wen 1931', HSSDX, p. 167.
[183] 'Handwritten notes in diary format by an unknown individual relating to the flood of Hankow', SOAS Archives 5/1201.
[184] Ibid.

Figure 6.1. A refugee camp in Wuhan in 1931. (*Report of the National Flood Relief Commission 1931–1932*. Shanghai: National Flood Relief Commission, 1933. Reproduced courtesy of Trinity College Library, Cambridge)

how many lives might have been saved had such policies been instituted prior to the forced resettlement of refugees.

Refugee camps were constructed using the same vernacular architectural techniques as squatter settlements, albeit with relief organisations distributing the matting. In some camps, such as the one pictured in Figure 6.1, families made individual huts, where they slept and prepared their own food.[185] In others, refugees lived together, with several thousand huddling under a single mat-shed roof and eating from large communal kitchens. By the autumn relief workers had managed to improve hygiene considerably. Sixty recruits from the local police academy were deputised as sanitary inspectors. They employed refugees to dig and disinfect latrines, establish sources of clean drinking water and conduct fly eradication campaigns.[186] Medical staff working in cooperation with the newly established quarantine service conducted an inoculation campaign. Wuhan soon boasted eight emergency hospitals and its

---

[185] RNFRC, pp. 69–70. Sister M. Patrick descibes a typical refugee hut in Barrett, *Red Lacquered Gate*, p. 275.

[186] RNFRC, pp. 147–8, 159–64; H. Owen Chapman 'Fighting Floods and Famine in China', SOAS Archives 10/7/15.

own bacteriological laboratory. Gradually these measures helped to reduce the level of flood-related diseases spreading through the refugee population.

Benevolence and Detention

Of all the modes of institutionalisation that emerged in the modern world, disaster relief camps would seem to be the most innocuous. Such institutions seemed to encapsulate the most benevolent intentions of modernising states, which sought to shelter their citizens from the capricious forces of the environment. There would seem, at first glance, little resemblance between relief camps and more infamous modes of institutionalisation, such as concentration or labour camps. Yet relief and detention have not always been neatly disaggregated. Today, the term concentration camp implies a facility in which people are incarcerated without legal process, as a result of their particular political or ethnic associations. This mode of institutionalisation is usually traced to the late nineteenth century. In Cuba, the Philippines and Southern Africa, colonial powers from Europe and America used concentration camps as weapons of war, detaining whole sections of the population during conflicts.[187] Until the Second World War, however, the term concentration camp was also routinely applied to facilities used to house disaster and conflict refugees. In fact, this may have been the original use of the term. British colonial officials in India were already describing the 'concentration' of relief labourers in camps during famines in the late 1870s. The fact that these starving refugees were compelled to undertake hard labour to receive minimal rations, demonstrates that the distinction between benevolence and detention was never quite as clear-cut as it might now appear.[188]

Scholars such as Giorgio Agamben and Jenny Edkins have made much of the conceptual overlaps between relief camps and concentration camps, seeing them as two incarnations of what Michel Foucault characterised as the biopolitical governance of the modern state.[189] It is not necessary to pursue this oblique Foucauldian approach to reveal the parallels between these two modes of institutionalisation. Modern history is rife with instances in which disaster relief camps functioned explicitly as

[187] Mühlhahn, 'Concentration Camp'.
[188] Hall-Matthews, *Peasants, Famine and the State*, p. 182.
[189] Agamben, *Means without Ends*; Edkins, *Trauma and the Memory of Politics*; Foucault, *History of Sexuality*.

institutions of pre-emptive detention. One of the most infamous examples occurred during the Mississippi flood of 1927, when a large number of African American refugees were accommodated in levee-top 'concentration camps'. The name given to these institutions was no mere linguistic slip. Fearing that African American sharecroppers would use the disaster as a pretext to migrate north and escape punitive debt arrangements, members of the white landowning elite detained their tenants in camps, encircled with barbed wire and policed by armed guards. Walter White, the leader of the National Association for the Advancement of Colored People, personally witnessed the treatment of African Americans displaced by the flood. He found

> Negro refugees penned in concentration camps from which they were not permitted by National Guardsmen to emerge without the consent of their landlords. I found also that Negroes in many instances were being forced to pay for relief that had been supplied gratis by the Red Cross. When they were unable to pay, many of them lost everything they owned, the 'debt' was assumed by the landlord of the near-by plantation and the Negro taken under guard to the plantation to work out his debt.[190]

Famine refugees were also pre-emptively detained during famines in Bengal during the early 1940s. Janam Mukherjee has described how impoverished refugees in Calcutta resisted attempts by the government to place them in ill-equipped poor houses. In response, the authorities ordered that thousands of refugees be cleared from the streets and placed in special 'repatriation camps', where they would no longer pose a threat to the social order and hygiene of the city.[191] The historian Klaus Mühlhahn has defined concentration camps as institutions in which members of a particular ethnic or political group are detained 'not for what they have done, but for who they are'.[192] It would seem that there are numerous instances in modern history in which simply being the victim of a disaster was considered sufficient grounds for an individual to find themselves incarcerated in an institution of benevolent detention.

In Chinese, the institutions constructed on the outskirts of Wuhan in 1931 were described using the innocuous term 'refugee relief shelters' 难民收容所 (nanmin shourongsuo). Foreign journalists and relief workers used the terms 'refugee camps,' 'segregation camps' and

---

[190] White, *Man Called White*, pp. 80–1; see also Patrick O'Daniel, *When the Levee Breaks*.
[191] Mukherjee, *Hungry Bengal.*   [192] Mühlhahn, 'Concentration Camp', p. 544.

'concentration camps' interchangeably.[193] This lack of linguistic preci-
sion betrayed the porous divisions between relief and detention. Camps
that were ostensibly places of refuge also facilitated various forms of
biological, social and political segregation. They consigned potentially
infectious people behind a *cordon sanitaire* of water and wire. This helped
arrest the trajectory of epidemics through the urban population yet
increased the exposure of refugees to infection. Camps also acted as a
mode of social segregation, relocating impoverished people away from
the city centre where they might be tempted to indulge in antisocial
or criminal activities. Once dispersed, refugees were subjected to further forms of internal segregation. Those who were deemed worthy of
official charity were sent to regular relief camps, while those considered immoral paupers were sent for punitive rehabilitation in prisons
or vagrant shelters. Relief camps functioned like workhouses, which
contained the poor while trying to teach them appropriate values.[194]

A final function of the relief camps was to suppress political sedition.
Military officials policed the refugee population, sending soldiers and
spies to patrol the camps.[195] Refugees were also subjected to political
propaganda designed to foster appropriate attitudes towards the government. Chiang Kai-shek himself wrote a manifesto that was read aloud to
refugees in the Wuhan camps explaining the political situation that faced
the government.

> My soldiers have killed almost all the revolutionaries, and are contin-
> uing to do so. I believe it will not be long before we have killed them
> all. It is very unfortunate that at this stage we have been struck by this
> natural disaster. The primary task of the government now is to safe-
> guard the refugee population and to eradicate the red bandits...I
> implore my fellow countrymen to be united and calm in this difficult
> environment...Refugees should not allow themselves to be tricked by
> evildoers but instead listen to the people who have been sent to assist
> them.[196]

The military were not content to rely on this persuasion. They also
resorted to coercion. One foreign journalist reported how the local
government had constructed a 'well-guarded refugee camp' to detain

[193] See *The Chinese Recorder*, November, 1931 and *The Chinese Recorder*, December 1931. See
    also Maze, *Documents Illustrative*, pp. 552, 557.
[194] Chen, *Guilty of Indigence*.
[195] In one instance a doctor was injured when he was blinded by the flashlight of a passing
    soldier causing him to fall into a cutting. See 'Handwritten notes in diary format by an
    unknown individual relating to the flood of Hankow', SOAS Archives 5/1201.
[196] Included as a preface to Xie, *Yi jiu san yi nian*.

'politically suspicious' people.[197] Beyond this brief reference, there is no record of this facility. Yet its existence suggests that some institutions during the flood were coming dangerously close to resembling concentration camps, in the modern sense of the term. Indeed, shortly after the flood, China gained its first actual concentration camp, built by the Japanese forces in Manchuria at Beiyinhe 背荫河.[198] The Nationalists soon followed suit, developing institutions that were known euphemistically as 'schools' 学校 (xuexiao), which confined inmates behind barbed wire and subjected them to routine torture and summary executions.[199] Meanwhile, the Communists were developing labour camps, based initially on the infamous Soviet model.[200] Despite their profound ideological differences, these various factions shared a predilection for political detention.

There is little doubt that for many members of the floating population, relief camps were truly a place of refuge. They offered access to food, shelter and medical assistance. The survival prospects of many inmates were improved because of the dedication of relief workers and volunteers, who at times placed themselves at considerable risk to minister to the needs of impoverished people. These volunteers were also responsible for recording much of the information that we have regarding the lives of ordinary refugees. There was, however, another side to the official response to the disaster, one instituted by individuals and groups who did not record their interactions with refugees. These were the people who created a regime of martial law, forcibly relocated squatters at gunpoint and either sent politically suspicious people to secure relief camps or had them executed. It was this latter group that made refugees suspicious of official assistance. As ordinary people realised that the divide separating benevolence from detention was only paper thin, they soon found it difficult to trust anyone in a uniform.

The experience of Wuhan in 1931 demonstrates the critical influence that political dynamics can have on a disaster regime. Violence, and the distrust it inspires, acts as an amplifier for humanitarian catastrophes. Political interactions are also a vital dimension of the disaster experience, having a profound influence on the way refugees behave. The dynamic within a community helps to determine the level of cooperation between the various actors involved in managing a crisis. If this dynamic becomes

---

[197] *North China Herald*, 25 August 1931 and *North China Herald*, 1 September 1931.
[198] Mühlhahn, 'Concentration Camp', p. 550.
[199] Wakeman, *Spymaster*, pp. 217–20, 457 [n. 51], p. 473 [n. 69]. See also Mühlhahn, 'Concentration Camp', p. 553.
[200] Mühlhahn, *Criminal Justice*, p. 147.

dysfunctional, then those who wish to exploit disasters for political or economic gain may feel emboldened to do so, without threat of legal or moral sanction. It is no coincidence that lethal disaster regimes often flourish in repressive political regimes. Such was the case in 1931.

Despite endemic distrust, millions of refugees throughout China ended up in camps. Others managed to avoid this fate. In early 1932, the streets of Wuhan were still awash with refugees who had somehow managed to evade the military and police and were now begging their wealthier counterparts for assistance.[201] With few clothes to keep out the bitter winter chill, these refugees were in a pitiful state.[202] At the time, the existence of these people was taken as evidence of the failure of the relief effort. Yet it is debatable whether they would have stood a better chance of survival in the infectious environments of the camps. Indeed, it is possible that the capacity to resist institutionalisation may have enhanced their prospects of survival. By January 1932, local journalists in Wuhan were expressing concerns about the threat that refugees posed to public order. One noted that although many refugees were genuinely 'impoverished and in difficulties' 贫困 (pinkun), there were also many 'cunning people' 狡黠者 (jiaoxiazhe) seeking to exploit the situation. To expedite agricultural recovery, so it was argued, the displaced population must be repatriated as soon as possible.[203]

The police began a campaign to register the remaining hut dwellers in the city.[204] At the same time divisions of water police were sent to monitor river dwellers, to ensure that no Communists were entering the city.[205] In late January 1932, the provincial authorities ordered that rice porridge kitchens should be closed, and that all forms of relief must but stopped within seven days.[206] The government issued an edict declaring that the organised camps were to be dispersed. Those with sufficient resources took down their huts and returned to their home districts. Others were shipped out to a smaller camp several miles upriver from Wuhan.[207] For the municipal authorities, the disaster was over. For the floating population, there was no neat closure. The acute difficulties of famine and epidemic disease would last until at least the summer of 1932. The devastating consequences of the flood would last for years.

---

[201] *The Chinese Recorder*, November 1932.
[202] *Wuhan Ribao*, 12 January 1932.   [203] *Wuhan Ribao*, 13 January 1932.
[204] *Wuhan Ribao*, 15 January 1932.   [205] *Wuhan Ribao*, 17 January 1932.
[206] *Wuhan Ribao*, 19 January 1932; *Wuhan Ribao*, 22 January 1932.
[207] Edith Wills, 'Hanyang 1931', SOAS Archives 10/7/15.

EPILOGUE

Only when the people become the masters of society in a new age, will we be able to turn a new page in the history of famine.

Deng Tuo[1]

By the late autumn 1931 most of the world had forgotten about the flood. The eye of the global media, which for a few months had been entranced by scenes of inundated China, had now shifted its focus north, and was gazing aghast at the Japanese annexation of Manchuria. It is for this act of international aggression that the year 1931 now stands in infamy in Chinese historical memory. If it is remembered at all, the flood – which had a far greater humanitarian impact – is seen merely as a background context for this invasion. For those living in the disaster zone, the inundation of their homes and communities proved harder to forget. After rivers had receded and streets had been pumped dry, the flood left a malodorous reminder of its presence, in the form of a thick residue of earth coating the landscape.[2] As it was no longer possible to use sampans to traverse the streets of Wuhan, pedestrians had to negotiate a path through this quagmire. Walkways soon became so slippery that people were forced to strap straw sandals to the bottoms of their boots.[3]

Observers of life in early twentieth century China often commented on the close affinity between the common people and the earth.[4] People lived in houses of tamped earth; they ate meals grown in earth fertilised with their own night soil – their fields and intestines locked in an

---

[1] Deng, *Zhongguo jiuhuang shi*, p. 397.
[2] *Wuhan Ribao*, 13 January 1932; *Hankow Herald*, 2 September 1931.
[3] Edith S. Wills 'Hanyang 1931', SOAS Archives 10/7/15.
[4] The most famous example being Buck, *The Good Earth*. Count Keyserling said 'There is no other peasantry in the world which gives such an impression of absolute genuineness and of belonging so much to the soil.' Quotes in Mallory, *China*, p. xi.

intimate nutrient cycle. When they died, their bodies joined this cycle, being buried in the earth of home, their graves guarded by a local Earth God. In extremis, people consumed certain types of earth to ward off the symptoms of hunger and disease. For the anthropologist Fei Xiao-tong 费孝通, although this intimate relationship between people and earth formed the bedrock of a 'glorious history', it was highly problematic. The 'earthbound' nature of Chinese life had created a sedentary and conservative society, which prevented 'the nation from moving forward' into the modern world.[5] Yet the flood had revealed that the earth – the very metaphor of stasis – was not as immobile as people supposed. What to the human eye appeared fixed, was, in fact, always moving, travelling in an imperceptible journey across the pedosphere. The flood had also revealed that the earthen world inhabited by most Chinese people remained painfully soluble. For the thick mud through which pedestrians now trudged had once been the material basis of communal life; the sediment the people washed off sturdy buildings contained the homes and bodies of their more vulnerable neighbours.

Some residues were less visible. For those who had lost their land, animals and homes, the flood lived on in the form of debt. The Sisyphean struggle against destitution that consumed the energy of recovering communities was rendered infinitely more difficult by the Great Depression, which had caused both a precipitous decline in the value of produce and a chronic shortage of money.[6] Gradually the epidemic of poverty caused by the flood was subsumed within a broader structure of endemic destitution, a slow-motion disaster in its own right. To make matters worse, pathogenic residues still lingered in the bodies of many flood victims. The malarial plasmodia and schistosome cercariae that had both flourished during the flood pulse found welcoming habitats in the intestinal tracts and livers of recovering communities. The flood had bequeathed a legacy of disease, by compromising individual and collective immune systems. The cholera outbreak of 1932 was probably the most obvious consequence, yet many conditions recently in remission enjoyed a resurgence in the aftermath of inundation. In Wuhan, the infection rate of smallpox, tetanus, diphtheria and meningitis had declined in the late 1920s. It rose again in the early 1930s.[7] This epidemiological trend was not caused by any single factor, but the flood had certainly helped to create conducive social and ecological conditions.

---

[5] Fei, *From the Soil*, pp. 38–40.   [6] Shiroyama, *China during the Great Depression.*
[7] Pi, *Wuhan Tongshi: Minguo juan (xia)*, pp. 322–4.

The flood also left political residues. The international networks that had been forged during the relief effort were solidified in the form of the National Economic Council 全国经济委员会 (Quanguo Jingji Weiyuan-hui), which was designed to facilitate the broader agenda of economic reconstruction.[8] So that it might operate free from the interference of the more militarist wings of the Nationalist regime, the Council required its own revenue stream. Song Ziwen, working, once again, in close collaboration with Ludwik Rajchman of the League of Nations, secured this by negotiating a series of cotton and wheat loans from the United States.[9] The American policy of agricultural surplus dumping, which had been pioneered during the flood, was now enshrined in a permanent bilateral relationship. During the Sino-Japanese War (1937–1945) the Chinese government leaned so heavily on loans from the United States that the wags of Washington dubbed Chiang Kai-shek with the humiliating moniker 'Cash My Check'.[10] Few reflected on how this checking account had originally been opened, as an earlier generation of American politicians had fostered an asymmetrical debtor relationship with China to balance their own ailing rural economy.

Even American financial assistance could not save the Nationalists. Few would have predicted in 1931 that the Communists, then being starved out of the hills and shot in the streets, would eventually rise to power. As bitter civil conflict continued to engulf China throughout the 1930s, the memory of the flood became intensely politicised. Both sides in the conflict saw their own actions vindicated by the motion picture 狂流 *Wild Torrent* (Kuangliu), which used actual newsreel footage of the flood shot in Hankou to frame a story of two lovers torn apart by disaster and parental expectations. The primary villains in the film were members of local gentry who absconded with funds intended for dyke reconstruction.[11] For the Communists this represented a 'proletarian melodrama', as Huang Xuelei has put it, which used disaster to frame class struggle under water. Yet as it reserved most of its venom for the gentry rather than government officials, this film also appealed to the Nationalists, who singled it out for praise, claiming that it demonstrated the didactic power of cinema.[12]

---

[8] Rajchman, *Report of the Technical Agent.*

[9] Zanasi, *Saving the Nation*, pp. 93–5. [10] Mitter, *China's War with Japan.*

[11] Unfortunately, no prints of this film have survived, but the script can still be read in Zheng and Liu, *Zhongguo wusheng dianying juben.* I am grateful to Huang Xuelei for providing me with this resource.

[12] Huang, *Shanghai Filmmaking*, pp. 117–18, 212–18.

There was far less ambiguity about the political intentions of the novella *Water* 水 (Shui), by the left-wing author Ding Ling 丁玲.[13] Having visited flood affected communities, Ding offered a stylistically experimental treatment of their experiences. In the first few paragraphs, readers are bombarded with disjointed sentences. Gradually, it becomes apparent that these are the voices of female villagers, who are holding panic-stricken vigils as their menfolk try to save the village dyke.[14] Though far less celebrated today, another short story entitled *Flood* 水灾 (Shuizai) by Kuang Lu 匡庐 explored very similar themes. It too presented an image of rural society riven by class divisions. At one stage a poor farmer remonstrates with his landlord, arguing that 'those with money should spend their money, and those with strength should use their strength, yet we spend our money and our strength, while you make profit and conserve your energy.'[15] Already, the flood was being used to consolidate the political ambitions of those determined to revolutionise rural life. Both Ding and Kuang used religion to symbolise the helplessness of the older generation, who were pictured making rambling prayers to Buddha and desperate pleas to the Dragon King. The village youths, by contrast, reject the spiritual realm and embrace a disenchanted world of class-consciousness.

Though more prosaic in style, academic treatments of the flood were no less politicised. Floodwater could be poured into any ideological vessel – providing evidence to reinforce all manner of pre-existing political opinions and policy prescriptions. For Wu Ruifeng 吴锐锋, the disaster highlighted the desperate need for rural education. Farmers needed to redirect their energy from gambling and chatting in teahouses to constructive hydraulic projects.[16] For She Ying 社英, the flood revealed the vital necessity for women to take a more active role in political life, as one of the most lamentable features of the disaster had been the failure of women to take the lead in organising the relief effort.[17] For the radical economist Qian Junrui 钱俊瑞 the flood was merely one aspect of a broader 'crisis of capitalism' 资本主义危机 (ziben zhuyi weiji), sweeping the world. Just as disasters had helped to consolidate revolutionary movements in Europe in 1848 and India in 1918, Qian believed that the 1931 flood would inspire the rural massess to overthrow the old social order.[18]

[13] Ding, 'Shui.' For a biographical sketch of Ding Ling see Rana Mitter, *Bitter Revolution.*
[14] Ding, 'Shui'.   [15] Kuang, 'Shuizai'.
[16] Wu, 'Tianzai renhuo'.   [17] She, 'Funü ying fu jiuji'.
[18] Qian Junrui wrote under the pseudonym Tao Zhifu 陶直夫. Tao, 'Yi jiu san yi nian'.

The historian Deng Tuo offered one of the most interesting analyses of the flood, considering it alongside other disasters is his seminal work, *A History of Chinese Famine Relief* 中国救荒史 (Zhongguo Jiuhuang Shi).[19] Written partly as a response to the neo-Malthusian interpretations of Walter Mallory and John Earl Baker, this monograph used a vast range of documents from throughout history to argue that, although the environment and demography had always been important, such factors had never been the sole causes of famine. Through a forensic analysis, Deng demonstrated the critical role played by politics, economics and culture. Though he would later go on to serve as a Maoist propagandist, his work at this stage was far removed from the shrill politicised screeds that would come to typify much official historiography after 1949.[20] It offered a fascinating glimpse of a classically trained historian making a transition to thoughtful Marxist analysis.

The flood carved a path through the natural as well as the social sciences. It inspired a generation of youths to study hydrology and hydraulic engineering. These included Huang Wanli 黄万里, who would later become a leading opponent of the rampant hydraulic interventionism of the Communist state.[21] It inspired a young meteorologist named Tu Changwang 涂长望 to search for an explanation for the excessive precipitation that had fallen on China in 1931. Tu identified that this was not an isolated incident, noting that several other world regions had also experienced heavy rainfall that year.[22] Rejecting popular theories that explained such synchronous meteorological activity with references to sunspots, he argued instead that there was a 'world weather system', driven by changing ocean pressure in the Pacific. He had not yet charted its comprehensive dynamics, but Tu had anticipated the later identification of the El Niño Southern Oscillation (ENSO). As subsequent generations of meteorologists would discover, however, merely determining the cause of extreme weather could not diminish its disastrous effects. Preventing climatic hazards from becoming humanitarian catastrophes required concerted political and economic action. Unfortunately, the Chinese people would have to wait decades before such comprehensive measures would be implemented.

The Party Leads the People to Victory over the Flood!

During the 1930s, the painful memory of the flood began to fade. As with all traumas, however, it could never been forgotten entirely. Not only

---

[19] Deng, *Zhongguo jiuhuang shi.*   [20] Cheek, *Propaganda and Culture.*
[21] Wei, 'Lamentation for the Yellow River'.   [22] Tu, 'On the Relation'.

did it live on in memories, but it was also invoked deliberately by propagandists, who used its spectre to haunt communities over subsequent
decades. Today, the 1931 flood is not even remembered as the most notorious deluge of the era. That dubious honour falls to the 1938 Yellow
River Flood. Though it killed fewer people and affected a much smaller
area, this later disaster enjoys an infamous reputation, largely because it
was attributable entirely to human actions.[23] The decision to breach the
dykes at Huayuankou 花园口 in Henan formed part of an attempt to slow
the advance of the Japanese army. Having witnessed the scenes of devastation in 1931, Chiang Kai-shek had written: 'I cannot but be painfully
aware of my deficiency in virtue and lack of ability, which have resulted in
my failure to take precautions to forestall this disaster.'[24] He must have
either supressed or forgotten this shame when, less than a decade later,
he deliberatley unleashed a river onto his own people.

   In fact, Chiang did not even have to look back as far 1931 to recall the
horrors of inundation. Just three years after the National Flood Relief
Commission 救济水灾委员会 (Jiuji Shuizai Weiyuanhui NFRC) had completed its lauded rehabilitation of the hydraulic system, dykes throughout the middle Yangzi had collapsed once again. The 1935 flood may not
have been as gargantuan as its predecessor, but it was a bitter reminder of
just how far China still had to travel before it could resolve its problems
with water. When the journalist Chen Gengya 陈赓雅 spoke to refugees
near Wuhan in 1935, he was bemused to find that they believed that fate
was the only factor determining whether one would experience 'disaster or fortune' 祸福 (huofu) during floods.[25] Given that their governors
had been unable to protect them from inundation, even when they mar-
shalled the brightest minds and the labour of more than a million workers, it would seem that these refugees had a point.

   Throughout the late 1930s and 1940s, China was gripped by first
international and then civil conflict. These conflicts not only caused profound destruction but also engendered a lack of administrative continu-
ity. These two factors rendered any significant reform of the hydraulic
system untenable. When heavy rain fell in 1948, forty-three counties in
Hubei once again found themselves under water.[26] Distracted by the
impending Communist invasion, neither the provincial government nor
local communities were able to repair the dykes properly. Hence, when

[23] Lary, 'Drowned Earth'; Muscolino, *Ecology of War*.
[24] *Hankow Herald*, 6 September 1931.
[25] Chen, *Jianghe shuizai*.   [26] *Hubei sheng zhi: Minzheng*, pp. 113–14.

the People's Liberation Army marched across Hubei the next summer, their soldiers found themselves wading through water. The inundation that struck the middle Yangzi in 1949 was the worst since 1935.[27] This baptism of floodwater served as an apt reminder for the new Communist government of the daunting resposibility of hydraulic management that they had just assumed. Taming rivers would assume paramount importance over the next decade. In Hubei, this process began in 1951, with the construction of the Jingjiang Flood Diversion Area 荆江分洪区 (Jingjiang Fenhong Qu).[28] Large sluice gates would allow governors to divert the Yangzi onto its erstwhile floodplains should the stream flow of the river reach dangerous levels. Heralded as a great victory for modern engineering, this was actually a rather ancient solution. The Song engineers who had first consolidated the river dyke system a millennium earlier had been careful to include sluice gates.[29]

The government did not have to wait long for a chance to test its new flood diversions. In the spring of 1954 it started to rain and did not stop for fifty-eight days. The water flowing through the Yangzi soon exceeded that of 1931, eventually reaching the highest point since records began in the late nineteenth century.[30] With water streaming down mountain tributaries and gathering on the plains, by the summer, 10 million people in Hubei had already been affected by the flood. Yet Wuhan, now a key centre of state-owned industry, had not been inundated.[31] The chief engineer Tao Shuzeng 陶述曾 declared war on water, claiming that Wuhan must be protected at all costs.[32] The flood had been propelled to the frontline of what Judith Shapiro has described as the 'war against nature' – a highly combative approach to environment management that prevailed during the Maoist era.[33] In mid-July, the provincial authorities unleashed their ultimate weapon in this war, opening the new flood diversions.[34] At the same time, in Wuhan tens of thousands of workers and soldiers were deployed to bolster the urban dykes. No longer helpless refugees provided with work as a form of charity, this was a flood prevention army, whose members, if the state media could be believed,

[27] *Hubei sheng zhi: Dashiji*, pp. 557, 565.   [28] Di, 'Xin Zhongguo'.

[29] Will, *State Intervention*. One significant difference was that one of the major objectives of the flood diversion was to safeguard urban industry. See Di, 'Xin Zhongguo'.

[30] Yu, Chen and Ren, 'Analysis of Historical Floods'.

[31] 'Hubei sheng zaiqing jiankuang,' 6 September 1954,' *HFKDX*, pp. 225–27. For a detailed analysis of the 1954 floods, see Courtney, *At War with Water*.

[32] Tao, 'Tao Shuzeng yu 1954'.   [33] Shapiro, *Mao's War against Nature*.

[34] Pi, *Wuhan tongshi: Zhonghua Remin Gongheguo*, p. 70.

risked life and limb battling against the flood, sometimes even blocking breached dykes with their own bodies.[35]

When not lionising the exploits of their heroic workers, propagandists were reminding people how much worse things had been in 1931. The memory of the flood was resuscitated to demonstrate the obvious superiority of Communist governance. Official publications reiterated such comparisons continually, printing photographs of inundated streets in 1931 alongside their dry equivalents in 1954. Pictures of starving refugees were juxtaposed with those of happy workers in shops brimming with produce.[36] Unlike in 1931, when an international community of journalists had conveyed descriptions of the disaster to a global audience, in 1954 those outside China had to rely on a trickle of highly dubious information. In the years that followed, practically the only evidence available was the bombastically titled *Man against Flood*, a book written by Rewi Alley. Having worked for the NFRC in Wuhan in 1931, and having also visited the city at the height of the flood 1954, Alley was well placed to make a comparison. Yet while his study of the 1954 flood was putatively based on eyewitness testimony, for the most part it merely recapitulated the unabashed hagiography found in the state media. In the battle of man against flood, there could be no victor, it would seem, other than Communist man.

The reality of the 1954 flood was markedly different. Triumphant propaganda heralding the salvation of Wuhan neglected to mention that large swathes of the city had been inundated. When the dykes surrounding Hanyang collapsed, around 26,300 refugees had been forced to head for the hills, just as they had in 1931.[37] Thankfully, conditions in camps were much better. In fact, many of those who lived on the hills of Hanyang remember the flood as an example of the honesty and diligence of early Communist governors.[38] To their credit, the government seems to have responded to the urban refugee crisis rapidly and efficiently, providing adequate food and arresting the transmission of epidemic diseases. The same was not true in the countryside. Contrary to the official statistics, which claimed a nationwide death toll of 30,000, an internal government

---

[35] There are articles describing flood exemplars throughout the year, for a typical example see *Changjiang Ribao*, 20 August 1954.

[36] WFZZ, *Dang lingdao renmin zhansheng le hong* shui.

[37] 'Kuikou fenhong qu mei ri qingkuang, Hubei sheng shengchan jiuji weiyuanhui bangongshi,' 29 July 1954, *HFKDX*.

[38] Courtney, *At War with Water*.

report written shortly after the flood reveals that the true figure was five times higher, with 149,507 dying in Hubei alone.[39]

Far from being a heroic victory over nature, this may have been the most lethal flood to strike China – perhaps the world – in the latter half of the twentieth century. Those living in the flood diversion area were the hardest hit, suffering 70 per cent of all fatalities. Engineers had opened the sluice gates before the land had been properly evacuated. In a painful echo of 1931, many villagers had refused to leave, though in this instance it was in part because they suspected that party cadres were using the threat of flooding as a ruse to collectivise their land. When they were finally convinced to evacuate, they found themselves living in highly unsanitary conditions. Dysentery and measles dispatched most of the immediate flood victims, with snail fever infecting many of the survivors.[40]

There were clear differences between the 1931 and 1954 disasters, not least the all-important urban dimension. Yet there were also significant similarities. Most obviously, the epidemiological aspects of the disaster regime had yet to be adequately addressed, meaning preventable diseases flourished during both floods. There were also political similarities. In each instance, distrust of the state had hampered official attempts to manage displaced populations – in one case this was caused by the context of war; in the other it was the result of the profound disruption of the revolution. Far from distinguishing the new society from the old, then, the 1954 flood revealed that while the political regime had changed many aspects of the disaster regime had not.

Ignoring these painful realities, propagandists tried to convince the people that the flood had revealed a critical difference between the two governance systems. The Nationalists had been venal and corrupt, whereas the Communists were upright and efficient. This argument accepted, if only implicitly, the socioeconomic model of disaster causation pioneered by the likes of Deng Tuo a generation earlier. In the hands of propagandists, however, this analytical model was reduced to the crudest of caricatures. The primary variable determining the outcome of a disaster was not the environmental profile of the hazard, but rather the

[39] For the official statistics see Zong and Chen, '1998 Flood'; The party investigation is 'Hubei sheng yijiuwusi nian shuizai qingkuang ji zaihou huifu qingkuang tongji,' HSD (Wuhan, 1954). The higher death toll is corroborated by other contemporary reports, see Courtney, *At War with Water*.
[40] Courtney, *At War with Water*.

political and economic system in which it occurred. The logical corollary of this position was that, if a society followed the right ideological prescriptions, any disaster could be averted.

By the end of the 1950s, the government was forced to perform an abrupt volte-face on this issue. When the Great Leap Forward of 1958–1962 plunged China into what was probably the most lethal famine in history, propagandists fell back on the old trick of pointing their fingers at the environment. Most historians today accept that this was an almost entirely anthropogenic famine, caused by the caustic political environment and the desperate mismanagement of the economy, yet at the time the regime attributed it to three years of natural disasters 三年自然灾害 (san nian ziran zaihai).[41] True to form, Deng Tuo was one of the few scholars courageous enough to point out that the famine had a clear political dimension. He was to pay a heavy price for his intellectual honesty. Seen as a critic of Maoist orthodoxy, Deng was subjected to a sustained period of political persecution during the Cultural Revolution (1966–1976). With the pressure eventually becoming too great, he took his own life.[42]

The Transformation of the Disaster Regime

Had Deng lived a few more years he would have witnessed China beginning to turn a new page in its history, just as he had dreamed in the 1930s. The latter half of the twentieth century witnessed a profound transformation of the disaster regime. Communities remained susceptible to hazards, including floods, earthquakes and droughts, yet their members were significantly less vulnerable to both their initial and secondary effects. China was not alone in experiencing this transformation. Some historians have characterised the late twentieth century as the Great Acceleration. Though people had been modifying the environment for countless millennia, and had been having an increasingly dramatic effect on the life systems of Earth since at least the beginning of the industrial revolution, it was in the late twentieth century that humanity plunged headlong into what some atmospheric scientists have begun to describe as the Anthropocene – a distinct geological era in which humanity has become a dominant force shaping Earth systems.[43] This

---

[41] Ens Manning and Wemheuer, *Eating Bitterness*; Thaxton, *Catastrophe and Contention*; Dikötter, *Mao's Great Famine*; Yang, *Tombstone*.

[42] Cheek, *Propaganda and Culture*.

[43] There is much debate regarding the timing – and even existence – of the Anthropocene. Although humans had clearly had an impact on the environment for millennia, I follow

transition has changed human life immeasurably, and in so doing has revolutionised the disaster regime.

Most obviously, the Chinese people have transformed their relationship with water – enacting probably the most significant alteration of the hydrosphere in human history. Historians have tended to focus on the monumental hydraulic interventions that facilitated this process, yet low-level interventions also played a key role. As the earthen world was solidified into brick and concrete, dykes grew stronger and higher, and reed huts and earth houses began to disappear from the landscape, though they can still be found if one knows where to look.[44] With labour-saving devices such as motorised and electrical water pumps replacing human- or ox-powered treadle pallet pumps, farmers were able to drain land much more efficiently, alleviating the low-level problem of waterlogging and reclaiming wetlands with much greater speed.[45] Politics was also vitally important. Tighter government control meant that the hydraulic network was regulated and standardised.[46] Thankfully, hydraulic failures are now much less common than they were at the time of the 1931 flood.

While these measures improved hydraulic security, the imperatives of economic growth also led to some spectacular mistakes in water management. The desire to increase agricultural production – driven by the state under Mao Zedong and increasingly by the market under Deng Xiaoping – encouraged the population of Hubei to reclaim lakes and marshes on an unprecedented scale.[47] The gradual assault on the wetlands that had been unfolding for millennia escalated exponentially. As nature was sacrificed on the altar of economic development, species such as alligators and dolphins were pushed to near extinction. The depletion of the environment also diminished cultural diversity. The fossilized remnants of wetland culture can still be found on dinner tables of Hubei. Locals relish delicacies such as steamed bream, lotus root soup and spicy duck neck, although now more often cultivated than foraged. Yet a meal

McNeill in recognising that there was a critical acceleration of anthropogenic influences during the latter half of the twentieth century. See McNeill, *Great Acceleration*. See also Christian, *Maps of Time*.

[44] I have spoken to many farmers in eastern Hubei over the past few years about flooding, many have stressed concrete reinforcement as the major factor improving hydraulic security.

[45] Li, *Village China*.

[46] Customary systems of hereditary management were replaced first by a system of production brigades, before being incorporated in an integrated state infrastructure. Gao, 'Transformation of the Water Regime'.

[47] Zhang et al., 'Possible influence of ENSO'; Ball, *Water Kingdom*, pp. 301–3.

would not be complete without rice – the semi-aquatic plant that has conquered wetlands throughout the world, and to which all other dishes in the middle Yangzi must perform obeisance.

The loss of wetlands deprived rivers of natural reservoirs, meaning that the land could no longer absorb large flood peaks. The official response was to invest in ever-more monumental hydraulic structures. In the 1990s, the government finally began to construct a dam at the Three Gorges in the west of Hubei. Often seen as an expression of the hubris of the Communist state, this grandiose scheme had enjoyed the support of every government in China, and of many Western engineers, since Sun Yat-sen had first proposed it in the 1910s.[48] Dams, as the ecologist Patrick McCully has observed, 'are much more than simply machines to generate electricity and store water. They are concrete, rock and earth expressions of the dominant ideology of the technological age.'[49] Nowhere has this ideology been embraced more deeply than in China, which is now home to half of the world's large dams.[50] The Three Gorges Dam was to be the largest of them all.

By the end of the twentieth century, an increasingly vocal environmentalist lobby had begun to question the ideology of damming. They pointed to the fact that the Three Gorges Dam would not only cause environmental destruction, but also displace more than 1.5 million people and cause the loss of countless precious cultural artefacts.[51] In response to this clamour of dissent, the government chose to invoke the memory of flooding. The 1931 disaster was trouped out once again, while the 1954 flood was reinvented not as a triumphant victory but as a tragic disaster that even the dedicated Communist state could not fully avert.[52] A wall of reinforced concrete would ensure that catastrophes such as these could never happen again. This argument ignored the fact that dam failures could now cause a flood that would be more physically destructive than anything previously witnessed in the region. Like dykes, dams are vulnerable to both environmental hazards and human negligence. When they fail, as they did at Banqiao 板桥 in Henan in 1975, for example, dams unleash waves of destruction far more dangerous than anything found in nature.[53] Those who constructed the Three Gorges Dam have bequeathed a formidable management task to future

[48] Yin, *Long Quest for Greatness.*   [49] McCully, *Silenced Rivers*, p. 2.
[50] Tilt, *Dams and Development*, pp. 3–4.   [51] Ibid., p. 146.
[52] See for example Tao, 'Features of the Three Gorges Dam.'
[53] Yi, 'World's Most Catastrophic Dam Failures'.

generations. They have locked them into a late twentieth century technology, which will require continual investment of economic resources, no matter whether the returns diminish over time. For better or worse, politics and economics have assumed even greater importance within the disaster regime.

The argument for the Three Gorges Dam was predicated on the assumption that the flooding of floodplains was somehow undesirable. It ignored the role that excessive human intervention had played in generating flood risks. In the latter half of the twentieth century the three major flood-generating processes – the channelisation of rivers, the deforestation of hillsides and the reclamation of wetlands – all increased dramatically.[54] The Three Gorges Dam would now permanently disrupt the flood pulse. As it became fully operational only in the late 2010s, insufficient time has passed to fully appreciate the ecological impact of the dam. There are worries that it will increase the deoxygenation and pollution of water, as the stream flow is slowed and toxic heavy metals flow up from the sediments on the riverbed, resulting in the permanent loss of many rare endemic species, including sturgeon and paddlefish.[55] The dam has also fragmented habitats, changing the distribution of flora and fauna. Some of the new islands in the dam reservoir now support massive populations of ground rodents, which threaten the survival of other small mammals.[56] Wetland reclamation and dam building have fundamentally disrupted the flood pulse. This has recalibrated the disaster regime, simultaneously removing both its beneficial and harmful effects – both its disaster risks and its ecological endowments. Were Hubei to experience a flood like that of 1931 today, it is unlikely that the local population would survive for long on depleted stocks of wild fish, fowl and plants.

Fortunately, the time in which Chinese people must fill their stomachs with wild produce to survive a period of want seems to have passed. The nutritional revolution that took place during the last few decades of the twentieth century was among the most profound changes to life on Earth during that period. Mao Zedong was fond of identifying contradictions. Few were more glaring than the fact that the same party that had precipitated the most lethal famine in history later initiated one of the

---

[54] Following the 1998 floods, even the government was forced to acknowledge that the denuding of old-growth forests was having deleterious consequences. See Marks, *China*, p. 249.

[55] Wu et al., 'Three Gorges Dam'; Jobin, *Dams and Disease*, pp. 463–4.

[56] Wang et al., 'Ecological Consequences'.

most successful policies of famine eradication. Even the virtuoso Qing administrators of the eighteenth century could not equal this boast. It was achieved through a combination of economics, politics and technology. Lillian Li has described how the government regulated the grain supply system, maintaining large reserves and controlling the import–export market.[57] At the same time, the agricultural sector witnessed a huge growth in productivity following the introduction of high-yielding crops and nitrogen-based chemical fertilisers.[58] The Chinese chapter of the Green Revolution began in earnest in the 1970s, but widespread hunger really began to fade only during the reform era.[59] Historians will no doubt continue to debate whether this was a happy coincidence of timing for Dengist policymakers, or whether the unfettering of agriculture from the collectivised economy acted as spur for production. What is clear is that, although food security may remain a pressing issue for policymakers, the Chinese people are now better fed than ever before.[60] Thankfully the threat of famine has largely been eradicated from the disaster regime.

Equally as profound as the nutritional revolution has been the epidemiological transition in the latter half of the twentieth century. This, more than any other factor, has diminished the fatalities caused by hazards. Though it is unlikely that the practical humanitarians of the NFRC would have approved of the politics, they may have admired the mass mobilisation used in public health campaigns during the Maoist years. Some historians have even argued that the nucleus of the famous barefoot doctor campaigns, in which minimally trained medical workers were set to work throughout rural districts, could be traced to pioneering public health workers such as John Grant, who dreamed of initiating similar policies around the time of the flood.[61] Preventive and emergency medicine have vastly improved the health of the population over the past seven decades, with medical and chemical interventions limiting or eradicating conditions such as smallpox, cholera and malaria.[62] One of the most celebrated achievements has been the campaign against snail

---

57 Li, *Fighting Famine.*   58 Smil, *China's Past.*

59 Many people in China still do not eat an adequate diet, while an increasing number are succumbing to obesity as a symptom of poverty. Yet the situation cannot compare with the widespread malnutrition of the Republican and early Maoist eras.

60 Smil, *China's Past.*   61 Brown Bullock, *American Transplant,* pp. 162–89.

62 Yip, 'Disease, Society and the State'; Gross, *Farewell to the God of Plague.* Schistosomiasis now infects only around 1 million people in China, still a serious problem but a startling decline from the 10 million affected in the 1950s, particularly given concurrent demographic growth. See Jobin, *Dams and Disease,* p. 467; Wagstaff et al., *Reforming China's Rural Health Care System.*

fever, in which millions of farmers were mobilised to kill molluscs using rudimentary techniques. This usually did not work, as Miriam Gross has observed, and it was medical treatment rather than mass mobilisation that turned the corner with snail fever.[63] Propagandists never allowed the truth get in the way of a good story. Whoever was truly responsible, the removal of schistosome cercariae from the disaster regime was a welcome relief for the Chinese people. It not only made floods less dangerous but also reduced the destitution suffered in wetland communities. The bitter coda to this story, however, is that infected snails have apparently colonised the reservoir above the Three Gorges Dam, meaning that China may not be as close to eradicating the dreaded big belly disease as many people had hoped.[64]

By the end of the twentieth century the residents of Hubei had much less to fear from flooding, not because they had tamed rivers with engineering but because they had eliminated many of the most lethal components of the disaster regime. This was demonstrated vividly in 1998, when the Yangzi unleashed it worst deluge in four decades. The amount of water flowing through the valley that year easily exceeded 1931, and caused significant economic losses and the destruction of nearly half a million homes. Despite its severity, the flood killed a mere 1,320.[65] The loss of any life during a disaster is tragic for those affected, yet over the course of the twentieth century flood mortality rates had been reduced from millions to thousands. Many of the worst social effects of inundation were also mercifully absent. Gone were the mass sales of children and farmers pulling ploughs on their own backs. The idea that food shortages would prompt people to resort to homicidal cannibalism, as they had as recently as the 1960s, was now entirely unthinkable.

Social and natural scientists often claim that the frequency and intensity of environmental disasters are increasing. There is a degree of truth in this. As population densities in disaster-prone regions have grown, the sheer number of people exposed to hazards has increased dramatically.[66] One element that is often overlooked in discussions of long-term trends is the demonstrable decline in disaster *intensity*. The experience of those living in Hubei is a case in point. In hydrological terms, hazards have increased over the twentieth century, and the number of people living in the basin has also grown dramatically. We might comfortably say that more people live under the threat of floods in the province than ever

[63] Gross, *Farewell to the God of Plague.*   [64] Jobin, *Dams and Disease*, p. 466.
[65] Zong and Chen, '1998 Flood'.   [66] Douglass, 'Urban Transition'.

before. This is simply a matter of demographic expansion. Since the 1950s, both the land flooded and the economic impact of inundation have also increased. Yet far fewer people die or become sick because of floods than was once the case.[67] This is the result of a fundamental reconfiguration of the disaster regime. The 1998 flood was devastating to the economy of Hubei, yet local communities were much less vulnerable. The major difference was not that hydraulic engineers had managed to tame rivers – they clearly had not. It was, rather, that the subsistence and health systems were no longer so acutely sensitive to shocks. Indeed, floods continue to occur in Hubei even now, with the Three Gorges Dam regulating the stream flow of the Yangzi. In the summer of 2016 the streets of Wuhan were filled with water. These inundations have become much less dangerous, largely because the local communities are no longer so profoundly impoverished.

China has by no means tackled its problem with disasters. This was demonstrated all too vividly when an earthquake struck Sichuan in 2008, killing at least 80,000 people. Much like in 1954, the state media presented its response in combative terms, depicting heroic soldiers pulling citizens out of the rubble, rescuing them from a dreadful seismic enemy. However, the state no longer enjoyed a monopoly on the dissemination of information, and soon there was a public outcry when it emerged that thousands of children had been killed when their poorly built schools had collapsed.[68] Poverty and corruption, it would seem, can still conspire to make communities vulnerable. While sudden hazards such as these have become relatively rare, the Chinese people now face an increased threat from emergent forms of slow disaster. River water may be less likely to carry cholera and snail fever, yet it often contains dangerously high levels of industrial waste, which, together with atmospheric pollution, has resulted in a cancer epidemic.[69] The dysfunctional modernity that poured petroleum and benzene into rivers in 1931 is now the norm. The disaster regime has not been rendered impotent – it has just been recalibrated. It will continue to evolve as humans find new ways to live in their environments. Climate change, easily the most terrifying by-product of the Anthropocene, now seems to be increasing the intensity and frequency of hydrological and meteorological shocks, including

---

[67] This finding is supported by Duan et al., 'Floods and Associated Socioeconomic Damages'.

[68] Paltemaa, *Managing Famine*, p. 185.

[69] Lora-Wainwright, *Fighting for Breath*; Ball, *Water Kingdom*.

Figure E.1. The Dragon King Temple. (Photograph by the author)

ENSO activity.[70] It would seem likely, therefore, that the people of Hubei have yet to see their last flood.

With the passing of the older generation the last living memories of the 1931 disaster are now being lost. The only public monument to the

---

[70] Shaw, Pulhin and Pereira, *Climate Change Adaptation*.

painful history of flooding in Wuhan is an obelisk on the riverside bund. This commemorates the supposed non-disaster of 1954. The face of Mao Zedong stares out magnanimously above socialist realist reliefs, depicting scenes of soldiers and workers fighting against water. There is no memorial to commemorate those who lost this fight in 1931. At the height of the disaster, the provincial authorities petitioned the Nanjing government to designate an annual Flood Commemoration Day, to remind citizens never again to allow such a calamity to occur.[71] Nothing came of this suggestion. In the years after the disaster, the only physical reminder that the flood had occurred was a beached sampan, which was left as an informal monument by the people Wuhan, acting as an indicator of the high-water level. When this was destroyed during a Japanese air raid, the last physical trace of the flood disappeared.[72]

In the last few years one relic of the past has re-emerged in the urban landscape. In 2010, the Dragon King Temple, pictured in Figure E.1, was reconstructed at the confluence of the Yangzi and Han Rivers. Eighty years since it was destroyed as an expression of ignorance and superstition, it was resurrected as a symbol of heritage. Standing adjacent to a shopping mall, it is one of the innumerable sites that have mushroomed up during the recent tourism revolution. Unlike other religious institutions that have been enjoying a renaissance over the last few decades, there is little to suggest that Dragon King Temple has been incorporated into a living religious tradition. If you chat with local people, most seem to be only vaguely aware of its existence. In the 1930s religious devotees found themselves lacking a temple – in the 2010s this temple lacks religious devotees. In time, perhaps, the citizens of this great river city might rediscover their lost Dragon King, and the rich ecological and cultural heritage that he once represented. We can only hope that they will never again be compelled to beg for his protection.

[71] *Hankow Herald*, 5 September 1931.   [72] Worcester, *Junks and Sampans*, p. 382.

APPENDIX

Nobody knows how many people died in the flood. Numbers commonly cited range from 140,000 to four million. The high-end estimate seems, as far as I can tell, to be based on the calculation of 3.6 million made by the Centre for Research on the Epidemiology (CRED).[1] This figure enjoys great currency online, helping the 1931 flood to secure its position on sensationalist lists of the world's deadliest disasters. The methodology CRED used in its calculation is unclear. The low-end estimate of 140,000 is based on a misreading of the NFRC report, which claimed that this many people had *drowned* during the initial phase of the flood.[2] The same report elsewhere claims that 2 million people died during the flood, having drowned or died from a lack of food.[3] Chinese language studies often cite 422,499 fatalities, which is based on a calculation made by Li Wenhai, Cheng Xiao, Liu Yangdong and Xia Mingfang. These historians used a variety of contemporary reports and statistics.[4] Though far more systematic than any other calculation, the authors do not seem to have consulted the Nanjing Survey, which was the only reliable contemporary attempt to calculate mortality. The survey suggested that 150,000 people had drowned, and that this number represented less than a quarter of all fatalities during the first 100 days of the flood. There are a number of problems with the Nanjing Survey, many of which were acknowledged by the authors. The figures provided

---

[1] Centre for Research on the Epidemiology of Disasters (CRED), *EMDAT Database*, http://www.emdat.be (accessed 11.03.2011). Philip Ball notes that the 1931 floods 'are thought to have killed up to 4 million people,' but does not provide a citation. Ball, *Water Kingdom*, p. 30.

[2] RNFRC, p. 6; This figure is cited in Hsu, *Rise of Modern China*, pp. 546–547; French, *Carl Crow*, p. 185; Winchester, *River at the Centre of the World*.

[3] RNFRC Facing p. 92.

[4] Li et al, *Zhongguo jindai shi da zaihuang*, p. 231; Cited by Li, *Fighting Famine*, p. 284. Yang, *Mubei* p. 396 [Not in English translation entitled *Tombstone*].

pertained only to the first 100 days of the flood, before the effects of famine and disease were fully felt. For reasons of safety, surveyors avoided conflict zones, and so did not travel to areas where famine was at its most intense The survey design also had a number of biases. It relied on surviving refugees to report the deaths of their own family members. This not only excluded those families killed outright, but also enabled people to underreport fatalities, particularly those that might raise accusations of infanticide. Given that all these biases imply an underestimation, it would seem that the figure of 2 million fatalities included in the NFRC report is far from unreasonable. Yet, as has already been noted, nobody knows how many people died in the flood.

BIBLIOGRAPHY

Abbreviations

DEP   Dwight W. Edwards Papers, *Yale Divinity School Library.*
HFKDX   *Hubei sheng yi jiu wu si nian fangxun kanghong dang'an xuanbian* 湖北
        省一九五四年防 汛抗洪档案选编 (The 1954 Flood Control and Fight
        Against the Flood – Selected Archival Documents), (Hubei sheng
        dang'an guan, Wuhan, 1998).
HSD   Hubei Sheng Dang'anguan 湖北省档案馆. (Hubei Provincial
        Archives)
HSSDX   Chen Zhongxing 陈仲兴, ed., *Hubei sheng yi jiu san yi nian shuizai
        dang'an xuanbian* 湖北省一九三一年水灾档案选编 (*The 1931 Hubei
        Flood – Selected Archival Documents*) (Wuhan: Hubei dang'an guan,
        1999).
HSSI   Hankou Jiujiang shouhui Ying zujie ziliao xuanbian 汉口九江收回英
        租界资料选编 (Selected Materials on the Retrocession of the British
        Concessions in Hankou and Jiujiang). Wuhan: Hubei renmin
        chubanshe, 1982.
JHS   John Hope Simpson Papers, *Balliol College Archives*, University of
        Oxford.
RNFRC   National Flood Relief Commission *Report of the National Flood Relief
        Commission 1931–1932* (Shanghai, 1933).
SOAS   School of Oriental and African Studies, University of London.
WFZZ   Wuhan shi fangxun zong zhihuibu 武汉市防汛指挥部 Wuhan Flood
        Control Committee.

Archives

Balliol College Archives

University of Oxford
Papers of John Hope Simpson
Folder 6 File i: Official Correspondence, China [JHS 6i]
Folder 6 File ii: China Family Letters, China [JHS 6ii]
Folder 10. Ian Hope Simpson, *Jack of All Trades: An Indian Civil
Servant in Retirement: Sir John Hope Simpson* [JHS 10]

Egyptian National Archives

Hubei Provincial Archives Hubei sheng dang'an guan 湖北省档案馆
[HPA]

Methodist Archives

University of Manchester

School of Oriental and African Studies

University of London
London Missionary Society
Subject 10, File 7 Box 15 [SOAS 10/7/15] 'Hankow Floods'
File 65 Box 10 [SOAS 65/10] 'Central China Reports, 1926–1931.'
(Wesleyan) Methodist Missionary Society
File 5 Box 1201 [SOAS 5/1201]
File 7 Box 1201 [SOAS 7/1202]
Presbyterian Church of England Foreign Missions Committee
File 6 Box 107a [SOAS 6/107a]

Shanghai Municipal Archives Shanghai shi dang'an guan 上海市档案馆
[SMA]

Yale Divinity School Library

Dwight W. Edwards Papers
Record Group 12 Box 14 Folder 153 [DEP 12/14/153]
Record Group 12 Box 7 Folder 97 [DEP 12/7/97]

Newspapers and Periodicals

Beidou 北斗 (1929)
Changjiang Ribao (1954)
The Chinese Recorder (1931–1932)
The Chinese Students' Monthly (1914)
Da Gongbao 大公报 (1931)
Daolu Yuekan 道路月刊 (1931)
Daxuesheng Yanlun 大学生言论 (1934)
Dongfang Huabao 东方画报 (1931)
Dongfang Zazhi 东方杂志 (1931)
Dongbei Wenhua 东北文化 (1931)
Funu Gongming 妇女共鸣 (1931)
Gaonong Qikan 高农期刊 (1931)
Gongshang Banyuekan 工商半月刊 (1931)
Guangming 光明 (1936)
Guowen Zhoukan 国闻周刊 (1931)
Guoji Maoyi Daobao 国际贸易导报 (1932)
Hankou Minguo Ribao 汉口民国日报 (1927)
Hankow Herald (1931)
Illustrated London News (1931)

Jiuguo Zhoukan 救国周刊 (1932)
Luxing Zazhi 旅行杂志 (1952)
Nanjing Shi Zhengfu Gongbao 南京市政府公报 (1931)
The New York Times (1931)
Nongmin Jiaoyu 农民教育 (1932)
North China Daily News (1931)
North China Herald (1872–1932)
The Religious Tract Society in China (1927)
Shanghai Wujia Yuebao 上海物价月报 (1937)
Shehui Xuekan 社会学刊 (1929)
Shenbao 申报 (1931)
Shenghuo 生活 (1926–1931)
Shoudu Shizheng Gongbao 首都市政公报 (1931)
The Singapore Free Press and Mercantile Advertiser (1931)
The Straits Times (1931)
Time Magazine (1931)
The Washington Post (1931)
Wuhan Ribao 武汉日报 (1932)
Wuhan Shizheng Gongbao 武汉市政公报 (1929)
Xin Chuangzao 新创造 (1932)
Xin Hankou 新汉口 (1927)
Xinminbao 新民报 (1931)
Xuesheng Wenyi Congkan 学生文艺丛刊 (1924)
Yaxi Yabao 亚细亚报 (1931)
Zhongyang Ribao 中央日报 (1931)
Ziqiang Zhoubao 自强周报 (1931)

Books and Articles

A Dong (阿栋). 'Hankou shuizai zhenxiang 汉口水灾真相 (The Truth about the Hankou Flood)'. *Shenghuo (生活)*, 6:37 (1931), 803–5.

Agamben, Giorgio. *Means without Ends: Notes on Politics*, trans. Vincenzo Binetti and Cesare Casarino. Minneapolis: University of Minnesota Press, 2000.

Ahlberg, Kristin L. *Transplanting the Great Society: Lyndon Johnson and Food for Peace*. Columbia: University of Missouri Press, 2008.

Aijmer, Göran. *The Dragon Boat Festival on the Hupeh-Hunan Plain, Central China: A Study in the Ceremonialism of the Transplantation of Rice*. Stockholm: Statens Etnografiska Museum, 1964.

Airey, Willis. *A Learner in China: A Life of Rewi Alley*. Christchurch: The Caxton Press & The Monthly Review Society, 1970.

Aldrete, Gregory S. *Floods of the Tiber in Ancient Rome*. Baltimore: Johns Hopkins University Press, 2007.

Alexander, David. 'Celebrity Culture, Entertainment Values . . . And Disaster'. In Fred Krüger, Greg Bankoff, Terry Cannon, Benedikt Orlowski and E. Lisa F. Schipper (eds.), *Cultures and Disasters:Understanding Cultural Framings in Disaster Risk Reduction*, pp. 179–92. London: Routledge, 2015.

Alley, Rewi. *Man Against Flood: A Story of the 1954 Flood on the Yangtse and of the Reconstruction That Followed It*. Peking: New World Press, 1956.

American Red Cross. *Report of the China Famine Relief, October, 1920–September, 1921.* Shanghai: The Commercial Press, 1921.

Anderson, E. N. *The Food of China.* New Haven: Yale University Press, 1990.

    Food and Environment in Early and Medieval China. Philadelphia: University of Pennsylvania Press, 2014.

Archer, C. S. *Hankow Return.* Boston: Houghton Mifflin Co., 1941.

Arnold, David. *Colonizing the Body: State Medicine and Epidemic Disease in Nineteenth Century India.* Berkeley: University of California Press, 1993.

Arthington, Angela H. *Environmental Flows: Saving Rivers in the Third Millennium.* Berkeley: University of California Press, 2012.

Atwell, William S. 'Volcanism and Short-Term Climatic Change in East Asian and World History, c. 1200–1699 '. *Journal of World History,* 12 (2001), 29–98.

Auden W. H. and Christopher Isherwood. *Journey to a War.* London: Faber and Faber, 1939.

Baker, John Earl. *Explaining China.* New York: Van Nostrand, 1927.

    'Transportation in China.' *Annals of the American Academy of Political and Social Science* 152 (November 1930), 160–72.

Ball, Philip. *The Water Kingdom: A Secret History of China.* London: Bodley Head, 2016.

Bankoff, Greg. 'Bodies on the Beach: Domesticates and Disasters in the Spanish Philippines 1750–1898 '. *Environment and History,* 13 (2007), 285–306.

    'Cultures of Disaster, Cultures of Coping: Hazard as a Frequent Life Experience in the Philippines'. In Christof Mauch and Christian Pfister (eds.), *Natural Disasters, Cultural Responses: Case Studies toward a Global Environmental History,* pp. 265–84. Lanham, MD: Lexington Books, 2009.

    Cultures of Disaster: Society and Natural Hazard in the Philippines. London and New York: Routledge Curzon, 2003.

    'Designed by Disaster: Seismic Architecture and Cultural Adaptation to Earthquakes'. In Fred Krüger, Greg Bankoff, Terry Cannon, Benedikt Orlowski and E. Lisa F. Schipper (eds.), *Cultures and Disasters: Understanding Cultural Framings in Disaster Risk Reduction.* London: Routledge, 2015.

    'Learning About Disasters from Animals'. In Heike Egner, Marén Schorch and Martin Voss (eds.), *Learning and Calamities: Practices, Interpretations, Patterns,* pp. 42–55. New York and London: Routledge, 2014.

Bankoff, Greg, Uwe Lübken and Jordan Sand. *Flammable Cities: Urban Conflagration and the Making of the Modern World.* Madison: The University of Wisconsin Press, 2012.

Barrett, William E. *The Red Lacquered Gate: The Early Days of the Columban Fathers and the Courage of Its Founder Fr. Edward Galvin.* New York: Sheed and Ward, 1967.

Bayley, Peter B. 'Understanding Large River-Floodplain Ecosystems'. *Bioscience* 45:3 (1995): 153–8.

Benton, Gregor. *Mountain Fires: The Red Army's Three-Year War in South China, 1934–1938.* Berkeley: University of California Press, 1992.

    New Fourth Army: Communist Resistance Along the Yangtze and the Huai, 1938–1941 Berkeley: University of California Press, 1999.

Berg, A. Scott. *Lindbergh.* London and New York: Simon and Schuster, 1998.

Bernard, Andreas. *Lifted: A Cultural History of the Elevator.* New York: New York University Press, 2014.

Bickers, Robert. *Britain in China: Community Culture and Colonialism, 1900–1949.* Manchester: Manchester University Press, 1999.
  Empire Made Me: An Englishman Adrift in Shanghai New York: Columbia University Press, 2003.

Biehler, Dawn Day. *Pests in the City: Flies, Bedbugs, Cockroaches, and Rats.* Washington: University of Washington Press, 2013.

Billingsley, Phil. *Bandits in Republican China.* Stanford: Stanford University Press, 1988.

Bird, Isabella. *The Yangtze Valley and Beyond.* Hong Kong: Earnshaw Books, 2008 [1899].

Birrell, Anne. *Chinese Mythology: An Introduction.* Baltimore and London: Johns Hopkins University Press, 1993).
  'The Four Flood Myth Traditions of Classical China'. *T'oung Pao* 83 1997), 213–59.

Blair, Danny and W. F. Rannie. '"Wading to Pembina": 1849 Spring and Summer Weather in the Valley of the Red River of the North and Some Climatic Implications'. *Great Plains Research: A Journal of Natural and Social Sciences,* 4:1 (1994), 3–26.

Blakiston, Thomas. *Five Months on the Yang-tsze: With a Narrative of Its Upper Waters and Notices of the Present Rebellions in China.* London: John Murray, 1862.

Boecking, Felix and Monika Scholz. 'Did the Nationalist Government Manipulate the Chinese Bond Market? A Quantitative Perspective on Short-Term Price Fluctuations of Domestic Government Bonds, 1932–1934'. *Frontiers of History in China,* 10 (2015), 126–44.

Borowy, Iris. 'Thinking Big: League of Nations Efforts towards a Reformed National Health System in China'. In Iris Borowy (ed.), *Uneasy Encounters: The Politics of Medicine and Health in China 1900–1937,* pp. 205–28. Frankfurt and New York: Peter Lang, 2009.

Bradshaw, C. J. A, N. S. Sodi, K. S. H. Peh and B. W. Brook. 'Global Evidence that Deforestation Amplifies Flood Risk and Severity in the Developing World'. *Global Change Biology* 13 (2007), 2379–95.

Brady, Anne-Marie. *Friend of China: The Myth of Rewi Alley.* London: Routledge Curzon, 2003.

Braudel, Fernand. *The Mediterranean and the Mediterranean World in the Age of Philip II,* trans. Siân Reynolds. New York: Harper and Row, 1972.

Brook, Timothy. *The Troubled Empire: China in the Yuan and Ming Dynasties.* Cambridge, MA: Harvard University Press, 2010).
  'Nine Sloughs: Profiling the Climate History of the Yuan and Ming Dynasties, 1260–1644'. *Journal of Chinese History* 1:1 (2017).

Brookes, Andrew. *Channelized Rivers: Perspectives for Environmental Management.* Chichester: John Wiley & Sons, 1988.

Bryrne, E. G. 'Yangtze Notes – Hankow 1910'. In Henling Thomas Wade (ed.), *With Boat and Gun in the Yangtze Valley,* pp. 199–200. Shanghai: Shanghai Mercury, 1910.

Buck, John Lossing. *Chinese Farm Economy: A Study of 2866 Farms in Seventeen Local-ities and Seven Provinces in China.* Chicago: University of Chicago Press, 1930.

Buck, John Lossing (ed.). *The 1931 Flood in China: An Economic Survey.* Nanking: The University of Nanking, 1932.

Buck, Pearl S. *The First Wife and Other Stories.* London: The Albatross, 1947.

The Good Earth. New York: John Day, 1931.

Bullock, Mary Brown. *An American Transplant: The Rockefeller Foundation and Peking Union Medical College.* Berkeley: University of California Press, 1980.

The Oil Prince's Legacy Rockefeller Philanthropy in China. Stanford: Stanford University Press, 2011.

'Buxing de tianzai 不幸的天灾 (An Unfortunate Natural Disaster)'. *Wenhua* 文华, 24 (1931).

Campbell, Cameron. 'Public Health Efforts in China before 1949 and Their Effects on Mortality: The Case of Beijing'. *Social Science History* 21:2 (1997), 179–281.

Camporesi, Piero. *Bread of Dreams: Food and Fantasy in Early Modern Europe,* trans. David Gentilcore Chicago: University of Chicago Press, 1989.

Carter, James. *Heart of Buddha, Heart of China: The Life of Tanxu, a Twentieth Century Monk.* Oxford: Oxford University Press, 2011.

Chabrowski, Igor Iwo. *Singing on the River: Sichuan Boatmen and Their Work Songs, 1880s–1930s.* Leiden and Boston: Brill, 2015.

Chang, Ning J. 'Tension within the Church: British Missionaries in Wuhan, 1913–28'. *Modern Asian Studies* 33 (1999): 421–44.

Chang, T. T. 'Domestication and Spread of Cultivated Rices'. In D. R. Harris and G. C. Hillman (eds.), *Foraging and Farming: The Evolution of Plant Exploitation,* pp. 408–17. London: Unwin Hyman, 1989.

'Changjiang yidai zhi shuizai canzhuang 长江一带之水灾惨状 (The Horrors of the Floods in the Yangzi Region)'. *Dongfang Huabao* 东方画报 28:20 (1931).

Chapman, H. Owen. 'Hodge Memorial Hospital (W.M.M.S.) Hankow Progress Report'. *The China Medical Journal XLI,* no. 5 (May 1927), 480–4.

Chapman, Owen. *The Chinese Revolution 1926–1927: A Record of the Period under Communist Control as Seen from the Nationalist Capital, Hankow.* London: Constable, 1928.

Chau, Adam Yuet. *Miraculous Response: Doing Popular Religion in Contemporary China.* Stanford: Stanford University Press, 2006.

Cheek, Timothy. *Propaganda and Culture in Mao's China: Deng Tuo and the Intelligensia.* Oxford: Clarendon Press, 1997.

Chen Bing 陈兵. 'Shi qu ludi xingzhou fuqiao lianjie 市区陆地行舟浮桥连接 (Land Connected by Pontoons in the City Area)'. *Wuhan Wenshi Ziliao* 武汉文史资料 Vol. 13, pp. 142–5. Hubei sheng Wuhan shi wenshi ziliao yanjiu weiyuanhui, 1983.

Chen Gengya 陈赓雅. *Jianghe shuizai shicha ji* 江河水灾视察记 (An Investigation into the Yangzi River Flood), reprinted in *Jindaishi Ziliao* 近代史资料. Beijing: Zhongguo shehui kexue yuan, 1987 (1935)

Chen Hesong 陈鹤松. 'Wuchang zaiqu shidi shichaji 武昌灾区实地视查记 (An Investigation of the Wuchang Disaster Area)'. *Yaxi Yabao* 亚细亚报 n.d, 1931, reprinted in HSSDX, 24–7.

Chen, Janet Y. *Guilty of Indigence: The Urban Poor in China, 1900–1953*. Princeton: Princeton University Press, 2012.

Chen Tinghong 陈汀泓. 'Zaihuang yu Zhongguo nongcun renkou wenti 灾荒与中国农村人口问题 (Famine and China's Rural Population Problem)'. *Daxuesheng Yanlun 大学生言论* 4 (1934).

Chen Wu 陈武. 'Zaimin jihan jiaopo wenyi liuxing 灾民饥寒交迫瘟疫流行 (Hunger, Cold and Epidemics Amongst Disaster Refugees)'. *Wuhan Wenshi Ziliao 武汉文史资料*, Vol. 13, pp. 145–6. Hubei sheng Wuhan shi wenshi ziliao yanjjiu weiyuanhui, 1983.

Chen Yuan-tsung. *Return to the Middle Kingdom: One Family, Three Revolutionaries, and the Birth of Modern China*. New York and London: Union Square Press, 2008.

Chou Huafei 仇华飞. '1931 nian Zhong-Mei xiaomai jiekuan deshi yanjiu 1931 年中美小麦借款得失研究 (The Advantages and Disadvantages of the 1931 Sino-American Wheat Loan)'. *Jianghai Xuekan 江海学刊*, no. 2 (2001), 144–9.

Christian, David. *Maps of Time: An Introduction to Big History*. Berkeley: University of California Press, 2011.

Clancey, Gregory. *Earthquake Nation: The Cultural Politics of Japanese Seismicity, 1868–1930*. Berkeley: University of California Press, 2006.

Clarke, Philip A. 'Australian Aboriginal Ethnometeorology and Seasonal Calendars'. *History and Anthropology*, 20:2 (2009), 79–106.

Classen, Constance, David Howes and Anthony Synnott. *Aroma: The Cultural History of Smell*. London: Routledge, 1994.

Clubb, O. Edmund. *Communism in China: As Reported from Hankow in 1932*. New York: Columbia University Press, 1968.

'The Floods of China, a National Disaster'. *Journal of Geography* 31 (January/December 1932), 199–206.

Cohen, Alvin P. 'Coercing the Rain Deities in Ancient China'. *History of Religions* 17:3/4 (1978), 244–65.

Cohen, Paul. *History in Three Keys: The Boxers as Event, Experience, and Myth*. New York: Columbia University Press, 1997.

Conkin, Paul. *Revolution Down on the Farm: the Transformation of American Agriculture since 1929*. Lexington: University of Kentucky Press, 2008.

Corbin, Alain. *The Foul and the Fragrant: Odor and the French Social Imagination*, trans. Miriam Kochan. Cambridge, MA: Harvard University Press, 1988.

Village Bells: Sound and Meaning in the 19th-Century French Countryside, trans. Martin Thom. New York: Columbia University Press, 1998.

Cornaby, William Arthur. *A String of Chinese Peach-Stones*. London: Charles H. Kelly, 1895.

'Morning Walks Around Hanyang'. *The East of Asia Magazine* 3 (1904), 232–7.

Courtney, Chris. 'At War with Water: The Maoist State and the 1954 Yangzi Flood'. *Modern Asian Studies* (in press).

Crabtree, Andrew. 'The Deep Roots of Nightmares'. In Fred Krüger, Greg Bankoff, Terry Cannon, Benedikt Orlowski and E. Lisa F. Schipper (eds.), *Cultures and Disasters: Understanding Cultural Framings in Disaster Risk Reduction*. London: Routledge, 2015.

Crawford, Dorothy H. *Deadly Companions: How Microbes Shaped Our History.* Oxford: Oxford University Press, 2007.

Cronon, William. 'A Place for Stories: Nature, History, and Narrative'. *The Journal of American History* 18:4 (March 1992), 1347–76.

Crosby, Alfred. *Ecological Imperialism: The Biological Expansion of Europe, 900–1900.* Cambridge: Cambridge University Press, 1986.

Crossley, Pamela. *The Wobbling Pivot – China since 1800: An Interpretive History.* Chichester: Wiley-Blackwell, 2010.

Crow, Carl. *Four Hundred Million Customers.* New York: Harper & Brothers, 1937.

Curtin, Philip D. *Disease and Empire: The Health of European Troops in the Conquest of Africa* Cambridge: Cambridge University Press, 1998.

Davis, J. A. *The Chinese Slave Girl: A Story of a Woman's Life in China.* Chicago: Student Missionary Campaign Library, 1880.

Davis, Mike. *Late Victorian Holocausts: El Niño Famines and the Making of the Third World.* London and New York: Verso, 2001.

De Bary, William. *Sources of Chinese Tradition.* New York: Columbia University Press, 2000.

De Visser, Marinus Willem. *The Dragon in China and Japan.* Amsterdam: J. Müller, 1913.

de Waal, Alex. 'AIDS, Hunger and Destitution: Theory and Evidence for the "New Variant Famines" Hypothesis in Africa'. In Stephen Devereux (ed.), *The New Famine: Why Famines Exist in an Era of Globalization*, pp. 90–126. London and New York: Routledge, 2007.

  Famine Crimes: Politics and the Disaster Relief Industry in Africa. Oxford: African Rights, 1997.

  Famine That Kills: Darfur, Sudan, 1984–1985. Oxford: Clarendon Press, 1989.

Dean, Britten. 'Sino-British Diplomacy in the 1860s: The Establishment of the British Concession at Hankou'. *Harvard Journal of Asiatic Studies* 32 (1972), 71–96.

Death, R. G. 'The Effect of Floods on Aquatic Invertebrate Communities'. In Jill Lancaster and Robert A. Briers (eds.), *Aquatic Insects: Challenges to Populations*, pp. 103–21. Wallingford: CAB International, 2008.

DeLanda, Manuel. *A New Philosophy of Society: Assemblage Theory and Social Complexity.* London: Continuum, 2006.

Del Moral, Roger and Lawrence R. Walker. *Environmental Disasters, Natural Recovery and Human Responses.* Cambridge: Cambridge University Press, 2007.

Del Ninno, Carlo, Paul A. Dorosh, Lisa C. Smith and Dilip K. Roy. *The 1998 Floods in Bangladesh: Disaster Impacts, Household Coping Strategies, and Response.* Washington, DC: International Food Policy Research Institute, 2001.

Deng Tuo 邓拓 [published as Deng Yunte 邓云特]. *Zhongguo jiuhuang shi* 中国救荒史 *(A History of Chinese Famine Relief).* Beijing: Shangwu yinshu guan, 2011 (1937).

Devereux, Stephen. 'Sen's Entitlement Approach: Critiques and Counter-critiques'. *Oxford Development Studies* 29:3 (2001), 245–63.

Devereux, Stephen and Paul Howe. 'Famine Intensity and Magnitude Scales: A Proposal for an Instrumental Definition of Famine'. *Disasters* 28:4 (2004), 353–72.

Diaz, Henry and George Kiladis. 'Atmospheric Teleconnections Associated with the Extreme Phase of the Southern Oscillation'. In Henry Diaz and Vera Markgraf (eds.), *El Niño: Historical and Paleoclimatic Aspects of the Southern Oscillation*, pp. 7–28. Cambridge: Cambridge University Press, 1992.

Dikötter, Frank. *Exotic Commodities: Modern Objects and Everyday Life in China*. New York: Columbia University Press, 2006.

Mao's Great Famine: The History of China's Most Devastating Catastrophe, 1958–62. London: Bloomsbury Publishing, 2010.

Sex Culture and Modernity in China: Medical Science and the Construction of Sexual Identities in the Early Republican Period. London: Hurst and Co, 1995.

Di Lei 迪雷. 'Xin Zhongguo weida de jianshe shiye-Jingjiang fenhong gongcheng 新中国伟大的建设事业-荆江分洪工程 (New China's Great Construction Project – Engineering the Jingjiang [Yangzi] Flood Diversion).' *Luxing Zazhi* 26:6 (1952), 25–30.

Ding Ling 丁玲. 'Shui 水 (Water)'. In *Ding Ling Quanji 丁玲全集 (The Collected Works of Ding Ling)*, Vol. 3. edited by 张炯 Zhang Jiong. Shijiazhuang: Hebei renmin chubanshe, 2001 (1933).

Dodgen, Randall A. *Controlling the Dragon: Confucian Engineers and the Yellow River in Late Imperial China*. Honolulu: University of Hawai'i Press, 2001.

Doolittle, Justus. *Social Life of the Chinese*. New York: Harper and Brothers, 1867.

Douglass, Mike. 'The Urban Transition of Disaster Governance in Asia'. In Michelle Ann Miller and Mike Douglass (eds.), *Disaster Governance in Urbanising Asia*, pp. 13–43. Singapore: Springer, 2015.

Duan Weili, He Bin, Daniel Nover, Fan Jingli, Yang Guishan, Chen Wen, Meng Huifang and Liu Chuanming. 'Floods and Associated Socioeconomic Damages in China over the Last Century'. *Natural Hazards* 82 (2016), 401–13.

Duara, Prasenjit. *Culture, Power and the State: Rural Northern China, 1900–1942*. Stanford: Stanford University Press, 1991.

The Global and Regional in China's Nation Formation. London and New York: Routledge, 2009.

'Transnationalism and the Predicament of Sovereignty: China, 1900–1945'. *American Historical Review* 102:4 (1997), 1030–52.

'Knowledge and Power in the Discourse of Modernity: The Campaigns against Popular Religion in Early Twentieth Century China'. *The Journal of Asian Studies* 50:1 (February 1991), 67–83.

'The Regime of Authenticity: Timelessness, Gender, and National History in Modern China'. *History and Theory* 37 (1998), 287–308.

Dyson, Tim and Cormac Ó Gráda. *Famine Demography: Perspectives from the Past and Present*. Oxford: Oxford University Press, 2006.

Ebrey, Patricia. *Chinese Civilization: A Sourcebook*. New York: The Free Press, 1993.

Edgerton-Tarpley, Kathryn. *Tears from Iron: Cultural Responses to Famine in Nineteenth-Century China*. Berkeley: University of California Press, 2008.

Edkins, Jenny. *Trauma and the Memory of Politics*. Cambridge: Cambridge University Press, 2003.

Whose Hunger: Concepts of Famine, Practices of Aid. Minneapolis: University of Minnesota Press, 2000.

Elgin, James Bruce Earl of. *Letters and Journals of James, Eighth Earl of Elgin.* Edited by Theodore Walrond. London: John Murray, 1872.

El Niño and La Niña. www.el-nino.com (Accessed 7 October 2015).

Elliot Smith, Grafton. *The Evolution of the Dragon.* Manchester: Manchester University Press, 1919.

Elvin, Mark. *The Pattern of the Chinese Past: A Social and Economic Interpretation.* Stanford: Stanford University Press, 1973.

The Retreat of the Elephants: An Environmental History of China. New Haven: Yale University Press, 2004.

'Three Thousand Years of Unsustainable Growth: China's Environment from Archaic Times to the Present'. *East Asian History* 6 (1993), 7–46.

'Who Was Responsible for the Weather? Moral Meteorology in Late Imperial China'. *Osiris* 13, no. 2nd Series (1998), 213–37.

Enarson, Elaine. 'Preface'. In Elaine Enarson and P. G. *Women, Gender and Disaster: Global Issues and Initiatives,* pp. xiv–xiii. Los Angeles: SAGE, 2009.

Ens Manning, Kimberley and Felix Wemheuer. *Eating Bitterness: New Perspectives on China's Great Leap Forward and Famine.* Vancouver: University of British Columbia Press, 2011.

Erikson, Kai T. *In the Wake of the Flood: With a Preface & Postscript on Buffalo Creek.* London: George Allen and Unwin, 1979.

'Fabiao Linbai kan zai baogao 发表林白勘灾报告 (Lindbergh's Disaster Report Published).' *Dongbei Wenhua* 东北文化 169 (1931).

Fang Fang 方方. 'Zhudong songhuan huilai de zujie – E Zujie 主动送还回来的租界—俄租界 (Foreign Concession Retrocession – The Russian Concession)'. *Wuhan Wenshi Ziliao* 武汉文史资料 Wuhan daxue, 2009.

Fang Qiumei 方秋梅. 'Difang bizhi, shizheng pianshi yu yi jiu san yi nian Hankou da shuizai 堤防弊制, 市政偏失与一九三一年汉口大水灾 (Systemic Faults in the Dike Network – Municipal Governance Failures and the 1931 Hankou Flood)'. *Renwen Luncong* 人文论丛, 2008.

Fan Kai 范锴. *Hankou Congtan* 汉口丛谈 *(Collected Writings on Hankou).* Wuhan: Hubei renmin chubanshe, 1990 (1822).

Fang Weide 方玮德. 'Da Yu zan 大禹赞 (In Praise of Yu the Great)'. *Xuesheng Wenyi Congkan* 学生文艺丛 *1002*; 1:2 (1924).

Fei Chengkang 费成康. *Zhongguo zujie shi* 中国租界史 *(A History of China's Foreign Concessions).* Shanghai: Shehui kexueyuan chubanshe, 1992.

Fei Xiaotong. *From the Soil: The Foundations of Chinese Society.* Berkeley: University of California Press, 1992.

Feng Jin. *Making of a Family Saga: The Ginling College.* New York: State University of New York Press, 2009.

Feng Shuidong, Tan Hongzhuan and Benjamin Abauku. 'Social Support and Posttraumatic Stress Disorder among Flood Victims in Hunan, China'. *Annals of Epidemiology* 17:10 (October 2007), 827–33.

Fiat, Antoine. *Life of Blessed John Gabriel Perboyre, Priest of the Congregation of the Mission.* Baltimore: John Murphy and Company, 1894.

Fitkin, Gretchen Mae. *The Great River: The Story of A Voyage on the Yangtze Kiang.* Shanghai: North China Daily News and Herald, 1922.

Flad, Rowan K. and Pochan Chen. *Ancient Central China Centers and Peripheries along the Yangzi River* Cambridge: Cambridge University Press, 2013.

Foucault, Michel. *The History of Sexuality, Vol. One: An Introduction,* trans. Robert Hurley. New York: Vintage Books, 1990 (1978).

French, Paul. *Carl Crow: A Tough Old China Hand.* Hong Kong: Hong Kong University Press, 2006.

Fuller, Pierre. '"Barren Soil, Fertile Minds": North China Famine and Visions of the "Callous Chinese" Circa 1920'. *The International History Review* 33:2 (September 2011), 453–72.

'Struggling with Famine in Warlord China: Social Networks, Achievements, and Limitations, 1920–21'. PhD thesis), University of California Irvine, 2011.

'North China Famine Revisited: Unsung Native Relief in the Warlord Era, 1920–21'. *Modern Asian Studies* 47:3 (2013), 820–50.

Fullerton, Carol and Robert Ursano. 'Psychological and Psychopathological Consequences of Disasters'. In Juan Jose López-Ibor, George Christodoulou, Mario Maj, Norman Sartorius and Ahmed Okasha (eds.), *Disasters and Mental Health,* pp. 13–36. Chichester: John Wiley & Sons, 2005.

Gao Yan. 'The Retreat of the Horses: The Manchus, Land Reclamation and Local Ecology in Eighteenth and Nineteenth Century Jianghan Plain'. In Tsui-jung Liu (ed.), *Environmental History in East Asia: Interdisciplinary Perspectives,* pp. 100–25. London: Routledge, 2014.

'Transformation of the Water Regime: State, Society and Ecology of the Jianghan Plain in Late Imperial and Modern China'. PhD thesis, Carnegie Mellon University, 24 April 2012.

Geil, William Edgar. *A Yankee on the Yangtze: Being a Narrative of a Journey from Shanghai through the Central Kingdom to Burma.* London: Hodder and Stoughton, 1904.

Gemmer, Marco, Jiang Tong, Su Buda and Zbigniew W. Kundzewicz. 'Seasonal Precipitation Changes in the Wet Season and Their Influence on Flood/Drought Hazards in the Yangtze River Basin, China'. *Quaternary International* 186 (2008), 12–21.

Godschalk, David R., David J. Brower and Timothy Beatley. *Catastrophic Coastal Storms: Hazard Mitigation and Development Management.* Durham and London: Duke University Press, 1989.

Goldberg, Jay M., Victor J. Wilson and Kathleen E. Cullen. *The Vestibular System: A Sixth Sense.* Oxford: Oxford University Press, 2012.

Goossaert, Vincent. 'The Beef Taboo and the Sacrificial Structure of Late Imperial Chinese Society'. In Roel Sterckx (ed.), *Of Tripod and Palate: Food, Politics, and Religion in Traditional China,* 237–48. New York: Palgrave Macmillan, 2005.

Goossaert, Vincent and David A. Palmer. *The Religious Question in Modern China.* Chicago and London: University of Chicago Press, 2011.

Gorman, Hugh S. *The Story of N: A Social History of the Nitrogen Cycle and the Challenge of Sustainability.* New Brunswick, NJ: Rutgers University Press, 2013.

Gottschang, Thomas R. 'Economic Change, Disasters, and Migration: The Historical Case of Manchuria'. *Economic Development and Cultural Change* 35 (1987), 461–90.

Gough, W. A. T. Jiang, H. T. Kung and Y. J. Wu. 'The Variation of Floods in the Middle Reaches of the Yangtze River and Its Teleconnection with El Niño Events'. *Advances in Geosciences* (February 2006), 201–5.

Gross, Miriam. *Chasing Snails: Anti-Schistosomiasis Campaigns in the People's Republic of China.* PhD thesis, University of California, San Diego, 2010.

   Farewell to the God of Plague Chairman Mao's Campaign to Deworm China. Berkeley: University of California Press, 2016.

Grove, Richard. 'The Great El Niño of 1789–93 and Its Global Consequences: Reconstructing an Extreme Climate Event in World Environmental History'. *The Medieval History Journal* 10:75 (2007), 76–98.

Grove, Richard and John Chappell. *El Niño – History and Crisis: Studies from the Asia Pacific Region* Cambridge: White Horse Press, 2000.

Guan Xuezhai 管雪斋. 'Shuishang san dian zhong 水上三点钟 (On the Water at Three O'Clock)'. *Yaxi Yabao* 亚细亚报, 1931 n.d. reprinted in HSSDX, 27–33.

Guo Jingrong 郭镜蓉. 'Wuhan zaihou pian pian lu 武汉灾后片片录 (Scenes in Wuhan After the Disaster)'. *Guowen Zhoukan* 国闻周刊 8:36 (1931).

Hall-Matthews, David. *Peasants, Famine and the State in Colonial Western India.* Basingstoke: Palgrave Macmillan, 2005.

Han Yuanyuan 韩媛媛. 'Jingjiang fenhong gongcheng sanbuqu 荆江分洪工程三部曲 (The Jingjiang Flood Diversion Trilogy)'. *Zhongguo Dang'an* 中国档案, 2010.

'Hankou pifa wujia zhishubiao 汉口批发物价指数表 (Index of Wholesale Prices in Hankou)'. *Shanghai Wujia Yuebao* 上海物价月报 13:5 (1937).

Hargett, James M. *Riding the River Home: A Complete Annotated Translation of Fan Chengda's (1126–1193) Diary of a Boat Trip to Wu.* Hong Kong: The Chinese University Press, 2008.

Harris, Marvin. 'The Cultural Ecology of India's Sacred Cattle'. *Current Anthropology* 7 (1966), 51–66.

Harrison, Mark. *Disease and the Modern World: 1500 to the Present Day.* Cambridge: Polity Press, 2004.

Hartman, Chester and Gregory D. Squires. 'Pre-Katrina, Post-Katrina'. In Chester Hartman and Gregory D. Squires (eds.), *There Is No Such Thing as a Natural Disaster: Race, Class, and Hurricane Katrina*, pp. 1–11. New York and London: Routledge, 2006.

Hayes, L. Newton. *The Chinese Dragon.* 3. Shanghai: Commercial Press, 1923.

Harrison, Henrietta. *The Making of the Republican Citizen: Political Ceremonies and Symbols in China 1911–1929.* Oxford: Oxford University Press, 2000.

   'A Penny for the Little Chinese: The French Holy Childhood Association in China, 1843–1951'. *American Historical Review* 113:1 (2008), 72–92.

Henriot, Christian. 'A Neighbourhood under Storm: Zhabei and Shanghai Wars'. *European Journal of East Asian Studies* 9:2 (2010), 291–319.

Hershatter, Gail. 'Modernizing Sex, Sexing Modernity'. In Christina K. Gilmartin, Gail Hershatter, Lisa Rofel and Tyrene White (eds.), *Engendering*

China: Women, Culture, and the State, pp. 147–74. Cambridge, MA: Harvard University Press, 1994.

Hodges, K. V. 'Tectonics of the Himalaya and Southern Tibet from Two Perspectives'. *Geological Society of America Bulletin* 112 (2000), 324–50.

Hong Liangji. 'China's Population Problem'. In William Theodore de Bary (ed.), *Sources of Chinese Tradition*, pp. 174–6. New York: Columbia University Press, 2001.

Hooda, Peter and Henry Jeya. 'Geophagia and Human Nutrition'. In Jeremy M. MacClancy, Jeya Henry and Helen Macbeth. (eds.), *Consuming the Inedible: Neglected Dimensions of Food Choice*, pp. 89–98. New York and Oxford: Berghahn Books, 2007.

Hou Houpei 侯厚培. 'Shuizai hou Wuhan zhi zhongyao chukou shangye 水灾后武汉之重要出口商业 (Wuhan's Important Export Businesses After the Flood)'. *Guoji Maoyi Daobao* 国际贸易导报 4:2 (1932).

Hsu, Francis. 'A Cholera Epidemic in a Chinese Town'. In David Paul Benjamin (ed.), *Health, Culture, and Community: Case Studies of Public Reactions to Health Programs*, pp. 135–54. New York: Russell Sage Foundation, 1955.

Hsu, Immanuel. *The Rise of Modern China*, 4th edn. New York: Oxford University Press, 1990.

Hu Xuehan 胡学汉. 'Zaimin jihan jiaopo wenyi liuxing 灾民饥寒交迫瘟疫流行 (Hunger, Cold, and Epidemics Amongst the Refugees)'. *Wuhan Wenshi Ziliao* 武汉文史资料, Vol. 13, 145. Hubei sheng Wuhan shi wenshi ziliao yanjjiu weiyuanhui, 1983.

Huang Xuelei. *Shanghai Filmmaking Crossing Borders, Connecting to the Globe, 1922–1938*. Leiden and Boston: Brill, 2014.

Hubei sheng zhi: Minzheng 湖北省志:民政 (Hubei Provincial Gazeteer: Civil Administration). Hubei renmin chubanshe, Wuhan, 1990.

Hubei sheng zhi: Dashi ji 湖北省志:大事记 (Hubei Provincial Gazeteer: Important Events). Hubei renmin chubanshe, Wuhan, 1990.

Huc, Évariste Régis. *A Journey through the Chinese Empire*, Vol. II. New York: Harper and Brothers, 1871.

Huntington, Ellsworth. *The Character of Races as Influenced by Physical Environment, Natural Selection and Historical Development*. New York: Scribner's, 1924.

Imperial Maritimes Customs Service. *Special Catalogue of the Chinese Collection of Exhibits for the International Fisheries Exhibition, London 1883*. Shanghai: Statistical Department of the Inspector General, 1883.

Isaacman, Allen F. and Barbara S. Isaacman. *Dams, Displacement, and the Delusion of Development: Cahora Bassa and Its Legacies in Mozambique, 1965–2007*. Athens, OH: Ohio University Press, 2013.

Isaacs, Harold. *The Tragedy of the Chinese Revolution*. London: Secker and Warburg, 1938.

Jachertz, Ruth and Alexander Nützenadel. 'Coping with Hunger? Visions of a Global Food System, 1930–1960'. *Journal of Global History* 6 (2011), 99–119.

Jackson, Innes. *China Only Yesterday*. London: Faber and Faber, 1938.

Jackson, Jeffrey H. *Paris Under Water: How the City of Light Survived the Great Flood of 1910*. New York: Palgrave Macmillan, 2010.

Jahn, Samia AI Azharia. 'Drinking Water from Chinese Rivers: Challenges of Clarification'. *Journal of Water Supply, Research, and Technology – AQUA* 50 (2001), 15–27.

Janku, Andrea. '"Heaven-Sent Disasters" in Late Imperial China: The Scope of the State and Beyond'. In Christof Mauch and Christian Pfister (eds.), *Natural Disasters, Cultural Responses: Case Studies Toward a Global Environmental History*, pp. 233–64. Lanham, MD: Lexington Books, 2009.

'From Natural to National Disaster: The Chinese Famine of 1928–1930'. In Andrea Janku, Gerrit J. Schenk and Franz Mauelshagen (eds.), *Historical Disasters in Context: Science, Religion, and Politics*, pp. 227–60. New York: Routledge, 2012.

The Internationalization of Disaster Relief in Early Twentieth-century China. In Mechthild Leutner and Goikhman Izabella (eds.), *State, Society and Governance in Republican China* Vol. 43, pp. 6–28. Berlin: Chinese History and Society, 2013.

Jernigan, Thomas R. *Shooting in China*. Shanghai: Methodist Publishing House, 1908.

Ji Xun 芰薰. 'Hankou renrou shichang – Shajia xiang 汉口人肉市场 – 沙家巷 (Hankou's Meat Market – Shajia Lane)'. *Guangming* 光明, 1936.

Jiang Tong, Zhang Qiang, Zhu Deming and Wu Yijin. 'Yangtze Floods and Droughts (China) and Teleconnections with ENSO Activities (1470–2003)'. *Quaternary International* no. 144 (2006), 29–37.

Jie Shan. 介山 'Hankou zhi kuli 汉口之苦力 (Hankou Coolies)'. *Shenghuo* 生活 19, 1926.

Jobin, William. *Dams and Disease: Ecological Design and Health Impacts of Large Dams, Canals and Irrigation Systems*. London and New York: E & FN Spon, 2003.

Johnson, Lonnie. *Broken Levee Blues*. OKeh 8618, 1928.

Jordan, Donald A. *China's Trial by Fire: The Shanghai War of 1932*. Ann Arbor: University of Michigan Press, 2001.

Junk, Wolfgang, Peter B. Bayley and Richard. E. Sparks. 'The Flood Pulse Concept in River-Floodplain Systems'. In D. P. Dodge (ed.), *Proceedings of the International Large River Symposium (LARS)*. Canadian Special Publication of Fisheries and Aquatic Sciences 106 (1989), 110–27.

Kelleher, Margaret. *The Feminization of Famine: Expressions of the Inexpressible?* Durham: Duke University Press, 1997.

Kellman, Martin C. and Rosanne Tackaberry. *Tropical Environments: The Functioning and Management of Tropical Ecosystems*. New York: Routledge, 1997.

Kilcourse, Carl. *Taiping Theology: The Localization of Christianity in China, 1843–64*. New York: Palgrave Macmillan, 2016.

Knapp, Ronald G. *China's Old Dwellings*. Honolulu: University of Hawai'i Press, 2000.

China's Vernacular Architecture: House Form and Culture. Honolulu: University of Hawai'i Press, 1989.

Kong Xiangcheng 孔祥成. 'Minguo Jiangsu shourong jizhi jiqi jiuzhu shixiao yanjiu – yi 1931 Jiang-Huai shuizai wei li 民国江苏收容机制及其救助实效

研究 —— 以 1931 年江淮水灾为例 (The Mechanisms and Effectivenesss of Relief in Republican Jiangsu – Using the Example of the 1931 Jiang-Huai Flood)'. *Zhongguo Nongshi* 中国农史, March 2003, 92–101.

'Kongzi danchen yu shuizai 孔子诞辰与水灾 (The Birthday of Confucius and Flood Disasters)'. *Guowen Zhoukan* 国闻周刊 8:35 (1931).

Koslofsky, Craig. *Evening's Empire: A History of the Night in Early Modern Europe.* Cambridge: Cambridge University Press, 2011.

Kotey, Phyllis. 'Judging Under Disaster: The Effect of Hurricane Katrina on the Criminal Justice System'. In Jeremy I. Levitt and Matthew C. Whitaker (eds.), *Hurricane Katrina: America's Unnatural Disaster*, pp. 105–31. Lincoln and London: University of of Nebraska Press, 2009.

Kuang Lu 匡庐. 'Shuizai 水灾 (Flood Disaster)'. *Beidou* 北斗 2:1 (1932), 129–44.

Kueh, Y. Y. *Agricultural Instability in China, 1931–1990: Weather, Technology, and Institutions.* Oxford: Oxford University Press, 1995.

Kuhlmann, Dirk. 'Negotiating Cultural and Religious Identities in the Encounter with the 'Other': Global and Local Perspectives in the Historiography of Late Qing/Early Republican Christian Missions'. In Thomas Jansen, Thoralf Klein and Christian Meyer (eds.), *Globalization and the Making of Religious Modernity in China: Transnational Religions, Local Agents, and the Study of Religion, 1800–Present.* Leiden: Brill, 2014.

Kum, Ayean. 'Some Chinese Methods of Shooting and Trapping Game'. In *With a Boat and Gun in the Yangtze Valley.* Shanghai: Shanghai Mercury, 1910.

Kuo, Huei-Ying. *Networks beyond Empires: Chinese Business and Nationalism in the Hong Kong-Singapore Corridor, 1914–1941.* Leiden and Boston: Brill, 2014.

Kutak, Robert I. 'The Sociology of Crises: The Louisville Flood of 1937'. *Social Forces* 17:1 (1938).

Lake, Phillip. S. *Drought and Aquatic Ecosystems: Effects and Responses.* Oxford: Wiley-Blackwell, 2011.

'Flow-generated Disturbances and Ecological Responses: Floods and Droughts'. In Paul J. Wood, David M. Hannah and Jonathan P. Sadler (eds.), *Hydroecology and Ecohydrology: Past, Present and Future*, pp. 75–92. Chichester: John Wiley & Sons, 2007.

Lambers, Hans, F. Stuart Chapin III and Thijs L. Pons. *Plant Physiological Ecology.* New York: Springer-Verlag, 1998.

Lander, Brian. 'State Management of River Dikes in Early China: New Sources on the Environmental History of the Central Yangzi Region'. *T'oung Pao* 100 (2014), 325–62.

Lanfranchi, Sania Sharawi. *Casting off the Veil: The Life of Huda Shaarawi, Egypt's First Feminist.* London and New York: I. B. Tauris, 2012.

Lary, Diana. 'Drowned Earth: The Strategic Breaching of the Yellow River Dyke, 1938'. *War and History* 8:2, (2001), 191–207.

Laufer, Berthold. *The Domestication of the Cormorant in China and Japan.* Chicago: Field Museum Press, 1931.

Lee, James Z. and Feng Wang. *One Quarter of Humanity: Malthusian Mythology and Chinese Realities.* Cambridge, MA: Harvard University Press, 1999.

Lee, Laurie. *I Can't Stay Long.* Harmondsworth: Penguin, 1975.

Leow, Rachel. '"Do You Own Non-Chinese Mui Tsai?" Re-examining Race and Female Servitude in Malaya and Hong Kong, 1919–1939'. *Modern Asian Studies* 46:06 (November 2012), 1736–63.

Lescot, Patrick. *Before Mao: The Untold Story of Li Lisan and the Creation of Communist China.* New York: Harper Collins, 2004.

Lewis, Mark Edward. *China between Empires: The Northern and Southern Dynasties.* Cambridge, MA: Harvard University Press, 2009.

The Early Chinese Empires: Qin and Han. Cambridge, MA, Harvard University Press, 2009.

Li Hui-lin. 'The Domestication of Plants in China: Ecogeographical Considerations'. In David N. Keightley (ed.), *The Origins of Chinese Civilization*, pp. 21–63. Berkeley: University of California Press, 1983.

Li Huaiyin. *Village China under Socialism and Reform: A Micro-History, 1948–2008.* Stanford: Stanford University Press, 2009.

Li, Lillian M. 'Life and Death in a Chinese Famine: Infanticide as a Demographic Consequence of the 1935 Yellow River Flood'. *Comparative Study of Society and History* 33:3 (1991), 466–510.

Fighting Famine in North China: State, Market, and Environmental Decline, 1690s–1990s. Stanford: Stanford University Press, 2007.

Li Qin 李勤. 'San shi nian dai shuizai dui zaimin shehui xinli de yingxiang – yi Liang Hu diqu wei li 三十年代水灾对灾民社会心理的影响—以两胡地区为例 (The Impact of 1930's Flooding Upon the Social Pschology of Refugees – Using Hubei and Hunan as an Example)'. *Jianghan Luntan* 江汉论坛 3 (2007), 101–3.

Li Wenhai 李文海, Cheng Xiao 程啸, Liu Yangdong 刘仰东 and Xia Mingfang 夏明方. *Zhongguo jindai shi da zaihuang* 中国近代史十大灾荒 (The Ten Great Disasters in Modern Chinese History). Shanghai: Shanghai renmin chubanshe, 1994.

Li Xia 黎霞. 'Fuhe rensheng: Minguo shiqi Wuhan matou gongren yanjiu 负荷人生: 民国时期武汉码头工人研究 (A Burdened Life: Dockers in Republican Wuhan)'. Doctoral thesis, Huazhong shifan daxue, 2007.

'Matou gongren qunti yu jindai Wuhan chengshi hua 码头工人群体与近代武汉城市化 (Docker Organisations and Urbanisation in Modern Wuhan)'. *Hubei Daxue Xuebao* 湖北大学学报 37 (March 2010), 25–9.

Liang, M. T. 'Combating the Famine Dragon'. *News Bulletin (Institute of Pacific Relations)*, April 1928.

Likens, Gene E. *River Ecosystem Ecology: A Global Perspective.* Amsterdam: Academic Press, 2010.

'Linbai suo she zhi Zhongguo shuizai zhaopian 林白所摄之中国水灾照片 (Lindbergh's Pictures of the Flood)'. *Dongfang Zazhi* 东方杂志, 29:2 (1932).

Lindbergh, Anne Morrow. *North to the Orient.* Orlando, FL: Harcourt Brace and Co., 2004 (1935).

Lipkin, Zwia. *Useless to the State 'Social Problems' and Social Engineering in Nationalist Nanjing, 1927–1937.* Cambridge MA: Harvard University Press, 2006.

Little, Archibold. *Through the Yang-tse Gorges or Trade and Travel in Western China.* London: Samson Low, Marston and Co, 1898.

Liu Fudao 刘富道. *Tianxia diyi jie: Wuhan Hanzheng jie* 天下第一街:武汉汉正街 (The First Street Under Heaven: Wuhan's Hanzheng Street). Wuhan: Chong wen shu ju, 2007.

Liu, Lydia. *Translingual Practice: Literature, National Culture, and Modernity – China, 1900–1937*. Stanford: Stanford University Press, 1995.

Liu Sijia 刘思佳. 'Hankou Zhongshan Gongyuan bainian huikan 汉口中山公园百年回看 (Looking Back on One Hundred Years of Sun Yat-sen Park).' *Wuhan Wenshi Ziliao* 武汉文史资料 9 (2010), 39–45.

'Liu Wendao tan Hankou shi muqian jianshe gaikuang 刘文岛谈汉口市目前建设概况 (Liu Wendao Discusses Wuhan's Recent Urban Planning)'. *Daolu Yuekan* 道路月刊, 33:3, 1931.

Liu, Ts'ui-jung. 'A Retrospection of Climate Changes and Their Impact in Chinese History'. In Carmen Meinert(ed.), *Nature, Environment and Culture in East Asia: The Challenge of Climate Change*. Leiden and Boston: Brill, 2013.

'Dike Construction in Ching-chou: A Study Based on the 'T'i-fang chin' Section of the Ching-chou fu-chih'. *Papers on China* 23 (1970), 1–28.

Lora-Wainwright, Anna. *Fighting for Breath: Cancer, Healing and Social Change in a Sichuan Village*. Honolulu: University of Hawai'i Press, 2013.

Lu Hanchao. *Beyond the Neon Lights: Everyday Shanghai in the Early Twentieth Century*. Berkeley: University of California Press, 1999.

Street Criers: A Cultural History of Chinese Beggars. Stanford: Stanford University Press, 2005.

Lu, Tracey Lie Dan. *The Transition from Foraging to Farming and the Origin of Agriculture in China*, BAR International Series, Vol. 774. Oxford: Hadrian Books, 1999.

Lu Xuegan 吕学赶, and Renmin Tang 唐仁民. 'Hankou Zhongshan Gongyuan dongwuyuan de pianduan huiyi 汉口中山公园动物园的片段回忆 (Some Memories of the Hankou Sun Yat-sen Park Zoo)'. *Wuhan Wenshi Ziliao* 武汉文史资料 9 (2006), 4–8.

Luo Han 罗汉. *Minchu Hankou zhuzhici jinzhu* 民初汉口竹枝词今注 (Early Republican Bamboo Branch Verses). Edited by Xu Mingting 徐明庭. Beijing: Zhongguo Dang'an Chubanshe, 2001.

Lynn, Madeleine. *Yangtze River: The Wildest, Wickedest River on Earth*. Oxford: Oxford University Press, 1997.

Ma Zhao. *Runaway Wives, Urban Crimes, and Survival Tactics in Wartime Beijing, 1937–1949*. Cambridge, MA: Harvard University Press, 2015.

Macintyre, Kate. 'Famine and the Female Mortality Advantage'. In Tim Dyson and Cormac Ó Gráda (eds.), *Famine Demography: Perspectives from the Past and Present*, pp. 240–43. Oxford: Oxford University Press, 2006.

Mackenzie, Donald A. *Myths of China and Japan*. London: Gresham Publishing Company, 1923.

Mackinnon, Stephen. 'Refugee Flight at the Outset of the Anti-Japanese War'. In Diana Lary and Stephen MacKinnon (eds.), *The Scars of War: The Impact of Warfare on Modern China*, pp. 118–35. Vancouver: University of British Columbia Press, 2001.

Wuhan, 1938: War, Refugees, and the Making of Modern China. Berkeley: University of California Press, 2008.

'Wuhan's Search for Identity in the Republican Period'. In Joseph W. Esherick (ed.), *Remaking the Chinese City: Modernity and National Identity, 1900–1950*. Honolulu: University of Hawai'i Press, 2000.

MacPherson, Kerrie. 'Cholera in China, 1820–1930: An Aspect of the Internationalization of Infectious Disease'. In Mark Elvin and Ts'ui-jung Liu (eds.), *Sediments of Time: Environment and Society in Chinese History*, 487–519. Cambridge: Cambridge University Press, 1998.

Major, John S. 'Characteristics of Late Chu Religion'. In Constance A. Cook and John S. Major (eds.), *Defining Chu: Image and Reality in Ancient China*, 121–44. Honolulu: University of Hawai'i Press, 1999.

Mallory, Walter H. *China: Land of Famine*. Worcester, MA: Commonwealth Press, 1926.

Mann, Susan. *Local Merchants and the Chinese Bureaucracy, 1750–1950*. Stanford: Stanford University Press, 1987.

Marks, Robert. *China: Its Environment and History*. Lanham, MD: Rowman and Littlefield, 2012.

Martin, G. Neil. *The Neuropsychology of Smell and Taste*. London and New York: Psychology Press, 2013.

Massumi, Brian. *Parables of the Virtual: Movement, Affect, Sensation*. Durham: Duke University Press, 2002.

Matt, Susan J. and Peter N. Stearns. *Doing Emotions History*. Urbana: University of Illinois Press, 2014.

Matthews, William J. *Patterns in Freshwater Fish Ecology*. London: Chapman and Hall, 1998.

Maxwell, James, M. 'The History of Cholera in China'. *The China Medical Journal*, XLI:7 (July 1927).

Maze, Frederick. *Documents Illustrative of the Origin, Development, and Activities of the Chinese Customs Service: Volume 4 – Inspector General's Circulars 1924 to 1931*. Shanghai, 1939.

McCord, Edward A. *Military Force and Elite Power in the Formation of Modern China*. London and New York: Routledge, 2014.

McCully, Patrick. *Silenced Rivers: The Ecology and Politics of Large Dams*. London: Zed Books, 1998.

McNeill, John. *Mosquito Empires: Ecology and War in the Greater Caribbean, 1620–1914*. Cambridge: Cambridge University Press, 2010.

'China's Environmental History in World Perspective'. In Mark Elvin and Ts'ui-jung Liu (eds.), *Sediments of Time: Environment and Society in Chinese History*, 31–52. Cambridge: Cambridge University Press, 1998.

The Great Acceleration: An Environmental History of the Anthropocene since 1945. Cambridge, MA: The Belknap Press of Harvard University Press, 2014.

Something New Under the Sun: An Environmental History of the Twentieth Century. London: Allen Lane, 2000.

Meissner, Daniel J. *Chinese Capitalists versus the American Flour Industry, 1890–1910*. Lewiston: The Edwin Meller Press, 2005.

Meyer-Fong, Tobie. *What Remains: Coming to Terms with Civil War in 19th Century China*. Stanford: Stanford University Press, 2013.

Middleton, Beth A. (ed.). *Flood Pulsing in Wetlands: Restoring the Natural Hydrological Balance.* New York: John Wiley & Sons, 2002.

Mikhail, Alan. *Nature and Empire in Ottoman Egypt: An Environmental History.* Cambridge: Cambridge University Press, 2011.

Mitsch, William J. and James G. Gosselink. *Wetlands.* 4. Hoboken, NJ: John Wiley & Sons, 2007.

Mitter, Rana. *A Bitter Revolution: China's Struggle with the Modern World.* Oxford: Oxford University Press, 2004.

   China's War with Japan, 1937–1945: The Struggle for Survival. London: Penguin, 2013.

Morris, Christopher. *The Big Muddy: An Environmental History of the Mississippi and Its Peoples from Hernando de Soto to Hurricane Katrina.* Oxford: Oxford University Press, 2012.

Mühlhahn, Klaus. 'The Concentration Camp in Global Historical Perspective'. *History Compass* 8:6 (2010), 543–61.

   Criminal Justice in China: A History. Cambridge, MA: Harvard University Press, 2009.

Mukherjee, Janam. *Hungry Bengal: War, Famine and the End of Empire.* Oxford: Oxford University Press, 2015.

Muscolino, Micah. *The Ecology of War in China: Henan Province, the Yellow River, and Beyond, 1938–1950.* Cambridge: Cambridge University Press, 2015.

Nathan, Andrew James. *A History of the China International Famine Relief Commission.* Cambridge, MA.: Harvard University Press, 1965.

National Flood Relief Commission. *Report of the National Flood Relief Commission 1931–1932.* Shanghai, 1933.

National Government of the Republic of China. 'Emergency Law for the Suppression of Crimes Against the Safety of the Republic'. In *The Search for Modern China: A Document Collection,* pp. 275–277. New York: W. W. Norton, 1999.

Nedostup, Rebecca. *Superstitious Regimes: Religion and the Politics of Chinese Modernity.* Cambridge, MA: Harvard University Asia Center, 2009.

Needham, Joseph, Kenneth Girdwood Robinson and Ray Huang. *Science and Civilisation in China: The Social Background Part 2 – General Conclusions and Reflections,* Vol. 7. Cambridge: Cambridge University Press, 2004.

Needham, Joseph, Gwei-djen Lu and Hsing-Tung Huang. *Science and Civilisation in China: Vol. 6 Pt. 1: Botany.* Cambridge: Cambridge University Press, 1986.

Newell, Barry and Robert Wasson. 'Social System vs Solar System: Why Policy Makers Need History'. In S. Castelein and A. Otte (eds.), *Conflict and Cooperation Related to International Water Resources: Historical Perspectices,* 3–17. Grenoble: UNESCO, 2002.

Notestein, Frank W. 'A Demographic Study of 38,256 Rural Families in China'. *The Milbank Memorial Fund Quarterly* 16:1 (January 1938), 57–79.

O'Daniel, Patrick. *When the Levee Breaks: Memphis and the Mississippi Valley Flood of 1927.* Charleston and London: The History Press, 2013.

Ó Gráda, Cormac. *Black '47 and Beyond: The Great Irish Famine in History, Economy, and Memory.* Princeton: Princeton University Press, 1999.

   Eating People Is Wrong, and Other Essays on Famine, Its Past, and Its Future. Princeton and Oxford: Princeton University Press, 2015.

Famine: A Short History. Princeton: Princeton University Press, 2009.

'Great Leap into Famine: A Review Essay'. *Population and Development Review* 37:1 (March 2011), 191–210.

Ó Gráda, Cormac and Joel Mokyr. 'Famine Disease and Famine Mortality: Lessons from the Irish Experience, 1845–1850'. In Cormac Ó Gráda and Tim Dyson (eds.), *Famine Demography: Perspectives from the Past and Present*, 19–43. Oxford: Oxford University Press, 2002.

Oliver-Smith, Anthony. 'Anthropological Research on Hazards and Disaster'. *Annual Review of Anthropology* 25 (1996): 303–28.

Orchard, Dorothy Johnson. 'Man-Power in China I'. *Political Science Quarterly* 50:4 (1935): 561–83.

Osborne, Anne. 'Highlands and Lowlands: Economic and Ecological Interactions in the Lower Yangzi Region under the Qing'. In Mark Elvin and Ts'ui-jung Liu (ed.), *Sediments of Time: Environment and Society in Chinese History*, pp. 203–34. Cambridge: Cambridge University Press, 1998.

Ouyang Tieguang 欧阳铁光. 'Zaihuang yu nongmin de shengcun weiji – yi 20 shiji 30 niandai qianqi Changjiang zhong xiayou diqu wei zhongxīn 灾荒与农民的生存危机 – 以20世纪30年代前期长江中下游地区为中心 (Disasters and the Crisis Survival of Peasants in the Middle and Lower Yangzi in the 1930s)'. *Huaihua Xueyuan Xuebao* 怀化学院学报 7 (2006).

Ouyang Wen 欧阳文. 'Xia siling guibai Longwang 夏司令跪拜龙王 (Commander Xia Kneels and Prays to the Dragon King)'. In *Wuhan Wenshi Ziliao* 武汉文史资料, Vol. 13, 144–5. Hubei sheng Wuhan shi wenshi ziliao yan-jjiu weiyuanhui, 1983.

Overmyer, Daniel L. *Local Religion in North China in the Twentieth Century: The Structure and Organization of Community Rituals and Beliefs.* Leiden: Brill, 2009.

Oxenham, E. L. 'History of Han Yang and Hankow'. *China Review* 1:6 (1873).

'On the Inundations of the Yang-tse-Kiang'. *Journal of the Royal Geographical Society of London* 45 (1875).

Paltemaa, Lauri. *Managing Famine, Flood, and Earthquake in China: Tianjin, 1958–1985.* New York: Routledge, 2016.

Paranjape, Makarand R. '"Natural Supernaturalism?" The Tagore–Gandhi Debate on the Bihar Earthquake'. *The Journal of Hindu Studies* 4:2 (2011), 176–204.

Peckham, Robert. *Epidemics in Modern Asia.* Cambridge: Cambridge University Press, 2016.

Pedersen, Susan. *The Guardians: The League of Nations and the Crisis of Empire.* Oxford: Oxford University Press, 2015.

Percival, William Spencer. *The Land of the Dragon: My Boating and Shooting Excursions to the Gorges of the Upper Yangtze.* London: Hurst and Blackett, 1889.

Perdue, Peter C. *Exhausting the Earth: State and Peasant in Hunan, 1500–1850.* Cambridge, MA: Harvard University Press, 1987.

Pfister, Christian. 'Learning from Nature-Induced Disasters Theoretical Considerations and Case Studies from Western Europe'. In Christof Mauch and Christian Pfister (eds.), *Natural Disasters, Cultural Responses Case Studies Toward a Global Environmental History*, 17–40. Lanham, MD: Lexington Books, 2009.

Pi Mingxiu 皮明庥 (ed.). *Wuhan tongshi: Minguo juan – shang* 武汉通史:民国卷-上 *A Comprehensive History of Wuhan: The Republican Period – Part One)*. Wuhan: Wuhan Chubanshe, 2006.

Wuhan tongshi: Minguo juan – xia 武汉通史:民国卷-下 (A Comprehensive History of Wuhan: The Republican Period – Part Two). Wuhan: Wuhan chubanshe, 2006.

Wuhan tongshi: Wan Qing juan – shang 武汉通史: 晚清卷-上 (*A Comprehensive History of Wuhan: The Late Qing – Part One*). Wuhan: Wuhan chubanshe, 2006.

Wuhan tongshi: wan Qing juan – xia 武汉通史: 晚清卷-下 (*A Comprehensive History of Wuhan: The Late Qing – Part Two*). Wuhan: Wuhan chubanshe, 2006.

Wuhan tongshi: Zhonghua Renmin Gongheguo – shang 武汉通史:中华人民共和国-上 (*A Comprehensive History of Wuhan: People's Republic of China – Part one*). Wuhan: Wuhan chubanshe, 2006.

Pi Zuoqiong 皮作琼. 'Senlin yu shuizai 森林与水灾. (Forests and Floods)' *Dongfang Zazhi* 东方杂志 20, no. 18 (1923).

Pickens, Claude. 'Rev. Claude L. Pickens, Jr. collection on Muslims in China' Album 3, ca. 1932–1947 Harvard-Yenching Library.

Pietz, David A. *Engineering the State: The Huai River and Reconstruction in Nationalist China, 1927–1937*. London: Routledge, 2002.

The Yellow River: The Problem of Water in Modern China. Cambridge, MA: Harvard University Press, 2015.

Pomeranz, Kenneth. 'Water to Iron, Widows to Warlords: The Handan Rain Shrine in Modern Chinese History'. *Late Imperial China* 12:1 (June 1991), 62–99.

Poon, Shuk-Wah. 'Cholera, Public Health, and the Politics of Water in Republican Guangzhou'. *Modern Asian Studies* (December 2012), 131.

Negotiating Religion in Modern China: State and Common People in Guangzhou: 1900–1937. Hong Kong: The Chinese University Press, 2011.

Quinn, W. H. and V. T. Neal. 'The Historical Record of El Niño Events.' In Raymond Bradley and Philip Jones (eds.), *Climate since A.D. 1500*, 623–48. London: Routledge, 1992.

Rahav, Shakhar. *The Rise of Political Intellectuals in Modern China: May Fourth Societies and the Roots of Mass-Party Politics*. Oxford: Oxford University Press, 2015.

Rajchman, Ludwik. *Report of the Technical Agent of the Council on His Mission to China*. Geneva: Council Committee on Technical Co-operation Between the League of Nations and China, 1934.

Rangasami, Amrita. '"Failure of Exchange Entitlements" Theory of Famine: A Response'. *Economic and Political Weekly* 20:42 (October 1985), 1797–1801.

Reeves, Caroline. 'The Red Cross Society of China, Past, Present, and Future'. In Jennifer Ryan, Lincoln C. Chen and Anthony J Saich (eds.), *Philanthropy for Health in China*, pp. 214–23. Bloomington: Indiana University Press, 2014.

Reice, Seth R. *The Silver Lining: The Benefits of Natural Disasters*. Princeton: Princeton University Press, 2001.

'Renhuo! Tianzai!! Waihuan!!! 人祸! 天灾!! 外患!!! (Human-Made Calamity! Natural Disaster!! Foreign Aggression!!!)'. *Ziqiang Zhoubao* 自强周报 1, no. 1 (1931).

Rensselaer, Catharina Van. *A Legacy of Historical Gleanings*. Albany, NY: J. Munsell, 1875.

Richards, John F. *The Unending Frontier: An Environmental History of the Early Modern World*. Berkeley: University of California Press, 2003.

Richards, Louis. *Comprehensive Geography of the Chinese Empire and Dependencies*, trans. M. Kennelly. Shanghai: Tusewei Press, 1908.

Ricklefs, M. C., Bruce Lockhart, Albert Lau, Portia Reyes and Maitrii Aung-Thwin. *A New History of Southeast Asia*. New York: Palgrave Macmillan, 2010.

Rogaski, Ruth. *Hygienic Modernity: Meanings of Health and Disease in Treaty-Port China*. Berkeley: University of California Press, 2004.

Ross, Stephen T. *Ecology of North American Freshwater Fishes*. Berkeley: University of California Press, 2013.

Rowe, William T. 'Bao Shichen and Agrarian Reform in Early Nineteenth-Century China'. *Frontiers in the History of China* 9:1 (2014), 1–31.

Crimson Rain: Seven Centuries of Violence in a Chinese County. Stanford: Stanford University Press, 2007.

Hankow: Commerce and Society in a Chinese City, 1796–1889. Stanford: Stanford University Press, 1984.

Hankow: Conflict and Community in a Chinese City, 1796–1895. Stanford: Stanford University Press, 1989.

'Water Control and the Qing Political Process: The Fankou Dam Controversy'. *Modern China* 14:4 (October 1988), 353–87.

Rozario, Kevin. *The Culture of Calamity: Disaster and the Making of Modern America*. Chicago: University of Chicago Press, 2007.

Sapio, Flora. *Sovereign Power and the Law in China*. Leiden: Brill, (2010).

Sautman, Bary. 'Myths of Descent, Racial Nationalism and Ethnic Minorities in the People's Republic of China'. In Frank Dikötter (ed.), *The Construction of Racial Identities in China and Japan: Historical and Contemporary Perspectives*, 75–95. London: C. Hurst & Co, 1997.

Schubert, S. D., M. J. Suarez, P. J. Region, R. D. Koster and J. T. Bacmeister. 'On the Cause of the 1930s Dust Bowl'. *Science* 303 (2004), 1855–9.

Scott, James C. *The Moral Economy of Peasants: Rebellion and Subsistence in South East Asia*. New Haven: Yale University Press, 1976.

Seigworth, Gregory and Melissa Gregg (eds.). *The Affect Theory Reader*. Durham: Duke University Press, 2010.

Sen, Amartya. *Poverty and Famines: An Essay on Entitlement and Deprivation*. Delhi: Oxford University Press, 1981.

Sha Qingqing 沙青青. 'Xinyang yu quanzheng: 1931 nian Gaoyou "da Chenghuang" fengchao zhi yanjiu, 信仰与权争: 1931 年高邮 "打城隍" 风潮之研究 (Faith and the Fight for Power: The 1931 "Beat the City God" Movement in Gaoyou)'. *Jindai Shi Yanjiu (近代史研究)*, 1 (2010), 115–27.

Shang Ruobing 商若冰. '"Gaibang" tanmi "丐帮" 探秘 (Secrets of "Beggar Guilds")'. In Xiao Zhihua 肖志华 and Yan Changhong 严昌洪 (eds.), *Wuhan Zhanggu* 武汉掌故. Wuhan: Wuhan chubanshe, 1994.

Shapiro, Judith. *Mao's War against Nature: Politics and the Environment in Revolutionary China.* Cambridge: Cambridge University Press, 2001.

Shaw, Rajib, Juan M. Pulhin, and Joy J. Pereira. *Climate Change Adaptation and Disaster Risk Reduction: An Asian Perspective.* Bingley: Emerald, 2010.

She Ying 社英. 'Funu ying fu jiuji shuizai zhi zeren 妇女应负救济水灾之责任 (Women Should Take Responsibility for Flood Relief)'. *Funu Gongming* 妇女共鸣, 1931.

Shiroyama, Tomoko. *China during the Great Depression: Market, State, and the World Economy, 1929–1937.* Cambridge, MA: Harvard University Press, 2008.

'Shourong 收容 (Refuge)' HSSDX pp. 52–7.

Shu, H. J. 'Some Attempts at Sanitary Reform at Hankow since the Revolution on 1911'. *Zhonghua Yixue Zazhi* 中华医学杂志, 2, no. 1 (1916), 43–9.

Shuiye Xingji 水野幸吉. [Mizuno Kokichi]. *Hankou – Zhongyang Zhina shiqing* 汉口—中央支那事情 (Hankou – Central China Affairs). Shanghai: wuming gongsi, 1908. This is the translation of the Japanese original published the previous year.

'Shuizai hou zhi liangshi wenti 水灾後之粮食问题 (The Post-Flood Food Problem)'. *Nanjing Shi Zhengfu Gongbao* 南京市政府公报 95 (1931).

Simoons, Frederick J. *Eat Not This Flesh: Food Avoidances from Prehistory to the Present.* Madison and London: University of Wisconsin Press, 1994.

Skinner, G. William. 'Regional Urbanization in Nineteenth-Century China'. In G. William Skinner (ed.). *The City in Late Imperial China*, pp. 211–49. Stanford: Stanford University Press, 1977.

Smil, Vaclav. *China's Past, China's Future: Energy, Food, Environment.* New York: RoutledgeCurzon, 2004.

Smith, Arthur. *Chinese Characteristics*, 96. New York: Revell, (1894).

Smith, Joanna Handlin. *The Art of Doing Good: Charity in Late Ming China.* Berkeley: University of California Press, 2009.

Smith, Mark M. *Sensory History.* Oxford: Berg, 2007.
    Sensing the Past: Seeing, Hearing, Smelling, Tasting, and Touching in History. Berkeley: University of California Press, 2007.

Snyder-Reinke, Jeffrey. *Dry Spells: State Rainmaking and Local Governance in Late Imperial China.* Cambridge, MA: Harvard University Asia Center, 2009.

Spence, Jonathan D. *God's Chinese Son: The Taiping Heavenly Kingdom of Hong Xiuquan*, 17. New York: W. W. Norton & Company, 1996.

Stark, Miriam T. (ed.). *Archeology of Asia.* Oxford: Blackwell, 2006.

Sterckx, Roel. *The Animal and the Daemon in Early China.* New York: State University of New York Press, 2002.

Stroebe, George. 'The General Problem of Relief from Floods'. *The China Weekly Review* 31 October 1931.

Su Shi'an 苏世安 'Gong'anju cheng nanmin taoji Guishan ji Binggongchang bei yan hou qingxing wen 公安局呈难民逃集龟山及兵工厂被淹后情形文 (Police Report on Refugees Sheltering on Turtle Mountain Following the Inundation of the [Hanyang] Arsenal)' HSSDX, 293–4.

Sun Yat-sen. *The International Development of China.* Shanghai: Commercial Press, 1920.

Suryadinata, Leo. *Prominent Indonesian Chinese: Biographical Sketches.* Singapore: Institute of Southeast Asian Studies, 1995.

Sutton, Donald S. 'Shamanism in the Eyes of Ming and Qing Elites'. In Kwang-Ching Liu and Richard Hon-Chun Shek (eds.), *Heterodoxy in Late Imperial China*, pp. 209–37. Honolulu: University of Hawai'i Press, 2004.

Tang Jian 唐建 (ed.). *Hong'an xian zhi* 红安县志 (Hong'an County Gazetteer). Shanghai: Shanghai Renmin Chubanshe, 1992.

Tao Dinglai 陶鼎来 (Oral Testimony), Li Senlin 李森林 and Zhou Yeqing 周叶青. 'Tao Shuzeng yu 1954 nian Wuhan da hongshui 陶述曾与1954年武汉大洪水 (Tao Shuzeng and the 1954 Wuhan Flood). *Wuhan Wenshi Ziliao* 武汉文史资料 12 (2005), 20–3.

Tao Jingliang. 'The Features of the Three Gorges Dam'. In Shui-Hung Luk and Joseph Whitney (eds.), *Megaproject: A Case Study of China's Three Gorges Dam.* Armonk, NY: M. E. Sharpe, 1993.

Tao Zhifu 陶直夫 [Junrui Qian 钱俊瑞]. 'Yi jiu san yi nian da shuizai zhong Zhongguo nongcun jingji de pochan 一九三一年大水灾中中国农村经济的破产 (The Bankruptcy of the Chinese Rural Economy During the Great 1931 Flood)'. *Xin Chuangzao* 新创造 1:2 (1932).

Tawney, Richard Henry. *The Attack And Other Papers.* New York: Books for Libraries Press, 1981.

Taylor, Jeremy E. 'The Bund: Littoral Space of Empire in the Treaty Ports of East Asia'. *Social History* 27:2 (2002), 125–42.

Thaxton, Ralph. *Catastrophe and Contention in Rural China: Mao's Great Leap Forward Famine and the Origins of Righteous Resistance in Da Fo Village.* Cambridge: Cambridge University Press, 2008.

Thomas, Amanda J. *The Lambeth Cholera Outbreak of 1848–1849: The Setting, Causes, Course and Aftermath of an Epidemic in London.* Jefferson, NC: McFarland and Company, 2010.

Thorbjarnarson, John, and Xiaoming Wang. *The Chinese Alligator: Ecology, Behavior, Conservation, and Culture.* Baltimore: Johns Hopkins University Press, 2010.

Tian Min. *Mei Lanfang and the Twentieth-Century International Stage: Chinese Theatre Placed and Displaced.* New York: Palgrave Macmillan, 2012.

Tian Ziyu 田子渝. *Wuhan Wusi Yundong shi* 武汉五四运动史 (The History of the May Fourth Movement in Wuhan). Wuhan: Changjiang chubanshe, 2009.

Tilt, Bryan. *Dams and Development in China: The Moral Economy of Water and Power.* New York: Columbia University Press, 2015.

Todd, Oliver J. *Two Decades in China.* Ch'eng Wen Publishing Company, 1971.

Toole, Micheal J. 'Refugees and Migrants'. In Jim Whitman (ed.), *The Politics of Emerging and Resurgent Infectious Diseases*, pp. 110–29. London: Macmillan, 2000.

Trescott, Paul B. 'Henry George, Sun Yat-Sen and China: More than Land Policy Was Involved'. *The American Journal of Economics and Sociology* 53 (1994).

Tu Chang-Wang [涂长望]. 'On the Relation between the Great Flood of 1931, the Drought of 1934 and the Centres of Action in the Far East'. *Guoli Zhongyang Yanjiu Yuan Qixiang Yanjiusuo Jikan* 国立中央研究院气象研究所集刊 10 (1937).

Tu Deshen 涂德深, and Yang Zhichao 杨志超. 'Wuhan Longwang Miao de bianqian 武汉龙王庙的变迁 (The Transformation of Wuhan's Dragon King Temple [Area])'. *Hubei Wenshi* 湖北文史 3 (2003).

Turvey, Samuel. *Witness to Extinction: How We Failed to Save the Yangtze River Dolphin.* Oxford: Oxford University Press, 2008.

Tyner, James. *Genocide and the Geographical Imagination: Life and Death in Germany, China, and Cambodia.* Lanham, MD: Rowman & Littlefield, 2012.

Upward, Bernard. *The Sons of Han: Stories of Chinese Life and Mission Work.* London: London Missionary Society, 1908.

Valdés, Helena Molin. 'A Gender Perspective on Disaster Risk Reduction'. In Elaine Enarson and P. G. Dhar Chakrabarti (eds.), *Women, Gender and Disaster: Global Issues and Initiatives*, 18–28. Los Angeles: SAGE, (2009).

Van de Ven, Hans J. *Breaking with the past: The Maritime Customs Service and the Global Origins of Modernity in China.* New York: Columbia University Press, 2014.

   'Globalizing Chinese History,'. *History Compass* 2 (2004), 1–5.

   War and Nationalism in China 1925–1945. London: RoutledgeCurzon, 2003.

Van Dijk, Albert, Meine Van Noordwijk, Ian Calder, Sampurno Bruijnzeel, Jaap Schellekens and Nick Chappell. 'Forest–Flood Relation Still Tenuous – Comment on "Global Evidence that Deforestation Amplifies Flood Risk and Severity in the Developing World" by C. J. A. Bradshaw, N. S. Sodi, K. S.-H. Peh and B. W. Brook'. *Global Change Biology* 15 (2009), 110–15.

Van Slyke, Lyman P. *Yangtze: Nature, History and the River.* New York: Addison-Wesley, 1988.

Vermeer, Eduard B. 'Population and Ecology along the Frontier in Qing China'. In Mark Elvin and T'sui-jung Liu (eds.), *Sediments of Time: Environment and Society in Chinese History*, pp. 235–79. Cambridge: Cambridge University Press, 1998.

Vishnyakova, Vera Vladimirovna. *Two Years in Revolutionary China, 1925–1927.* Cambridge, MA: Harvard University Press, 1971.

Von Glahn, Richard. 'Household Registration, Property Rights, and Social Obligations in Imperial China: Principles and Practices'. In Keith Breckenridge and Simon Szreter (eds.), *Registration and Recognition: Documenting the Person in World History*, pp. 39–66. Oxford: Oxford University Press, 2012.

Wade, Henling Thomas. *With Boat and Gun in the Yangtze Valley.* Shanghai: Shanghai Mercury, 1910.

Wagstaff, Adam, Magnus Lindelow, Shiyong Wang and Shuo Zhang. *Reforming China's Rural Health Care System.* Washington, DC: The World Bank, 2009.

Wakeman, Frederic. *Policing Shanghai, 1927–1937.* Berkeley: University of California Press, 1995.

   Spymaster: Dai Li and the Chinese Secret Service. Berkeley: University of California Press, 2003.

Walsh, James A. *Observations in the Orient: The Account of a Journey to Catholic Mission Fields in Japan, Korea, Manchuria, China, Indo-China, and the Philippines.* Ossining and New York: Catholic Foreign Mission Society of America, 1919.

Wang Guowei 王国威. 'Fu xiu difang tanwu fen fei 复修堤防贪污分肥 (The Rehabilitation of the Dyke Network Spoiled by Corruption)'. *Wuhan Wenshi*

Ziliao 武汉文史资料, Vol. 13, 146–7. Hubei sheng Wuhan shi wenshi ziliao yanjjiu weiyuanhui, 1983.

Wang Huazhen 汪华贞. 'Hankou tebie shi furu jiuji yuan de guoqu xianzai he jianglai 汉口特别市妇孺救济院的过去现在和将来 (Hankou Special City Women and Children's Relief Institution, Past, Present, and Future)'. *Xin Hankou* 新汉口 1, no. 4 (1929).

Wang Jianzhu, Huang Jianhui, Wu Jianguo, Han Xingguo and Lin Guanghui. 'Ecological Consequences of the Three Gorges Dam: Insularization Affects Foraging Behavior and Dynamics of Rodent Populations'. *Frontiers in Ecology and the Environment* 8:1 (February 2010), 13–19.

Wang Jianzhu, Gu Binhe, Huang Jianhui, Han Xingguo, Lin Guanghui, Zheng Fawen and Li Yuncong. 'Terrestrial Contributions to the Aquatic Food Web in the Middle Yangtze River'. *PLoS ONE* 9:7 (2014).

Wang Lin 王林. 'Ping 1931 nian Jiang-Huai shuizai jiuji zhong de meimai jiekuan, 评1931年江淮水灾救济中的美麦借款 (Analysis of the American Wheat Loan during the 1931 Jiang-Huai Flood)'. *Shangong Shifan Daxue Xuebao* 山东师范大学学报, 56, no. 1 (2011), 77–81.

Wang Weiyin 王维骃. 'Jiuji shuizai zhong zhi xiaomai wenti 救济水灾中之小麦问题 (The Flood Relief Wheat Problem)'. *Gongshang Banyuekan* 工商半月刊 21 (1931).

Wang Wensheng. *White Lotus Rebels and South China Pirates*. Cambridge, MA: Harvard University Press, 2014.

Warren, James. 'A Tale of Two Decades: Typhoons and Floods, Manila and the Provinces, and the Marcos Years'. *The Asia Pacific Journal: Japan Focus* 11 (2013), 1–11.

Watson, Philip. *Grand Canal, Great River: The Travel Diary of a Twelfth-Century Poet*. London: Francis Lincoln Limited, 2007.

Watts, Michael J. and Hans G. Bohle. 'The Space of Vulnerability: The Causal Structure of Hunger and Famine'. *Progress in Human Geography* 17:1 (1993), 43–67.

Weatherley, Robert. *Making China Strong: The Role of Nationalism in Chinese Thinking on Democracy and Human Rights*. Basingstoke and New York: Palgrave Macmillan, 2014.

Webb, James L. A. *Humanity's Burden: A Global History of Malaria*. Cambridge: Cambridge University Press, 2009.

Weber, Max. *The Protestant Ethic and the Spirit of Capitalism*. London: Routledge, 2005 (1905).

'Wei daishou gongfei qu nei nanmin zaikuan qishi 为代收共匪区内难民灾款启 (Collecting Funds for the Refugees in the Communist Bandit Area)'. *Jiuguo Zhoukan* 救国周刊 1, no. 5 (1932).

Wei, Shang. 'A Lamentation for the Yellow River: The Three Gate Gorge Dam (Sanmenxia)'. In Dai Qing (ed.), *The River Dragon Has Come!: The Three Gorges Dam and the Fate of China's Yangtze River and Its People*, 143–59. Armonk, NY: M. E. Sharpe, 1998.

Wei Yuan 魏源. 'Hubei difang yi 湖北堤防议 (Dykes in Hubei)'. In *Wei yuan quan ji 魏源全集 (The Collected Works of Wei Yuan)*, Vol. 12, 368–9. Changsha: Yuelu shushe, 2004 (Qing).

'Huguang shuili lun 湖广水利论 (Water Conservancy in Huguang)'. In *Wei yuan quan ji* 魏源全集 *(The Collected Works of Wei Yuan),* Vol. 12 365–7. Changsha: Yuelu shushe, 2004 (Qing).

Weyl, Walter E. 'The Chicago of China'. *Harper's Monthly Magazine* (1918 October), 716–24.

WFZZ, Dang lingdao renmin zhansheng le hongshui 党领导人民战胜了洪水 (The Party Leads the People to Victory over the Flood). Wuhan: Hubei renmin chubanshe, 1954.

Wheatcroft, S. G. 'Towards Explaining Soviet Famine of 1931–33: Political and Natural Factors in Perspective'. *Food & Foodways* 12 (2004), 107–36.

White, Gilbert F. *Human Adjustment to Floods.* Chicago: Department of Geography, University of Chicago, 1945.

Natural Hazards: Local, National, Global. New York: Oxford University Press, 1974.

White, Richard. *It's Your Misfortune and None of My Own: A New History of the American West.* Norman: University of Oklahoma Press, 1991.

White, Walter. *A Man Called White: The Autobiography of Walter White.* New York: Viking Press, 1948.

Who's Who in China: Biographies of Chinese Leaders. Shanghai: Shanghai China Weekly Review, 1936.

Wilbur, C. Martin. *The Nationalist Revolution in China, 1923–1928.* Cambridge: Cambridge University Press, 1983.

The Cambridge History of China: Vol. 12: Republican China, 1912–1949, Part One, edited by Denis Twitchet and John Fairbank. Cambridge: Cambridge University Press.

Wilde, Oscar. *The Soul of Man under Socialism.* New York: Max N. Maisel, 1914 (1891).

Will, Pierre-Étienne. *Bureaucracy and Famine in Eighteenth-Century China,* trans. Elborg Forster. Stanford: Stanford University Press, 1990.

'State Intervention in the Administration of a Hydraulic Infrastructure: The Example of Hubei Province in Late Imperial Times'. In Stuart R. Schram (ed.), *The Scope of State Power in China,* pp. 295–347. Hong Kong: Chinese University Press, 1985.

'Un cycle hydraulique en Chine: la province du Hubei du XVIe au XIXe siècles (A Hydraulic Cycle in China: Hubei Province from the Sixteenth to Nineteenth Centuries)'. *Bulletin de l'école Française d'Extreme Orient* 68 (1980), 261–88.

Will, Pierre-Étienne and R. Bin Wong. *Nourish the People: The State Civilian Granary System in China, 1650 – 1850.* Ann Arbor: Center for Chinese Studies, 1991.

Willmott, Donald E. *The National Status of the Chinese in Indonesia 1900–1958.* Ithaca, NY: Cornell University Press, 1961.

Winchester, Simon. *The River at the Centre of the World: A Journey Up the Yangtze, and Back in Chinese Time.* London: Penguin, 1998.

Wisner, Ben, Piers Blaikie, Terry Cannon and Ian Davis. *At Risk: Natural Hazards, People's Vulnerability and Disasters.* London and New York: Routledge, 1994.

Wittfogel, Karl A. *Oriental Despotism: A Comparative Study of Total Power.* New Haven: Yale University Press, 1957.

Wolf, Arthur. 'Gods, Ghosts, and Ancestors'. In Arthur Wolf (ed.), *Religion and Ritual in Chinese Society*, 131–82. Stanford: Stanford University Press, 1974.

Worcester, G. R. G. *The Junkman Smiles*. London: Chatto and Windus, 1959.

The Junks and Sampans of the Yangtze. Annapolis: Naval Institute Press, 1971.

Worster, Donald. *Dust Bowl: The Southern Plains in the 1930s*. Oxford: Oxford University Press, 1979.

Wright, Arnold. *Twentieth Century Impressions of Hong-kong, Shanghai, and Other Treaty Ports of China*. London: Lloyd's Greater Britain Publishing Company, 1908.

Wu Jianguo, Huang Jianhui, Han Xingguo, Gao Xianming, He Fangliang, Jiang Mingxi, Jiang Zhigang, Richard B. Primack and Shen Zehao. 'The Three Gorges Dam: An Ecological Perspective'. *Frontiers in Ecology and the Environment* 2 (2004), 241–8.

Wu Jingchao 吴景超. 'China-Land of Famine (Walter H. Mallory)'. *Shehui Xuekan* 社会学刊 11 (1929).

Wu Liande 伍连德 and Wu Changyao 伍长耀 *Haigang jianyi guanli chu baogao shu* 海港检疫管理处报告书 (Port Quarantine Service Report), II. Shanghai: Shanghai tushuguan cangshu, 1932.

[Wu Lien-Teh], J. W. H. Chun, R. Pollitzer and C. Y. Wu. *Cholera: A Manual for the Medical Profession in China*. Shanghai: National Quarantine Service, 1934.

Wu Ruifeng 吴锐锋. 'Tianzai renhuo zhong de nongmin jiaoyu 天灾人祸中的农民教育 (Educating Farmers during a Natural Disaster and Human-Made Calamity)'. *Nongmin Jiaoyu* 农民教育 *(Farmers Education)* 2, no. 8 (1932).

Wuchang xian zhi 武昌县志 (Wuchang County Gazetteer). Wuhan: Wuhan daxue chubanshe, 1989.

Wuhan shi zhi: Minzheng zhi 武汉市志: 民政志 (*Wuhan City Gazetteer: Civil Administration*). Wuhan: Wuhan daxue chubanshi, 1991.

Wuhan shi zhi: Junshi zhi 武汉市志·军事志 (Wuhan City Gazetteer: Military Affairs). Wuhan: Wuhan daxue chuban she, 1992.

Wuhan shi zhi: Shehui zhi 武汉市志: 社会志 (*Wuhan City Gazetteer: Social Life*). Wuhan: Wuhan daxue chubanshe, 1997.

'Wuhan yi cheng canghai' 武汉已成沧海 (The City of Wuhan Becomes a Sea). *Guowen Zhoukan* 国闻周刊, 8 (1931).

Xia Mingfang 夏明方. *Minguo shiqi ziran zaihai yu nongcun shehui* 民国时期自然灾害与农村社会 (*Natural Disasters and Rural Society in Republican China*). Beijing: Zhonghua shuju, 2000.

Xiao Yaonan 蕭耀南. *Hubei difang jiyao* 湖北堤防纪要 (A Study of Hubei's Dykes). Wuchang, 1924.

Xie Chuheng 谢楚珩. 'Hankou shuizai shidi shicha ji 汉口水灾实地视察记 (An Investigation of the Hankou Flood)' *Xinminbao* 新民报 n.d. 1931, reprinted in HSSDX: 22–4.

Xie Qianmao 谢茜茂. *Yi jiu san yi nian Hankou dashui ji* 一九三一年汉口大水记 *(A Record of the Great 1931 Hankou Flood)*. Hankou: Hankou Jianghan yinshuguan, 1931.

Xu Huandou 徐焕斗 (ed.). *Hankou xiaozhi* 汉口小志 (Hankou gazetteer). Wuhan: Aiguo tushu gongsi, 1915.

Xu Mingting 徐明庭. 'Fangxun xianduan Longwang Miao 防汛险段龙王庙 (Flood Control Danger Area the Dragon King Temple)'. In Xiao Zhihua 肖志华 and Yan Changhong 严昌洪 (eds.), *Wuhan Zhanggu*, 武汉掌故, 287. Wuhan: Wuhan chubanshe, 1994.

Yan Changhong 严昌洪. 'Dashui chongle Longwang Miao – jindai Wuhan da shuizai 大水冲了龙王庙-近代武汉大水灾 (A Flood Inundates the Dragon King Temple – Modern Wuhan's Flood Disasters)'. In Xiao Zhihua 肖志华 and Yan Changhong 严昌洪 (eds.), *Wuhan Zhanggu* 武汉掌故, 233–6. Wuhan: Wuhan chubanshe, 1994.

Yan Wenmin. 'The Origin of Rice Agriculture, Pottery and Cities'. In Yoshinori Yashuda (ed.), *The Origins of Pottery and Agriculture*. New Delhi: Lustre Press and Roli Books, 2002.

Yan Yizhou 严仪周 (ed.). *Macheng xian zhi* 麻城县志 (Macheng County Gazetteer). Beijing: Hongqi chubanshe, 1993.

Yan Yunxiang. *The Flow of Gifts: Reciprocity and Social Networks in a Chinese Village*. Stanford: Stanford University Press, 1996.

Yang Chunbo 杨春波. 'Yisan can'an yu shouhui Ying zujie de douzheng 一三惨案与收回英租界的斗争 (The January 3rd Massacre and the Fight for the Retrocession of the British Concession)'. *Wuhan Wenshi Ziliao* 武汉文史资料 14, 1983.

Yang Guoan 杨国安. 'Qing dai Liang-Hu Pingyuan de shecang yu nongcun shehui 清代两湖平原的社仓与农村社会 (Social Organisation and Rural Society on the Hubei-Hunan Plains in the Qing Dynasty)'. In Chen Feng 陈锋 (ed.), *Ming Qing yilai Changjiang liuyu shehui fazhan shi lun* 明清以来长江流域社会发展史论 (Social Development in the Yangzi River Area during the Ming and Qing Dynasties), pp. 335–81. Wuhan: Wuhan daxue chubanshe, 2006.

Yang Jisheng 杨继绳. *Mubei: Zhongguo liu shi nian dai da jihuang jishi* 墓碑: 中国六十年代大饥荒纪实 (Tombstone: Documenting China's Great 1960s Famine). Hong Kong: Cosmos Books, 2008.
    Tombstone: The Great Chinese Famine, 1958–1962, trans. Stacy Mosher and Jian Guo. London: Allen Lane, 2012.

Yao Ting 耀庭 (Oral Testimony) and Yu Chun 玉纯. '30 wan ren 75 tian dazao jianguochu zui da shuili gongcheng 3万人75天打造建国初最大水利工程 (Thirty Thousand People in Seventy Five Days Construct the Biggest Water Conservancy Project in the Early Communist Period)'. *Wenshi Bolan* 文史博览, August 2009.

Ye Diaoyuan 叶调元. *Hankou zhuzhici jiaozhu* 汉口竹枝词校注 (Hankou Bamboo Branch Verses), edited by Xu Mingting 徐明庭 and Ma Changsong 马昌松. Wuhan: Hubei Renmin Chubanshe, 1985 (Late Qing).

Ye Zhiguo. 'Big Is Modern: The Making of Wuhan as a Mega-City in Early Twentieth Century China, 1889–1957'. PhD thesis, University of Minnesota, 2010.

Yeh Wen-hsin. *Shanghai Splendor: Economic Sentiments and the Making of Modern China, 1843–1949*. Berkeley: University of California Press, 2007.

Yi Si. 'The World's Most Catastrophic Dam Failures: The August 1975 Collapse of the Banqiao and Shimantan Dams'. In Dai Qing (ed.), *The River Dragon Has Come!: The Three Gorges Dam and the Fate of China's Yangtze River and Its People*, pp. 25–38. Armonk, NY: M. E. Sharpe, 1998.

Yin Hongfu and Li Changan. 'Human Impact on Floods and Flood Disasters on the Yangtze River'. *Geomorphology* no. 41 (2001), 105–9.

Yin Hongfu, Liu Guangrun, Pi Jianguo, Chen Guojin and Li Changan. 'On the River–Lake Relationship of the Middle Yangtze Reaches'. *Geomorphology* 85 (2007), 197–207.

Yin Liangwu. 'The Long Quest For Greatness: China's Decision to Launch the Three Gorges Project'. PhD thesis, Washington University, 1996.

Yip, Ka-Che. 'Disease, Society and the State: Malaria and Healthcare in Mainland China'. In Ka-Che Yip (ed.), *Disease, Colonialism, and the State: Malaria in Modern East Asian History*, 103–120. Hong Kong: Hong Kong University Press, 2009.

  Health and National Reconstruction in Nationalist China: The Development of Modern Health Services, 1928–1937. Ann Arbor: Association for Asian Studies, 1995.

  'Health and Nationalist Reconstruction: Rural Health in Nationalist China, 1928–1937'. *Modern Asian Studies* 26:2 (May 1992), 395–415.

Yorke, Gerald. *China Changes*. London: Jonathan Cape, 1935.

Young, Sera L. *Craving Earth: Understanding Pica the Urge to Eat Clay, Starch, Ice and Chalk*. New York: Columbia University Press, 2011.

Yu, Anthony C. (trans.). *The Monkey and the Monk: An Abridgment of the Journey to the West*. Chicago: University of Chicago Press, 2008.

Yu Fengling, Chen Zhongyuan and Ren Xianyou. 'Analysis of Historical Floods on the Yangtze River, China: Characteristics and Explanations'. *Geomorphology* 113 (2009): 210–16.

Yu, Shiyong, Zhu Cheng and Wang Fubao. 'Radiocarbon Constraints on the Holocene Flood Deposits of the Ning-Zhen Mountains, Lower Yangtze River area of China'. *Journal of Quaternary Science* 18 (2003), 521–5.

Yuan Jicheng 袁继成 (ed.). *Hankou zujie zhi* 汉口租界志 (Hankou Foreign Concessions Gazetteer) Wuhan: Wuhan Chubanshe, 2003.

Yue Qianhou 岳谦厚 and Dong Yuan 董媛. 'Zai lun 1931 nian E—Yu—Wan sansheng da shui 再论1931年鄂豫皖三省大水 (Further Discussion of the Flood Disaster in the E-Yu-Wan Area)'. *Anhui Shixue* 安徽史学 5 (2012), 116–26.

Yun Daiying 恽代英. *Yun Daiying wenji* 恽代英文集 (*Yun Daiying Anthology*). Beijing: Renmin chubanshe, 1984.

'Zaizhen zhong zhi zhi'an 灾赈中之治安 (Public Order During Disaster Relief)'. In HSSDX: 41

Zaman, Mohammed Q. 'Rivers of Life: Living with Floods in Bangladesh'. *Asian Survey* 33:10 (1993), 37–44.

Zanasi, Margherita. *Saving the Nation: Economic Modernity in Republican China*. Chicago: University of Chicago Press, 2006.

Zeng Xianhe 曾宪和. 'Nanmin ku 难民苦 (The Bitterness of Refugees)'. *Gaonong Qikan* 高农期刊 1:1 (1931), 26–27.

Zhang Bo 章博. 'Lun zhengfu zai zaihuang jiuji zhong de zuoyong – yi Wuhan 1931 nian shuizai wei ge'an de kaocha 论政府在灾荒救济中的作用 – 以武汉 1931 年水灾为个案的考察 (Analysis of the Effectiveness of Government Disaster Relief – Using the Wuhan flood 1931 as a Case Study).,' Jianghan Luntan 江汉论坛 (December 2006), 87–90.

Zhang Jiayan. *Coping with Calamity: Environmental Change and Peasant Response in Central China, 1736–1949*. Vancouver: University of British Columbia Press, 2014.

'Environment, Market, and Peasant Choice: The Ecological Relationships in the Jianghan Plain in the Qing and the Republic'. *Modern China* 32:1 (2006), 31–63.

'Water Calamities and Dike Management in the Jianghan Plain in the Qing and the Republic'. *Late Imperial China* 27:1 (June 2006), 66–108.

Zhang Qiang, Xu Chongyu, Tong Jiang and Wu Yijin. 'Possible Influence of ENSO on Annual Maximum Streamflow of the Yangtze River, China'. *Journal of Hydrology* no. 333 (2007), 265–74.

Zhang Taishan 张泰山. *Minguo shiqi de chuanran bing yu shehui* 民国时期的传染病与社会 *(Infection and Society in Republican China)*. Shanghai: Shehui kexue wenxian chuban she, 2008.

Zhang, X., Wang D., Liu R., Wei Z., Hua Y., Wang Y., Chen Z. and Wang, L. 'The Yangtze River Dolphin or Baiji (Lipotes Vexillifer): Population Status and Conservation Issues in the Yangtze River, China'. *Aquatic Conservation: Marine and Freshwater Ecosystems* 13 (2003), 51–64.

Zhao Qiguang. 'Chinese Mythology in the Context of Hydraulic Society'. *Asian Folktales Studies* 48:2 (1989), 239.

Zhe Fu 哲夫, Yu Lansheng 余兰生 and Di Yuedong 翟跃东 (eds.). *Wan Qing-Minchu Wuhan yingxiang* 晚清民初武汉映像 *(Images of late Qing and Early Republican Wuhan)*. Shanghai: Sanlian shudian, 2010.

Zheng Daolin 郑道霖. 'Shijie hongwanzi hui Si xian fen hui 世界红卍字会泗县分会. (World Red Swastika Society Si County Committee)'. *Q120-4-302* (December 1931). [SMA]

Zheng Peiwei 郑培为 and Liu Guiqing 刘桂清. *Zhongguo wusheng dianying juben* 中国无声电影剧本 *Chinese Silent Film Scripts*. Beijing: Zhongguo dianying chubanshe, 1996.

'Zhongguo Hongshizihui Hankou fenhui cheng yanmai gongzuo wen 中国红十字会汉口分会呈掩埋工作文 (The Chinese Red Cross Society Hankou Branch Working Paper on Burials)'. 28 September 1931. In HSSDX: 167.

Zhongguo jingji xue she 中国经济学社 (China Economics Society). 'Jiuzai yijian shu 救灾意见书 (Opinion on Disaster Relief)' *Dongfang Zazhi* 东方杂志 28:22 (1931).

Zito, Angela. 'City Gods, Filiality and Hegemony in Late Imperial China'. *Modern China* 17 (1987). 333–71.

Zong Yongqiang and Chen Xiqing. 'The 1998 Flood on the Yangtze, China'. *Natural Hazards* 22 (2000): 165–84.

INDEX

famine, 188, 226
flood adaptations, 24
flooding, 41, 63
gender, 212
inoculation campaigns, 185
religion, 69, 93, 95
Indus River, 19
industry, 51, 198, 214, 240
inoculation, 78, 116, 161
(1931) campaigns, 183–6
of foreigners, 78
propaganda techniques, 185–6
in refugee camps, 225
resistance to, 184
Ireland, 75, 198

Jackson, Innes, foreign student, 145
Jackson, Jeffrey, 137
Jade Emperor, deity, 98, 99
Japan, 171
bombing Zhabei refugee camp, 178
charitable donations, 172
concentration camps, 229
earthquake, 11
invasion of China, 15, 120, 168, 172,
175, 186, 231, 236
Jardine Matheson Estate, flooded, 62
Ji Xun, journalist, 210, 211
Jianghan Plain, 28–37, 55
Jiangsu, 6, 20, 59, 64, 67, 153, 188
Jiangxi, 5, 32, 63, 194
Jin Baoshan, NFRC medical commitee, 159
Jingjiang Flood Diversion Area, 237
Johnson, Lonnie, blues musician, 153
junks, 30, 37, 45, 58, 121, 133
Justus Doolittle, missionary, 102

kerosene, 51, 121, 137
kidnapping
Communist, 86, 180, 190
for prostitution, 211
Kuang Lu, author, 234
Kutak, Robert, 134

La Niña. *See* ENSO
labour
emotional, 169
labourers
agricultural, 66
child labour, 214
Communist labour policies, 190

coolies, 119, 124, 198
corvée labour, 166
flood prevention, 125
flood reconstruction, 186
imperial labour relief policies, 188
labour market, 188
labour relief, 165, 181
refugee camps, 182
trade unions, 108, 110
wharf labourers, 101, 108
Lander, Brian, 27
landlords, 63, 183, 234
League of Nations, 81, 172, 178, 192,
233
technical league, 160
Lei Gong, god of thunder, 99
Leow, Rachel, 215
Li Bai, poet, 153
Li Bing, hydraulic master, 96
Li Jinfang, murdered soy milk seller, 217
Li Lisan, Communist leader, 108, 218
Li Qin, 151
Li Wenhai, Cheng Xiao, Liu Yangdong and
Xia Mingfang, 249
Li Yuanhong, Hubei governor, 105
Li, Lillian, 10, 64, 162, 182, 244
Liang Ruhao, politician and relief worker,
163
Lindberghs, 31, 33–4
Little, Archibald, foreign traveller, 40, 47
liturgical governance, 201
Liu Fudao, 114
Liu Ruiheng, health minister, 76, 155, 158,
159, 160, 183, 202, 224
Liu Wendao, Wuhan mayor, 111, 114
Liu Xinsheng, businessman, 49
Lockhart, William Bruce, journalist, 116,
170–1
lotus, 25, 30, 39, 64, 241
Lu Hanchao, 137, 204
Lu You, Song dynasty traveller, 11, 30, 37
Luo Han, poet, 40, 145, 210

Ma Zhao, 211
Mae Fitkin, Gretchen, foreign traveller,
139, 145, 146
magistrates, 98, 107, 114, 118, 130
malaria, 26, 42, 48, 76, 81, 88, 232, 244
Malaya, 86, 172, 198
Mallory, Walter, relief worker, 163, 188,
202, 203, 235

Other Books in the Series (continued from page ii)

CPSIA information can be obtained
at www.ICGtesting.com
Printed in the USA
LVHW020450041220
673324LV00014B/281